D1035610

God and Humanity in Auschwitz

DONALD J. DIETRICH

God and Humanity in Auschwitz

Jewish-Christian Relations and Sanctioned Murder

Transaction Publishers
New Brunswick (USA) and London (UK)

Library of Congress Catalog Number: 93-35689
ISBN: 1-56000-147-X
Printed in the United States of America

Library of Congress Cataloging-in-Publication Data
Dietrich, Donald J., 1941-
    God and humanity in Auschwitz : Jewish-Christian relations and sanctioned murder /Donald J. Dietrich.
        p.   cm.
    Includes bibliographical references (p.   ) and index.
    ISBN 1-5600-147-X
    1. Judaism--Relations--Christianity. 2. Christianity and other religions--Judaism. 3. Christianity and antisemitism. 4. Holocaust (Christian theology) 5. Holocaust (Jewish theology) I. Title.
    BM535.D54 1994
    261.2'6--dc20   93-35689
                                                             CIP

To Tom, Sue, Emily, Sara, and Elizabeth

Contents

     Scriptures as Products of Living Communities   103
     Continuity or Discontinuity in the Scriptures   109
     Proleptic Christology   115

4.   Theology and the Christian-Jewish Dialogue:
     The Spectrum of Issues   125

     Christian Theology and Judaism   126
     Christian Identity and the Jewish Revelatory
        Experience   133
     The Formation of Christian Identity   145

5.   Christology and Antisemitism   159

     Discontinuity and Covenants   162
     Rethinking the Discontinuity Thesis   165
     The Christ-event and Human Dignity   177
     The Single Covenant and the Eclipse of Fulfillment   182
     Pluralism and Complementarity   187

6.   Jewish Faith After the Holocaust:
     The God-of-History   199

     Richard Rubenstein   201
     Emil Fackenheim   209
     Ignaz Maybaum   212
     Eliezer Berkovits   214
     Humanity and God as the Architects of Society   217

7.   Political Theology and Foundational Values   227

     The Event and Authentic Theology   231
     Praxis and Theory   236
     Action as Concretized Knowledge   243
     Theory-Praxis and its Potential Impact   248

Acknowledgments

This work is a product of two decades of teaching courses on the Holocaust and of reflecting on the tragic behavior of those Christian men and women who helped develop the antisemitic tradition in our culture. My own thoughts on the religious and cultural antisemitism that became institutionalized have been stimulated, broadened, and refined by the undergraduates and graduates in my lecture courses and seminars. Papers given at conferences have elicited comments from colleagues who have thoughtfully directed my attention to the pertinent questions posed by the Christian responsibility for this policy of sanctioned murder. Interactions with varied Jewish-Christian study groups in the United States and Europe as well as with "Facing History and Ourselves," a Boston-based organization devoted to introducing Holocaust educational materials into our schools, has continuously sensitized me to the historical development of the deeply rooted antisemitism in our society.

Two men, however, have especially supported my scholarly work throughout these years. Irving Louis Horowitz, Hannah Arendt, distinguished professor of sociology at Rutgers University, and Otto P. Pflanze, now retired but formerly editor of the *American Historical*

Review as well as my *Doktorvater,* have contributed to the scholarly dimension of my career. I would also be remiss if I did not thank my new colleagues at Boston College for their support as I made my transition from the University of Wisconsin-Stevens Point to my new academic home in Chestnut Hill. Several faculty research grants from Boston College have made the research and writing of this work possible. Additionally, the Bernard A. Stotsky/George and Bess Stotsky Endowed Research Fund has helped support my research and promises continued financing of Holocaust studies in the Department of Theology at Boston College. I would like to thank Stephen Cannella, a student at Boston College, for his work on organizing the details, which made the manuscript complete. Finally, I would like to express my appreciation to Susan Sweetser, my secretary, who managed to find time among all of our projects to type and correct several drafts. Without her, this book would not have been possible. Naturally, I acknowledge any errors in this work as my own.

Introduction

Implemented as a political and racial policy and nurtured by an antisemitic cultural paradigm, the Holocaust emerged as a systematized program of cruelty and destruction that has hermeneutically informed post-1945 theological reflection and social science research. This tragic horror, perpetrated in a supposedly Christian civilization, has given rise to a critical and unrelenting inquiry into historical as well as contemporary Jewish-Christian relations, into the political and psychological nature and behavior of individuals and groups, and into the meaning of the roles that have been assigned to all of us in society. For some, the evil embodied in this unprecedented tragedy is incomprehensible because it poses theodicy-related questions, which they feel cannot be resolved. In general, however, we assume that we can comprehend our world. We may not like to think that as rational beings we have freely committed such carnage or created an environment within which such a tragedy could unfold, because our past actions can have very real implications for our future. But most of us understand that the Holocaust was intentionally implemented as a policy, and we have spent decades trying to understand the "why" and the "how." Comprehension of the

1

tragedy, of course, would seem to imply that methods of preventing future disasters have to be found. Normative standards would have to be institutionalized and theological systems reconfigured. Ultimately, when faced with such dissonance as "good" Christians exterminating Jews or creating an environment that permitted the Shoah, we have increasingly been finding that we can no longer manipulate information, emotions, and attitudes to compel theological consistency.[1] Only by revealing the roots of and comprehending modern genocidal evil can there even be a possibility of shaping the future so that sanctioned murder will not happen again. The Holocaust offers us an example, upon which we can reflect, so that we can seek ways to avoid further genocide and incidents of sanctioned murder.

The religious and antisemitic roots of our civilization can be found embedded in Christianity from its very inception and have been consistently reinforced thereafter by the political, social, and cultural infrastructure that has supported European civilization. Scholars from varied theological traditions, therefore, have probed and analyzed the very essence of historical Jewish-Christian relations with an intent to see if Christianity by its very nature is antisemitic. Such a scholarly enterprise is necessary since the sociopolitical roots of and the psychological mechanisms supporting our civilization have matured in a religious and anti-Jewish context. Even in the modern era, this anti-Jewish bias has supported secularized ideologies resembling through terminology and imagery the historically Christian culture that was contemptuous of the Jewish people.[2] Any solution that hopes to avoid such catastrophes as the Shoah in the future must go back to the roots of the religious commingling in the first century C.E., must respond to the theological axioms that evolved in Jewish-Christian relations, and must also explore the sociopolitical antisemitic paradigm that emerged during and after the Enlightenment as Europe adjusted to the industrial revolution. Given the research already published in a panoply of books and journals, the time has come to analyze systematically the scholarly efforts and their concomitant results, which have accumulated during the last twenty-five years, in order to suggest ways to reconfigure the values at the base of our society so that such disasters can be avoided in the future. The underlying premise in this work, therefore, is that to be human means to have the ability to shape the religious, social, and political conversations that converge as the "human condition."

Addressing our normative structure, Auschwitz has insisted that we question some of the basic value assumptions at the core of our culture — the nature of progress, the effect of science and technology on society, the role of the nation-state, and certainly the concept of morality that has emerged through the speculative reflections that have developed during the past centuries of human interaction. What does freedom mean? How is the individual to relate to the group? Along with uncovering the historical facticity, reflecting on the conceptual ethical embodiments that have guided our past decisions and isolating the psychological principles that have helped support this monstrous deed can in the long run help us to begin reconfiguring our moral horizons so that future sanctioned murder can be avoided. The actual transformation of values, of conceptual structures, and of the institutions that respond to our commands is a task infinitely more complex and demanding than merely identifying what went wrong in our past. Being faced with taking prescriptive action seems to require that we rethink the human meaning of morality and of the God-man relationship from psychological, moral, and theological perspectives.

As a complex event that has meaning, it seems necessary to consider the Holocaust a discrete, unique event in the death and now life of the Jewish people, as well as one with lessons for the entire human race. This Nazi program of destruction has been seen by many as morally and theologically seminal because it represents a crisis of faith for Jews as well as Christians, both of whom have been forced to face directly theological antisemitism because the ongoing existence of the Republic of Israel obtrudes on a daily basis, which some have suggested is God's latest revelation. One of the dominant themes that has shaped this book is that Christian theology of necessity has to be reconstructed in this post-Holocaust era and has to make a conscious effort to end Christian triumphalism. Any attempt to discuss the Nazi genocide, which restricts its meaning solely to the Jewish people, cannot communicate its universal message. Knowing the full ramifications of the Nazi policy, which sought the extermination of non-Jewish peoples as well, can help us better understand the Holocaust and its meaning for the Jewish people. Although the historical and sociopolitical lessons of the Holocaust can be compared to parallel developments drawn from other twentieth-century genocides, any dialogue on the Holocaust that ignores its moral and theological meaning for all of us would provide only a truncated explanation. Merely academic study, moreover, without an impact on current human actions, would rob the Holocaust of its full import for human history.

When the question is posed, How have Christians responded to the Holocaust? a complex and nuanced answer can be discerned because certain milestones have already been passed. First, as the plethora of literature indicates, the significance of the Holocaust as a seminal event has been and is being probed. Research focusing on genocide can almost be categorized as an academic growth industry with its own journal and array of annual conferences. There is an abundance of research and commentary on the pervasive religious and sociopolitical issues, which are viewed as causally connected. Studies rooted in a variety of disciplines have responded to the challenges produced by the Nazi Holocaust policy and have readily been made available to scholars and the general public.[3] Secondly, interest in the Holocaust has extended beyond a fascination with the macabre; the compulsive need to know has passed beyond merely delineating the dates of orders or the Nazi organizational structure.[4] These latter topical interests have been and still are necessary research areas because only in knowing the historical details can we reflect on this value-laden event. No longer is the question What happened? crucial. Now, the question How and why did the Shoah happen? seems to motivate research, even though such questions will probably never be satisfactorily answered because subtle human motives and dynamics are not easily explicated. The constantly shifting perspectives guiding research on this topic suggest the complexity of a civilization and culture that provided the soil for the growth of religious and political antisemitism.

Responding to the Holocaust has also become vital for both Christians and Jews as they reflect on God and the human person, who both have had a role in shaping our civilization. Auschwitz has created a breach in our theodicy tradition and has affected the theoretical level of theological discourse. With Auschwitz was completed a paradigm change because clearly Leibniz's idea of the best of all possible worlds does not agree with our own experience. The new theodicy that is becoming prominent characteristically does not provide absolute answers, but rather is suggesting that God wants us to oppose evil. It is designed to make possible human decisions that would deny neither the experienced evil nor the possibility of a living faith. Such a theological innovation is worth reflection because in the past theodicy has only tried to account for the existence of evil. If theodicy can now support opposition to evil as well, then major theological conceptions have been changing. That Christian theologians have to confront the enormous evil of the Holocaust has helped to account for this change. For Christians, this critical reflection has led to a struggle to comprehend the Holocaust as a historical phenomenon rooted to an unfortunate extent in their own faith. For them it has led to a realization and acceptance that Christianity has had an integral role in making the Shoah a reality. Thinking about the *Endlösung* (final solution), therefore, has posed stark questions that not only condemn the Nazis as murderers but call Christianity and modern civilization before the bar of historical and ethical judgment. Elie Wiesel's very cogent and now almost habitually cited observation is useful in summing up the issue: "In Auschwitz all the Jews were victims, all the killers were Christian." Wiesel adds: "As surely as the victims are a problem for the Jews, the killers are a problem for the Christians."[5]

Simply put, Christians who think about the Holocaust have to deal with the murderers and bystanders who are the end-products of a two-thousand-year-old civilization. Approaching the issue from such a historical direction can be devastating as the implications become clear. When we ask, "Why was this racial genocide implemented by European Christians?" "Why did many in Europe accept, almost passively, the systematic bureaucratic destruction of millions of Jews and millions of others in factories designed to produce death?" we are asking for answers that require an extended discernment. What Jules Isaac has called "the teaching of contempt" has been part of the Christian churches for so long that this very teaching and its associated practices, it is now almost universally recognized, helped prepare the ground that made Hitler's attempted "Final Solution" possible.[6] Why did Christians develop this teaching? How can they deal with their own history?

Irving Greenberg has related a story from the Holocaust event that more than any mere recitation of facts can help illuminate the connection between the teaching of contempt and the Shoah:

> In 1942, the Nietra Rebbe went to Archbishop Kametka of Nietra to plead for Catholic intervention against the deportation of Slovakian Jews. Tiso, the head of the Slovakian government, had been Kametka's secretary for

many years, and the rebbe had hoped that Kametka could persuade Tiso not to allow the deportations. Since the rebbe did not yet know of the gas chambers, he stressed the dangers of hunger and disease, especially for women, old people and children. The Archbishop replied: "It is not just a matter of deportation. You will not die there of hunger and disease. They will slaughter all of you there, old and young alike, women and children, at once — it is the punishment that you deserve for the death of our Lord and Redeemer, Jesus Christ — you have only one solution. Come over to our religion and I will work to annul this decree."[7]

The archbishop's statement pointedly summarizes the tradition of Christian antisemitic theology. This theology took its theme from a series of tracts or books written by classical Christian theologians and bearing the title *Adversus Judaeos*.[8] Such an antagonistic theology cannot be viewed as merely confined to specific esoteric tracts; it evolved as a historically reinforced conceptual model for understanding the theological and ultimately even the secular relations between Christianity and Judaism. This prejudiced outlook has permeated, at least until recently, virtually all aspects of theology from biblical exegesis to dogmatic theology as well as, of course, the political, social, and cultural formulae that have been evolved to regulate the relations between Christians and Jews.[9] But theological antisemitism is not sufficient to explain the Shoah.

With respect to the Holocaust as a historical phenomenon, what motives directed the actors and how they translated their wishes or fantasies into reality depend on the characteristics of the specific culture and societies under consideration. The Nazis, for example, were convinced that through biopolitics they could reshape their environment, perhaps humanity itself, to a degree rarely deemed imaginable in the past. The Holocaust, therefore, has also raised profound ethical questions that have focused on humankind's responsibility for the organization of society. It has also highlighted serious "faults" in our social environment because the Nazi aim to transform human values cannot be considered an unrealistic threat in light of our own cultural ethos. How do we establish, therefore, moral responsibility in an impersonal civil society established through technological and bureaucratic axioms, in which the dignity of human life itself appears to be eroding in virtually every dimension? How can theology and the social sciences be made subject-centered and used to re-create a social environment that can support personal dignity?[10] If historically formed cultural values helped legitimize Nazi policy, then to avoid future disasters a sociocultural metamorphosis would seem to be necessary in order to redirect the psychological mechanisms that affect human behavior. Some responses to such issues and some lines of development, which can be briefly mentioned here, serve as a preview to the final chapters and should be kept in mind while exploring the theological reflections demanded by the Shoah.

Along with other Europeans, many Germans had long devalued the Jewish people as a group and had discriminated against its members. Among the European communities, Germans seemed to have a particularly strong respect for authority as well as an overly superior and/or vulnerable self-concept which, some scholars feel, made them more likely to turn against the indigenous Jewish subgroup in their country when pressured or threatened. But the issue is more broadly based because the Germans were not alone in implementing this horror; others in Europe readily lent their skills and were instrumental to the near success of the policy. Why did "normal" people support the nefarious Nazi policies? How can we explain their behavior? Psychological mechanisms leading to genocide have been isolated. Such harmful patterned activities were nurtured in a culture that gave birth to European social thought and "Christian" values as well as in historically documented actions against the "outsider." From a psychological perspective, earlier, less harmful acts seem to inoculate individual perpetrators, bystanders, and even the victims in such a way that more devastating acts become possible. This continuum of destruction, according to Ervin Staub, can help create a historical and progressive devaluation of the victim. Even the self-concept of the perpetrators may change as they dehumanize outsiders and implement a "guilt-free massacre." Ultimately, in the case of the Jews, a governmentally formulated commitment to genocide provided a "legal" justification. But the Final Solution was at its deepest level based on latent and blatant antisemitic motivations, reinforced by the psychological dispositions and behavioral dynamics common to humanity, only in this instance rooted and shaped within the historical European culture.[11]

To enable moral predispositions to support physical assault, a number of political and sociocultural variables apparently have to be oper-

ant given that conceptual ideas in a vacuum cannot power the historical events. Within the European historical environment, specific psychological dynamics seem to have been operant and can be briefly
mentioned to sensitize us as we examine theological and moral traditions. Scapegoating, for example, diminishes our own responsibility.
By pointing to a cause of societal problems, scapegoating has great
psychological usefulness in the process of dehumanization. Aggression seems to promise a solution to sociopolitical problems by focusing action against the scapegoat and allowing people to feel connected
as they join against others. Devaluation of a subgroup can help raise
the injured self-esteem of the dominant group. Adopting an ideology
— i.e., a comprehensive vision that explains or makes sense of the
various dimensions of human life — can provide a meaningful
worldview that helps portray a better and hoped-for society, which can
presumably be attained by manipulating the political, social, and economic realities at hand. Even currently accepted biological principles
can help sensitize us to our sociocultural environment, because humans have genetic propensities for both altruism and aggression.
Which of these propensities dominates at any specific point in time
seems to depend on cultural socialization practices. A person, for example, in a society that is highly aggressive toward a targeted group
has a good chance of inculcating that socializing hostile value. [12] The
above psychological principles can serve to remind us that moral formation is very intricately connected to our social activities.

Psychological research also seems to suggest that persons may
exhibit refined moral characteristics but that these can be obliterated
when individuals identify with a group, which may emphasize serving
the interests of its members without moral obligations toward others.
Thus, a diffusion of responsibility can typify group activity. Members
often also relinquish authority and control to the group and its leaders.
In some cases, they abandon themselves to the group decision, even if
only articulated by an individual, and develop a commitment that can
enable them to sacrifice even their lives. [13] It would seem, then, that
some values normally accepted by an individual may not suffice to
safeguard a society unless we recognize the communitarian nature of
personal morality. A structural morality may have to counterbalance
the varieties of potential institutional evil, which have become more
discernible in this century.

In light of the Holocaust and other similar massacres, the basic factors that seem to signal genocide can be broadly characterized as historically conditioned cultural characteristics, stressful life situations, and the needs and motives that emanate as people interact within their milieu. The Holocaust as a horrifying lesson, therefore, can help us elaborate a basic political and cultural agenda for the future that necessitates the creation of caring, nonaggressive people and societies, since we gain much of our identity from groups. We incorporate the social systems, to which we belong, into our own self-conceptions.[14] To prevent future political disasters as well as to promote healthy sociopsychological identity, therefore, the rethinking of Jewish and Christian relations, which has already developed some very fruitful perspectives, can be viewed as a positive step in redefining religious and cultural socialization with its attached normative practices. The scholarly research and reflection used in creating this new religious identity can become part of the bedrock useful for supporting a more altruistic social morality.

Religious antisemitism was not a sufficient condition for the Holocaust, but it was a necessary one. What happened at Auschwitz would be inconceivable without the beliefs about God held by Christians. For some, especially Jews, who have lived after Auschwitz, it has been God as a caring being and not genocide that has proven inconceivable. In fact, the Holocaust makes the traditional Jewish and Christian religious affirmations both difficult and problematic. As a result, both Jews and Christians have been driven to rethink the sources of their religious affirmations as well as their relations to God. For some, the Shoah has impugned the claims about God that Christians and Jews have historically made. For some it calls the existence of God into doubt.[15] The Holocaust managed to shatter faiths that had endured for centuries, and it compelled a critical rethinking of the meaning of God, the cogency and accuracy of theological principles, and the implications of religious traditions along with the whole nature of the God-human relationship. The Holocaust, then, certainly qualifies as a watershed event.

Philosophers and theologians usually claim to ground their arguments in appeals to actual human experience. These appeals, of course, go beyond the tangible empirical knowledge of individual cases or the statistically documented studies of human behavior and attitudinal belief, which are carried out by social scientists. Philosophers and theologians draw on such databases as well as historical material, but their efforts often require them to raise and reflect on questions that are spiritual in nature, which touch on the very essence of humanity — for example, as the concretized image of God. On the theological and philosophical level, the facts do not always speak clearly for themselves; nor are they self-interpreting. Philosophers and theologians have unpacked the Holocaust experience so that its most basic features — structural and normative — can be clarified. Along with social scientists, they have been seeking to comprehend the Holocaust in order to shed light on past experiences and to develop theological and socioethical normative principles and methodologies, which can help us plumb the depths of the mysteries of God and humanity more sensitively. The result of this research, it is hoped, can enable us to form and nurture societies that will be able to provide an environment for "true" human development.

The Holocaust has compelled a rethinking of theological-ethical, political, and socialization principles and, thus, of the holistic human condition. Scholarly attempts in disparate areas seem to be converging on common questions, reflections, and values as men and women analyze the Shoah and work to erect defenses against a recurrence. Social science contributions can be diagnostic and predictive because they focus on agents with specific values able to incite genocide. If values are known, what prediction can be made? What can be done to elaborate a value structure that can safeguard us? Any relevant and comprehensive analysis today virtually has to include theological, political, psychological, and social dimensions if a future disaster of this magnitude is to be averted. Since the Holocaust did occur in what could be termed a nominal Christian culture that supported the values developed through two thousand years of European history, the response of post-World War II Christian thinkers and institutions has initially been to assess the derailment from Jesus' original message of love and compassion. They have sought critically to analyze historical Jewish-Christian relations in order to understand the symbiosis that produced the hatred toward the Jewish people.

The object in the following chapters is to illuminate the routes being taken by disparate theologians and social scientists as they reflect on the Holocaust and its significance. Their work and their conclusions seem to be converging. This phenomenon may mean that a new consensus on the human condition with its operant value grid, even if not a new cultural paradigm yet, is beginning to emerge. In comprehending God and humanity at Auschwitz, I shall initially survey Christian antisemitism and then outline the changing post-Holocaust Christian, in particular Catholic, institutional attitudes as well as the biblical and theological scholarship that has helped support this institutional change. Here is a classic case of scholars affecting institutional policy, which in turn reinforces specific scholarly thrusts. The result of these efforts has led to an analysis of moral values and where they find their legitimacy. Jewish scholars have also provided some provocative studies on identity issues, in which humanity's responsibility for creation has emerged as a counterpart to Christian reflections. Theologians from both the Jewish and Christian traditions appear to be grappling with fundamental theodicy issues. Finally, two chapters will deal with the articulation of the ethical and sociopolitical norms that seem to be foundational for the construction of a society in which values are rooted in the dignity of the human person who exists in a relational and institutionalized community. In essence, the scholarly research in several fields has posed some very provocative challenges for the future construction of our culture and civilization, which can actively counter the genocidal potential that seems to be as alive today as it was during World War II.

Notes

1. Ervin Staub, *Positive Social Behavior and Morality*, vol. 1, *Social and Personal Influences*, vol. 2, *Socialization and Development* (New York: Academic Press, 1978-79); Emil Fackenheim, *The Jewish Return into History: Reflection in the Age of Auschwitz and a New Jerusalem* (New York: Schocken Books, 1978), 279; Emil Fackenheim, *God's Presence in History. Jewish Affirmation and Philosophical Reflections* (New York: New York University Press, 1970), 84-92; Amos Funkenstein, "Theological Interpretations of the Holocaust: A Balance," in Francois Furet, ed., *Unanswered Questions: Nazi Germany and the Genocide of the Jews* (New York: Schocken Books, 1989), 302; Richard Rubenstein, *The Age of Triage: Fear and Hope in an Overcrowded World* (Boston: Beacon Press, 1983), 131; Leon Festinger, *A Theory of Cognitive*

Dissonance (Stanford: Stanford University Press, 1957), 3. Two recent works have begun to connect the research insights produced by theologians and social scientists; see Darrell J. Fasching, *Narrative Theology after Auschwitz: From Alienation to Ethics* (Minneapolis: Fortress Press, 1992) and Christine Gudorf, *Victimization: Examining Christian Complicity* (Philadelphia: Trinity Press International, 1992).

2. Zygmunt Bauman, *Modernity and the Holocaust* (Ithaca, NY: Cornell University Press, 1989).

3. For a recent and excellent review of the literature, see Michael Marrus, *The Holocaust in History* (Hanover: University Press of New England, 1987). To keep current with research on the Holocaust, see the journal *Holocaust and Genocide Studies* and Yehuda Bauer et al., eds., *Remembering for the Future: Working Papers and Addenda*, 3 vols. (Oxford: Pergamon Press, 1989). Although many definitions of genocide have been offered, Helen Fein has delineated one that aims at inclusivity: "Genocide is sustained purposeful action by a perpetrator to physically destroy a collectivity directly or indirectly, through interdiction of the biological and social reproduction of group members, sustained regardless of the surrender or lack of threat offered by the victim." See Helen Fein, "Introduction," in Helen Fein, ed., *Genocide Watch* (New Haven: Yale University Press, 1992).

4. Saul Friedländer, "From Anti-Semitism to Extermination: A Historiographical Study of Nazi Policies toward the Jews and an Essay in Interpretation," in Furet, *Unanswered Questions*, 3-32; Christopher Browning, "The Decision Concerning the Final Solution," in Furet, *Unanswered Questions*, 96-118; Raul Hilberg, *The Destruction of the European Jews* (New York: Holmes and Meier, 1985). For a recent collection of essays that probe the religious and philosophical issues growing from the Holocaust experience, see Michael Berenbaum and John K. Roth, *Holocaust: Religious and Philosophical Implications* (New York: Paragon House, 1989).

5. Regina Ammicht-Quinn, *Von Lissabon bis Auschwitz. Zum Paradigmawechsel in der Theodizeefrage* (Freiburg: Herder, 1992); Elie Wiesel, *A Jew Today* (New York: Random House, 1978), 13-14; Barry Whitney, *Theodicy: An Annotated Bibliography of the Problem of Evil, 1960-1990* (Hamden, CT: Garland, 1993).

6. Jules Isaac, *The Teaching of Contempt* (New York: Holt, Rinehart, and Winston, 1964).

7. Irving Greenberg, "Cloud of Smoke, Pillar of Fire: Judaism, Christianity, and Modernity after the Holocaust," in Eva Fleischner, ed., *Auschwitz: Beginning of a New Era?* (New York: KTAV Pub. House, 1977), 11-12.

8. Rosemary Ruether, *Faith and Fratricide: The Theological Roots of Anti-Semitism* (New York: Seabury Press, 1974); Clark Williamson, "The *Adversus Judaeos* Tradition in Christian Theology," *Encounter* 39 (1978): 273-96; John Gager, *The Origins of Anti-Semitism. Attitudes toward Judaism in Pagan and Christian Antiquity* (New York: Oxford University Press, 1983); Jacob Neusner, *Judaism and Christianity in the Age of Constantine. History, Messiah, Israel, and the Initial Confrontation* (Chicago: University of Chicago Press, 1987); Louis Feldman, *Jew and Gentile in the Ancient World: Attitudes and Interactions from Alexander to Justinian* (Princeton: Princeton University Press, 1993). For works that analyze this *Adversus Judaeos* tradition, see A. Lukyn Williams, *Adversus Judaeos: A Bird's-Eye View of Christian Apologiae until the Renaissance* (London: Cambridge University Press, 1935); K.H. Rengstorf and S. von Kortzfleisch, eds., *Kirche und Synagogue Handbuch zur Geschichte von Christen und Juden, Darstellung mit Quellen* (Stuttgart: Klett, 1968); Kurt Hruby, *Juden und Judentum bei der Kirchenvätern* (Zurich: Theologischer Verlag, 1971); Bernhard Blumenkranz, *Die Judenpredigt Augustins. Ein Beitrag zur Geschichte der Jüdisch-Christlichen Beziehungen in der ersten Jahrhunderten* (Paris: Études Augustiniennes, 1973).
9. Jacob Katz, *From Prejudice to Destruction: Anti-Semitism, 1700-1933* (Cambridge: Harvard University Press, 1980); Helen Fein, ed., *The Persisting Question: Sociological Perspectives and Social Contexts of Modern Antisemitism* (New York: DeGruyter, 1987); R. Po-chia Hsia, *The Myth of Ritual Murder: Jews and Magic in Reformation Germany* (New Haven: Yale University Press, 1988).
10. Joseph Bernardin, "Emerging Catholic Attitudes toward Judaism," *Journal of Ecumenical Studies* 26 (1989): 445-46.
11. Yehuda Bauer, *A History of the Holocaust* (New York: F. Watts, 1982); Lucy Davidowicz, *The War Against the Jews, 1933-1945* (New York: Holt, Rinehart, and Winston, 1975); George Mosse, *Toward the Final Solution: A History of European Racism* (New York: F. Fertig, 1978); Leon Poliakov, *Harvest of Hate* (Syracuse: Syracuse University Press, 1954); Walter Laqueur, *The Terrible Secret: An Investigation into the Suppression of Information about Hitler's "Final Solution"* (London: Weidenfeld and Nicolson, 1980). For insights into the "insider-outsider" phenomenon, see H. Tajfel, *Social Identity and Intergroup Relations* (Cambridge, England: Cambridge University Press, 1982); Ervin Staub, *The Roots of Evil: The Origins of Genocide and Other Group Violence* (Cambridge, England: Cambridge University Press, 1989), 5.
12. Staub, *The Roots of Evil*, 17, 24. For the genetic issues impacting on altruism and aggression, see Staub, *The Roots of Evil*, chap. 4.

13. M.A. Wallach et al., "Group Influences on Individual Risk Taking," *Journal of Abnormal and Social Psychology* 65 (1962): 75-86; B. Latane and J.M. Darley, *The Unresponsive Bystander: Why Doesn't He Help?* (New York: Appleton-Century Crofts, 1970); D.T. Campbell, "Ethnocentric and Other Altruistic Motives," in David Levine, ed., *Nebraska Symposium on Motivation* (Lincoln: University of Nebraska Press, 1966).
14. David Abraham, *The Collapse of the Weimar Republic* (New York: Holmes and Meier, 1986); R.H. Dekmejian, "Determinants of Genocide: Armenians and Jews as Case Studies," in R.G. Hovannisian, ed., *The Armenian Genocide: A Perspective* (New Brunswick, NJ: Transaction Books, 1986); Staub, *The Roots of Evil*, 42.
15. Richard Rubenstein, *After Auschwitz: Radical Theology and Contemporary Judaism* (Indianapolis: Bobbs-Merrill, 1966).

1

Christian Antisemitism and European Civilization

Ever since Christianity and Judaism diverged and started to compete with each other, they have affirmed their separate confrontational identities. As a result of this relationship, the teachings of the Christian churches and societies have designated the Jewish people as "different." Very early in the common era, Jews were also assigned a defined place in "salvation history," and their ultimate conversion was viewed by Christians as validating the contemporary divine superiority of Jesus' message. The alleged involvement of "the Jewish people" in the death of Jesus with everything involved in that accusation, as well as their so-called "collective guilt," demanded that Jews in subsequent generations were consigned to live in communities and in a demeaned state as punishment for those deeds labeled diabolical by Christians.[1] Fortunately, such a view is now characterized as antediluvian.

For centuries before 1945, Christian antisemitism (anti-Judaism) thrived and was reinforced as a religious as well as cultural norm, which ultimately became a self-fulfilling social and political prophecy.

Ironically, even the philosophers during the Enlightenment found that they could utilize the traditional Christian defamation of the Jew as a weapon useful in the attack on Christianity, an example which the Nazis would subsequently emulate. Modern nationalism, ethnocentrism, and racism continued to stress the stateless situation of the Jewish people as well as the "insider-outsider" distinction earlier nurtured and developed by Christianity. Scholars, therefore, can make a good case that strong continuities exist between Christian anti-Judaism and racial antisemitism, at least with respect to terminology and images, even though the former was not based on biology.[2]

The term "antisemitism" as such was first used publicly by a German racist, Wilhelm Marr, in 1879. In the increasingly secularized and modernized society in which faith in Jesus was shrinking, the question of who was responsible for his death began to seem irrelevant, and so a biological basis for the prejudice was advanced. Such anti-Christian racists as Houston Stewart Chamberlain, for example, saw a Christianity derived from Judaism as condemnable for factors other than the alleged deicide. They needed a "scientific" term that would not include the word "Jew" but would suggest an empirical biological category. Antisemitism was the term chosen, although everyone knew that it meant only Jews and not other Semitic ethnic groups. Such antisemites as Richard Wagner and Hitler found comfort in a secularized antisemitism, which was sustained by science as a substitute for religion and theology.[3]

The foundational elements of the prejudice may have changed through expansion, but the terminology and stereotypes remained the same. There has been no post-Holocaust inquiry more critical for Christian self-understanding than that into the nature of the relationship between the anti-Judaism of theological pronouncements and the antisemitism of racist denunciation and murder. The terms anti-Judaic and antisemitic cannot technically be used interchangeably because the latter includes modern biological racism as well as a note of hatred or contempt for Jewish blood as such. Thus, in racial antisemitism, religious conversions would not deal with the issue of the Jews as outsiders. In a sense, early Christianity can be characterized as premodern antisemitism because in such cases as John's Gospel the Jewish people as a whole were historically demonized. Group hatred became increasingly endemic to Christianity over time, and such animosity ultimately was biologically based on blood itself in the nineteenth century. For the purpose of this study the more familiar term antisemitism rather than anti-Judaism will be used, although we have to be aware that the term is a late entry into this historical hatred.[4]

A vast scholarly literature on antisemitism and Christianity has developed. Here, the roots and branches of antisemitism in classical Christianity will be briefly recounted. Following this, a survey will offer the outlines of the current and in-depth scholarship that has addressed the nineteen hundred years of antisemitism. It seems crucial for this study to understand the complexity of antisemitism as it has historically engaged our civilization and to become familiar with some of the major analyses that have probed the historical entanglements that have bound this prejudice to our culture. A broad-stroke review of the research on Christian antisemitism and the scholarly conclusions of the last four decades also seems necessary to set the stage for the more explicit analyses offered by today's theologians and to realize that institutional religious changes, which are now countercultural, have not occurred in a vacuum.

Early Christian Antisemitism

In the abundant literature on antisemitism within the early Christian European culture, two historically ongoing themes of this *adversus Judaeos* theology have emerged: (1) rejection/election and (2) inferiority/fulfillment. In brief, the Jews were purportedly rejected while the Gentiles were elected. This motif was constructed on the "two peoples" allegory and the unsubstantiated claim of a "trail of crimes" ending in deicide. After a sustained period of cultural, social, and political confrontation, some Christian thinkers concluded that Christianity had fulfilled the biblical promises and was superior to Judaism. Only Christians, early commentators concluded, could rightly interpret the "Old" Testament, and even then its meaning had to be seen in light of the "New" Testament. Jewish approaches to interpreting their own Bible were portrayed as invalid. Ultimately, this anti-Jewish, apologetic argument helped establish the claim that Christianity had superseded Judaism. Antisemitism was a component of popular prejudice, theological commentary, and legalistic enactments. When church councils articulated anti-Jewish regulations, they did it through legislation to maintain order, but not to formulate doctrine.[5] As a result, until recently there has been little sustained theological reflection on this issue and its potential for harm. Prior to the comprehensive analysis of the Christian Scriptures as the contextual source of antisemitism in the "Modern Theologians on Early Antisemitism" section of this chapter as well as in chapter 3, several borings from the strata of Christian and secular history can concretely illustrate this culturally embedded antisemitism and will help suggest the historical continuity flowing from the postcanonical period into the twentieth century.

According to the Epistle of Barnabas (author unknown) from the late first or early second century, God had absolutely repudiated Judaism as the true faith that could enliven a theological, ritual, and social system. This author's theology was exclusivistic and intolerant as it appropriated the significant meaning of scripture for Christianity and denied it to Judaism. Contextually, Barnabas' anti-Jewish tract was apparently an ideological response to the needs of the Christian community in Alexandria. Presumably, the youthful church must have felt the challenge of a vibrant and threatening Judaism as well as the need to respond.[6]

In the late second century, Melito, Bishop of Sardis in Syria, wrote a sermon, "On the Passover."[7] Melito listed the categories of Judaism that in his opinion were worthless: rabbinic teaching, worship, ethics, and biblical interpretation. His sermon concluded with a reminder of the suffering of Christ, which he saw as deicide:

> He who hung the earth was hung;
> he who fixed the heavens was affixed;
> he who sustained all was suspended on the tree;
> the master has been outraged;
> God has been murdered;
> the king of Israel slain by an Israelite hand.[8]

A number of theologians, attracted by this invective tone, included the direct charge of deicide into their own works to help explain the role of the Jews in salvation.[9] Among them was Justin Martyr (c. 100-165), who delineated themes that continued as Christians advanced their identity by suggesting that Jewish law was emptied of significance after the Crucifixion, for which "the Jews" were to continue suffering. Bitterly, he stated:

> For the circumcision according to the flesh, which is from Abraham, was given for a sign; that you may be separated from other nations, and from us; and that you alone may suffer that which you now justly suffer; and that your land may be desolate, and your cities burned with fire; and that strangers may eat your fruit in your presence, and not one of you may go up to Jerusalem.[10]

Not surprisingly, some wanted to rid the religion of the Hebrew Bible. In the middle of the second century, Marcion rejected the Hebrew Bible as valid revelation, which forced an official response. Significantly, the church fathers rejected his suggestion, but in the process unfortunately separated the Jewish and Christian revelatory experiences. Thereafter, the church reinforced this ambivalence. God's revelation, it was asserted, was contained in both Scriptures, but through separation an argument could be made that one historical revelation had ended and another begun. Antisemitism, of course, was not necessarily the reverse side of Christianity; but the very concept of a "New" Testament as distinct from the "Old" helped legitimate, at least subliminally, Marcion's repudiation of the Jewish Bible as valid in itself. For centuries the Jewish Bible was seen as valuable only because it prepared the way for Christ's coming.

Irenaeus (c. 136-202) also can serve to represent the path taken by Christianity as it rejected the Hebrew Bible on the one hand while continuing to validate the experience of the Jewish people on the other. Irenaeus tried to oppose both Marcion and Judaism. For Irenaeus, the two covenants have one author but are successive. The Hebrew Bible was to be kept but interpreted in light of the Christian message, which would, as a result, continue to undercut its validity for the Jewish people. Marcion's explicit heresy was rejected, but his ideas continued to configure Christian thinking. Tertullian (late second and early third centuries) reinforced this now persisting theme. The Jews deserted God; the Gentiles quit the idols they had served and converted to the same God, from whom Israel had departed. Thus, triumphalism reared its head.[11]

Origen (185-254) transcendentalized the politics of the ancient world as he pointed to the "true" significance of the events around him. He insisted that the Jews suffered calamities because they were a wicked nation guilty of many sins, including deicide.[12] Increasingly, by the fourth century, the tone adopted became one of contempt — witness St. Gregory of Nyssa (c. 331-96):

> Slayers of the Lord, murderers of the prophets, adversaries of God, men who show contempt for the law, foes of grace, enemies of their fathers' faith, advocates of the Devil, brood of vipers, slanderers, scoffers, men whose minds are in darkness, leaven of the Pharisees, assembly of demons, sinners, wicked men, stoners and haters of goodness.[13]

In the Western church, Augustine's (354-430) views of the role of Judaism definitively guided Christianity into the Middle Ages. In his *Reply to Faustus*, Augustine outlined his distinctive contribution to anti-Jewish theology by stressing the notion of the wandering Jew as a homeless creature who served as a witness to unbelief. Cain and the Jews, he insisted, had been found in disfavor by God and rejected, while faith in the "new covenant" was preferred to the ossified, materialistic observances of the Old. The Jews were to wander and "… the continued preservation of the Jews will be a proof to believing Christians of the subjection merited by those who … put the Lord to death."[14] During this same era in Antioch, John Chrysostom (344-407) launched eight sermons against the Jews, thus setting the tone and providing the vocabulary for future generations. Apparently, Chrysostom was disturbed by the ongoing Christian fascination with Judaism and felt very keenly the rivalry between church and synagogue. Imitating the classical rhetoric of his era, he descended to new lows in speaking of Jews as "dogs" and "wild animals … suited for slaughter." Drunken and gluttonous, the Jews had murdered their master, he exclaimed. These theologians are not exceptions, but rather typical of those dedicated to condemning Judaism in order to support Christianity as it assumed its leadership role in the ancient world.[15]

Corresponding to the theological formulations, church councils legislated against the Jews from Constantine until the nineteenth century. A brief sampling will illustrate the consistency of the antisemitism that was being institutionalized during these millennia.

306 C.E. — The Council of Elvira forbade intermarriages between Christians and Jews, banned adultery between Christians and Jews, and

ordered Christian farmers not to have their fields and crops blessed by Jews. This latter prohibition was repeated for several more centuries, suggesting that apparently Judaism proved quite attractive, at least to farmers, despite the antisemitic theology and legislation that characterized this period. Pathological antisemitism, however, did not seem to be lurking within the Christian populace.

325 C.E. — In an effort to de-Judaize Christianity, the Council of Nicea legislated that Easter was to be celebrated on a Sunday and was not to be determined by the Passover celebration but rather by the phases of the moon.

341 C.E. — The Council of Antioch passed rules that forbade Christians from entering a synagogue.

581 C.E. — The Council of Macon insisted that Jews were not to be judges or tax collectors.

638 C.E. — The Council of Toledo proclaimed that Jews remaining in Spain were to be baptized.

1215 C.E. — The Lateran Council voted that Jews and Saracens were to be separated from Christians by their clothing.

1267 C.E. — The Synod of Breslau made ghettoes compulsory for Jews.

1870 C.E. — In Vatican I, 510 fathers of the council proposed that the Jewish people were to acknowledge Jesus as the Messiah and Savior.[16]

Adhering to the lead of the church, kings and nobles were encouraged to design further restrictions on the Jews. In 534, for example, Justinian abolished the legality of Judaism. Subsequent crusades led to physical assaults on Jewish communities. Accusations of ritual murder funneled the antisemitic virulent hatred, based on fear and envy, into modern times. This latter indictment appeared for the first time in Norwich, England, in 1144, persisted through the Middle Ages and even reappeared in Kielce, Poland, in 1946.[17]

Although Hitler's attempted Final Solution has been interpreted by scholars as anti-Christian as well as anti-Jewish, the Nazis could and did claim that they were merely imitating Christianity's historical practice. Hatred, dislike, and distrust of the Jews had been historically learned through two millennia and had become part of the "normal" intellectual baggage for most Europeans. Nazi antisemitism, were it to be analyzed outside of the long Christian tradition of teaching and practice against the Jews, would be nearly inconceivable. [18]

The Holocaust was launched in Christian Europe. Since 1945, this basic fact has posed fundamental questions focused on the theology and praxis of Christianity, which presumably was instrumental in socializing the perpetrators and the bystanders through both religious and secular historical channels. How could a gospel message originating in love and forgiveness end in brutal murder? Among others, John Paul II has called for a thorough exegetical revision of the historical Christian teaching that deals with the Jewish people and Judaism. He has insisted:

> It is necessary to get to the point where such teaching at the various levels of religious instruction and catechesis with children and adolescents will not only present the Jews and Judaism in an honest and objective manner, but will also do so without prejudice or offense to anyone and, even more, with a lively awareness of ... our common spiritual heritage [which is] above all important at the level of our faith.... Certainly, since a new bough appeared from the common root 2,000 years ago, we know that relations between our two communities have been marked by resentments and a lack of understanding. If there have been misunderstandings, errors, and even insults since the day of separation, it is now a question of overcoming them with understanding, peace, and mutual esteem. The terrible persecutions suffered by the Jews in various periods of history have finally opened many eyes and disturbed many hearts. [19]

This recent challenge to traditional Christian teaching has not developed in a vacuum but has been supported over the last four decades by a body of scholarship that has been probing the ambivalences of a complex past in order to design an authentic dialogue for the future. [20] Where can antisemitism be located in our culture and what has been its genesis? The scholarly responses to this question have also prepared the ground for substantive theological reflection.

Modern Theologians on Early Antisemitism

Even while Nazi Germany was constructing the death machine, such scholars as Jules Isaac, Karl Barth, and Jacques Maritain were calling upon Christians to review the fundamental Christian positions on Judaism. Engaged in research and reflection during World War II and in written works thereafter, for example, Jules Isaac had traced Christian antisemitism back to the very early Christian theses of supersession and deicide, which by the fourth century he felt could be labeled as the "teaching of contempt" that would subsequently permeate European culture.[21] Isaac's schema sketched out a Christianity that had too effectively embellished and reinforced the pagan anti-Judaism that had emerged in the classical era. Religious antisemitism, it seemed to him, had nourished and formed a cultural environment that ultimately supported the implementation of the Nazi biological *Endlösung*. Since Isaac's work, a growing and refined literature has tested this hypothesis both historically and theologically. Given the sheer bulk of the literature and the nature of this foundational question that goes to the very inception of Christianity, a consensus initially was unnaturally slow in growing. Some purely factual issues, of course, could be easily resolved; those remaining, which have gone to the heart of the Christian identity-formation process, have now been given sharper focus and can effectively be outlined. The systematically elaborated analyses have led scholars increasingly into the genesis and development of Christian antisemitism. The analyses have been extended beyond the birthing and formative years of Christianity into the present in order to illuminate the fusion between religion and politics.

Introducing his 1961 study, *The Jews and the Gospel*, Gregory Baum asserted that his book was designed to continue the conversation begun by Jules Isaac's work. Baum did not try to refute Isaac's central thesis that the teaching of contempt was the keystone in the edifice of modern antisemitism, which had persisted with its negative portrayal of the Jewish people. On the contrary, Baum argued that the real or essential meaning of the Christian Testament should be clarified. According to Isaac, the beginning of a movement to stigmatize the Jews as an outcast people could be located in the Christian Scriptures. This stream was fused with other currents of thought into the calculated hatred of the Jewish people. Baum maintained, however, that a Christian had to reject any position that maintained that the Christian Testament was essentially antisemitic. Baum considered it unthinkable for anyone who accepted the Gospels as the ultimate revelation of divine love to suggest that any part of the

Christian Scriptures had been designed to encourage contempt for any people and to have contributed to the growth of hatred in the world.[22] In reaching this conclusion, Baum had meticulously analyzed the Christian Testament, book by book, concluding with the very problematic Epistle of Paul to the Romans, chapters 9-11. He was reasonably successful in illustrating, at least for himself and those of like mind, that the Christian Testament *as a whole*, exegetically analyzed, did not necessarily need to lead to antisemitism. But the point is that in the eyes of some it could and, indeed, had. Baum's revised 1966 edition suggests that he perceived the issue at the time as a totally exclusivistic choice; the title defensively had asked *Is the New Testament Anti-Semitic?*

Isaac's work, however, had not labeled the Christian Testament as antisemitic — he had only stressed that in the process of its decades-long development after the death of Jesus, various polemical strands had become embedded into the Christian Scriptures for a variety of culturally contextual reasons. When such phrases and words subsequently were exploited by Christians, these culturally rooted attacks on Jewish communities in the one hundred years after the Resurrection could be used to justify universal antisemitic assaults. Isaac pointed out, for example, that the later Gospels seemed to whitewash the role of Pilate, and so magnified the prominence of the Jewish actors. This helped prepare the way for the devastating deicide accusation that became the architectonic keystone of the contempt teaching.[23] But the question focusing on a Christianity that for some by its very nature *had* to be antisemitic continued to haunt the scholarship of the late 1960s and the 1970s.

In *Faith and Fratricide,* Rosemary Ruether dramatically posed an answer from a very radical Christian point of view when she asserted that Christianity was antisemitic because of its christological foundations. Her study asserted that the anti-Judaic polemics in the Christian Testament were intimately related to the development of "high" Christology. Within this historical milieu, therefore, antisemitism became the "left hand" of Christology so that, in the eyes of early Christians, according to Ruether, one could not exist without the other. She maintained that the anti-Jewish milieu was neither a superficial nor a secondary element in Christian thought. The foundations of antisemitism were embedded into the Christian

Scriptures and, during the first three centuries of the common era, had been articulated with premeditation so that the basis for attitudes and practices, which subsequently produced such frightful results, was established. [24] She laid bare the crucial issue with which Christian scholars would have to wrestle.

Ruether's thesis appears to draw a straight line from John's Gospel to Auschwitz. She has exceeded Isaac's less threatening theses by arguing that Christianity and antisemitism have historically and so inevitably been linked of necessity. Introducing Ruether's book, Baum as well had now decisively rejected his own earlier defensive and moderate posture toward the Scriptures, which he had seen as rooted in real historical communities responding to very specific issues. Very explicitly, Ruether posed the issue for the Christian in its starkest fashion: Must one repudiate Christianity in order to extirpate antisemitism? But Samuel Sandmel has insisted that this was a false dichotomy.

Sandmel subtly modified the title of his 1978 parallel study, *Anti-Semitism in the New Testament*, to reframe the issue. While Baum's question challenged the extent of God's inspiration of the apostolic writings, Sandmel hermeneutically challenged Christians by asking them to analyze the ambiguous early Christian attitudes toward the Jews. Contemporary Christians were not being asked to accept the Christian Testament verbatim, he insisted, but were being warned that they should carefully delineate its message, which through scholarship could and should be shorn of historically conditioned prejudice. The question that has to be asked is: Why did specific groups of Christians use antisemitic diatribes to define their own faith? Isaac had already asked Christians to revisit the implications of their faith and to analyze biblical texts from that vantage point. From this somewhat more scholarly perspective, Sandmel concluded his analytical portrait of the Gospels' antisemitic material on a positive note: "I firmly believe on the basis of my experience with Christians ... that once full recognition [of the problem] takes place and the will exists, the solution will be found."[25] Approaches that focused on the context of these comments seemed to be needed.

Along this line, some thoughtful critiques of Ruether's thesis can also be found in the essays in Alan Davies' *Anti-Semitism and the Foundation of Christianity*. In general, the authors represented in this collection have acknowledged that the religious polemic directed against Jewish communities had been primarily constructed to deal with specific issues peculiar to the Christian communities. These localized responses then became part of the Christian Scriptures as these were formalized into the canon. To further confuse the issue, other theological opinions that positively depicted the Jews were also embodied in the apostolic writings. The positive attitude toward Jews contained in the early chapters of John's Gospel as well as in some of Paul's letters would seem to suggest that these authors were not axiomatically antisemitic. Early Christianity was not an antisemitically focused religion. Ambivalence and lack of closure among the early Christians in their attitude toward the Jewish people seem to be the order of the day in these canonical texts, which were living reflections of and messages to the early Christian communities. An array of modern commentators have examined the emergence of the Christian faith within the polemical and tumultuous atmosphere of the classical world. Christian, Jewish, and pagan attitudes intersected in a disorderly fashion to form classical culture. The common motif organizing these essays as well as subsequent scholarship has asserted that Christians rooted in their tradition do not have to choose between a theological defense of the total Christian Scriptures, which automatically would demand a repudiation of lethally damaging criticism, and the equally debilitating conclusion that would insist that these texts are essentially so contaminated by antisemitism that they would lose all of their moral authority. The result of the scholarship has helped clarify the issue posed so dramatically by Ruether. Defective traditions do exist and did gain predominant positions in Christian history as the result of cultural interactions. Through hermeneutical analyses, Christian scholars have been encouraged, however, to segregate the culturally induced antisemitism in these major writings and to ask why antisemitic outbursts were embedded in these classical texts. By disclosing the historical genesis and context of these themes, theologians could declare that such views had to be declared unacceptable to any Christian believing in a loving God.[26] The contamination of the Christian message with antisemitism does offer an object lesson, however, in the construction of prejudice within a cultural context and the subsequent universalization of the particular bias.[27]

A further prominent issue that scholars have been analyzing is the actual influence of pagan anti-Jewishness on the emerging Christian prejudice. Some Christian apologists have maintained that because anti-Jewish writings were also produced by the classical pagan authors, Christianity cannot be accused, at least exclusively, of inventing antisemitism. From this perspective, Christianity would only serve as one historical conduit for the virulent antisemitic strain that had actually originated in the earlier clash between monotheism and polytheism. As Salo Baron has expressed it, "Almost every note in the cacophony of medieval and modern anti-Semitism was sounded by a chorus of ancient writers." Marcel Simon, however, has suggested that there has also arisen a tendency to make this purely literary and economic pagan antisemitism incidental and thus acquit pagan authors of hard-core antisemitism in order to burden Christianity with the entire responsibility.[28] Clearly, this issue is complex and in part depends on the agenda being developed.

How the question is posed is relevant when interpreting the literature. When the bias of the historian is Christian, the Egyptian or Persian remarks are stressed to mitigate the attitude of Christians; when the author is biased against Christianity, classical pagan antisemitism is examined with an eye to burdening Christianity with this diabolical prejudice. Rational discussion has not been easy. Warning against the dangers of specific agendas, Edward Flannery, a Catholic scholar, has attempted a presentation in which the theological anti-Jewish tradition is seen to reinforce the antisemitism that can already be glimpsed in pagan anti-Judaism, and he has suggested the ongoing growth of this insider-outsider phenomenon.[29] Ruether has asserted that the differences between pagan and Christian anti-Jewish writings prove that each is independent, but that one could certainly reinforce the other. Presumably the pagan attitude was rooted in psychological and economic issues, while the Christian attitude emerged as its religious identity was solidified. Despite interest in pagan antisemitism, most current scholars seem to agree that the overall attitude toward Judaism in the ancient world featured only intermittent hostility and in general respected the Jewish "way of life."[30] What should be stressed, however, is that the sheer act of separation and pointing to differences can help create hostility over an extended period of time and in a supportive environment.

During the last decade or so, scholars not engaged in apologetics have reinforced the idea that Christian antisemitism has to be studied

within its historical milieu and with an eye to the psychological needs
of the involved individuals and groups, who were struggling to
establish an identity. Wilken's study of John Chrysostom, for
example, whose diatribes contributed much to solidifying anti-Judaic
views in the Middle Ages, declaimed against the Jews in the context
of a pluralistic and prosperous Antioch, where Jews, Christians, and
pagans all thrived. The Jewish community apparently was so
creatively dynamic that its rituals and practices attracted both pagans
and Christians. Chrysostom developed his homilies against the Jews
from this defensive posture as he was trying to urge Christian
"Judaizers" to return to their churches. He was not aiming at a
triumphant destruction of Judaism. In delineating the original intent of
Chrysostom, Wilken has blamed his alleged virulent antisemitism on
subsequent generations of Christians who, ignorant of the rhetorical
devices that the "golden mouth" employed, saw and imbibed his
writings as directed universally against the Jews. Wilken admitted that
he had initially studied Chrysostom's sermons on the Jews and was
intent on judging their meaning from the vantage point of the
Holocaust. His experience should remind us that later events should
not be retrojected into earlier eras. Medieval and modern images
cannot be superimposed on antiquity.[31]

The obvious parallel between the revisionist defense of Chrysostom
— as well as of the early fathers who reinforced this *adversus Judaeos*
tradition — and Gregory Baum's initial defensive analysis of the
Christian Testament is inescapable. Wilken's position supports the
consensus of the contributors to the Davies collection, a retrospective
of Ruetherian scholars, when he argues that Chrysostom's rhetorical
declamations are not designed to demonize the Jews and that his
sermons should be subjected to hermeneutical and contextual
criticism. Like many early Christian thinkers, John Chrysostom
assumed that the ascendance of Christianity, coupled with the
destruction of Jerusalem, which to many seemed coterminous even
though they really occurred more than a generation apart, signified
that Judaism had lost its theological legitimacy. The theological
implications of the fall of Jerusalem seemed self-evident to many
Christians of John Chrysostom's day. If a religious meaning could be
attached to the fall of Jerusalem in those early centuries, however, in
our contemporary setting it may be equally reasonable to view the

crucial events of the survival of the post-Holocaust Jewish people as well as the establishment of the modern Republic of Israel as religiously significant.[32]

In a vein similar to his colleagues in the Davies collection, Baum by the late 1970s also saw the biblical message of life as a basic hermeneutical principle that should be used in evaluating the Christian Testament's didactic and polemical strata. Since, historically, the negation of Jewish spiritual existence in Christian society has led to contempt, injustice, and physical extermination, this perennial antisemitism should be condemned by the superior principle of God's redemption of human life. This principle is the vital spirit that enlivens the entire Bible. In light of this central revelatory teaching, specific culturally formulated interpretations of scripture and tradition should, he has insisted, be reexamined and interpreted, as it is clear that they have led, even though indirectly, to the destruction of life. Along these lines, Raymond Brown has argued, for example, that the entire Passion may be read during Holy Week, but that an accompanying commentary should stress that the centuries-old, culturally reinforced hostility between Christians and Jews can no longer persist as it would be diametrically opposed to the fundamental spiritual impetus of Christianity. In practice, such explanations, of course, might well be impossible to coordinate with the services.[33]

Sensitive to this plethora of analyses, John Gager has also asserted that the distance between Ruether and her critics may be more apparent than real, as she has also admitted that the disciples of Jesus did not think that his death and Resurrection significantly restricted their membership in the local Judaic communities. In her opinion, the early Christians did not think that their faith in Christ automatically compelled an antisemitic stance. The antisemitism seemingly endemic to the Scriptures has actually emerged through historical contingencies. If the scriptural texts are approached from this angle, the polemical strains of the Christian Testament seem to be more a search for identity than a virulent antisemitism constructed for malevolent reasons or because Christian revelation demands it. The early Christian authors may have viewed themselves more as reformers in the prophetic mold. The onus for the developing religious and cultural antisemitism appears to fall on the subsequent generations of gentile Christians who read their Testament without the context of the Jewish tradition and metamorphosed a limited internal debate into an absolute condemnation of Judaism. Gager has sought a more realistic middle ground between exonerating the Christian Scriptures of responsibility and mandating their guilt for nineteen hundred years of antisemitism. In the Synoptic Gospels and John, Gager has isolated varying degrees or strata of "gentilizing" anti-Judaism that was attached to the prophetic intra-Jewish variety of criticism. In this context, the Epistle to the Hebrews, for example, was "well on its way toward Marcion," and this constricted Jewish-Christian debate could be seen as planting the seeds that blossomed initially under very specific conditions into a later, full-blown, anti-Jewish diatribe.[34] The original intention may bear only a very limited resemblance to the final result.

Pursuing Lloyd Gaston's reappraisal of the controversial Pauline corpus, which he feels challenges the linkage between Christology and anti-Judaism, Gager has contributed to the ongoing discourse on Paul's arguments, many of which were aimed at Christians — Gentile by origin — and not at Jews. The relationship between the Torah and Christ, therefore, seems to be such that neither should invalidate the other. The Torah still would remain the path of righteousness for Israel, while Christ could be seen as the promised way of righteousness for Gentiles.[35] Most of these scholars are marketing the idea that the supersessionist argument was not vital for the original enlivening of Christianity but now has to be investigated in light of what has occurred.

Along with other contemporary scholars, Gager has emphatically maintained that the categories of "anti-Semite" or "anti-Judaic" do not adequately mirror the complex socioreligious configuration of Jewish-Gentile relationships in the ancient world. Indeed, Gager has noted that unfortunately the Christian-Jewish conflict is more evident in texts than is the Christian-Jewish harmony, which may well have been as common in the pre-Constantinian era. Basically, the winners in the rivalry controlled which texts would be passed on. Along with Wilken, Gager's balanced scholarship helps support the position that Judaism positively attracted pagans and Christians even into the fourth century. One of the real problems shaping modern scholarship has been the tendency to apply such labels as antisemitism globally, as if they included the total spectrum of interactions between Jews and non-Jews in antiquity. Antisemitism and anti-Judaism reveal only partially the complexities of the ancient world. Specifically selected aspects of Jewish-Gentile interaction originated in pagan and Christian antiquity, and these trends were subsequently reinforced, universalized, and made dominant. Any universal "hatred of Jews" in antiquity — pagan or Christian — would be possible only by suppressing the nonconforming evidence. Greeks and Romans, for example, typically exhibited a marked attraction toward Judaism.[36]

Whether the Christian Testament is in part antisemitic has been debated, as we will see more extensively in chapter 3, but generally agreement has been reached that antisemitic tones and vestiges were introduced within a specific cultural milieu as the Jews and those who followed Jesus constructed their mutual identities. Most scholars today seem to favor the position that the harsh polemics in the Christian canon can be interpreted as the result of a Jewish intramural struggle and would be used to support future prejudice. Jesus and his early disciples were Jewish, and there is certainly enough evidence to indicate that from 70 C.E. into the patristic era a theological antisemitism useful in procuring an identity, which was culturally reinforced, gradually began emerging. There was no overwhelming or exclusively anti-Christian policy among Jews before the Bar Kochba revolt (135 C.E.) and no irremediable separation between Jews and Christians before this revolt. This fact holds in spite of the famous malediction against all heretics supplied by Rabbi Samuel the Small. It is important to realize that both modern Judaism and Christianity have the same origin: early Judaism. Moreover, early Judaism was a variegated panorama that can be discerned only by analyzing Rabbinic Judaism and post-second-century Christianity. Judaism can be characterized by its creative responses to God's will as portrayed in the Torah. The tendency to see Jewish Christianity as a major concern of the sages has to be rejected. Disagreements existed, but Jews, Jewish Christians, and gentile Christians prolonged their conversations into the second century without major and irreparable fissures, except perhaps in local situations. Gradually, Christians and Jews concretized their identities in relation to and in confrontation with one another, and the cleavage continued to widen over several decades.[37] But even so, the split was not finalized for several centuries.

Well into the fifth century the church and synagogue interacted in dialogue, although often on mutually antagonistic levels. First,

Judaism persisted in exercising a strong appeal to Christians who were attracted to such Jewish observances as the Sabbath, even though church leaders persistently and loudly proclaimed that such attractions were undermining Christianity. Conciliar and legal denunciations over the centuries would suggest that the intermingling of Jewish and Christian populations continued at least on the popular level. Second, Jewish preaching to pagans was persistently effective. Josephus has written, for example, that many pagans persisted enthusiastically in adopting Jewish religious observances and that the custom of abstaining from work on the seventh day had spread throughout the empire.[38] Judaism and Christianity were competing for the loyalty of pagans. While some pagans became Christians, Jewish practices remained attractive to this group, just as they did to Christians who formerly were Jews. But Jews were also *perceived* by some in the early church as associated with such heresies as Ebiontism within Christianity. Tertullian, for example, almost without fail labeled as Jewish any Christian viewpoint with which he disagreed.[39]

The antisemitic theme in Christianity, therefore, was a dynamically evolving, systematic pattern of relationships designed to help articulate the Christian faith. The texts indicate that Judaism was increasingly portrayed as an ossified model of barrenness, defiance, and antiquarianism; representing for many both a religious system and a people who had rejected their own election, repudiated God, and eventually committed deicide. Rooted within an increasingly monolithic Christianity, the anti-Jewish model predicated a stereotype of a church that was both a religious system and a *new* people of innovation — spiritual and obedient — rather than, in contrast to stereotypic Judaism, a particularistic, carnal, and obtuse people. This successor people, it was opined, had inherited all the promises spoken to the prophets, and Christians had left the "residue" (the Jewish people) behind.

What role has the Christian Testament had in promoting antisemitism? Recent analyses of Paul's Epistle to the Romans, chapters 9-11, for example, suggest that even this controversial passage cannot be understood through a word-by-word exegesis, but only in the context of Paul, his audience, and the issues being addressed. The scholarly work on this passage would seem to suggest what is necessary for the exegesis of other scriptural passages before condemning the entire New Testament as the birthplace of antisemitism. Certainly some portions of even the Gospels can be seen as nurturing future antisemitism, and they demand condemnation for their bias, but such an unequivocal denunciation of the Christian Scriptures as a whole seems to ignore the historical reality of the setting. John's Gospel is a good example of a document that begins by praising and concludes by condemning "the Jews." The term "the Jews" permeates John's Gospel, and by the end it seems to signify a faithless people devoid of spiritual insight and consumed with hostility and hatred toward Jesus. The Jews become synonymous with the world. This polemic against "the Jews" seemed to result from the interaction involving the historical and theological forces in the Evangelist's own day. More than an expression or reflection of ontological hostility between church and synagogue, the term "the Jews" and the theology slowly developing behind its use were on their way to that antagonism which ultimately became foundational in Christian culture. Through investigating the dialectical relationship between the Evangelist's Christology and the concrete social situation of the Johannine Christians, the hostility behind this term, "the Jews," can be understood. In John's Gospel the roots of the conflict were theological and probably lay within the synagogue, between Jews who believed in Jesus and the nonbelieving majority. Understanding does not neutralize the antisemitic potential of John's Gospel. Until the Christian churches today engage in an ideology critique that can show that antisemitism originally crept in as a result of social and political interaction, early Christianity cannot be liberated from its own active complicity in this "symbolic dehumanization" of the Jewish people.[40] Whether or not the Christian faith inevitably led to the Holocaust has become the crucial question. A brief selection of historical data is necessary to set the stage for the more expansively scholarly discussion of this issue in the section entitled "Antisemitism and the Christian Faith-Experience" later in this chapter. In advance, a couple of thoughts should probably be offered that will help direct the inquiry. That the laudable religious dialogue of the early Christians was tainted by historical actors should not negate the validity of Christianity as a faith founded on love and compassion. What has been suggested by scholars is that God's revelation was warped by historical actors and that Christian belief was being expressed imperfectly. This issue will be explicated more thoroughly as we progress.

Medieval and Modern Antisemitism

One support for a balanced view of early Jewish-Christian relations can actually be found in the High Middle Ages. Yosef Yerushalmi, of course, has affirmed the tragic effects of the Christian anti-Jewish polemic on Western history. Like Gager and Wilken, he has cited the other variables that Ruether tended to omit from her story. The real question, he has insisted, is not why Christians treated the Jews in such a hateful manner, but rather, supported by the teaching of contempt, why the Christians did not simply expunge the Jews when they had the chance through their control of society in medieval Europe.[41] Contempt clearly did not necessarily lead to destruction, which, as will be seen in subsequent chapters, demands sociopolitical and psychological explanations as well. Yerushalmi has noted that Ruether's approach focuses on "the reprobation of the Jews." But the Augustinian theory of preservation of a remnant for the future of Christianity can also be observed because Jews lived in Christian society. Although the pagan temples and institutions were confiscated or destroyed by Christianity after Constantine, Judaism did not suffer a similar fate. Synagogues were legally protected even though the Jews were popularly depicted in orations as persons without honor or civil rights. Medieval Jews enjoyed delineated rights that generally meant that in the secular world the socioeconomic status of the Jewish communities was more elevated than that of the Christian peasantry. The church did not seem to be the monolithic institution that has sometimes been portrayed. Under specific conditions, popes and kings frequently protected their local Jewish communities, even when the fantastic blood libel charge was at issue. Although attitudinally ambiguous toward Jews, papal legislation traditionally made available a court of appeal to protect Jewish rights.[42]

For Ruether and others, genocide seemed to be the inexorable consequence of Christian theology. Yerushalmi has countered this by reminding his readers of the church's physical control during the Middle Ages. Had Christianity sought extermination, that would have been the time, although one could perhaps argue that the necessary technology did not exist. Even though not dedicated to genocide, Christian antisemitism through the ages helped generate the climate and mentality in which sanctioned massacre could be planned and then achieved with virtually no opposition. The crucial issue here in the shift from medieval to modern antisemitism seems to be that while Christian reprobation perdured, that of preservation ultimately evaporated under the pressure of racism. Modern antisemitism was not simply a transformed medieval prejudice. A quantum leap had to be made in the post-Enlightenment period because the Holocaust erupted in our secular society and *not* in that of the Middle Ages. The most serious anti-Jewish assault that the medieval Christian state launched was sporadic murder, expulsion, and, in rare circumstances, forced conversions because this latter act resolved at least the religious issue.[43] Ruether has focused on the discontinuity between the anti-Jewish polemics of the pagan world and the theological polemics of the patristic period; Yerushalmi has highlighted the discontinuity that separated the ambivalent attitudes of Christian theory dealing with the Jews and the genocidal antisemitism that has its roots in the technological modern era.[44] But he has ignored the significant attitudinal metamorphosis in the Middle Ages, a type of sea change which potentially endangered the Jewish communities in Christian society and introduced a more aggressive intolerance.

Jeremy Cohen has recalled the darker side of Christian theology in the Middle Ages and has analyzed the intensification of Christian antisemitism. To achieve cultural homogeneity, he has shown that the Dominicans and Franciscans, as newly established and missionizing orders of friars in the thirteenth century, promoted a dangerous anti-Jewish theology that took root so well by the end of the sixteenth century that, combined with the expulsion from France (1290), England (1390), and Spain (1492), it led to the near disappearance of the Jews from Western Europe. Following in the steps of Wilken and Gager, Cohen has accepted an overall environment of tolerance and mutual interaction until the thirteenth century. Despite their marginal and reprobate status, the Jewish communities performed the positive role of witnesses useful to the Christian church as it expanded and accepted its responsibility of preserving the Hebrew Bible.[45]

Intolerant toward any type of heterogeneous society, the Dominicans and the Franciscans devised a more dramatic theology to relate the church and the Jewish people. This new schema corresponded to the needs of the inquisitorial and missionary efforts of the friars. Unfortunately, this desired Christianization of the Jewish people took an ugly turn, which reinforced what the Crusades had begun. Jews were massacred, for example, throughout Europe in the wake of the Black Plague. Blood libel charges became more widespread; Passion Plays stressing the deicide charge became more common. During this period the ghettos now began to be more rigidly enforced in Italy. The Fourth Lateran Council significantly and negatively undermined the traditional tolerance so apparent in earlier canonical legislation by mandating that distinctive clothing be worn so that the Jewish people could be distinguished within the Christian communities.

The Dominicans introduced this theological shift by encouraging the study of the Talmud as a prooftext useful in disputation against Jewish scholars, who had purportedly abandoned their roots in the Jewish Bible. The Talmud could be used as a documented source of heresy. Thus, the Jewish community would no longer be depicted merely as a remnant of biblical Israel awaiting conversion before the Last Judgment, or as a fossilized vestige useful in reaffirming the Christian triumph. Rabbinic literature was labeled as heresy for the Jews and then subsequently for any Christians who might be attracted to it. As the Talmud burned, Christians simultaneously developed a more coherent vision of a society unified by one faith, in which dissidents were to have no place.

The thirteenth century, then, appears to be a turning point in Christian history as Jews and Christians now were separated by impenetrable walls and, even more significantly from an ideological standpoint, by an aggressive theology that demanded homogeneity. From the High Middle Ages onward, anti-Jewish physical violence intensified in all of Europe, with Jews portrayed as active agents of Satan and charged with crimes against Christianity. Blood libels frequently coupled with charges of host desecration appeared with increasing frequency from the twelfth century onward. Visually, the representation of Jews in art assumed noticeably more hostile and demeaning features that highlighted the infamous *Judensau* along with the frequent juxtaposition of Jews and the devil. Jews were no longer depicted in a fashion similar to their Christian neighbors or as merely symbols in the historical religious drama. They had now become pernicious enemies of Christian civilization as such.[46] New and irrational elements had accrued to the antisemitic tradition undergirding the now developing popularized prejudice, which would give the nineteenth- and twentieth-century antisemites a treasure trove of hate imagery at their disposal. This demonization of the Jews in popular Christian thought perdured through the Reformation into modern times.

Martin Luther ultimately proposed such ruthless measures as the burning of Jewish books and of synagogues after he became convinced that Europe's Jews were not about to join the Protestant sects that opposed the Roman Church. His theological themes had already been stated in prior centuries. What seems to be unique was his vitriolic and vulgar tone combined with appeals to the political authorities to suppress the Jews. His remarks about the Jews were every bit as vicious and obscene as his assaults on the Anabaptists and the pope. Scholars have therefore suggested that for the older Luther the Jews were not a separate category but rather belonged with such other groups as the Catholics generally and the Turks who had misinterpreted or falsified the true gospel. The Reformation had introduced or religiously legitimized the fragmentation of Christian European civilization and also intensified the antisemitism that was cancerously present in Christianity.

Heiko Obermann has carefully linked the medieval and modern periods in the development of anti-Jewish theory and practice within Christianity by concisely analyzing the attitudes toward the Jews that were promoted by the leading humanists of the Renaissance, by the major reformers, and by their principal scholastic antagonists. The Jewish question was a central theme in Luther's own theology. Even Reuchlin's defense of the Hebrew texts as vital for scholarship, Obermann mentions, was motivated not so much by disinterested research as by the phobias concerning "Jewish magic," which obsessed the aggressive polemicists of the era. Reuchlin was also convinced that in the cabala Jewish scholars had demonstrated the hidden power of the Hebrew Bible.[47]

On the sociopolitical level, anti-Jewish diatribes became a key element for cultural identification in this acrimonious era. Polemical themes initially launched against the Jews were soon refocused by the reformers and Catholics alike on each other. Popular pamphleteers used antisemitism as a bludgeon against all their perceived enemies, whether peasants or nobility. Antisemitism was woven with renewed intensity into the fabric of modern society during the Reformation, which became one more stage in the reinforcement of the Jewish danger to Christian society. In *Of the Jews and Their Lies*, Martin Luther urged that his readers practice a merciful severity toward the Jews. Christians were exhorted to raze the synagogues, burn Jewish homes, remove Talmuds, forbid rabbis to teach by threatening death, forbid traveling privileges, consign the Jews to hard labor, and, in the event of a continued threat, expel the Jewish communities from Germany. Thus, Luther hoped that all could be free of this insufferable devilish burden. His anti-Jewish diatribes ironically represented a late blossoming of that same mendicant tradition that he had already attacked on other grounds.

Anomalies, of course, persisted, which reflected the apparently irrepressible ambivalence of both Protestant and Catholic behavior toward the Jews. In Calvin's Geneva, for example, Jews were forbidden to have homes; in papal Rome, they were allowed to reside. Jews fled from the Inquisition in Catholic Spain and Portugal, but found refuge in the "Protestant" Netherlands. The degree of antisemitism seems to have been rooted in specific cultural contexts and in the needs that people felt. The reformers analytically and effectively challenged varied elements of their medieval heritage, but anti-Jewishness was not one of those cultural residues that either side was ready to jettison.[48] Christian antisemitism had become endemic to modern culture as a whole. The line from the sixteenth century to Auschwitz, however, cannot easily be drawn solely along religious lines because the forces behind modernity also reinforced this bias. With the birth of the modern era, secular antisemitism began to assume a convoluted life of its own, although it increasingly reappropriated the traditional imagery.

Jewish emancipation from the ghetto was finally realized during the Enlightenment. This period also marks the beginning of the removal of the "Jewish problem" from the realm of Christian theorists, as secular ideologists moved to a new level. Enlightenment secularism was initially perceived as an improvement in the environment within which the Jewish population lived. In fact, religious antisemitism was merely reclothed in a secular costume.[49] Recent scholarship has brought to light a religious antisemitism that mutated with frightening ease into the secular culture and that infected even the egalitarians who advocated emancipating the Jews from the ghettos. Older Christian attitudes became secularized as "enlightened" thinkers translated the Christian demand for Jewish conversion into a conviction that Jews should now lose their particular social and cultural identity, which was rooted in their religion, by being assimilated into secular culture. But this did not mean that antisemitism had died. Such anti-Christian figures as Diderot sought to embarrass Christianity by delineating its Jewish roots. In a more poisonous attack on Christianity, Voltaire posited that the Jewish people and their descendants, the Christians, represented a major threat that impeded the progress of European culture. His aim was to combat the dominant Christian religion by challenging the foundations that were built on biblical revelation by suggesting that the Jews by their very nature would always be outside European society. This polemical shift from the Christian stance is significant. Along with antisemitism, Christianity had also offered the possibility of conversion and so a resolution of the insider-outsider issue. If logically pursued, Voltaire's approach of excluding the Jews as Jews or even as converted Christians from European society would serve to dehumanize the Jews to the extent that their very nature could exclude them from any universal sense of obligation. From the standpoint of psychologically conditioning Europeans for a resolution of the "Jewish problem," Voltaire's suggestion was a radical departure from the Christian desire for conversion. Voltaire's preracist invectives had a very isolated precedent in late-fifteenth-century Catholic Spain. Concerned about the Jewish blood in the lineage of so many of their leading families, which had been introduced through intermarriage with converted Jews, the Spaniards promulgated the infamous "purity of blood" laws. Such a legal step was peculiar to Spain, but enough precedents can help create a pattern.

Typical of the flavor of early modern antisemitism is this quote from Bossuet:

A monstrous people, having neither hearth nor home, without a country and of all countries; once the most fortunate people in the world, now the evil spirit and the detestation of the world; wretched, scorned by all, having become in their wretchedness by a curse the mockery of even the most moderate.[50]

Such intellectual fulminations following expulsions and ghettoizations show how religious and secular antisemitism were beginning to blend. During this period, there was even at least one notable effort to restrict systematically the growth of the Jewish population, when the Hapsburg government decreed in 1726 that only the eldest son of a Jewish family had the right legally to marry. This radical method of birth control was short-lived, but it does suggest that enlightened culture could focus on demographic contours, although the decree had nothing, of course, to do with genetic manipulation in the modern sense.[51] Intellectual antisemitism was also complemented in the popular culture.

The popular image of the Jew, which permeated European culture, by 1789 featured a deformed monster with horns, tail, hooves, and a sulfuric odor that betrayed a fundamentally diabolic character. Such an image was stamped into European popular culture, where it remained until the Third Reich and even until recently in the popular Passion Plays that have attracted tourists. This popular antisemitism, of course, seemed to be sublimated among the more educated groups after the French Revolution, who now became concerned with the development of the nation-state. The earlier religious prejudice was significantly different from the political antisemitism derived from the ethnocentric aspects of nationalism, which found its sustenance in the insecurity that characterized European socioeconomic groups that had been displaced by the process of industrialization. Secular antisemitism seemed to rely on stereotypes derived from popular folk culture that has prospered through the centuries. The potency of the old images left the Jews particularly susceptible to being isolated as scapegoats by modern demagogues who could now embellish "scientific" conclusions with the colorful lore of the past.[52] In an age when political life was powered by nationalism, to be stateless was to be by political definition the outsider — a secular reiteration of earlier religious viewpoints.

By the nineteenth century, Jews continued to be the victims of antisemitic abuse along virtually the entire European ideological spectrum. A variety of examples are available. To French ultraconservatives, including many clergy, Jewish emancipation symbolized everything despicable about modern liberalism. German nationalists viewed the Jewish non-Aryan as a threat to cultural unity. Radical secularists of every nation despised Jews for giving birth to Christianity. The ancient teaching of contempt was also positively promoted by Protestant and Catholic preachers alike. Religiously and ideologically splintered, Europeans did seem to be united around their fear and hatred of the Jews, who were "different" even though they offered witness to the one God. The Protestant *Realenzyklopädie* around the turn of the century, for example, noted that one could feel the Jews' undue importance, sense the racial difference, and resent their aggressiveness.[53] While theological ideas did not directly cause the Holocaust, they could legitimize and help reinforce conclusions reached on other grounds. They seemed to help "sanctify" decisions for those individuals who still took religion seriously in the secular post-Enlightenment era.

European nations were nominally Christian to a similar degree, but only Germany precipitated the Holocaust, in which subsequently other states cooperated. An argument can be made that specific traditions in German romanticism, historicism, and cultural pessimism helped create the pagan and anti-Christian elements that found a political home in Hitler's Nazi *Weltanschauung* and differentiated German antisemitism from European Christian antisemitism. Such secular elements built upon a historically Christian antisemitic culture a political machine of mass murder.

The development of a German neopagan antisemitism based in part on romanticism and historicism gave a new and decidedly secular vitality to the religiously negative stereotype of the Jew, who seemed to epitomize reason and enlightened values. Paul de Lagarde and Richard Wagner, for example, insisted that there were no simple and rational solutions to the sociopolitical, cultural, and economic problems of the era because the roots of these challenges were nourished by an overweening Jewish political, financial, and cultural control that went against the true spirit of the German *Volk*. With his deft use of the German language, Friedrich Nietzsche also tied the sterility of his culture with its "bourgeois ethics" to the frightening emergence of the political and financial despotism of the Jews and so struck a theme similar to that of other antisemites.[54] Richard Wagner was concerned as well with the penetration of Jews into European, and especially German, culture. For Wagner, the artist was to be inspired by the tradition of the national group to which he belonged. German culture, he opined, had deteriorated because of the predominance of Jews in his nation. Wagner himself was not a biological racist and so could conclude that only absolute and unreserved assimilation could resolve the "Jewish problem" in economics, politics, and music. Wagner's son-in-law, Houston Stewart Chamberlain, completely ignored physical data and defined races by mental characteristics: the creative, loyal responsible race is German; the corrupt parasitic race is Jewish. Biologically based conclusions were muted in his work with only the racial terminology left behind. Chamberlain's book, *The Foundations of the Nineteenth Century*, enjoyed mass circulation.[55] By 1927, Felix Goldmann could succinctly pinpoint the fatal attraction of racial antisemitism when he wrote: "Racial antisemitism then is rooted in the belief in the irrational."[56]

An array of nineteenth-century intellectuals indicted the era after they had experienced a profound disillusionment with the Enlightenment's heritage of liberalism and nationalism.[57] Ludwig Feuerbach and Karl Marx felt that they had proven that past and current manifestations of the spirit were merely projections of material needs and socioeconomic interests. As a result of this materialistic assault, the stress on "will" by Schopenhauer and others, as well as the denigration of any "next world," proved attractive to students imbued with realism and suspicious of religious or secular ideologies. By the end of the century, an eclectic *Weltanschauung* was gaining strength in Germany. This worldview tied together the concept of self found in Fichte, the ontological *Urgrund* of Schelling, romantic German mythology, historicist jurisprudence (which viewed natural law as illusory), and Nietzsche's glorification of the superman, who epitomized a will to power coupled with moral freedom).[58]

Nineteenth-century liberals had originally placed their faith in education, rational morality, tolerance, and the perfectibility of humanity and society. By the end of the century, they felt that these values could no longer provide sustenance to a society that distrusted abstract and speculative reason. In 1867, Nietzsche had already voiced this cultural despair (*Kulturpessimismus*) when he proclaimed: "What is there in history except the endless war of conflicting interests and the struggle for self-preservation?"[59] Anti-intellectuals and antisemites felt that spiritual goals were merely effete responses to humanity's basic animal desires, which in the opinion of some needed a Führer before they could be embodied and articulated. Using such a Führer principle in the nineteenth and twentieth centuries to organize society meant that spiritual or charismatic qualities would not be amenable to rational exposition; such phenomena would be *felt* by the leader.[60]

Those intellectuals engaged in refining "cultural despair" rejected religion as one of the corrosive institutions that had perverted natural instinct. Christianity was seen as the religion of the poor and the weak, who articulated hypocritical ideals of selflessness and sacrifice. They felt that such ideals undermined the life-enhancing qualities of pride and vital spontaneity, which simultaneously seemed to support racial antisemitism and endow it with a non-Christian or even an anti-Christian significance.[61]

Eugen Dühring, a Social Darwinist, and Paul de Lagarde lent their voices to the development of an anti-Christian antisemitism. De Lagarde, for example, wrote that one should "despise those who — out of humanity! — defend these Jews or who are too cowardly to trample this usurious vermin to death. With trichinae and bacilli one does not negotiate, nor are trichinae and bacilli to be educated: they are exterminated as quickly and thoroughly as possible."[62] The earlier Christian image of the Jew as devil now coupled with the Jew as parasite completely dehumanized Jews and opened the way for theories of physical destruction. Thus, anti-Christian antisemitism became a reality in this era of cultural critique.

With prophetic fervor, de Lagarde surged beyond what he referred to as the narrow limits of scholastic Catholicism and Lutheranism. He insisted that the dangers of his time demanded a wholesale renewal that would resurrect the ancient Germanic virtues and the vigor of the Teutonic soul. The whole process of this romantic historicism and cultural despair had managed by the end of the century to incorporate Jesus and Christianity into a racialist Aryan ideology that could simultaneously retain non-Christian and even anti-Christian elements.[63] Racial antisemites sought to liberate Christianity from what they perceived as Jewish control. From a theological point of view, traditional Christianity depended on the Jewish people as a living witness of its beliefs. Such a theological stance, the cultural antisemites insisted, actually managed to support the diabolical power of the Jews. Paradoxically, an antisemitic movement intent on liberating Christianity from Judaism had to use the racialist principle to succeed, just as the anti-Christian antisemites did. As the future would illustrate, Christianity without its Jewish roots could easily be fused with Nazi neopaganism and lose its uniqueness as a religion. Historically, as the Third Reich would show, modern antisemitism was equally anti-Christian.

The traditional Christian bias against the Jews — which was composed of such elements as the collective guilt tied to deicide, discriminatory policies laid down by such church councils as the Fourth Lateran (1215), and the concept of the "wandering Jew" as a symbol of abomination — helped create the Christian pattern of hatred and prejudice. The anti-Christian elements of racial antisemitism did not reject these Christian patterns but only transformed their meanings by using pseudoscientific jargon that could be fused with earlier, romantic historicist themes that had become fused in German culture.[64] Unfortunately, Christian discipline and faith were lost in the process of creating this pagan ideology. In the Third Reich, such pagan antisemitism led to an emphasis on a pseudoreligious Aryanism and on the creation of a feeling of blood and mystical unity (*Volk*). Germans focused on the historically unified community (*Reich*), *Volk*, fatherland (*Vaterland*), and, increasingly, race (*Rasse*). Such values would serve to certify that the speaker or writer was a "true" German.[65]

Antisemitism could be and was a political tool. Czarist Russians, for example, had concocted the infamous forgery *The Protocols of the Elders of Zion* to help further domestic policies. This text apparently was instrumental in forging Hitler's own hatred of the Jews. Houston Stewart Chamberlain also found support for his own popular racist philosophy in the *Protocols*. The Jew could be seen as the archcommunist as well as the arch-capitalist — an almost stunning contradiction that could resonate with virtually all economic classes. To say the least, Nazism was birthed in a cultural swamp of antisemitic hatred. Ironically, this milieu was supported by the Christian tradition of contempt and by the secular ideologies that held Christianity in contempt. Such scholars as Uriel Tal have even suggested that it was precisely to attack Christianity's roots that the secular venom of hatred was directed toward the Jews.[66]

Even if still subject to cultural and religious diatribes, Jews had made some progress on the political front. Between 1848 and 1870, European ghettos were disbanded and full citizenship could finally be attained by the Jewish people in Western Europe. Even with such positive policies, all disabilities were not eliminated in such nations as Germany until the Weimar Republic. In Eastern Europe, the religious-political pogroms of the late nineteenth and early twentieth centuries were responses to the old religious images, which were now given renewed life with the national and racial charges against the Jews. The infamous *Protocols*, for example, continued the myth of the "carnal Jew" as conspirator against the faith and the industrial wealth of Christendom. Everything threatening in this newly industrializing society became "Jewish." The *Protocols* were built on the concept that the Jewish Messiah would in fact be the anti-Christ. According to this fantasy, a Jewish secret government in existence since the time of Christ continued to plot the overthrow of Christendom and hoped to inaugurate the reign of the devil, which would last to the end of time. The *Protocols* were only legally disproven in 1934, but they served to link earlier anti-Jewish forms and modern ethnoracial antisemitism. [67]

Social Darwinism, biological racism, and eugenics served to give religious and cultural antisemitism a scientific veneer. If the belief were that blood determined history, then extermination would and did become the only viable solution for those who believed in biological racism. But most Europeans were not such fanatics, although they generally seemed to use populistic imagery and terminology. Christian antisemitism solved the "Jewish Problem" by conversion; nationalism could resolve the issue through assimilation or acculturation. Biological racists feared that assimilation might result in blood pollution. Thus, physical discrimination became necessary to isolate the Jew, and it logically could lead to extermination in order to preserve the valued biological identity of the "superior" race. Along with the transmutations of this antisemitic prejudice, the solutions were becoming more radical. Antisemitism could be a latent or virulent prejudice, but no matter what direction the bias took, it did seem to be a part of the general culture, even though it might not be the primary political motivation that moved the masses politically. As post-1933 Germany has shown, virulent legalized hatred need only be present in a few to wreak legalized murder.

Any virulent antisemitic hatred driving the masses was illusory as well as unnecessary in Nazi Germany.[68] The Germans' latent antisemitism seemed to allow the increasingly criminal "dynamic" hatred inspiring the Nazi true believers the autonomy that they needed to implement the Final Solution. The fanatics could proceed because few Germans viewed their fellow Jewish citizens as valued members of the community. The Jewish people had historically been marginalized in European culture. It has, of course, been argued from the spontaneous physical assaults on the Jews as well as the large membership in the Sturmabteilung (SA) that a significant number of Germans were not exactly latent; rather they were blatant antisemites, even if normally quiescent. As always, however, the argument could be made that people join organizations for a variety of reasons and that one might not have been antisemitic even in joining the SA. Comradeship and career opportunities presumably would play a role in motivating individuals to join such a highly visible organization in the Third Reich, but antisemitism served to validate one's membership in the Nazi party, whether it was an expressed or passive bias. The mythical Jew, after all, had been molded throughout Christian history to serve as the symbol of the "disease" that Christians had to expunge to save their world. Since both legitimate Christians and the Nazis used similar terminology, religious and racist antisemitism could be used by the Nazi gangsters of mass propaganda to purge the body politic of this "misfortune," and its use would not offend even the German who had no affinities to biological racism. Germans could vote for the Nazi party and join its organizations despite its virulent antisemitism because they and their ancestors had been exposed to milder Christian forms of this disease for centuries and had been raised in a romantic historicist culture that supported cultural stereotyping. This cultural immunization may help to suggest why bystanders might be very slow to react to antisemitism — they could identify with Hitler on other levels. The romanticized *Volk* of the nineteenth century created the environment that allowed Rudolf Hess in the 1934 film *Triumph of the Will* to proclaim the mystical unity of leader, party, and people: "The Party is Hitler. But Hitler is Germany, just as Germany is Hitler. Hitler! Sieg Heil!"[69] The emotion of the Nuremberg Rally of 1934 not surprisingly emerged into bureaucratic language. The constitutional lawyers in Nazi Germany agreed that all power lay with the Führer alone. This viewpoint was stated in a memo from the Reich Ministry of the Interior in November 1935, which said that the Führer state had replaced the constitutional state as an entity of law and no longer recognized the existence of many wills, but just the single will.[70] Judges were to make value judgments that corresponded to the will of the political leadership.[71] German political leaders may have instigated the Final Solution more easily because of specific trends and factors in their culture, but the executions were carried out in an at least nominally Christian environment. Sensitive to that responsibility, Christians have been reflecting on their past and present roles.

Antisemitism and the Christian Faith-Experience

The issue that Christian theologians have to deal with has been cogently put forward by Rabbi Eliezer Berkovits:

> Christianity's New Testament has been the most dangerous antisemitic tract in history. Its hatred-charged diatribes against the "Pharisees" and the Jews have poisoned the hearts and minds of millions and millions of Christians for almost two millennia now.... No matter what the deeper theological meaning of the hate passages against the Jews might be, in the history of the Jewish people the New Testament lent its inspiring support to oppression, persecution and mass murder of an intensity and duration that were unparalleled in the entire history of man's degradation. Without Christianity's New Testament, Hitler's *Mein Kampf* could never have been written.[72]

In the light of historical documentation, it is nearly impossible to deny that an unbroken line of cultural socialization exists from John's portrayal of the Jews as progeny of the devil, eagerly doing their "father's desires," through the medieval antisemitic tracts illustrated with woodcuts of the Jews with their father the devil, right up to a child's book (1936) whose first page prominently asserts: "the father of the Jews is the devil."[73] To oppose in a rational fashion this long history of hatred and contempt, these Christian roots and the soil from which they sprang have to be examined in great depth to help clarify the meaning of Christianity as a faith-experience that does not necessarily have to be nourished by hatred. It must generally be recognized that Christians have frequently expressed God's revelations in a manner not approved by the Spirit.

The role of Judaism in the Christian world that has traditionally maintained its position as the fulfillment of revelation must be scrupulously delineated. Both Jews and Christians have begun to re-create an authentic Jewish-Christian relationship. Christians have begun critically reflecting on the meaning of their Scriptures as thcsc were interpreted during the patristic era. Christians have also begun to forge an identity that does not depend on hatred. Other scholars have been seeking also to analyze how the Christian antisemitic strands became secularized and led to the disaster of the Shoah. A great deal of research is still necessary to expose the entanglements that have mingled Christians and Jews as well as to understand how and why they developed, the critical turning points in our common history, and the means to forge new cultural patterns. The antisemitic story is complex. Christian antisemitic images were joined to popular culture and gained concrete legitimacy in the postemancipation world of the nineteenth century. The religious portrayal of the Jew could be given this secular foundation because of the thrusts of modern nationalism and ideology. Earlier images had associated the Jew with Satan, witches, well poisoners, financial manipulators, and ritual murderers. Such images were antisocial and in European communities placed the Jewish communities frequently beyond the pale of societal obligation. Historical and popular religious imagery helped feed the "modern" needs of portraying Jews as manipulating capitalists or communists who endangered society. In the age of biological science beginning in the nineteenth century, virtually every image of eugenic pollution could be associated with the alien Jew living in the ethnocentric society of modern Europe. How can a less hostile society be reconstructed out of this fabric woven with such intricate complexity?

One of the obvious tasks for the concerned Christian has been to reopen the dialogue with the Jewish people, which was severed so early in the common era. Scripture and historical tradition have to be reexamined to understand how these antisemitic images emerged because this has to be the necessary prelude to extricating this prejudice from the social fabric of our culture. In particular, the question or issue that stands at the forefront challenges the Christian to discover whether antisemitism originally was the reverse side of

Christology, and if so how this can be handled, before dealing with such long-term issues as covenant and fulfillment. Earlier religious prejudice was different from the political antisemitism connected to the ethnocentric aspects of modern nation building and the insecurity arising among social groups displaced by the industrialization process. Modern secular antisemitism relies on needs distinct from those of past popular culture, although the stereotypic residue of historically conditioned contempt has left the Jews especially vulnerable to being singled out as scapegoats by popular demagogues right up to the present.[74] In an age when European politics has been powered by nationalism, to be stateless was to be by political definition the "outsider." The psychological mechanisms that supported the perpetration of the Holocaust were nurtured in the ideological and cultural milieu of our civilization that seemed to contain both "insiders" and "outsiders." To direct our attitudes and behaviors for the good of our society, cultural values and stereotypes have to be changed. Several connections between cultural antisemitism and murder can be briefly mentioned here and then developed as the study proceeds.

Since major cultural changes in the patterns of a society take time to become established, presumably years if not decades may elapse before the antisemitic stereotypes can be dissolved. Sensitivity to the issues may help us in the future to prevent sanctioned massacre in our own culture and in that of others. Harming or killing members of a minority group by the dominant society becomes possible when a feeling of responsibility for their welfare has been lost as a result of the profound devaluation of a minority group and of the values it espouses. The pattern of characteristics, i.e., culture, that enhances the potential for group violence has to be studied. The psychological processes leading to extreme destructiveness apparently can be energized when a cultural pattern that supports marginalization, combines with social and political stress. To excise an antisemitism that has been inculturated, therefore, small and intermediate goals may have to be achieved along the way.

Since at least the 1950s we have begun achieving the intermediate goals of excising antisemitism, at least intellectually, which could lead to a lessening of aggression. Institutionalized support for Jewish-Christian dialogue has reinforced scriptural and theological scholarship, which in turn has served to inform institutional leaders. Such scholarship can help further institutional reform. Scriptural scholarship, for example, has apparently been seen by many as a step on the path to eliminate the teaching of contempt. Many see it as important to understand the earliest experiences of the first Christians and to analyze how antisemitism became rooted in a religious tradition that purportedly was designed to reward love and compassion. What went wrong in those first centuries after the Resurrection? Reinforced by scriptural scholarship, theological reflection has begun rethinking the Christian message so that it can respond to the cultural environment of our era, as we will see in chapters 3, 4, and 5.

No solution to the disastrous linkage of Christianity and antisemitism can be viable if it proposes a non-Jewish Christianity that would acknowledge the Jews as Jews but simultaneously understand Christianity apart from the Jews. Christianity is dependent upon Judaism for its own self-understanding. The result is that Judaism cannot be viewed as a limiting or ossified religion. Antisemitism cannot be the obverse side of Christology. Antisemitism, according to Robert Osborn,[75] has its roots not in Christian faith but in Christian faithlessness. The way out of this conundrum[76] may be to declare that no individual religious community possesses *the* truth and that each community must humbly recognize its contextual limitations in appropriating *the* truth. From this perspective, there seems to be the notion that religious communities in general are related to *the* truth in valid ways. Osborn may go too far for some, but the Catholic and Protestant Churches as institutions have begun testing their own faith boundaries. Reexamining Jewish-Christian relations has gone hand-in-hand with scriptural scholarship and theological analyses. The result of all three initiatives has been a rethinking of basic human values from a religious perspective. What was God's message and how has it been institutionalized? Scholarship and institutional reflection have proceeded simultaneously, nourished by one another for the last thirty-five years. But scholarship without an institutionalization of its insights would be like a voice crying in the desert and a message unheard outside of arcane academic circles. How have the churches reflected on their past and reformed their attitudes toward the Jewish people? How can the results of Jewish-Christian reflections be institutionalized in our culture?

Notes

1. Helen Fein, *Accounting for Genocide: National Responses and Jewish Victimization During the Holocaust* (New York: Free Press, 1979), 4. For the relations between Jewish communities and the early Christians, see Gager, *The Origins of Anti-Semitism*; Alan Segal, *Rebecca's Children: Judaism and Christianity in the Roman World* (Cambridge: Harvard University Press, 1986); Neusner, *Judaism and Christianity in the Age of Constantine*; Randolph Braham, ed., *The Origins of the Holocaust: Christian Anti-Semitism* (New York: Columbia University Press, 1986); James H. Charlesworth, *Jesus within Judaism. New Light from Exciting Archaeological Discoveries* (New York: Doubleday, 1988); Franz Mussner, *Tractate on the Jews: The Significance of Judaism for Christian Faith* (Philadelphia: Fortress Press, 1984); Edward H. Flannery, *The Anguish of the Jews: Twenty-Three Centuries of Anti-Semitism* (New York: Paulist Press, 1985), 33. Flannery has distinguished theological anti-Judaism and negative prophetic statements delivered within a Jewish ambiance "from modern antisemitism" and candidly acknowledges that the New Testament has reflected an anti-Judaic theology and anti-Jewish pronouncement, prophetic in nature, which has made it a seedbed of antisemitism; see Herbert Strauss, ed., *Der Antisemitismus der Gegenwart* (Frankfurt: Campus Verlag, 1990); Frank Manuel, *The Broken Staff: Judaism Through Christian Eyes* (Cambridge: Harvard University Press, 1992).

2. Jacob Katz, *Out of the Ghetto: The Social Background of Jewish Emancipation: 1770-1870* (Cambridge: Harvard University Press, 1973), 57-79; Uriel Tal, *Christians and Jews in Germany: Religion, Politics, and Ideology in the Second Reich, 1870-1914* (Ithaca: Cornell University Press, 1975); John Pawlikowski, "Christian Ethics and the Holocaust: A Dialogue with Post-Auschwitz Judaism," *Theological Studies* 49 (1988): 649-70.

3. Bauer, *A History of the Holocaust,* 43-44; Eberhard Bethge, *Am Gegebenen Ort* (München: Kaiser, 1979).

4. For an example of this "theological antisemitism," see Janis Leibig, "John and 'the Jews': Theological Antisemitism in the Fourth Gospel," *Journal of Ecumenical Studies* 20 (1983): 226-27. Robert Kaysar has recently insisted that the Gospel itself is not antisemitic but that it historically has nurtured antisemitism. The Gospel has been read and interpreted outside of its original situation and beyond its original purpose. Such an approach would compel us to differentiate between the normative and the situational; see Kayser's essay in Craig A. Evans and

Donald A. Hager, eds., *Antisemitism and Early Christianity: Issues of Polemic and Faith* (Minneapolis: Fortress Press, 1993).

5. For an exception proving the rule, see Jaroslav Pelikan, *The Emergence of the Christian Tradition (100-600)* (Chicago: University of Chicago Press, 1971), esp. chap. 1.

6. James Donaldson and Alexander Roberts, eds., *Ante-Nicene Christian Library: Translations of the Writings of the Fathers Down to AD 325* (Edinburgh: T. and T. Clark, 1882), vol. 1, chaps. 7-12.

7. Melito of Sardis, *Sermon "On the Passover,"* (Lexington, KY: Lexington Theological Seminary Library, 1976), 4.

8. Ibid., p. 47.

9. To ask who and how many invoked the theme of deicide does not get to the root of the problem. The theological origins of the Christ-killer motif developed and flourished as an expression of a real and/or perceived Jewish hostility after the Crucifixion and did not necessarily reflect the events of Jesus' life; see Jeremy Cohen, "Introduction," in Jeremy Cohen, ed., *Essential Papers on Judaism and Christianity in Conflict: From Late Antiquity to the Reformation* (New York: New York University Press, 1991), 9-11.

10. Donaldson and Roberts, *Ante-Nicene Christian Library*, 1: 200-2, 215.

11. Norman Perrin, *New Testament: An Introduction: Proclamation and Parnesis, Myth and History* (New York: Harcourt Brace Jovanovich, 1974), 331; Donaldson and Roberts, *Ante-Nicene Christian Library*, 1: 466, 470, 472, 481; 3: 151-52.

12. Donaldson and Roberts, *Ante-Nicene Christian Library*, 4: 433.

13. Flannery, *The Anguish of the Jews* (1985), 50; see also Fred Bratton, *The Crime of Christendom: The Theological Sources of Christian Anti-Semitism* (Boston: Beacon Press, 1969), 83.

14. *Reply to Faustus*, in Frank Talmage, ed., *Disputation and Dialogue: Readings on the Jewish-Christian Encounter* (New York: KTAV Pub. House, 1975), 28-32.

15. Wayne A. Meeks and Robert Wilken, *Jews and Christians in Antioch in the First Four Centuries of the Common Era* (Missoula, MT: Scholars Press, 1978), 87-89; Williams, *Adversus Judaeos*. For a recent study, see Robert Wilken, *John Chrysostom and the Jews: Rhetoric and Reality in the Late Fourth Century* (Berkeley: University of California Press, 1983).

16. Cited in Jacob R. Marcus, ed., *The Jew in the Medieval World: A Source Book* (Cincinnati: The Sinai Press, 1938), 138; Clark Williamson, *Has God Rejected His People? Anti-Judaism in the Christian Church* (Nashville: Abingdon, 1982), 108-10; Hilberg, *The Destruction*, has

carefully connected early Christian legislation to the laws passed during the Third Reich. The similarity makes clear that Hitler's actions had precedents.

17. Flannery, *The Anguish of the Jews* (1965), 56, 98-99; James William Parkes, *The Conflict of the Church and the Synagogue: A Study on the Origins of Antisemitism* (London: The Soncino Press, 1934), 252; Marcus, *The Jew in the Medieval World*, 115-20, 127-30; Nicholas Berdyaev, *Christianity and Anti-Semitism* (Kent, England: Hand and Flower Press, 1952), 12; Leon Poliakov, *The History of Anti-Semitism* (New York: Schocken Books, 1974), 58, 62; Bernard Malamud, *The Fixer* (New York: Farrar, Strauss, and Giroux, 1966); Hilberg, *The Destruction*, 678.

18. Ruether, *Faith and Fratricide*. For responses to Ruether's ideas, see Alan Davies, ed., *Antisemitism and the Foundations of Christianity* (New York: Paulist Press, 1979).

19. Pope John Paul II, Address to Representatives of the Catholic Bishop's Conference and Other Christian Churches, March 6, 1982, *National Catholic News Service* translation, 17 March 1982.

20. For a review of the literature up to 1976, see John T. Townsend, *The Study of Judaism: Bibliographical Essays* (New York: Anti-Defamation League of B'nai B'rith, 1976), vol. 2. For works up to 1984, see Eugene Fisher, "A New Maturity in Christian-Jewish Dialogue: A Bibliographical Essay," *Face to Face* 11 (Spring 1984): 29-43. After 1984, an ongoing review of the literature can be found in the journal *Jewish-Christian Relations*.

21. See Bernard Doering, *Jacques Maritain and the French Catholic Intellectuals* (Notre Dame, IN: University of Notre Dame Press, 1983), 126-27. On theological ambiguities at the time of the Holocaust, see Eugene Fisher, "Ani Ma'amin: Theological Responses to the Holocaust," *Interface* (December 1980), 1-8; Jules Isaac, *Jesus and Israel* (New York: Holt, Rinehart, and Winston, 1971); Isaac, *The Teaching of Contempt*.

22. Gregory Baum, *Is the New Testament Anti-Semitic? A Re-Examination of the New Testament* (Glen Rock, NJ: Paulist Press, 1965), 15-16.

23. See Charlotte Klein, *Anti-Judaism in Christian Theology* (Philadelphia: Fortress Press, 1978) and Franklin Littell, *The Crucifixion of the Jews* (New York: Harper & Row, 1975).

24. Ruether, *Faith and Fratricide*, 226.

25. See Gregory Baum in Ruether, *Faith and Fratricide*, 3-4; Samuel Sandmel, *Anti-Semitism in the New Testament* (Philadelphia: Fortress Press, 1978), 164.

26. Davies, *Antisemitism and the Foundations of Christianity*, xv; Flannery, *The Anguish of the Jews* (1985), 33; see also John Townsend, "The Gospel of John and the Jews: The Story of a Religious Divorce," pp. 72-97, and Lloyd Gaston, "Paul and the Torah," in Davies, *Antisemitism and the Foundations of Christianity*, 48-71.

27. John 9: 22-35, 12: 42, 16: 2-3. See, for example, Justin Martyr, *Dialogue with Trypho* (New York: MacMillan, 1930); Leibig, "John and 'the Jews.'" Asher Finkel, "Yavneh's Liturgy and Early Christianity," *Journal of Ecumenical Studies* 18 (Spring 1981): 231-50; Steven Katz, "Issues on the Separation of Judaism and Christianity," *Journal of Biblical Literature* 103 (1984): 43-76.

28. Charles Journet, *Destinée d'Israël, A Propos du Salut par les Juifs* (Paris: Egloff, 1945), 199-200; Salo Baron, *A Social and Religious History of the Jews* (New York: Columbia University Press, 1952), 1: 194; Marcel Simon, *Verus Israel: A Study of the Relations between Christians and Jews in the Roman Empire* (New York: Oxford University Press, 1986), 263; Flannery, *The Anguish of the Jews* (1985), 62.

29. Flannery, *The Anguish of the Jews* (1965), 3-43, 281; F. Lovsky, *Antisémitisme et mystère d'Israël* (Paris: A. Michel, 1955), 45.

30. Ruether, *Faith and Fratricide*, 27. An understanding of the dynamics behind the emerging Christian identity can assist educators today; see Mary Boys, "A More Faithful Portrait of Judaism: An Imperative for Christian Educators," in David Effroymson et al., eds., *Within Context: Essays on Jews and Judaism in the New Testament* (Collegeville, MN: Liturgical Press, 1993).

31. Wilken, *John Chrysostom and the Jews*, 163; Eugene Fisher, "The Origins of Anti-Semitism in Christian Theology: A Reaction and Critique," in Braham, *The Origins of the Holocaust*, 17-29.

32. Joshua Trachtenberg, *The Devil and the Jews: The Medieval Conception of the Jews and Its Relation to Modern Anti-Semitism* (New Haven: Yale University Press, 1943); Jeremy Cohen, *The Friars and the Jew: The Evolution of Medieval Anti-Semitism* (Ithaca: Cornell University Press, 1982); Wilken, *John Chrysostom and the Jews*, 163.

33. Gregory Baum, "Catholic Dogma after Auschwitz," in Davies, *Antisemitism and the Foundations of Christianity*, 140-41; Raymond Brown, cited in Eugene Fisher, *Seminary Education and Christian-Jewish Relations: A Curriculum and Resource Handbook* (Washington, DC: National Catholic Educational Association, 1983), 38.

34. Gager, *The Origins of Anti-Semitism*, 25, 141-53, 159, 183.

35. Lloyd Gaston, "Paul and the Torah," in Davies, *Antisemitism and the Foundations of Christianity*, 48-71; Krister Stendahl, *Paul among the*

Jews and Gentiles (Philadelphia: Fortress Press, 1976); John Koenig, *Jews and Christians in Dialogue: New Testament Foundations* (Philadelphia: Westminster Press, 1979); E.P. Sanders, *Paul, the Law and the Jewish People* (Philadelphia: Fortress Press, 1983); Gager, *The Origins of Anti-Semitism*, 202, 247.

36. Gager, *The Origins of Anti-Semitism*, 9, 33, 36. A deep-seated antisemitism has pervaded Western history, but this must be seen in a wider, albeit more confusing, context.

37. See Gager, *The Origins of Anti-Semitism*; Neusner, *Judaism and Christianity in the Age of Constantine*. For an analysis of the post-70 C.E. relations between Christians and Jews, see Katz, "Issues": 43-76, and Douglas Hare, *The Theme of Jewish Persecution of Christians in the Gospel according to St. Matthew* (Cambridge: Cambridge University Press, 1967), 37-38. For an analysis of the "benediction of the heretics," see Leibig, "John and 'the Jews'": 217-19; James Charlesworth, "Exploring Opportunities for Rethinking Relations among Jews and Christians," in James H. Charlesworth, ed., *Jews and Christians: Exploring the Past, Present, and Future* (New York: Crossroad, 1990), 42; Craig A. Evans and Donald A. Hagner, *Anti-Semitism and Early Christianity: Issues of Polemic and Faith* (Minneapolis: Fortress Press, 1993).

38. H. Thackeray, trans., *Josephus* (Cambridge: Harvard University Press, 1926), 1: 405-7.

39. Williamson, *Has God Rejected His People?*, 89-90; Poliakov, *The History of Anti-Semitism*; Frederick Schweitzer, *A History of the Jews since the First Century A.D.* (New York: Macmillan, 1971).

40. Clemens Thoma, *Christliche Theologie des Judentums* (Aschaffenburg: P. Pattloch Verlag, 1978), 14; Leibig, "John and 'the Jews'": 209-34; E.J. Epp, "Anti-Semitism and the Popularity of the Fourth Gospel in Christianity," *Journal of the Central Conference of American Rabbis* 22 (1975): 35; R.A. Culpepper, "The Gospel of John and the Jews," *Review and Expositor* 84 (1987): 273-88; Sidney Hall, *Christian Antisemitism and Paul's Theology* (Minneapolis: Fortress Press, 1993).

41. Yosef Hayim Yerushalmi, "Response to Rosemary Ruether," in Fleischner, *Auschwitz: Beginning of a New Era?*, 98.

42. Ibid., 99-101. For an analysis of Christianity's theological and practical ambivalence toward the Jews, see Edward Synan, *The Popes and the Jews in the Middle Ages* (New York: Macmillan, 1965).

43. Yosef Hayim Yerushalmi, "Response to Rosemary Ruether," in Fleischner, *Auschwitz: Beginning of a New Era?*, 102-3.

44. For an analysis of the discontinuity between classic Christian antisemitism and biological or racist antisemitism, see Tal, *Christians*

and Jews in Germany, and such works as Flannery, *The Anguish of the Jews* (1965), 3-43. For the connection between the biological and anthropological disciplines and antisemitism, see Robert Proctor, *Racial Hygiene: Medicine under the Nazis* (Cambridge: Harvard University Press, 1988) and Sheila Weiss, *Race Hygiene and National Efficiency: The Eugenics of Wilhelm Schallmayer* (Berkeley: University of California Press, 1987).

45. Cohen, *The Friars and the Jew*, 20-21, for an analysis of Augustine in the context of Medieval antisemitism; see also Robert Chazan, *Barcelona and Beyond: The Disputation of 1263 and Its Aftermath* (Berkeley: University of California Press, 1992).

46. Cohen, *The Friars and the Jew*, 244.

47. For recent monographs delineating Luther's perspective on the Jews, see E.W. Gritsch, *Martin—God's Court Jester: Luther in Retrospect* (Philadelphia: Fortress Press, 1983); H. Kremers, ed., *Die Juden und Martin Luther—Martin Luther und die Juden* (Neukirchener: Neukirchener Verlag, 1985); Walther Bienert, *Martin Luther und die Juden* (Wuppertal: Evangelisches Verlagswerk, 1982); J. Halpérin and A. Sovik, eds., *Luther, Lutheranism, and the Jews* (Geneva: Dept. of Studies, Lutheran World Federation, 1984); Heiko Obermann, *The Roots of Anti-Semitism in the Age of the Renaissance and Reformation* (Philadelphia: Fortress Press, 1984), 12; J.S. Oyer, *Lutheran Reformers against Anabaptists: Luther, Melanchton, and Menius, and the Anabaptists of Central Germany* (The Hague: M. Nijhoff, 1964); E. Gritsch, "Luther and the Jews: Toward a Judgment of History," in E. Gritsch, *Luther and the Jews: Toward a Judgment of History* (New York: Lutheran Council in the USA, 1983), 7; Hans J. Hillerbrand, "Martin Luther and the Jews," in Charlesworth, *Jews and Christians*, 127-45.

48. Talmage, *Disputation and Dialogue*, 35-36; A. Roy Eckardt, "The Mutual Plight of the Churches," in A. Roy Eckardt, *Your People, My People: The Meeting of Jews and Christians* (New York: Quadrangle, 1974), 21, 68-77.

49. Katz, *From Prejudice to Destruction*; Arthur Hertzberg, *The French Enlightenment and the Jews* (New York: Columbia University Press, 1968); Yizhak Heinemann et al., eds., *Antisemitismus* (Stuttgart: J.B. Metzler, 1929).

50. Poliakov, *The History of Anti-Semitism*, 184.

51. Ibid., 239.

52. Frederick Weil, "The Extent and Structure of Anti-Semitism in Western Populations since the Holocaust," in Fein, *The Persisting Question*, 164-65.

53. Peter J.G. Pulzer, *The Rise of Political Anti-Semitism in Germany and Austria* (New York: Wiley, 1964); George Mosse, *The Crisis of German Ideology; Intellectual Origins of the Third Reich* (New York: Schocken Books, 1981); Eugen Weber, "Jews, Antisemitism, and the Origins of the Holocaust," *Historical Reflections* 5 (1978): 1-17; *Realenzyklopädie für Theologie und Kirche*, 9: 510.

54. Shmuel Ettinger, "The Secular Roots of Antisemitism," in Otto Dov Kulka and Paul R. Mendes-Flohr, *Judaism and Christianity under the Impact of National Socialism* (Jerusalem: Historical Society of Israel and Zalman Shazar Center for Jewish History, 1987), 47; Tal, *Christians and Jews in Germany*, 47; Fritz Stern, *The Politics of Cultural Despair: A Study in the Rise of Germanic Ideology* (Berkeley: University of California Press, 1961), 285; Hans Liebeschütz, *Das Judentum in deutschen Geschichtsbild von Hegel bis Max Weber* (Tübingen: Mohr, 1967), 157ff.

55. Katz, *From Prejudice to Destruction*, 194-95. On Chamberlain, see Geoffrey Field, *Evangelist of Race: The Germanic Vision of Houston Stewart Chamberlain* (New York: Columbia University Press, 1981). Wilhelm Marr coined the term antisemitism; see Moshe Zimmermann, *Wilhelm Marr: The Patriarch of Anti-Semitism* (New York: Oxford University Press, 1986).

56. Felix Goldmann, "Das Irrationale im Antisemitismus," *Der Morgan* August 1927: 314.

57. Harry Pross, *Die Zerstörung der deutschen Politik, Dokumente 1871-1933* (Frankfurt: Fischer Bücherei, 1959), especially chaps. 1, 2, and 7; Ernst Weyman, "Die 'deutsche Sendung' als Leitgedanke im Geschichtsunterricht in der höheren Schulen," *Tribüne* 5 (1966): 1820ff. For the role of romanticism in nineteenth- and twentieth-century German culture, see Mosse, *The Crisis of German Ideology*, especially chap. 1, "From Romanticism to the Volk," 13-30; and George Mosse, *Germans and Jews: The Right, the Left, and the Search for a "Third Force" in Pre-Nazi Germany* (New York: H. Fertig, 1970); Paul Rose, *Revolutionary Antisemitism from Kant to Wagner* (Princeton: Princeton University Press, 1990).

58. Tal, *Christians and Jews in Germany*, 69, 76-77; Donald J. Dietrich, *The Goethezeit and the Metamorphosis of Catholic Theology in the Age of Idealism* (Berne: Lang, 1979), 137.

59. Friedrich Nietzsche, *Aufzeichnungen über Geschichte und historische Wissenschaften* (München: Musarion Gesamtausgabe, 1922), 1: 286; Leopold Auerbach, *Das Judentum und seine Bekenner in Preussen und in anderen deutschen Bundesstaaten* (Berlin: S. Mehring, 1890), 39.

60. Robert Waite, *Vanguard of Nazism: The Free Corps Movement in Post-war Germany, 1918-1923* (Cambridge: Harvard University Press, 1952); Friedrich Wilhelm Heinz, *Die Nation greift an: Geschichte und Kritik des soldatischen Nationalismus* (Berlin: Verlag Das Reich, 1933), 88.

61. Hannah Arendt, *Elemente und Ursprünge totaler Herrschaft* (Frankfurt: Europäische Verlagsanstalt, 1955), 10; Flannery, *The Anguish of the Jews* (1965), 180-81.

62. Davidowicz, *The War Against the Jews*, 32.

63. Stern, *The Politics of Cultural Despair*, 35ff., 53ff.; Theodor Lindström, *Paul de Lagarde, Ein Vorkämpfer Deutschsozialen Reform, Antisemitisches Jahrbuch* (Berlin: Humboldt, 1898), 4ff.; Tal, *Christians and Jews in Germany*, 272.

64. "Typical for all *völkisch* opponents of Judaism is their radical alienation from Christianity"; see Karl Thieme, ed., *Judenfeindschaft: Darstellung und Analysen* (Frankfurt: Fischer Bücherei, 1963), 232, as quoted in Tal, *Christians and Jews in Germany*, 305.

65. Juan J. Linz, "Totalitarian and Authoritarian Regimes," in Fred I. Weinstein and Nelson Polsby, eds., *Macropolitical Theory*, vol. 3, *Handbook of Political Science* (Reading, MA: Addison-Wesley Pub. Co., 1975), 237; Peter Merkl, *Political Violence under the Swastika. 581 Early Nazis* (Princeton: Princeton University Press, 1975).

66. Tal, *Christians and Jews in Germany*; Norman Cohn, *Warrant for Genocide: The Myth of the Jewish World-Conspiracy and the Protocols of the Elders of Zion* (New York: Harper & Row, 1967); Merkl, *Political Violence under the Swastika*, 517; Hermann Huss and Andreas Schroeder, eds., *Antisemitismus: Zur Pathologie der Bürgerlichen Gesellschaft* (Frankfurt: Europäische Verlagsanstalt, 1965).

67. Schweitzer, *A History of the Jews*, 185-280.

68. Ian Kershaw, "The Persecution of the Jews and German Popular Opinion in the Third Reich," *Leo Baeck Yearbook* 26 (1981): 261-89; Donald J. Dietrich, "Holocaust as Public Policy: The Third Reich," *Human Relations* 34 (1981): 445-62. For an analysis of the role that antisemitism played in the creation of the post-1918 identity of an array of German socioeconomic and political groups, see Donald J. Dietrich, "National Renewal, Anti-Semitism, and Political Continuity: A Psychological Assessment," *Political Psychology* 9 (1988): 385-411.

69. Cited in D. Welch, *Propaganda and the German Cinema, 1933-1945* (Oxford: Clarendon Press, 1983), 157.

70. Commentary on the draft of a law on the announcement of legal regulations of the Reich sent by the Reich minister of the interior to the departments, Bundesarchiv Koblenz, 43 II/694.

71. Ingo Müller, *Hitler's Justice: The Courts of the Third Reich*, trans. by Deborah Lucas Schneider (London: Tauris and Co., 1991), 73. For an analysis of the relationship between the concept of Führer and the Holocaust, see Fred Weinstein, *The Dynamics of Nazism: Leadership, Ideology, and the Holocaust* (New York: Academic Press, 1980) and Marrus, *The Holocaust*, 17.

72. Eliezer Berkovits, "Facing the Truth," *Judaism* 27 (1978): 324-25.

73. Richard Lowry, "The Rejected-Suitor Syndrome: Human Sources of the New Testament's Antisemitism," *Journal of Ecumenical Studies* 14 (1977): 229.

74. Reinhard Rürup, *Emanzipation und Antisemitismus* (Göttingen: Vandenhoeck und Ruprecht, 1975); David Schoenbaum, *Hitler's Social Revolution: Class and Status in Nazi Germany, 1933-1939* (Garden City, NJ: Doubleday, 1966); Richard Hamilton, *Who Voted for Hitler?* (Princeton: Princeton University Press, 1982).

75. Robert Osborn, "The Christian Blasphemy: A Non-Jewish Jesus," in Charlesworth, *Jews and Christians*, 214.

76. Jacob Agus, "Revelation as Quest," *Journal of Ecumenical Studies* 9 (1972): 537-38; Jacob Agus, "The Covenant Concept—Particularistic, Pluralistic, or Futuristic," *Journal of Ecumenical Studies* 18 (1981): 217ff.

2

Institutional Catholic Attitudes to Judaism and the Jewish People

Before the Second World War, only rare voices foreshadowed the post-1945 revisionist trends. In 1933, Paul Tillich, confronting Nazism, discerned in the Hebrew prophets a tantalizing political eschatology that he felt could be instrumental in saving Germany and the world from the barbaric Nazi movement. In the United States, Reinhold Niebuhr attacked antisemitism in every form and began to mold a case for the abandonment of Christian triumphalism. Most prominently, however, James Parkes published a study of antisemitism that demanded a new reflection on Jewish history and has subsequently led to the scholarly study of Judaism as an integral socioreligious phenomenon that does not depend on Christianity. He concluded that Christianity based its theology on a gross historical misrepresentation of the role of the Jews in God's salvific plan.[1] Unfortunately, these were lonely voices, and their initiatives would not be advanced until after the Holocaust.

Simultaneously, while the above scholars were probing a new *Weltanschauung*, Dietrich Bonhoeffer could still in a more traditional vein write: "The Church of Christ has never lost sight of the thought that the 'Chosen People' who nailed the redeemer of the world to the cross must bear the curse for its action through a long history of suffering. The final return of the people of Israel can only take place through the conversion of Israel to Christ." Or to cite a sermon preached by Martin Niemoeller in 1937: "The gospel for the day throws light upon the dark and sinister history of this people that can neither live nor die because it is under a curse which forbids it to do either. Until the end of its days, the Jewish people must go its own way under the burden which Jesus' decree has laid upon it." Gustav Gundlach, SJ, argued that a political antisemitism fighting the Jews' "exaggerated and harmful influence" was permitted as long as it utilized morally admissible means.[2] These men wrote and preached in Nazi Germany, and their sentiments were not unfamiliar in our culture.

After the shock caused by the slaying of approximately 6 million Jews, Christians and Jews alike raised their voices and urged the churches to combat antisemitism as an evil in itself and to work toward establishing a positive attitude toward the Jewish people. In 1947, at a conference at Seeligsberg, Switzerland, the International Conference of Christians and Jews drew up a document that would have a historic impact as the initial institutional assault on antisemitism. While hiding from the Germans during the war, Jules Isaac had studied and analyzed the Christian sources of antisemitism and brought his results to this conference. The "Ten Points of Seeligsberg" became the stimulus for the ensuing dialogue between Christians and Jews. These points included the fact that God speaks to all, that Jesus was Jewish, that he loved and forgave all mankind, and that the apostles as well as early martyrs were Jews. Readers of these ten points were reminded that the foundational injunction of Christianity is love of neighbor — a commandment that was already proclaimed in the Hebrew Bible. Judaism was not to be distorted by extolling Christianity. The document emphasized that the word "Jew" was not to be used in the exclusivistic sense of the enemies of Jesus. Equally important was the insistence that the contemptuous attitude toward the Jewish people as reprobate, accursed, and destined for suffering was to be deleted from religious materials.[3]

From this opening offensive against religious antisemitism and coupled with the Christian consciousness-raising activity, church-affiliated groups have continued to denounce antisemitism. Even so, the condemnations were frequently ambivalent. The World Council of Churches, for example, in 1948 stressed the unique role of the Jewish people and the contribution of Israel to the design of God, but then stated: "The church has received this spiritual heritage from Israel and is therefore in honor bound to render it back in the light of the Cross. We have, therefore, to proclaim to the Jews 'The Messiah for whom you wait has come. The promise has been fulfilled by the coming of Jesus Christ.'"[4] The World Council subsequently urged churches to continue their traditional mission to the Jews.

The newly founded Republic of Israel not surprisingly only seemed to complicate the issue of Jewish-Christian relations. Fortunately, other themes began to intrude in the 1950s as the Christian churches continued wrestling with the problems of Christian antisemitism, Jewish survival and self-identity, the relation between the Hebrew Bible and Christian Testament, the relevance of mission, and God's role in history. The issues became more theologically exciting and ceased focusing merely on the older, pragmatic Christian-Jewish interaction as the churches realized that the relational problems were not superficial but had deep roots and went to the very essence of the Christian faith. The newly sensitive openness in virtually all theological disciplines, combined with a critically grounded repudiation of triumphalism in a recognizably multicultural world, mandated the rethinking of deeply embedded traditions and doctrines as well as forced new perspectives to emerge, which would have been almost inconceivable before the war and the Holocaust. Several issues were hotly debated, set the agenda for future dialogue, and helped create the boundaries for this new theological pattern that seemed to be emerging in several Christian denominations, including the Catholic Church.

The Modern Catholic Church and Antisemitism prior to John Paul II

For the Catholic Church, the road to the Second Vatican Council's *Nostra Aetate* has been convoluted. Virtually no church council, for example, had taken up the questions left unresolved by St. Paul in Romans, chapters 9-11, until Vatican II approached the entire

Christian tradition of antisemitism with an eye toward essentially reexamining its roots and growth. Institutional antisemitism pervaded its ecclesial culture and its sociopolitical reactions. Only when the Italians occupied Rome in 1870, for example, were the Jews liberated from their ghetto, to which they had been consigned three centuries earlier and condemned to live in abject deprivation. Even thereafter, the Vatican had continued to support religious antisemitism, which harbored the traditional stereotypes, and was convinced that the Jews were destined for eternal punishment. A frequently related episode, which sheds light on this attitude, occurred in 1904 when Theodor Herzl, father of modern Zionism, was admitted to an audience with Pius X to explain the objectives of this new movement. The pope's reaction was unequivocally negative:

> The Jews have not recognized our Lord; therefore, we cannot recognize the Jewish people. It is not pleasant to see the Turks in possession of our Holy Places, but we have to put up with it; but we could not possibly support the Jews in the acquisition of the Holy Places. If you come to Palestine and settle your people there, we shall have churches and priests ready to baptize all of you.[5]

This supersessionism was the lodestar of the pre-Vatican II Catholic perspective.

To the Catholic Church, the Jewish people remained accursed for their rejection of Jesus. This act had led to permanent exile and degradation, which would only end when salvation was realized. The humiliation of the Jews had been inculcated into succeeding generations, leading to the cultural despisal that Jules Isaac had referred to as the "teaching of contempt." A pastoral letter of the Dutch Catholic Church, for example, continued to decree: "Parish priests must take care that Christians do not work for Jews. The faithful must take care never to need the help or support of Jews." This regulation was only annulled in 1970.[6]

Little changed in the church's pre-World War II public attitude. In 1936, for example, Cardinal Hlond called for a strengthening of Poland's anti-Jewish legislation, already noted for its severity. But among the hierarchy there was emerging a growing awareness that historical Christian antisemitism could potentially have dire consequences; the activities of Nazi Germany reinforced this apprehension.

In his 1937 encyclical, *Mit Brennender Sorge*, Pius XI condemned racism. In a 1938 speech he said: "Anti-Semitism is unacceptable. Spiritually we are all Semites." The pope also had requested two Jesuits, Gustav Gundlach in Germany, now apparently seeing the error of past statements, and John LaFarge in the United States to prepare an encyclical text for a solid scholarly denunciation of racism and specifically antisemitism. Unfortunately, Pius XI died before the encyclical could be published, and his successor, Pius XII, preferred a more prudent course, especially in light of the oncoming conflict. During the war, however, the controversial pope unobtrusively worked to save Italian Jewry and other national groups when he could, but he failed to take a public stand against Nazism and the *Endlösung*. Few actually defended Jews as human beings. The record of the church in Europe seemed to depend on the courage of its individual members without overt leadership from the top. Jews were saved in those countries where a sense of obligation or toleration existed.[7]

Papal delegates in countries where the Holocaust horror was implemented usually failed to protest publicly. When they did quietly intervene, it was usually only on behalf of those Jews who had become baptized Christians.[8] To Hitler, of course, these converted men and women were still Jews, but to the church they were on the road to salvation and so merited protection. The pope never took a spiritual stance publicly and clearly against the extermination, although he certainly knew what was transpiring. The silence of the church in the face of this evil has been loudly criticized, even though there were virtually no other public defenders of Jewish lives during these years. In hindsight, of course, critics can now insist that a more rigorous moral stance should have been developed by Christian church leaders and their secular counterparts, but few at the time could realize the extent of Hitler's plans. Only from our perspective has it become clear that the devastation had been nourished by traditional Christian antisemitism.

After the war, it took time for the religious implications of the Holocaust to be fully realized; then, gradually, the haunting questions as well as its challenges had to be faced. As time went on, it became clear that the Holocaust was rooted in two thousand years of contempt that had been funneled into the cultural, political, and social environment of modern Europe. For many it seemed clear that the perception of the Jewish people as spiritual and social outsiders had to be extirpated before progress in Jewish-Christian relations could be made. Pius XII invited Jules Isaac to the Vatican to discuss Nazi antisemitism as the secular radicalization of the biased impulses of historical Christianity. The pope agreed as a first step to change the Good Friday prayer, which read: "Let us pray for the perfidious Jews that our Lord and God will remove the veil from their hearts so that they too may acknowledge our Lord, Jesus Christ. Heed the prayers we offer for the blindness of that people that they may be delivered from that darkness." By the late 1950s "perfidious Jews" would read "the unbelieving Jews."[9] To say the least, only a small beginning had been made. But consciousness of the problem was growing and legitimate concern was being expressed.

The real revolution in the attitude of the Vatican and thus the institutional Catholic Church was launched by John XXIII, who had been influenced by Isaac and who had also been the apostolic delegate in the Balkans during the war. When he convened Vatican II, he insisted that the agenda include a statement on the Jews, a document he entrusted to Augustin Cardinal Bea of Germany. Bea labored on the "Declaration on the Jews," one of the most bitterly contested pronouncements of the council. As he began, Bea explained that the document was to be solely religious and its purpose spiritual, as he correctly anticipated opposition from the Arab Catholics. He stressed that the declaration should not be considered political, i.e., pro-Zionist, because for a variety of reasons, used until recently, the Holy See did not feel drawn to recognize the Republic of Israel. Arab Catholics for their part seemed to fear that if the guilt of deicide were expunged, then the Jews would no longer have to suffer exile and could return legally and morally to Israel. Equally bitter hostility, although on theological grounds, was encountered within the conservative ranks, including influential members of the Curia. To them, the Jews had remained spiritually blind, reprobate, and accursed because they had turned their backs on God. The church, these men felt, had no obligation to the Jews other than that which it had to all peoples — to confront them with Christ's truth. The opposing elements succeeded in preventing the adoption of the pro-Jewish document until the final phase of the council, and then it was accepted only after very specific modifications. In the original statement, for example, "May Christians never present the Jewish people as one rejected, cursed or guilty of deicide," the words "guilty of deicide" were omitted. The conservatives had felt that any public renunciation of deicide would amount to a denial of the gospel, even though scriptural research had increasingly suggested that the Gospel had been read for generations through antisemitic cultural lenses. In their view, what was not renounced could still be accepted. Care was taken, therefore, to state explicitly that some Jews and their followers had pressed for the death of Christ. Also, in response to pressure, antisemitism was no longer "condemned" in the document, but only "deplored." Nowhere in this initial document was there any expression of contrition or repentance for the two-thousand-year record of Jewish suffering at the hands of the church — no recognition of the nature of God's covenant with the Jewish people right up to the present. In fact, the document highlighted the notion that the Christian Scriptures had superseded the Hebrew Bible. The committee drafting the document, moreover, did not refer to the continuing role of the Jewish communities up to the present and did not support the idea that they still had a God-ordained mission. While setting an important tone for future dialogue, the document unfortunately avoided mentioning the Holocaust, much less the Republic of Israel.[10] *Nostra Aetate* was creatively vague, merely opening the door for the clearer explications of the "Guidelines" ("Guidelines and Suggestions for Implementing the Conciliar Declarations, *Nostra Aetate*, n. 4," [1974]) and the "Notes" ("Notes on the Correct Way to Present the Jews and Judaism in Preaching and Catechesis in the Catholic Church" [1985]), the second and third major documents on Jewish-Christian relations.

With its fifteen carefully modulated sentences, however, *Nostra Aetate* was finally passed by an overwhelming majority. Denoting this changed attitude itself was a breakthrough. The stress on the spiritual bond between the church and the Jewish people, as well as the statement that the church "received the Old Testament through the people with whom God concluded the Ancient Covenant," were unprecedented and crucial for any future potential theological metamorphoses. The acknowledgment of the obviously Judaic roots of Christianity, including the Jewish ancestry of Jesus, unlocked vistas not previously exposed in public ecclesial discussions. Stating that the Jews were not rejected by God or in essence an accursed people reversed the church's traditional position. The teaching that "what happened in the passion of Christ cannot be charged against all Jews without distinction living at that time and certainly not against the Jews living today" was an important change of course. This repudiation of historical antisemitism as well as an insistence on mutual understanding through fraternal dialogue opened a new era in Catholic-Jewish relations.[11]

The publication of *Nostra Aetate* led to significant developments in the Catholic understanding of its Jewish heritage and of the role of the Hebrew Bible for contemporary Christianity. Not surprisingly, some problems were still outstanding. The Hebrew Bible, for example, had to be reconsidered as a text with its own integrity, and some have suggested that even the words "Old Testament/New Testament" should be rejected, proposing, for example, "Jewish Bible" and "Christian Scriptures." The term "Old," they have suggested, is pejorative and implies replacement by the "New," but then, that depends on one's perspective as some persons value old objects or ways. Some Christian theologians have continued to contend that there have been crucial events in Jewish history that have created distinctions. Martin Noth, for example, has suggested that the covenant ended with the destruction of the first temple (586 B.C.E.) and that this rejection was confirmed in 70 C.E.[12] In fact, the word "new" may be rooted in Jer. 31:31-34: "Behold, the days are coming, says the Lord, when I will make a new covenant with the house of Israel and the House of Judah." The discussion of this issue indicates a healthy reexamination of Jewish-Christian relations, even though no agreement on the use of "Old" or "New" may be forthcoming.

Thanks to the insights of modern biblical scholarship, some of which will be seen in the next chapter, recent decades have experienced a return to the original meaning and significance of the Hebrew Bible. In *Nostra Aetate*, n. 4, Vatican II, for example, proclaimed:

> The Church acknowledges that the beginnings of her faith and election are already found among the patriarchs, Moses and the prophets. The Church cannot forget that she received the revelation of the Old Testament through the people with whom God deigned to establish the ancient covenant.

A residue from this past has remained. In 1973, for example, the French Committee for Catholic-Jewish Relations reaffirmed that Christians were to understand Jewish tradition through study of the Bible and that the initial covenant was not invalidated by the latter. But it continued: "It is true that the Old Testament renders its meaning to us only in the light of the New Testament, but we must receive it and understand it by itself."[13] Such statements were probably designed to please both conservatives and liberals, but they leave a lot to be desired in providing unambiguous direction. Still, greater understanding seemed to be developing within the church, and this was encapsulated in *Nostra Aetate* and reinforced in subsequent documents. In their own reflection, theologians and others have been emboldened to be more critical in their work.

Cornelius Rijk, for example, suggested that the entire Bible is good news because the whole text throws the light of God's spirit on human history and reveals God in a covenantal relationship with the human race.[14] The Vatican "Guidelines" of 1974 state: "The same God speaks in the Old Testament and the New Testament."[15] Explaining this extension of *Nostra Aetate*, Eugene Fisher has said: "Stripped of its basis in the Hebrew Scriptures, the New Testament makes little sense."[16] Even so, these statements fail to recognize explicitly the Hebrew Bible as an authentic, *independent* religious document.

Protestant theologians, however, did move more forcefully in this direction and have exhibited some very creative initiatives that served to stimulate Catholic scholars. Along this line, Paul van Buren has offered a provocative nuance that may enable us to get to the heart of the question. The Hebrew Bible serves as a reminder that Christians were not the first to be called.[17] Rolf Rendtorff, professor of theology at Heidelberg, has concluded that the question that confronts Christian theologians is whether they can continue to claim an abbreviated "de-Judaized" Hebrew Bible as Christian. Since, presumably, they cannot, they should have the honesty and courage to declare that the Hebrew Bible must be accepted in its entirety. They should concede its Jewish character and should refrain from challenging the right of the Jews to their own interpretation of their Bible.[18]

The discussion of the relationship of the Hebrew Bible and the Christian Scriptures to one another has served to sensitize theologians to the obviously more profound problem of the interaction among the

Jewish people, the covenant, Jesus Christ, and Christianity in God's plan of salvation. Institutionally, the Christian churches came to grips with the relationship between Christianity and Judaism as well as the Christian role in developing historical antisemitism. They simultaneously worked to redefine theological parameters and to establish an intellectual ambiance, which could lend support for more thorough analyses of Judaism within the Christian *Weltanschauung*.

Such liberal Catholic critics as A.C. Ramselaar and Cornelius Rijk noted that whenever the entire Vatican II document ("Declaration of the Church to Non-Christian Religions") discussed Hinduism or Islam, for example, it described them in the authentic terms of those religions. Only Judaism had not been extended this right. Where the church acknowledged the truths of Judaism, the Hebrew revelatory experience did not attain autonomous status and depended for its validity on the Christian Scriptures. Similarly, although Judaism may well have become a partner in the dialogue, it still did not seem to exist in its own right; it was only relevant through its connection to Christianity. This connection was prominent in two motifs:

1.   the historical interpretation, articulated by the church, that the "New" Testament was basically latent in the "Old"; and
2.   the eschatological conception that insisted that redemption could be complete only when Judaism acknowledged that salvation had been foreseen by the prophets and others and was the explicit reason behind Judaism.[19]

Other statements of Vatican II seemed to support traditional viewpoints. The documents of the Dogmatic Constitution stated that the election of Israel was to be seen as merely preparatory because it prefigured the new and perfect covenant that was ratified in Christ, who originated the new people of God. While addressing with eloquence and understanding the Hebrew Bible, the Dogmatic Constitution on Divine Revelation concluded that this Hebrew origin of the Bible only revealed its full meaning in the Christian portion. The supersessionist implications of these documents were subsequently transfused into other Vatican pronouncements and seem to indicate the continuing ambivalence within church circles during these years of halting advance.

A cautious Paul VI abolished the Good Friday prayer about the unbelieving Jews. Simultaneously, in a Lenten homily delivered to the council, however, he described the Jews as a people who fought, slandered, injured, and, finally, killed Christ! Exhibiting his finely honed diplomacy, he appeared more sensitive to the conservative bent of his colleagues than to the spirit of *Nostra Aetate*, which he was implementing. The really long-lasting impact of the "Declaration" was not so much in what it actually said than in the new supportive attitudes that it initiated. Its very ambivalence helped open the way for discussion.

A creatively new vocabulary could now be deployed for a constructive reflection on Jewish-Christian relations, and the emerging referent could help contribute to the creation of an open atmosphere that was conducive to legitimate dialogue. Still, obstacles persisted. Even Cardinal Bea, who had piloted the "Declaration" to a positive vote, remained somewhat hostage to the historical religious patterns of thought. Writing in a positive spirit in his book *The Church and the Jewish People*, he asserted that deicide could only be properly imputed to the guilty officials who were aware of Christ's dual nature. Such knowledge would be unlikely, of course, because Christ's nature was dogmatically explicated only at a later date and after a great deal of debate. Using such quotes from Christ as "Father forgive them for they know not what they do" (Luke 23:24), he presumed that the members of the Sanhedrin did not have such knowledge. But Bea also tended to ignore Jewish self-understanding through history, and he supported theologians who continued to interpret Judaism from a supersessionist perspective that neglected the ongoing vitality of Judaism up to the present. He stated: "Evidently the Jewish people is no longer the people of God in the sense of an institution of the salvation of mankind, not because it is rejected, but [because] its function in preparing the kingdom of God finished with the advent of Christ and the founding of the Church."[20] With the foundation of the church, he insisted, the nature of the "people of God" was no longer propagated by descent but by faith. No longer were the people of God confined to a single nation. Certainly, he contended, no one could take from the Jews the past honor in preparation for redemption. The church was and is rooted in this people's experience. The Jewish people, he continued, have God's assurance that their lack of faith would not last forever. In *Nostra Aetate* a start had been made, but old forms die hard. The institutional modifications could now be nurtured by and could interact with the theological reflections that had begun delineating new boundaries that could encourage the creative stages of the Jewish-Christian dialogue that was beginning.

An impasse had seemingly been reached because old formulae still enjoyed support even though new theological explorations also seemed viable. Even one of the most well-disposed members of the Catholic hierarchy, Cardinal Bea, seemed to maintain that the mission and purpose of the Jewish people had ceased with the advent of Christ and that the church now was merely waiting for them eventually to accept Jesus. Not surprisingly, the church's traditional self-definition had led to this conclusion. If one were to accept the popularized premise that outside the church there is no salvation, which was not really understood in either its roots or original and proper meaning, then a non-Christian as such could not be saved, unless one could manage to portray Christianity as a spiritual and not institutional movement. Some initiatives on this front were actively developing through Karl Rahner's proposal that "anonymous Christians" could be saved, but this was a very paternalistic approach because it defined the integrity of others in terms of Christian "truth." The council had begun interpreting the stringent and oppressive perspective, at least in the popular mind, but still insisted that the church seek — or at least anticipate — the ultimate ideal in which all people, including the Jews, could find salvation in Christ. Meanwhile, Bea and others felt that the Jewish people should be respected as they had accomplished God's mission in preparing for Jesus. But this line of thought, although more commendable than the earlier, very narrow views, would be unacceptable to Jews in light of work by such scholars as Franz Rosenzweig, Paul van Buren, and John Pawlikowski, who saw both Judaism and Christianity as legitimate, both having their origin in God and both maintaining an integral and living tradition. Jews and Christians were seen to stand equally before God. Rosenzweig's dual-covenant approach, for example, has had profound implications on Jewish-Christian dialogue. Acceptance of one faith would not necessarily mean rejection of the other. Paul van Buren also has insisted that Judaism should not be assimilated into Christianity. Pawlikowski has pointed out that even a warrant for toleration would not suffice because toleration has the connotation of a superior-inferior relationship.[21] The choice of words and models seems crucial here.

Because of such mixed and even contradictory signals stemming from the church and various Christian theologians, some Jewish commentators resented the 1965 "Declaration," which they felt had still not grappled with reality and had led to ambivalent statements. How, they asked, could they be absolved from guilt for the Crucifixion when the act could never be recognized as a crime in the first place by the contemporary civil or religious authorities? Even had it been recognized as a crime, it was an act committed, of course, by individuals and not by a whole people. Guilt, moreover, could not be transmitted through generations. Despite the fact that the negative religious baggage had not been discarded, opportunities for dialogue had at least been exposed, and the problematic issues could now be confronted more openly. As the points of contention were discussed, the creative seeds of *Nostra Aetate* blossomed into more refined documents, reflecting a deeper understanding of the issues.

Paul VI took a number of steps that reinforced the changes that had been initiated. He extensively revised the prayer "For the Conversion of the Jews" into a prayer "For the Jews." He also stopped the veneration of Simon of Trent, the boy beatified in the sixteenth century because of a popular belief that he had been ritually murdered by the Jews. A new relationship between Jews and Christians was being institutionalized as historically ossified values were being shattered. The first formal meeting between representatives of the church and world Jewry was held in Rome in 1970. The Jews were represented by the newly constituted International Jewish Committee for Interreligious Consultations, which thereafter has maintained an ongoing dialogue between the Jewish world and Christian groups. The Vatican Liaison Committee was its counterpart and has regularly met to discuss broad themes and examine contemporary developments. While the Vatican would have preferred an exclusively religious dialogue, Jewish leaders persistently raised such political issues as the recognition of the Republic of Israel, which in the eyes of many Jews was seen as the cornerstone of Christian sincerity. Catholic leaders, however, have seen this political recognition as fraught with danger. In 1974, Paul VI established a Commission for Religious Relations with Judaism, which was officially described as "attached to but independent of the Secretariat for Christian Unity." This anomalous linkage originated from both historical and theological motivations. Historically, the committee title and institutional association developed from the traditional view that the first schism in the church was the break with Judaism. Thus, unity within the church seemed to presume some form of reconciliation with the Jewish people. Theologically, the intimate, yet traditionally acrimonious, bond with the Jews precluded a connection with the Secretariat for Relations with Non-Christian Religions. The Commission was independent of the Christian Unity Secretariat, and its objective was not to seek union but to engage in dialogue.

In 1974, the Vatican issued a second document on Jewish-Christian relations, entitled "Guidelines for the Implementation of *Nostra Aetate*." The "Guidelines" provided explicit and formal expression to accommodate the new attitudes that were taking shape as Jews and Christians examined their past and present relationships with an intent to design the parameters for future interchanges. The document asserted that Christians should begin learning how Jews have historically defined themselves within the context of their own integral religious experience. Judaism was no longer to be seen as a religion of fear and legalistic justice that ignored the love of God and neighbor, both of which traditionally had been viewed by Christians as the unique contribution of their own faith community. The document also repudiated the familiar presumptive fossilization of Judaism by insisting that Jewish history had not ended with the destruction of Jerusalem. The Jewish people, it asserted, have continued to develop a rich religious tradition that can even now help support Christians who are reflecting on their own salvific history. Antisemitism, moreover, was now to be condemned and not merely deplored. Supersessionist implications were to be excised, and Christians were "to strive to understand the difficulties which arise for the Jewish soul — rightly imbued with an extremely high, pure notion of the divine transcendence when faced with the mystery of the incarnate word."[22]

One of the most divisive issues on the Jewish-Christian agenda has been that of sending missionaries to convert the Jewish people. The traditional Christian attitude has been that Jews were stubbornly avoiding conversion and that such behavior justified a continuing mission, which was to reinforce Christian identity. The fact that the

Jewish people did not convert in the first centuries of Christianity was used to explain the delayed Second Coming. This conversion mission became integral to the Christian worldview that was focused on the coming Parousia. The aggressive, although not the theoretical, mission, of course, had long been obviated. After Vatican II, Christians were asked to be aware of Jewish sensitivities toward the so-called need for a mission, which had in the past contributed to antisemitism. Many Christians, however, still rejected a broad and inclusive view of God's salvific plan and could not accept the fact that God had not acted in an exclusively redemptive way in world history. Jacob Jocz, for example, insisted that in confronting the Synagogue, the church was being true to itself as a missionary force that proclaimed the centrality of Jesus Christ. The moment that Christ was professed as Lord, he maintained, the church had developed a missionary agenda with the Jewish people as the object. If Christianity did not extend to the Jews, some felt it could have no gospel for the world.[23] To improve relations, such inaccurate, myopic views had to be expunged. Christianity would have to reject its conversion model in order to understand the meaning and end of God's people. Christians were now being asked to search for an identity rooted in God's salvific plan for all humanity.

The winds of change were increasing in velocity. In 1977, with the approbation of the Holy See, Thomaso Federici presented a paper at a meeting of the Catholic-Jewish Liaison Committee. Federici distinguished between "witness" and "proselytism." "Witness" he defined as the Christian proclamation of the ongoing action of God-in-history and of the continual struggle to show how Christ has provided a valuable insight into God's plan. Even in the twentieth century, "proselytism" has retained its original zealous emphasis on propagating the faith, but through the years it has also acquired a pejorative dimension that Federici asserted should aptly now be labeled "unwarranted proselytism." This "unwarranted proselytism" should stand outside Christian witness because it has included aggressive actions that violated the human right to be free from any religious constrictions. Federici insisted that the church publicly reject any preaching that would be derogatory toward the Jews as individuals or as a community and that would impinge on personal religious decisions as well as free will. Contempt toward or prejudice against

Jews or Judaism, he asserted, were to be excluded, as were all forms of discussion that sought to exalt Christianity at the expense of Judaism. Any action seeking to convert Jews singly or as groups by offering advantages or using threats and coercion was to be condemned because liberty of conscience had been given by God. Very explicitly stated, the attempt to convert the Jewish people was to be rejected totally. [24] This statement enunciated a position that was not consistent with other contemporary documents issued by various Vatican offices, and so suggested that the church was not yet prepared to follow a uniform path that would risk losing the support of its more conservative constituencies.

The Vatican Council Decree on the Missionary Activity of the Church, for example, viewed the church as a missionary organization in its very nature when it said: "It is God's plan that the whole body of men which makes up the human race should form one people of God and be joined in one body of Christ."[25] At the same time, the "Declaration on Human Freedom" had indicated an appreciation for religious pluralism as a God-given reality. Even before Federici's statement, Catholic theologians had been moving in a direction that was more congruent with the realities of the world. Earlier, some theologians had distinguished between Israel and those other religious groups, to whom a mission was appropriate, and had maintained that the Christian task was to implant the seed of faith and to give flesh to the gospel in alien soil. Since Israel could be viewed as the "mother-soil" for Christianity, the concept of mission did not seem to apply and ought to be replaced by an ecumenical outlook. [26] This newly shaped position might appeal to Jews but easily could also alienate others who had more traditional perspectives. In a similar vein, Hans Küng had written: "The Church can never seriously take up the task of missionizing the Jews. The Gospel cannot be presented to them as something alien and external. They have never been guilty of false faith. In fact before the Church existed, they believed in the one, true God."[27] A consensus seemed to be building that God's revelation was not to be viewed so narrowly that missionary activities could be justified.

The Vatican initiatives were reinforced by several national episcopal synods. Frequently, these efforts testified to the positive encounter between Catholic and Jewish communities as they have interacted with one another. In 1980, the German bishops stated: "He who encounters Jesus Christ encounters Judaism." They encouraged changes in the New Testament interpretations relating to the Jews, insisting that negative Christian scriptural statements on Jews must always be balanced with corrective canonical insights and that the *Sitz in Leben* (contextual environment) of the text must be probed to understand the statements. There is, proclaimed the bishops, a common ground between Christians and Jews; in a swipe at Marxism, they insisted that the Judaic-Christian religion is the "anti-opium of the people."[28] In 1984 and 1986, the Brazilian bishops also stressed that Catholics should learn the essential religious and ethnic traits that Jews used to define themselves and should cease relying on the residue of outdated and obviously dangerous stereotypes. Judaism was not, they insisted, to be equated with other religions, because it had historically been the first human experience with monotheism. God had constituted the Hebrews as a people by making a covenant with them. The Brazilians reminded all Christians that God gave Canaan to Abraham and proclaimed the rights of the Jews to a definitive political existence in their country of origin. The Republic of Israel, therefore, was to be acknowledged, the bishops felt, but not at the expense of injustice to others.[29] This latter notion added a provocative factor to the ongoing dialogue.

The French bishops also penetrated to the very heart of the issue: "The existence of the Jewish people and its partial ingathering in the land of the Bible constitute increasingly for the Christian the basis of a better understanding of his own faith and a greater enlightenment for his own life." A return to the scriptural sources, marking a break with the attitude of an entire past, was at the base of this declaration. Christians were to adopt a new attitude toward the Jewish people not only in secular affairs but also in their understanding of revelatory faith, which was to be probed for its most profound meaning. The bishops' statement correctly attributed at least one form of antisemitism to the pagan world and so suggested that this was a prejudice already embedded in early Christianity, at least partially through acculturation. The classical stereotypes, they felt, were subsequently intensified in Christian times by pseudotheological arguments. Contrary to the very ancient, but very contested, exegesis, the bishops insisted that the Christian Testament, seen in its cultural and historical context, had originally not taught that the Jews had been deprived of their election. Whether this testament was or was not antisemitic became a controversial topic during the 1970s and 1980s.[30] The Dutch bishops also affirmed that the church should reflect on Jewish self-understanding and that the Bible could not be comprehended without a positive familiarity with the Jewish awareness of God, which had been proclaimed in the Hebrew Bible. The Belgian bishops also maintained that the church could not fully be the people of the covenant until the end of time, and they insisted that the church had not displaced the Jews in God's plan. The bishops of the United States and other national groups have issued documents along similar lines.[31] Institutionally, then, the Catholic Church had begun to rethink the meaning of the Christian experience as lived by successive communities.

John Paul II and the Church's Ambivalent Positions

This general upbeat development was reinforced by John Paul II. Speaking to an international group of Jewish leaders in Rome in 1979, the pope again highlighted the "spiritual bond" that served to unite the church to the people of Israel. He reaffirmed that "both communities were connected and that both were closely related at the very level of their respective identities." The need for "fraternal dialogue" between them was seen as of primary importance because the Jewish-Christian relationship was not a merely marginal matter for the church's own identity. Subsequently addressing the German Jewish community in Mainz in 1980, he pointed to "the depth and richness of our common inheritance bringing us together in mutually trustful collaboration." Judaism was now described as a *living* legacy that had to be understood by Christians if they hoped to understand their own faith. He spoke of a dialogue between today's churches and today's people of the covenant concluded with Moses.

Several points stand out in the pope's remarks. The first is that he affirmed that the common origins and roots of Christianity sprang from Judaism. The original covenant was never retracted by God, and so the way for an entirely new relationship between the two living traditions on the basis of mutual respect for each other's essential religious claims had now to be reforged from this new perspective. The pope also insisted that the church enthusiastically should accept the continuing and permanent election of the Jewish people. A Christian appreciation for Judaism's unique self-definition and the sensitive awareness that the church has a very real stake in the survival and prosperity of the Jewish people had become preconditions for legitimate dialogue.[32]

In a 1982 address, the pope reaffirmed that the two religious communities were linked in God's revelation. This symbiosis between the church and the Jewish people was grounded in the design of the covenantal God. John Paul II went on record as deploring the ancient and recent persecutions endured by the Jews, and he called for Christians and Jews to explore their unique yet common identities. "Our common spiritual heritage is considerable and we can find help in understanding certain aspects of the Church's life by taking into account the faith and religious life of the Jewish people as professed and lived now as well." Both groups, he continued, should be able "to go by diverse — but in the end convergent — paths with the help of the Lord who has never ceased living with his people, to reach true brotherhood in reconciliation, respect, and the full accomplishment of God's plan in history."[33]

In 1985, the Vatican published its third document on Christian-Jewish relations, entitled "Notes on the Correct Way to Present the Jews and Judaism in the Preaching and Catechesis of the Catholic Church," later called "The Common Bond" or "Notes."[34] As a successor statement, the "Notes" were somewhat disappointing. The document contained some significant advances but simultaneously also restated some traditional positions which by that time should have been abandoned. Apparently, the document was once again a political statement that attempted to include bold liberal and conservative opinions, which probably reflected other enduring post-Vatican II controversies swirling through the church.

On the positive side, the "Notes" incorporated the pope's statement at Mainz, focusing on "The people of God and the Old Covenant that has never been revoked." The incorporation of this statement into an official Vatican document constituted an important step forward, and one whose full significance continues to be explored. A further statement with profound implications warned that care had to be taken in reading some of the traditional Christian scriptural texts because, as "Notes" indicates, some hostile references to the Jews are rooted in

conflicts between the early church and the Jewish community. Certain
controversies emerged within cultures after the time of Jesus. The
Gospels and other canonical works were to be accepted not as
eyewitness accounts but rather as written documents reflecting the
times and contexts in which the fledgling communities were seeking
self-understanding. Those reading the classical Christian texts were
asked to remember that the theological speculations of the patristic age
often were retrojected into the testament text. The enunciation of this
warning, supported by modern scholarship, would seem to indicate the
new openness of the church to these historical permutations. The
serious attention paid to this recommendation has done much to help
explain the sources of historical friction that had developed between
Catholics and Jews as well as the antisemitic stereotypes that were
formed. In the process, such scholarship has helped delineate the
Christian identity of these early communities engaged in an intra-
Jewish struggle.

Jews could also see a new opening in "Notes." The text stated that
Christians must accept their responsibility to prepare the world for the
coming of the Messiah. They should also cooperate to create the
conditions for the rights of persons and nations and for social and
international reconciliation. Jews and Christians were commanded to
love their neighbors, to participate in a common hope for the Kingdom
of God, and to be aware of the great heritage of the Prophets. The
directives also provided some contextual signposts for dealing with
the early Christian period. They establish clear theological guidelines
that could help, it was felt, to eliminate biases that in the past had led
to anti-Jewish prejudices. Jesus was Jewish, the text reminded its
readers; the Pharisees received some positive references. The
document, moreover, emphasized that Judaism is even today a
contemporary vibrant way of life and of communion with God and not
just a historical reality. Judaism is anything but ossified and can, in
fact, help elucidate Christian revelation.

Beside these positive contributions, however, the "Notes" continued
to stress some of the boundaries that presumably had to be respected
in Catholic-Jewish dialogue. At least for those conservatives who
helped shape this document, the basic problem obviously has
remained the nature of salvation. Unfortunately, the document states
that the church and Judaism cannot be perceived as two parallel and

equal roads to salvation and that the church *must* witness Christ as the redeemer for *all*.[35] Although this is subsequently qualified by an expression pledging respect for religious liberty, its implications are clear for Judaism as well as for all other non-Christian faiths that have been allowed existential, but not theological, legitimation. The authors of the document also have tried to qualify their reform by insisting that in any Christian reflection on Judaism such opposites as promise/fulfillment and continuity/newness have to be balanced, but always in favor of Christianity. The document seems to rest on a Hegelian dialectic that has not reached final synthesis. At least the thesis and antithesis seem to be stated so that the tension can persist, as perhaps no legitimate synthesis is possible that would maintain both faiths intact. Still, even though there appears to be theological movement here, there is also the subtext that the church alone has the ultimate truth and that the sole path to salvation for all is through Jesus. Some of the proclamations of Vatican II as well as those embedded in succeeding documents had suggested the possibility that traditional positions could be reexamined in light of the more sensitive historical consciousness of the Christian communities. John Paul II himself seemed to acknowledge the legitimacy of divergence and the mystery of convergence. The "Notes," however, strongly suggest that divergence can only be seen as temporary and that convergence is a precondition for salvation. The dialectical tension understandably persists because theologians, bishops, and the pope have recognized that God's revelation may not be as clear as once thought. Since a final synthesis has not been offered, the dialogue can continue.

The "Notes" seem to reinforce, however, a traditional missionizing tendency regarding the salvific will. On one hand, both Jews and Christians are working toward the *eschaton* — the coming or return of the Messiah. On the other hand, the church is seen as the all-embracing means of the fullness of salvation. Christians can only get to the Father through Christ. This seems to mean that the road to salvation lies through Jesus and the church.[36] Jews seemingly were denied their own validity, and the initial issue at the base of antisemitism was yet to be resolved completely. Religious faith, almost by its nature, of course, insists that it has the exclusive path to holiness, and so it is very difficult to be open to others. The Holocaust serves as a silent witness to the disasters associated with such exclusivity. But such a human cultural trait may be difficult to expunge.

Although Judaism is frequently accused of particularism, Christians have to remember that it contains a universal doctrine of salvation teaching that the righteousness of all nations has its place in the world to come — i.e., salvation comes through righteous living. In this context, David Flusser[37] has argued that in reflecting on salvation, Judaism's pluralism and universalism could profitably be contrasted to Christianity's historical exclusivity and particularism. From the patristic era, Christianity has insisted on faith in Jesus as essential for full salvation. Unless Christianity, many seem to be suggesting, is prepared to reconfigure this axiomatic attitudinal and behavioral pattern, which was constructed in response to other faiths, and rely on a faith rooted in mystery and eschatology, triumphalism will probably persist. Such a predictable result appears to conflict with the insistence of the "Notes" that significant dialogue can only occur if respect for the essential traits, by which the Jews define themselves in light of their own religious experience, is embraced by Christians. Running counter to Federici's critique of mission, the "Notes" still seem to imply implicitly, if not explicitly, a conversionist hope that has made Jewish communities uncomfortable and uncertain of the real motives shaping their dialogue partner. The document may well be an umbrella or committee report designed to cover all the theological bases. Eugene Fisher suggests that more appropriate sentiments have to be present if dialogue is to develop, when he asserts that "the point to be remembered is not who is 'most dear' to God, but rather what God has called us both, Jews and Christians, to do in and for the world." Essentially, Christians and Jews are to build God's Kingdom and not carve out spheres of interest or develop isolated agendas.[38]

Linked to any position on salvation is the legitimacy of election. In repudiating antisemitism, the "Notes" remind the faithful to learn to appreciate and love the Jews as an ongoing chosen people. Unfortunately, the document then adds that the Jewish people have been chosen to prepare the way for the coming of Christ. The definitive meaning of the election of Israel, therefore, is only illumined by the complete fulfillment in Christ. Not surprisingly, this statement has been found objectionable. Fisher has suggested another interpretation. This statement may only mean that Israel's election is a final witness to and finds its ultimate destiny in God's Kingdom. But then what is Christianity if Israel's election is the final witness? Sounding a cautionary note, scholars have been quick to point out that the nineteenth- and twentieth-century missionaries developed their normative case based on the Christian definition of Kingdom, and so it is important to come to grips with this issue.[39]

The "Notes" do not resolve issues. Rather, they raise them, because the document appears to affirm two equally valid covenants. What is not made clear is the status of the Mosaic covenant after the coming of Christ. Is it still valid as an integral entity? The Israeli Catholic theologian Marcel Dubois has commented that many Christians and Jews have pondered whether there is one covenant or two. Do two peoples of God exist, spiritually linked, or one people composed of both Jews and Christians whose mission is to proclaim the one God? In the final analysis, the question may be unanswerable because it probes the most profound mystery at the very base of revelation. But it does have to be explored to help unpack the mystery. In general, the continuity as well as the discontinuity between Christianity and Judaism have now been recognized as issues foundational to an understanding of the interactions in the Christian Scriptures that reflect on such sensitive issues as "covenant," Paul's conversion-call, and the use of the title "Israel."[40]

On the relation between the Hebrew Bible and the Christian Scriptures, the "Notes" state emphatically that the Hebrew Bible has permanent value for the Christian faith expression. But no hint emerges that the Jewish proclamation of monotheism, the glory of the Psalms, and the social and ethical message of the prophets have a permanent value in their own right as fruitful insights for all persons, even though there is admittedly a general agreement that the Hebrew covenant has never been revoked. The "Notes" stress what Judaism historically has provided and can still extend to Christianity. Unfortunately, a typology is again endorsed. The Hebrew Bible, it is emphasized, must not be read for its own value but merely as a document forecasting and prefiguring the Christian Testament. From this standpoint, Jewish texts would again lose their intrinsic value and would merely serve as models or prototypes. Thus, Jesus would be the culminating point for the Hebrew Bible; only Christ seems to liberate through the sacraments. Contemporary theological interpretations of

Christian faith were to be used to elucidate an understanding of the Hebrew Bible, and the supersessionist assumptions of the approved exegesis have remained the controlling agents. Historically, the use of typology has constituted for the Jewish people an obstacle, and its reaffirmation as a legitimate exegetical tool can be seen as disquieting. The "Notes" as a document merely seems to be pouring new wine into old vessels. The Vatican's leading ideologist, Cardinal Ratzinger, has stated: "We must again have the courage to say clearly that the Bible taken as a whole is Catholic." Given his position in the Curia, such a statement was unfortunate and disquieting. But the "Notes", while unfortunately highlighting typology, also insist that there is a Christian and a Jewish identity, that the Hebrew Bible maintain an intrinsic value, and that the Christian Testament should be read in light of earlier revelation because this was the context within which Christian catechesis was formed. Using typology could well evoke past problems, but carefully understood within the newly emerging interpretative context, the approach does not necessarily have to produce anxiety as long as the supersessionist imperative is excised. Typology could be seen as the result of the common culture out of which sprang Christian and Jewish reflections, and perhaps a new term or model must now be used to achieve more positive results. Care in usage until a new model can be uncovered, which expresses the post-Vatican II reality of openness more exactly, should be the order of the day.[41] Many scholars would like to see severance made with the past, but institutions rarely move that rapidly. For Jews, of course, the "Old" Testament cannot prefigure Christianity. The Hebrew Bible is axiomatically Jewish and the only recognized revelation. Other approaches could have been articulated. In December 1969, for example, a document had been prepared for the Office for Relations with Judaism but unfortunately was not officially accepted. The text has been printed, however, elsewhere. "The Old Testament should not be understood exclusively in reference to the New nor reduced to an allegorical significance as is so often done in Christian liturgy."[42] Setting a course using this norm could have resulted in a more positive direction for the development of healthy Jewish-Christian relations.

In dealing with the death of Jesus, the "Notes" continued the directional line of *Nostra Aetate,* but still did not fully break with past errors. To move away from the church's historical tradition of laying the blame for Jesus' death on all Jews then living and who have lived subsequently, it says that "there is no putting the Jews who knew Jesus and who did not believe in him on the same plane with Jews who came after him or those of today." The intent is clear, but it fails to recall in an explicitly positive fashion the significance of the historical continuity in Judaism, which is fundamental to Jewish self-conception. Presumably the Jews of today do not wish to be seen on a plane distinct from their ancestors in the time of Jesus. Although historically no universal group has been officially accused of executing Jesus, the Jewish nonacceptance of Jesus has been popularly seen in this light by successive generations. The problem is that having suggested and subsequently reinforced the deicide myth, even if not in doctrine, and now recognizing its dangers, church leaders cannot see how to uproot and destroy it expeditiously. Instead, straddling the issue, the church has aimed at explaining the past, which only has involved it in further historical distortions. The deicide myth has developed over centuries and will take time to dissolve, but a clear-cut condemnation should have been made.

The "Notes" do not directly confront the Christian responsibility for the creation of antisemitism; they only deplore it. The real question is why antisemitism was created and how it can now be expunged. How can Christianity "deconstruct" what it has created? The document also treats the Holocaust in an offhand manner. Particularly unfortunate is the restriction of the significance of the Holocaust to its "meaning for the Jews," which seems to ignore its meaning for the church and Christendom or its universal implications for all humans. The document's stance can in part be praised, because it retains the uniqueness of the Shoah, a premeditated assault on the Jewish people. But the Holocaust has more universal implications that impact on society as a whole and on Christianity, the nominal religion of the perpetrators and one of the sources of the "insider-outsider" nexus that set the stage for the disaster.[43] For all its positive statements and subsequent clarifications by Catholic representatives, key sections of the document understandably disappointed Jewish leaders because they failed to meet the declared need to conduct a dialogue based on the foundation that each religious group should mutually recognize the other's self-definition. What has been missed is that in theological dialogue, the goal is not necessarily agreement but an understanding of the implications of an issue, and while progress has been made, outstanding problems need further explication.

Such concrete problems were only underlined by an astonishing series of papal statements during the months after the "Notes" were issued. In October 1985, John Paul II received the Jewish-Catholic Liaison Committee. While the pope assured them that *Nostra Aetate* would be an irrevocable pronouncement binding on the church for the future, he later spoke to a general audience and referred to the Jews as having killed Christ.[44] The eradication of this deeply rooted prejudice was supposed to have been the main achievement of *Nostra Aetate*, but old patterns of thought persisted. Concern was also heightened by a series of three Lenten sermons delivered by the pope in March 1986. Traditional displacement theology appeared to be reinforced through his statement:

> Because of the many transgressions of the Covenant, God promises His chosen people a new covenant, ratified with the blood of His own Son, Jesus, on the cross. The Church, expression of the New Covenant, represents the continuity of Israel, which had wandered in search of salvation. It is the new Israel; it presupposes the old and goes beyond it, to the extent that it has the necessary strength to live not through obedience to the ancient laws, that gave knowledge of God but not his salvation, but through faith in Jesus.[45]

All these speeches contained residues from older attitudes. Jews as well as representative Catholic theologians, who saw the reversal to a pre-Vatican II mentality, were alarmed. Jewish organizations were considering an appropriately critical response, when they learned that the pope, for the first time in history, would visit the synagogue in Rome. Although papal representatives stated that this visit had been previously discussed, the actual precipitate scheduling may have been related to the growing confusion and malaise in Jewish circles due to John Paul's pronouncements. Papal remarks seemed to reflect varied agendas and suggested the continuing conflict in the hierarchy on post-Vatican II directions.

The pope's visit to and comments in the synagogue in April of 1986, however, gave renewed impetus to the dialogue. The speech cautiously praised the progressive theological discernments that had been achieved, and so the pope seemed to detach himself from the conservatives. Such statements as "each of our religions wishes to be respected and recognized in its own identity" and "the Lord will judge each one according to his own works, Jew and Christian alike" helped to counter some of the negative Jewish reactions to the "Notes" and papal homilies as well as to acknowledge that Jewish identity was sacrosanct and not to be threatened by any Christian appropriation. His observations supported his 6 May 1982 statement that had asserted the importance for Christians to know "the faith and religious life of the Jewish people as they are professed and practiced today." Similarly, the compelling reference to Judaism as "our elder brother" and to Jews as "irrevocably the beloved of God" supported a renewed effort for dialogue, while the statement that "faith cannot be the object of exterior pressure" continued Federici's denunciation of "unwarranted proselytism." The Jewish audience was disappointed, however, by the absence of any reference to the Republic of Israel. Some Jews hoped, although probably unrealistically at the time, that the pope would make some dramatic gesture on the subject. Even a reaffirmation of his 1984 statement acknowledging the right of the Jews in Israel to security and tranquillity would have been welcome. In general, the speech was a positive and much needed stimulus to the ongoing dialogue. The pope's address reflected the conclusion of the 1985 meeting of the Catholic-Jewish Liaison Committee, which had suggested as vital for future reflection the dissemination of the achievements of the preceding two decades of Jewish-Christian dialogue. The hope was to overcome the residues of indifference, resistance, and suspicion. By the 1980s, joint action in resisting religious extremism and fanaticism as well as mutual efforts pursuing justice and peace were accepted as necessary by both Jewish and Christian groups. The Catholic-Jewish Committee agreed with others as well that a joint and comprehensive study of the historical events and theological implications of the Holocaust was clearly needed.[46]

Since 1965, the Christian-Jewish dialogue and intra-Christian discussions have been candid as they have tackled the underlying issues that have historically matured through past Jewish-Christian interactions. The past, it was felt, had to be understood so that the future could be shaped. Activists in this dialogue recognized that the originality of the new patterns of thought could result in changing the parameters that also seemed to control Catholic relationships with other non-Christian religions and could help the church develop a theological voice to relate to other faith communities and even to the secular problematic. Theologians and ecclesial leaders have also shifted from an ahistorical frame of reference to one sensitive to the event, and that has been supportive of dialogue as well. Relying on the documents of Vatican II, Uriel Tal has maintained that the church in recent decades has consistently been affirming the theological relevance of the created world, of life, and of survival, which he feels will subsequently help render the traditional preoccupation of the Torah and Judaism with the earth more understandable to Christians.[47] The official church pronouncements, at least for Catholics, have helped remove some of the theological encrustations or obstacles and have helped establish the intellectual ambiance necessary for more thorough analyses. But the more expansive theological understanding has not until recently led to Vatican acceptance of the Republic of Israel, and so one more stumbling block has recently been removed.

The gap between the Jews' bond to and identity with this land and the Christian difficulty in seeing religious meaning to it still remains wide. A. Roy Eckardt, a leading Protestant theologian in the study of Christian antisemitism, has maintained that the overall Christian ambivalence to Zionism and Israel simply replicates the traditional Christian negative approach toward Judaism and Jewishness. The Christian difficulty in accepting a political Israel is only the most recent variation upon the historical Christian denial of Jewish rights and integrity. Eckardt further has asserted that the Christian treatment of Israel has merely recapitulated the traditional treatment of the Jewish people. Such behavior is unfortunate because there are no theological reasons in doctrine, which should have inhibited relations with a sovereign Jewish state.[48]

Catholic theologians such as John Oesterreicher have also dealt with the question of Israel by delineating the differences between the Jewish and Christian views of the Promised Land. In this context, Catholics have been asked to remember their anxieties when the papal states were threatened, and all Christians should generally remember that politics, land, and religion went together in the sixteenth century. Christians, of course, now see no political state as particularly holy and necessary, but they should nevertheless be able to respect the Jewish religious attachment to Israel. A further point that should probably be kept in mind is that Christians do not have to be neutral toward the real world wherein the Jews have established their own state; Israeli political policies can be critiqued. The creation of Israel, Oesterreicher has insisted, indicates "God's love and the vitality of the Jewish people and is a sign of God's concern for His people."[49]

Edward Flannery has also emphasized that the Vatican's former reluctance to accept the Republic of Israel with enthusiasm was disappointing and surprising. The roots of this negative attitude run deep, specifically into anti-Zionism, antisemitism, and theological anti-Judaism. The politicization of the Jewish religious ethos and the mythologization of those aspects that are truly political were the primary obstacles that have retarded dialogue. Critics of Israel have to be seen realistically by the Jewish people because Israel as a state will have to undergo the same types of critiques as do other political entities. A Christian theology of Israel and its statehood scarcely exists and cannot really be advanced without an in-depth Christian theology of Judaism as well as a sensitive and reconfigured attitude toward the volatile atmosphere in the Middle East. In essence, what are the religious and political issues that should focus the attention of the Christian churches as they deal with Middle Eastern political realities? Prior to political theologizing, an authentic repentance for Christianity's contribution to antisemitism is needed because the traditional Christian response has helped reinforce the impasse in the Middle East.[50] Dealing with Israel as a political and religious community will test the sincerity of the Catholic Church's dedication to rooting out antisemitism and rethinking its own theology that presumably, at least partially, guides the institution politically.

Catholic Institutional Identity and Antisemitism

The past couple of decades have offered a minute time span for eradication of the mistrust and hatred of centuries. Genuine dialogue that does not espouse conversion is a novel Christian religious experience and lacks guiding precedents within the traditional Christian-Jewish context. Misunderstandings have occurred, and inevitably many suspicions have continued to linger along with residues of prejudice on both sides. Various dialogical themes and theological interpretations, however, have emerged to direct the new

Christian-Jewish relationship, and some solid foundations for mutual interaction have been erected.[51]

The goal of this Jewish-Christian dialogue is to foster mutual and appreciative understanding based on what is held in common, coupled with a respect for points of difference. Such commonalities include mutual roots and the monotheistic faith that stresses such ethical and social corollaries as the principle of human community. Since the ways of Christians and Jews to God are varied, presumably no artificial syncretism should be encouraged. The Jewish-Christian relationship, many feel, should visibly assert as a prerequisite the principle of equality between the two faiths and the integrity of each. This mutual understanding should be grounded in the self-definition of the partner, which can be comprehended but should not be questioned. Such a dialogue would be asymmetrical because the relationship of Christianity to Judaism presumably contains one-way elements of dependency and causality. From a post-Holocaust perspective, moreover, Jews have particular expectations and needs due to the extended history of Christian antisemitism. Conversely, Jewish thinkers should increasingly be asked to react to the world of Christian ideas, although history and the Holocaust certainly would not mandate this. If dialogue is to emerge, then Christians must recall that they have more for which to atone.

In recent decades, much has been accomplished in rebutting the cruder forms of theological antisemitism. A brief mention of major themes here will suggest that institutional and theological transformations have gone hand in hand. Chapters 3 and 4 contain a more expansive articulation of the theological developments. Positive responses to the Jewish roots of Christianity have helped neutralize the blatant prejudice that has evolved in the past. In many cases, however, the popular prejudice has merely been sublimated and the roots covered. The literal story of the Crucifixion, unaccompanied by contextual analyses or by any indoctrination on the implications of supersessionism, will continue to foster negative attitudes toward Jews and Judaism as a whole. In the popular culture, such an extrication of bias will be a massive undertaking. To obliterate antisemitism methodically in theology, a conscious condemnation of the prejudice must probably be coupled with a hermeneutic that reappropriates a legitimate Christian theology devoid of any anti-Jewish bias. The Holocaust can become such a hermeneutical tool. Discontinuity in God's revelation to Jews and Christians has been accepted as one possibility, but an overnight disappearance of all the problems hitched to antisemitism is unrealistic. Some theologians and John Paul II have begun rethinking the meaning of chapters 9-11 in Romans, for example, but their views have not yet been widely enough crystallized and disseminated. The past Christian *Weltanschauung* stresses discontinuity and triumphalism. Transferring this triumphalism to the eschatological plane, as some have tried, does not really convince many Jews of Christian sincerity because essentially nothing has been changed, only postponed. The church's ultimate perception of the role of the Jews in God's salvific plan has not yet become congruent with the Jews' own self-definition. Theologically and institutionally progress has been made, but periodically residues of the past still bubble up.

The Catholic abandonment of mission, of course, has helped constitute a historic external step forward in the Christian-Jewish encounter. Now the arguments supporting mission and the exclusivity of the Christian identity can be eroded and expunged. The Jews' centuries-long yearning for a return to Israel has also acquired a new urgency because of the Holocaust and the vulnerability of the Republic of Israel. Thus, Jews now expect Christian theological and political recognition of this essential element of their own self-definition. But the response has not been quickly forthcoming because the connection between the Jewish people and Israel is somewhat perplexing to the Christian mind, which frequently does not see any crucial relationship between land and the religious community. Perhaps those in the Catholic Church would do well to recall the tenacity of Pius IX during the Italian Unification, when control of the papal states was deemed vital.

The diverse forms of Judaism also preclude a unified approach to the resolution of political problems. Such postwar developments as the acceptance of pluralism and the emergence of the Republic of Israel have helped reinforce a self-confidence among Diaspora Jews, who view themselves no longer as merely a minority with its implications of inferiority but now as one more ethnic element within the society in which we all live. The resultant self-assertiveness of the Jewish people has helped propel the dialogue into surprising directions because for the first time in the common history of Christians and Jews relationships can be constructed on a basis of equality and impartiality. Crucial for this future relationship will be an education devoted to weeding out latent and blatant antisemitism.

Normalized and regular forms for dialogue seem to be necessary to cleanse our culture of this antisemitic bias. Secular and Christian textbooks, for example, still largely ignore any mention of postbiblical Judaism, antisemitism in general, and its Christian implications in particular. Jewish works on Europe tend to be restricted to the long history of Christian antisemitism. Both groups unfortunately seem to observe history through their own lenses. One approach may be to affirm that there are situations when such Jewish experiences as the Holocaust and historical victimization can be more pertinent for Christians than their own experiences as they develop their fundamental theology. In treating the Palestinians, the Israelis may be able also to learn a great deal from the Christian treatment of theological issues. Both Christianity and Judaism, therefore, should not keep from each other their experiences but should engage in mutual constructive exchanges similar to those, as A. Roy Eckardt suggests, of an elder and younger brother.

The dialogue between Jews and Christians may now have to be enhanced and deepen its discernment before a further refinement of Christian institutional identity can be realized. The ongoing stress should now probably be on the common religious heritage and not exclusively on an obsession with the ills of the past, although these should not be forgotten. The historical and social science studies on antisemitism, its origin, and its meaning, have revealed the depth of Christian responsibility for the Shoah and have begun to lead to a rethinking of the Christian faith. Making the current shift in rethinking Jewish-Christian relations possible was the openness of major theologians to the concept of pluralism. After Vatican II, Karl Rahner, for example, suggested that the issue of pluralism was "a new problem" and "a genuine disputed question" which he saw confronting the church and theology just as it had troubled past political thinkers. For Rahner, a receptiveness to what had been forgotten or even suppressed in the reflections on dogmatic theology in history became the order of the day. In Bernard Lonergan's opinion, the phenomenon of pluralism also emerged due to a shift from the traditionally normative classicist view of culture to an empirical or modernist one, which now required a deeper appreciation of the dialectical process of historical flux that was involved. For Schillebeeckx, recent historical, critical, and hermeneutical thought has revealed the varied interpretative frameworks that could prove useful to help explain Christian history and move into the future. Discussion of a specific developmental line is probably still impossible. Schillebeeckx called for the delineation of new, more detailed maps so that the "traditioning process" in its many intricacies can be more readily understood and the untapped resources of the past reappropriated in an appreciative manner.[52] Such views, coupled with institutional initiatives, have set the church in a new direction as it has immersed itself in the world after Vatican II. Both Catholic and Protestant theologians have devoted a great deal of energy to trying to understand the "traditioning process."

Resting on a number of central conclusions tentatively formulated by Jews and Christians of all persuasions, a consensus has been emerging within Catholicism during the last 25 years:

1. The movement begun by Jesus and institutionalized in the Christian church originally was a reform movement within Judaism during his own lifetime. Certainly Jesus and his disciples displayed no wish to break away from their Jewish environment.
2. Paul's missionary movement was a Jewish mission to the Gentiles as an integral part of God's continuing summons to Israel.
3. Conflicts between Jesus and certain Jews clearly existed.
4. Church and synagogue began to divide more visibly after 70 C.E. as Jesus' disciples gained a self-understanding of themselves as a unique religious community.

Even so, several scholars have noted that the later writings of the Christian Scriptures, while showing signs of the movement toward separation, not surprisingly seem to prefer dialogue with the original Jewish tradition. The rupture between Judaism and the early church did not and does not now eradicate the spiritual bond to which *Nostra Aetate* refers, but this common root must now be rediscovered.

Judaism and Christianity owe their origins to their respective perceptions of God's revelation. This was the central message of Vatican II and one that demands recommitment on a daily basis. There is a deep bond at the level of religious identity that has not destroyed but validated the two communities and their individual members in their specific differences as well as in their common values. This general consensus, of course, obscures the discussion around a myriad of perspectives and distinctions within such issues as the meaning of covenant and Christology. It would seem wise, therefore, to look more closely at the nuanced research that has developed as the consensus for more dialogue has been formed through scriptural scholarship and theological discernment. The research has helped clarify both the continuities and the discontinuities that exist between the two faith communities. Since the conversation includes such topics as scapegoating, insider-outsider tension, the Holocaust, and the "factual" basis of theology, this issue of antisemitism has become part of a broader rethinking of the meaning of morality and of the human condition. These dimensions will become more apparent as we move forward.

Notes

1. For an early analysis of Jewish-Christian relations, see Parkes, *The Conflict*; B. Martin, "Paul Tillich and Judaism," *Judaism* 15 (1966): 180ff.; Geoffrey Wigoder, *Jewish-Christian Relations since the Second World War* (Manchester, England: Manchester University Press, 1988), 2.
2. For Bonhoeffer, see Eva Fleischner, *Judaism in German Christian Theology since 1945: Christianity and Israel Considered in Terms of Mission* (Metuchen, NJ: Scarecrow Press, 1975), 24. For Niemoeller, see Alan Davies, ed., *Anti-Semitism and the Christian Mind* (New York: Herder and Herder, 1969), 110; Donald J. Dietrich, *Catholic Citizens in the Third Reich: Psycho-Social Principles and Moral Reasoning* (New Brunswick, NJ: Transaction Books, 1988); Gustav Gundlach, SJ, "Antisemitismus," in Michael Buchberger, ed., *Lexikon für Theologie und Kirche*, 2nd ed. (Freiburg: Herder, 1930), 1: 504.
3. Helga Croner, ed., *More Stepping-Stones to Jewish-Christian Relations: An Unabridged Collection of Christian Documents, 1975-1983* (New York: Paulist Press, 1985), 32-33.
4. See, for example, the journal *Christian-Jewish Relations*; Helga Croner, ed., *Stepping-Stones to Jewish-Christian Relations* (London: Stimulus Books, 1977), 69-72; documents published by the World Council of Churches, Programme Unit in Faith and Witness, March 1974; World Council of Churches' Report on Consultation on the Church and the Jewish People, 10-14 February 1986; *Erwangungen zur kirchlichen*

Handsreichung zur Erneuerung des Verhältnisses von Christen und Juden, Evangelisch-Theologisches Seminar der Rheinischen Friedrich Wilhelm Universität, Bonn, May 1980.

5. Theodor Herzl, *Complete Diaries*, ed. by Raphael Patai (New York: Herzl Press, 1960), 4: 1601ff.

6. Wigoder, *Jewish-Christian Relations*, 75-76.

7. The effect of the course of World War II and of Germany's policies in European countries were factors accounting for the success or failure of genocide as Nazi policy. Helen Fein's book *Accounting for Genocide* is invaluable for analyzing the principle of a "universe of obligation" as a decisive concept in political life. Without this operative political principle, individuals and groups can be capriciously subjected to the power of the state. A Catholic response to racism was constructed by Gustav Gundlach, SJ, and John LaFarge, SJ, but not issued by the Pope. Gordon Zahn, "The Unpublished Encyclical—An Opportunity Missed," *National Catholic Reporter* 9 (8) (15 December 1972): 9. For an incisive book on how deeply antisemitic roots extend, see Wladyslaw Bartoszewski, *The Convent at Auschwitz* (New York: G. Braziller, 1991) and Adam Michnik, "Poland and the Jews," an address given at Central Synagogue in New York, April 1991.

8. John Morley, *Vatican Diplomacy and the Jews during the Holocaust, 1939-1943* (New York: KTAV Pub. House, 1980); Saul Friedländer, *Pius XII and the Third Reich* (New York: Knopf, 1966).

9. Wigoder, *Jewish-Christian Relations*, 76-77.

10. Arthur Gilbert, *The Vatican Council and the Jews* (Cleveland: World Pub. Co., 1968). For the text of *Nostra Aetate*, see Wigoder, *Jewish-Christian Relations*, 143-44.

11. Wigoder, *Jewish-Christian Relations*, 78-79. For further analyses of *Nostra Aetate* and its significance, see Eugene Fisher, "The Evolution of a Tradition: From *Nostra Aetate* to the 'Notes'," *Christian-Jewish Relations* 18 (1985): 32-47; Pynchas Brener et al., "*Nostra Aetate* Twenty Years On: A Symposium," *Christian-Jewish Relations* 18 (1985): 5-46; Johannes Cardinal Willebrands, "Vatican II and the Jews: Twenty Years Later," *Christian-Jewish Relations* 18 (1985): 16-30.

12. Martin Noth, *The History of Israel* (New York: Harper, 1958), 447ff.

13. Croner, *Stepping-Stones*, 1, 32-33, 62. The text of *Nostra Aetate* may be found in Johannes Cardinal Willebrands, *Church and Jewish People: New Considerations* (New York: Paulist Press, 1992), 202-6; n. 4 appears on p. 204.

14. In an unpublished paper, "The Theology of Judaism."

15. Croner, *Stepping-Stones*, 13.

16. Eugene Fisher, *Faith without Prejudice* (New York: Crossroad, 1977), 33.
17. Paul van Buren, *Discerning the Way: A Theology of the Jewish Christian Reality* (New York: Seabury Press, 1980), 156.
18. Rolf Rendtorff, in *Christian-Jewish Relations* 16 (1983): 18.
19. Wigoder, *Jewish-Christian Relations*, 79.
20. Augustin Bea, *The Church and the Jewish People* (New York: Harper & Row, 1966), 96.
21. Walter Jacob, *Christianity through Jewish Eyes: The Quest for Common Ground* (New York: Hebrew Union College, 1974); John Pawlikowski, "Toward a Theology for Religious Diversity: Perspectives from the Christian-Jewish Dialogue," *Journal of Ecumenical Studies* 26 (1989): 138-53; Paul van Buren, *A Christian Theology of the People of Israel* (New York: Seabury Press, 1983); van Buren, *Discerning the Way*, part 1, 25ff. For a thorough analysis of the concept "no salvation outside of the Church" and the reasons for its repudiation as a legitimate position, see Francis A. Sullivan, SJ, *Salvation Outside the Church? Tracing the History of the Catholic Response* (New York: Paulist Press, 1992). Although inadequate because others are identified only in relation to Catholicism, see one approach to non-Catholic religions in Rahner's model of the "anonymous Christian": Karl Rahner, "Christianity and the Non-Christian Religions," in Karl Rahner, *Theological Investigations*, vol. 5, *Later Writings* (Baltimore: Helicon Press, 1966): 115-34; Ronald Miller, *Dialogue and Disagreement: Franz Rosenzweig's Relevance to Contemporary Jewish-Christian Understanding* (Lanham, MD: University Press of America, 1989).
22. For the complete text, see Wigoder, *Jewish-Christian Relations*, 144-49; John Pawlikowski, "Ethical Issues in the Israeli-Palestinian Conflict: One Christian Viewpoint," unpublished paper, 1988.
23. For an incisive analysis of this issue, see Jakob Jocz, *Christians and Jews: Encounter and Mission* (London: SPCK, 1966).
24. Croner, *More Stepping-Stones,* 37ff.
25. In Martin A. Cohen and Helga Croner, eds., *Christian Mission—Jewish Mission* (New York: Paulist Press, 1982), 30.
26. Fleischner, *Judaism in German Christian Theology*, 89.
27. Hans Küng, *The Church* (New York: Sheed & Ward, 1967), 142.
28. Ibid., 124ff.
29. Croner, *More Stepping-Stones*, 151ff.
30. Bernard Dupuy and Marie-Therese Hoch, eds., *Les Églises devant le Judaisme* (Paris: Éditions du Cerf, 1980), 171ff.
31. Croner, *Stepping-Stones*, 54; Croner, *More Stepping-Stones*, 29-30.

32. Bernardin, "Emerging Catholic Attitudes": 441-42; *Osservatore Romano* (English Edition), 9 December 1980; Eugene Fisher et al., eds., *Twenty Years of Jewish-Christian Relations* (New York: Paulist Press, 1986), 218ff.

33. Fisher, *Twenty Years*, 215ff.

34. For "Notes," see Wigoder, *Jewish-Christian Relations*, 149-59.

35. For a recent exploration of this issue, see Reidar Hvalvik, "A 'Sonderweg' for Israel: A Critical Examination of a Current Interpretation of Romans 11: 25-27," *Journal for the Study of the New Testament* 38 (1990): 87-107.

36. *Midstream* June/July 1986: 11ff.

37. David Flusser in Arthur A. Cohen and Paul Mendes-Flohr, eds., *Contemporary Jewish Religious Thought: Original Essays on Critical Concepts, Movements, and Beliefs* (New York: Scribner, 1987), 61ff.

38. Fisher, *Twenty Years*, 2.

39. Wigoder, *Jewish-Christian Relations*, 95; Fisher, *Twenty Years*, note 30.

40. Marcel Dubois, in *Face to Face* Fall 1985: 31; N.S. Campbell, "Christianity and Judaism: Continuity and Discontinuity," *Christian-Jewish Relations* 18 (1985): 3-14.

41. Wigoder, *Jewish-Christian Relations*, 96; see "Notes" in Wigoder, *Jewish-Christian Relations*, 153. For Ratzinger's statement, see *The Tablet*, 7 September 1985, editorial.

42. Michael B. McGarry, *Christology after Auschwitz* (New York: Paulist Press, 1977), 21ff.

43. Gavin D'Costa, "Elephants, Ropes, and a Christian Theology of Religions," *Theology* 68 (1985): 259-68. For an analysis of the Holocaust as an example of the genocidal possibility present in the modern nation-state, see Irving Louis Horowitz, *Taking Lives: Genocide and State Power*, 3rd ed. (New Brunswick, NJ: Transaction Books, 1982).

44. *Osservatore Romano* (weekly English edition), 28 October 1985, p. 2.

45. Ibid., 3 March 1986, p. 5; 10 March 1986, pp. 2, 11.

46. Bernard Dupuy and Jean Halperin, eds., *Juifs et Chrétiens "pour une entente nouvelle"* (Paris: Éditions du Cerf, 1986); Bernardin, "Emerging Catholic Attitudes": 443; *Christian-Jewish Relations* 18 (1985): 6; Giacomo Saban, Chief Rabbi Elia Toaff, and Pope John Paul II, "Documentation: Pope John Paul II's Visit to the Synagogue in Rome," *Christian-Jewish Relations* 19 (1986): 46-56.

47. *Ecumenical Trends* April 1986: 66; Uriel Tal in Walter Kasper and Hans Küng, eds., *Christians and Jews* (New York: Seabury Press, 1974), 80-87; Nora Levin, "A Jewish View of the Dialogue," *Christian-Jewish Relations* 17 (1984): 35-42.

48. A. Roy Eckardt, *Jews and Christians, The Contemporary Meeting* (Bloomington: Indiana University Press, 1986), 74; Eugene J. Fisher, "The Holy See and the State of Israel: The Evolution of Attitudes and Policies," *Journal of Ecumenical Studies* 24 (1987): 191-211; Edgar Bronfman et al., "Catholic-Jewish Relations—Tension and Intention," *Christian-Jewish Relations* 20 (1987): 33.

49. For Oesterreicher, see Wigoder, *Jewish-Christian Relations*, 120.

50. Edward Flannery in Fisher, *Twenty Years*, 76-85.

51. For several cogent analyses on the directions that Jewish-Christian relations have taken and should pursue, see Bernardin, "Emerging Catholic Attitudes," 439-40; Monsignor Pietro Rossano, Rector of the Pontifical Lateran University, Rome, in an address in Jerusalem, 1987, p. 67; David Flusser in Clemens Thoma, *A Christian Theology of Judaism* (New York: Paulist Press, 1980), 10-12; Arthur Hertzberg on the Jewish-Catholic dialogue in *Christian-Jewish Relations* 18 (1985): 21.

52. Karl Rahner, "Pluralism in Theology and the Unity of the Creed in the Church," in *Theological Investigations* (London: DLT, 1969), 11; Bernard Lonergan, *Method in Theology* (New York: Herder and Herder, 1972); Bernard Lonergan, *Doctrinal Pluralism* (Milwaukee: Marquette University Press, 1971); Edward Schillebeeckx, *The Understanding of Faith: Interpretation and Criticism* (New York: Seabury Press, 1974); Edward Schillebeeckx, *Jesus: An Experiment in Christology* (New York: Seabury Press, 1979); Edward Schillebeeckx, *Christ: The Experience of Jesus as Lord* (New York: Crossroad, 1981); Edward Schillebeeckx, *The Church with a Human Face: A New and Expanded Theology of Ministry* (New York: Crossroad, 1985).

3

Scripture and Contextual Antisemitism

In uncovering Christian antisemitism, the Christian Scriptures are the first place to look. But is Christianity in its earliest phase really biased? In the pre-Vatican II Catholic tradition, the Hebrew Bible was interpreted by exegetes who had imbibed the supersessionist theology that elevated Christianity over a Judaism that had supposedly stopped living with the death and Resurrection of Jesus Christ. Traditionally, the Hebrew Bible was subjected to an allegorical and spiritual interpretation that was designed to uncover the "true meaning" of God's message. Using the more refined, historicocritical method in the biblical sciences, as well as accepting the premise that God does not take back what was given, has enabled this generation's biblical scholars in both the Hebrew Bible and Christian Testament to interact on the same wavelength with one another in such scholarly associations as the Society of Biblical Literature and the Catholic Biblical Association.[1] Such cross-fertilization experiences have deeply enriched Christian and especially Catholic biblical awareness by directing attention to the cultures and literary genres that had an effect on the authors of the canonical works. Virtually all of the official documents in the post-Vatican II church have called on Christians and

Jews to explore the Scriptures with an intent to expand the dialogue and to eradicate supersessionism.

In general, biblical translations are now being used in which apologetical and exegetical footnotes, as well as "chapter titles" that trumpeted confessional orientations, have been removed in an attempt to erase triumphalism. In a good example of the former supersessionism, the old Confraternity-Douay edition, for example, entitled Gen. 3: 14-20 "Punishment: The Promise of a Redeemer" and maintained through a footnote that these verses prophesied "Jesus Christ, the Conqueror of Satan" and that the Hebrew words included also the faithful children of God in every age who share in Christ's victory. Dropping this exclusivistic orientation, the New American Bible, currently widely used, asserts that Christian scriptural references can be useful for theologically comprehending this passage for Christians alone and by Christians alone. In this way, Christians can establish their own horizon while the Hebrew text can simultaneously engage the reader on the originally intended level. The same passage can have distinct meanings for different peoples. One tradition, therefore, would not obviate the other because a specific text can be rich in meaning to a variety of readers.

This new use of Jewish sources has resulted in an exegetical revolution in Christian scriptural studies. E.P. Sanders, for example, has maintained that varied assumptions of first-century Judaism, historically supported by earlier scholars, must now be suspect on the basis of the Jewish sources. Thus, no longer does it seem possible to substantiate the apologetic views that insist that sharp dichotomies existed between Jesus' teaching and the now clearly vibrant, but complex, environment of early Judaism. Such authors as Daniel Harrington and Sean Freyne[2] have offered some of the historical interconnections among these groups and have provided very balanced as well as readable interpretations that make Jesus and his followers one of many groups at the time.

Likewise, a plethora of scholarly work has helped to abolish the earlier and abysmal portrait of the Pharisees that was embedded in the pejorative sayings collected in Matthew's and John's Gospels. Studying the Pauline corpus and focusing seriously on Judaism and Jewish sources has helped scholars systematically reevaluate the varied misconceptions swirling around the pharisaic/rabbinic understanding of the Law, which Jesus and Paul supposedly condemned. Recent works, for example, have gone to the heart of the ancient question of Paul's view of the Law by using more historicocritical tools of research.[3] In general, most scholars seem to agree that the Hebrew Bible did not yield a monolithic faith by the first century but rather resulted in a dynamic and ongoing process characterized by the reappropriation and reinterpretation of the earlier traditions. Through archaeology, Christians have also been challenged to respect the setting of the Hebrew Bible in its own times and not to see the Jewish experience merely as a foreshadowing of the Christian Scriptures. The Jewish faith can now be portrayed as an ongoing, living community of belief, integral in itself.

Christian-Jewish relations over the centuries have also been shaped by a major misunderstanding of the Christian texts and their relationship to the Hebrew Bible given that historically the former have been used, although this was not their major intention, to support the charge that the Jewish people were collectively responsible for the death of Jesus. Theological scholars are now convinced that the charge is untenable and certainly could not be "proven" from the early canonical writings, which can be seen as addressing very specific agendas. One potential antisemitic textual exception may be the latter part of John, but even that must be interpreted within the context of the embattled Johannine community. The texts, of course, may not have been written with an intent to support deicide, but that did not prohibit later readers from utilizing them for their own nefarious purposes. If the texts were analyzed with an already formed agenda in mind, a notion of collective guilt could be found at least implicitly in some scriptural texts, although such an explicit condemnation does not seem intended by the early Christian communities. Presumably, therefore, later Christians used the texts to bolster their own identity. The Christian texts are now perceived by an array of scholars who are contextually viewing the Jewish sources as the products of the *Sitz im Leben* and are being reinforced in their own work by the theological insights derived from the Jewish-Christian dialogue.[4]

Beginning especially with the Second Vatican Council and stimulated by an ongoing scholarly and popular dialogue, the "teaching of contempt" has been systematically dismantled and condemned because, as most scholars insist, it was rooted in historical and theological misdevelopments. The council itself condemned the deicide accusation and insisted that scholars develop a normative hermeneutic for future Catholic exegetical analyses of the Christian Scriptures. Quite simply, "the Jews should not be represented as rejected by God or accursed as if this followed from Holy Scripture."[5] John Paul II has reaffirmed this document as an "expression of the Faith" and "word of the Divine Wisdom."[6]

Nearly all recent studies have diagnosed and condemned the earlier interpretations that have fanned theological and intellectual offensives through the centuries. The construction of the negative stereotype of the Jewish people will take time to unmask and dismantle, but a foundation has now been biblically constructed. Jesus and Paul were both members in good standing of the variegated Jewish community. Both had views of the Law that seem to be congruent with those of their respected contemporaries. Unfortunately, their intent became obscured because the original content of their words in their specific communities historically became ambiguous. Research over the last three decades has now helped clarify the context and has shown how Jesus and Paul, along with their contemporaries, dealt with issues of common concern. It is hardly their fault that their words were subsequently misconstrued by others who were searching for a viable Christian identity. Seeking self-identity, the early Christian church reinforced specific strands of anti-Judaism, which were made in a very specific context, until the strengthening "gentilization" expunged the religious dissonance by distinguishing, for example, between ethical and ceremonial/dietary commands. Such initiatives ignored the original religious linkage between both. Certainly, the earliest Christians did not directly assault the Law as such; later generations apparently projected their own views back into the texts. Research has helped make clear that the conviction of an immanent eschatology and dynamic soteriology, for example, combined to "relativize" and question, though not denigrate or abrogate, the Jewish Law for the early church leaders as they institutionalized Christianity into the dominant religion after Constantine's rule was extended to the empire. In the views of Gager, Wilken, and others, early Christian commentators cannot legitimately be read as if they were disciples or precursors of Wilhelm Marr, the nineteenth-century writer who coined the term "antisemitism."[7]

By focusing on the evolving and historically conditioned nature of the strata of traditions locked into the Gospel texts, students of the Christian canon have helped clarify our understanding of the complex relationship that existed between Jesus and his followers as well as between the nascent church and the vital Rabbinic Judaism of this period. Models based on the earlier, defensive, and simplistic interpretation of Jesus' teaching with respect to his contemporary Jewish milieu are now being abandoned as completely inadequate. Jesus and the initial Christians were good Jews. Replacing the pre-Vatican II perceptions of the early Christian communities embattled with the synagogue are the more intricate portrayals of the complex interaction that apparently resulted as Jews and the Jewish followers of Jesus enriched their self-identities while frequently venting hostility toward one another as part of this psychological process.[8] The communities giving birth to the living traditions of both religions, integral in themselves, have had to be analyzed from a contextual perspective to comprehend the reasons for the presence of these biased texts.

A clearer understanding of the Hebrew Bible can be observed by uncovering the world of the rabbis, which can help situate Jesus and Paul in their Jewish environments. From scholarly discussions, such hermeneutical schema as promise/fulfillment, salvation history, Law/grace, and replacement (Old/New Testaments) can be seen to have severe shortcomings as models when they are used to organize both scriptural traditions, because each religious community, it is now conceded, has to speak for itself. Hence, the focus has been shifting to the context in which the Scriptures were written in order to understand the passages that contributed to the theology of contempt. A survey of some of the research that has engaged these issues can help us see that Judaism and Christianity have, at least to a degree, a common core and can help us understand the context of early antisemitic outbursts.

Scriptures as Products of Living Communities

Source-oriented and historicocritical styles of scholarship have focused on the biblical texts as the products of living communities. Such an approach can free biblical scholarship that in the past has utilized a retrojective method by reading modern biases into the early Christian period. Current research has helped identify and control some of the potent abuses of past biblical scholarship. To be intellectually responsible not only to those of one's Christian community but also to those of diverse traditions, which have a valid claim to the specific biblical passages under study, seems to demand that the insights of the Jewish traditions be respected in themselves. The Jewish texts should not be used to further apologetically the theological agenda of Christians.

This is a radical break from the earlier Christian tradition. In this older tradition, Matthew Black's essay, for example, had castigated pharisaic/Rabbinic Judaism as a "sterile religion of codified tradition, regulating every part of life by a *holachah*, observing a strict *apartheid*." Responding to Black's essay, which was even then becoming an inappropriate approach, Samuel Sandmel asserted the following in his 1961 presidential address to the Society of Biblical Literature: "I am personally a descendant of the Rabbinic tradition, the sterility of which was not so complete as to prevent my being born. Black's article is not only unreliable. It is disgraceful that it should have appeared in the same dictionary to which I and some dozen other Jews contributed."[9] Loyalty to the integral traditions of both Christians and Jews has since then become the hallmark of scholarship. One tradition cannot be allowed to secure its identity at the expense of the other. Tracing a few of the paths that have been followed and focusing on selected insights that have been gained can help suggest how scholars have been trying to understand the Hebrew Bible and Christian Scriptures. From this perspective, then, antisemitism seems to have been reinforced by historical conditions at a specific point in time and does not seem vital to Christianity as such, even though this bias may have been useful to specific Christians confronting a unique historical issue in their own era. This contextual approach has been found useful in uncovering how antisemitism evolved as well as in explicating the original meaning of the Jewish and Christian canonical books. Such analyses seem necessary to foster an open dialogue along with dissecting and isolating the antisemitism endemic to our culture.

In focusing on the persistence of misinformation used in former analyses of New Testament Judaism, E.P. Sanders has suggested that a focus on legalistic Judaism helped support later pejorative Christian interpretations. Such scholarship as that of Max Weber constructed a model against which so-called "superior forms" of religion could be measured. Within this framework, theology would then be written as if it were history. In essence, later religions seemed to be superior to earlier religions. Protestant scholars, for example, were able to project onto Judaism the view which historically they had used to assault Roman Catholicism: the existence of a treasury of merits established by legalistic works. In this example of the retrojection of the Protestant-Catholic debate utilizing patriotic history, Judaism assumed the role of Catholicism, and enlightened Christianity the role of Protestantism.[10]

One antidote against such apologetic and anachronistic scriptural abuses has been offered by the collaborative or dialogical efforts of Christian and Jewish scholars. Their impetus has helped create a critical mass of solid knowledge that has furthered the ecumenical dialogue among Protestants, Catholics, and Jews, who perhaps have more in common than had previously been thought. This interchange has also managed to foster an unbiased self-consciousness among the participants, which in turn has counterbalanced their own religious orientations when they write for their denominational journals. Significant dialogues apparently can increase the specific horizons available to scholars and have helped produce a spectrum of ecumenical perspectives, which was nonexistent when only sectarian apologetical efforts predominated.[11] The deconstruction of the antisemitic tradition that has formerly thrived in our culture is being accelerated in part through a more scientific approach to biblical scholarship.

In this context, Fuchs-Kreimer has asserted that earlier biblical scholarship tended to focus on theological issues, partially because traditional biblical theology was used to produce viable foundations that supported Christian apologetic positions and so antisemitism was ignored. But the creative scholarly insights of such Protestant scholars as Paul van Buren have reinforced the driving need for recasting biblical theology so that it can now be nourished by a dialogical interaction between Christians and Jews. Transcending the obstructions born of the Jewish-Christian estrangement in past research initiatives, Jews and Christians are now working to construct theologies informed by the current pluralistic era.[12] Calls to Christian scholars to reevaluate scriptural research have been reinforced on a regular basis through such Catholic pronouncements as *Nostra Aetate* (1965), the Vatican's "Guidelines" (1974), the position papers of local episcopates (U.S., France, Germany), statements from the World Council of Churches, and the "Notes" (1985) as well as such journals as *Holocaust and Genocide Studies* and *The Journal of Ecumenical Studies*. Recalling that earlier Catholics distrusted scriptural research, this new interest signifies a sea change in Catholic scholarship.

Why did antisemitism sprout from the Christian Scriptures and how was it nurtured in the early Christian communities? Despite the textual evidence of anti-Judaic outbursts, some earlier studies[13] did try to defend the Gospels against the accusation that they were antisemitic because it was felt that it would be unchristian to foster hate. Such scholars were only relatively successful until it was accepted that Christians were indeed defining themselves because they were in competition with their Jewish contemporaries. Christians used polemical statements to respond to local issues but were certainly not constructing an antisemitic theology.[14] Rosemary Ruether's theory that antisemitism is the opposite side of Christology focused this whole discussion most radically and demanded a response. Reactions to her thesis have reinforced a general sensitivity to the polemical strata lodged in the New Testament due to the historical context of the era, and have also led to an awareness of the continuity, rather than the discontinuity, in the Christian tradition. The straight line between the Christian canon and Auschwitz as well as the somewhat simplistic method of Ruether and her supporters in the early stages of the debate did not adequately explain the historical realities and ambiguities, which have intersected through the centuries. Antisemitic positions have really been nourished, although not intentionally caused, by the ambivalent Christian Testament and the patristic attitudes. Her work may be too reductionistic and overdetermined. A highly charged negative perspective among early Christians, reacting to a specific community's problems, cannot alone account for the actual behavior toward Jews during the ensuing centuries because other sociopolitical needs among the Christian communities may have also intruded. The fact that the scriptural and classical terminology and imagery originated in response to very specific issues has to be taken into account.[15] The goal now is to dissect these original contexts to show that misdirected Christians, who may have set the tone and funneled biased values into our civilization, were not inspired by the legitimate Christian core message. This would seem to be a necessary initiative before the historically seminal values in our culture can be articulated.[16]

To say the least, the scriptural and historical waters are very muddy. What may be said is that the initially ambivalent attitude and subsequent pattern of behavior have helped make Christianity one of the causal links to the Holocaust. Since Vatican II, the biblical expressions of the revelatory message have been analyzed and the seminal issues refined as the fundamental historical questions have been more surgically delineated. [17] What now seems clear is that the Christian anti-Jewish polemic was a necessary, even though not complete, cause for the Nazi assault and so needs to be explained along with the theological and liturgical antisemitism so that the essential Christian faith can be separated from some of its disastrous manifestations. Thus, Christians have to assume responsibility for their teachings, which effectively could be used by some to justify the Nazi murders. They have to know what their actual teachings were as well as what they were supposed to be. The Christian Scriptures and the ensuing tradition had a role in generating antisemitism because the canonical texts did not send a clear message.

Within the New Testament, alongside Matthew's polemic against the Pharisees, for example, can be found a reasonably positive por-trayal in Luke, who indicates that some Pharisees sought to save Jesus' life by warning him of the plot. In Acts they even succeeded in saving the lives of the apostles. In the Gospel of John as well there are distinct strata of development beginning with positive and concluding with negative views toward the Jewish people and Judaism. Initially, the author insists that salvation comes from the Jews; by the end of the Gospel, the Jewish people as a whole are virtually condemned.[18] The question, then, is not the simplistic, earlier question — Is the New Testament antisemitic? — but the more subtle — Are the roots of anti-semitism in the Gospels? Complicating the issue, from its inception the church has revealed a tendency toward what Robert Osborn has suggested was a "sinful self-centered ecclesiasticism." He has asserted that this pride was given credence by an antisemitism that denied the dependence of the church on any Jewish heritage by suggesting that Jesus had broken with his own communities.[19] The contextual issue has now become framed from a more hermeneutical perspective of suspicion, which has only become accepted in some quarters as the Catholic Church initiated a reexamination of its own roots.

Given its extended stress on tradition, the Catholic Church's *magisterium* has had a unique role in this exploration. In 1975, the National Conference of Catholic Bishops, for example, issued a statement on the Pauline corpus in which they said that Paul's theology of Judaism has its more negative aspects that have been overemphasized through the centuries in Catholic teaching. Perhaps now is the time to explore the positive Pauline elements. Paul's letters were presumably directed to specific groups for explicit purposes and presumably written in the heat of the moment. Chapters 9-11 of Romans, for example, offers one of the best examples of Pauline ambivalence. Mussner, Van Buren, and others[20] have labored over the negativity of the passage, which still manages to culminate with Paul's conclusion that the Jews are saved. The debate on Paul's meaning in this and other letters has been and is being explored in greater depth so that we can understand Paul's real significance as a loyal follower of Jesus within the Jewish community. Paul's struggle in Romans is rooted in the identity problem that Christians had from the very inception of their faith. Paul almost seems to epitomize the struggle that early Christians had in establishing their identity.

By 1979 a great deal of discussion had occurred on Ruether's work because it threatened the meaning of the Christian message. In his volume of collected essays, Alan Davies and his colleagues pointed out that the question of anti-Judaism appears to be more than a few notorious and incidental passages from Matthew, Paul, and John. In the light of Ruether's work, questions related to antisemitism seemed to deal foundationally with the basic meaning of New Testament theology. But the contributors to this volume contended that Christians did not have to defend their Scriptures *in toto* ideologically and were not really compelled to repudiate justifiable criticism as if it would automatically lead to the horrifying conclusion that the New Testament is so antisemitic that it was in danger of losing all moral authority. Through careful literary and historical study, scholars began isolating the genuine contextual and cultural roots of anti-Judaism that was nourished in the Christian Scriptures. By examining the historical genesis of these antisemitic texts within the original Christian communities, they have continued separating the real meaning of Christianity from the literary expressions used by the authors to announce God's salvation and to construct their identity within their Jewish environment.[21]

Continuity or Discontinuity in the Scriptures

How are the Scriptures connected? Does the New supersede the Old Testament?[22] John Paul II focused on this issue when he defined the parameters of the Jewish-Christian dialogue:

> The first dimension of this dialogue, that is, the meeting between the people of God of the covenant never revoked by God (Rom. 11:29), on the one hand, and the people of the New Covenant on the other is at the same time a dialogue within our own Church, so to speak, a dialogue between the first and second parts of the Bible. (17 November 1980, Mainz)

The pope's words go to the heart of the hermeneutical question and seek answers to the myriad issues that lie behind the failure until the last couple of decades to formulate a theology that legitimately focuses on the Hebrew Bible. In light of *Nostra Aetate* and other documents, Catholics have now been urged to view the Hebrew Bible less as merely background material for the Christian gospel and more as a text worthy of study in itself. Jesus and the early Christian teachings tend now to be seen as a not atypical reform movement within the context of a vibrant Judaism. In its origins, Christianity was not just a new set of post-Judaic or Hellenic doctrines.

Scholars[23] have still not adequately balanced and appreciated theologically the delicate tension mediating continuity and discontinuity on the historically textual level. Earlier scholars of the Hebrew Bible suggested that Judaism in the common era was an entity culturally separate from earlier Judaism and basically manifested a disintegration of the religious unity that seemed to reign in the pre-Christian era. From their perspective, a Christianity emerged from this Jewish milieu that no longer reflected God's favor. Post-Christian Judaism had purportedly separated from its own roots and no longer proclaimed revelation. Jewish communities of the first century C.E. were not the problem to which purportedly the New Testament was responding. The authors of the Christian canonical texts were presumably stating that the Jewish covenant had now been superseded by the Christian.[24] This issue of continuity/discontinuity seems woven into the fabric of past Jewish-Christian relations, and most recent commentators have concluded that such a perspective, in what some see as a dialectic, should be denigrated. Improperly understood, the dialectic can produce a model that warps legitimate dialogue and supports supersessionism by yielding a synthesis that eliminates the viability of at least one of its original elements.

Accepting an *a priori* religious tension could lead to placing the histories of Israel and Christianity into a Hegelian dialectical model. The experience of the Jewish people would then be seen as a chronological sequence during which the original spiritual treasure of the Hebrew Bible (thesis) was shattered through the revelation of sin and the failure of Judaism's "legalistic morbidity" (antithesis). This clash would culminate then in Christ providing true salvation (synthesis), and the earlier elements would be sublimated into the final result. This historical discontinuity could be seen simply as a version of the "salvation history" offered by Irenaeus, who recounted that continuous providential history had reached its climax or goal in Christ and the church. Such supersessionist arguments would virtually negate any life in Judaism after the inception of Christianity and could help explain nineteen hundred years of antisemitism. How did this supersessionism emerge? Supersessionism, or promise/fulfillment, coupled with the extensive genealogies in Matthew and Luke, were designed to locate Jesus in the Hebrew Bible and cement the continuity between Him, and so by implication the early Christians, and Israel. Such a strategy at an early stage in the Christian communities helped classify the Christian revelation as an outgrowth of that of the Jewish people. First, Jesus could be legitimated with an Israelite pedigree. Second, his death could be seen as a component of a larger predetermined plan. Third, the early Christian community seemed to emerge in God-ordained fashion from an established tradition. Jaroslav Pelikan has remarked that the "struggle over the authority of the Old Testament and over the nature of the continuity between Judaism and Christianity was the earliest form of a quest for a tradition that has, in other forms, recurred throughout Christian history."[25] The success and implications of using this not surprising tactic had very significant results because the process in hindsight seems one of development from a primitive to a more sophisticated and inclusive stage.

To sustain this religious model of discontinuity seemed to compel theologians to ignore the pluralism present in both the Hebrew experience and in early Christianity and to ignore the fact that the latter should logically be perceived as an organic development rooted within Second Temple Judaism. If Judaism evolved into an ossified religious system merely preparing the way for the gospel, then virtually no defense against Marcion's extrapolated assertion of the promise/fulfillment theme could logically be mounted. The Hebrew Bible could be ignored as a revelation experience that was still necessary. Historically, such eminent scholars of the discontinuous model as Schleiermacher and Harnack based their systems on a Christianity that historically and essentially emerged from Judaism but left this sterile system behind, thus ignoring the immutable and continuing bond between the two. In this context, Wellhausen also had asserted that Judaism at the time of Jesus was an empty chasm between the "Old Testament" and the "New."[26]

By asserting the continuity of Jewish and Christian history along with a dialogue-responsive model rather than a supersessionist approach, a more fruitful hermeneutic could result. Following the fruitful model of "continuity," a modified promise/fulfillment theme could further the dialogue, if a more nuanced or corrective interpretation could be offered. The promise theme (Rom. 1:2; 4:14ff; Gal. 3:17ff.), if solipsistically accepted, would negate using the Hebrew Bible as an ongoing source of God's word that would still be relevant today. The unique role of the Jewish people would evaporate into allegorical interpretations of "hidden meanings" leading to subsequent fulfillment. Embedded in this traditional and popular promise/fulfillment schema was a lethal supersessionist perspective that historically became instrumentalized in the catechetical and liturgical formulae of the churches. Left dangling and generally ignored is how Christians can continue to theologize if God's plan had been consummated in Jesus Christ two millennia ago. What's left? One solution to any circumscribed view of revelation would be to stress that God's revelation in each human experience can be seen as complete within that specific historical context. Thus, the promise/fulfillment model would be re-

viewed from the perspective that the process would not be stopped at
any point. The challenge would be to see Jesus Christ not as the
chronological culmination of the Hebrew Bible but rather as its
"axiological meaning." Fulfillment would not mean that the promise
had been achieved and that the Jewish covenant was now to be replaced by a new revelation. Rather, at the onset of Christianity the
promise had become only more clearly known to and finally effective
for others. Israel was the light of the nations.[27] God's revelation could
now be understood and accepted by others.

Such a redefinition of the model does not offer a really new
unambiguous theological terminology that can evoke a constructive
affirmation of the authentic elements in the promise/fulfillment model
while avoiding the difficulties of that schema. Keeping the term and
changing the meaning seems to be an artificial solution. This type of
problem solving has become endemic to theological reflection on
Jewish-Christian relations. The goal seems to be to keep the traditional
term and to use theological "spin doctors" to resolve the issue. This is
a "new wine into old skins" approach that furthers the dialogue but
does not provide a legitimate solution because it does not adequately
join with the real issue. Shading the meaning of models and retaining
the terms in order to justify theological tradition may simply be a
desire on the Christian side to maintain consistency while responding
to this challenge. That is, Christians seem to be saying that the
traditional terminology and classifications can remain valid, but only
now is their true meaning being explicated. The alternative is to seek a
new model. Here lies the real challenge. Understanding the problem,
at least, is already a significant step beyond the standard, pejorative
Christian perspectives. Analyzing revelation through the lens of
continuity, i.e., its openness to God's persisting activity, which
materializes into beliefs, doctrines, and faith statements, can offer
excellent opportunities for constructive considerations of God's
ongoing self-revelation as it has appeared along pluralistic horizons. A
continuity model would seem to suggest that God's plan is not subject
to fits and starts and that he does not take back his gifts.

The 1974 Vatican "Guidelines" have suggested that when
explicating biblical texts, the continuity of the Christian faith with that
of the earlier covenant should be highlighted. The full cognizance of
God's promises would be exhibited, and the original elements that

have been contributed by Christianity would not be minimized. Unfortunately, even the "Guidelines" assert that God's promises were "fulfilled" to some extent with Christ, although the perfect fulfillment will only emerge at the end of time.[28] The document does succeed in offering a more nuanced understanding of the concept of fulfillment, but perhaps a new word has to be found.

This distinction between "partial fulfillment" and "perfect fulfillment" is problematic and nebulous, and appears to be more of a semantic solution. But it does at least suggest even today that there can be "unfulfilled" horizons of the Christ-event that seem to demand that we reconsider the historical pattern of Jewish-Christian relations. Two World Wars, the Holocaust, potential nuclear annihilation, and ecological degradation are convincing that the messianic age has not arrived. Such actual and potential disasters justify the ongoing Jewish "no" to the triumphalist and ahistorical elements of Christian hubris. It seems clear that God's plan has not yet been fulfilled, and this has implications because it may mean that we have to keep preparing. The drama is not yet finished. "Fulfillment," for example, has historically meant that the past can be discarded. Liberation and political theologians, as we will see, have maintained that humans are responsible for the good and evil resulting from political and socioeconomic acts, and these tragedies have not ceased. Limited and warped interpretations of Scripture, which assisted in reinforcing political bias, helped prepare the way for the Holocaust, which would imply for most of us that nothing truly revelatory has been fulfilled. Such systematicians as Pannenberg, Moltmann, Küng, Gutiérrez, and Boff have found valuable and enriching material in the works of such scholars actively engaged in this Jewish-Christian dialogue as Franklin Littell, Roy and Alice Eckardt, Paul van Buren, and Eva Fleischner. For all of these scholars, the messianic Kingdom looms in the future. We are responsible for creating the Kingdom. Jesus was not simply the fulfillment of the Hebrew messianic prophecies because even these are in themselves not all that clear. John Pawlikowski has summed up well the emerging consensus: "The Christ-event did not invalidate the Jewish faith perspective. Christianity is not superior to Judaism; nor is it the fulfillment of Judaism as previously maintained."[29] In this context, Judaism has to be taken with absolute theological seriousness as a continuing and living revelation of God's will, and this leads to a reflection on the meaning of Messiah.

What can also be seen in the earliest extant Christian writings and Paul's letters is that the issue of Jesus as Messiah was hardly pivotal for the kerygma. In the oldest strata of the gospel traditions, in fact, the concern about the Messiah is either nonexistent or is only of a tangential concern. In the Gospels of Mark and John, it seems possible to argue that as the label *Christian* became progressively more central to the early communities, the notion of Jesus as "Messiah" evolved from the Jewish understanding of the Messiah. In the Gospels, Jesus was designated under the categories of Son of Man or Son of God or even both together understood in very specific ways. Certainly these categories may be located in the Jewish views of the Messiah, but not as the central ones in the Judaism of the period. Indeed, an early Christian interpretation of the Messiah concept exists, but it is neither as simple nor as completely standardized as later Christian texts would suggest. [30] Thus, for the early Christians the notion of fulfillment may not have been as clear as later commentators thought.

The complex messianic perspectives in the Hebrew Testament, coupled with the fact that no individual version mandates inexorably an application to Jesus as its fulfillment, suggest that scholars have to be cautious about interpreting the Hebrew Bible merely from the vantage point of the Christian Scriptures and later exegesis. Faith in Jesus as the Messiah cannot find sustenance in the Hebrew Bible. The followers of Jesus metamorphosed the complex idea of Messiah, contained in Judaism, when he partially fulfilled it or began fulfilling it or when they began suggesting new perspectives on the Jewish traditions. The development of the Christ-event into a "Messiah orientation" took decades and was not perceived as clearly and as early as historical hindsight may suggest. Jesus as "the" Messiah cannot be found as a fully articulated prediction in the Hebrew Bible or even as a definitive concept in the Christian Scriptures.

A more fruitful approach, it is now recognized, may be to posit that the full messianic meaning can only be reached in the eschaton. Neither Jews nor Christians know what the total meaning is. An unbiased study of the Hebrew Scriptures, then, cannot find Jesus as Messiah explicitly or implicitly in God's revelation to the Jewish people. Christianity cannot filter out this concept. The Christ-event occurred in Israel, and the Christian Scriptures were formed out of the interaction of the early communities within this environment. Both testaments are spiritually linked in concrete historical terms that gain sustenance from the divine mystery, and each illumines the other. Covenantal linkage occurs through dialogue within the historical context rather than in absorption or supersession. Thus, the spiritual connection between Christianity and the Jewish people is located where their respective identities meet in the ongoing revelation experience. In other words, introducing such a process perspective can provide a dynamic for the continuous interaction that remains even now necessary and can help move beyond the obstacle of fulfillment. To "do" biblical theology, then, requires dialogical involvement with "today's people of the covenant established with Moses,"[31] It also means identifying hermeneutical tools that can gain access to the text so that a dialogue can be constructed and revelation can be contextually understood.

Proleptic Christology

Such prominent Catholic scholars as David Tracy have argued for the construction of a "hermeneutics of suspicion." Based on such a model, suspicion would be directed at all spirituality and texts that seemed to point to a specific contemporary reality as the final and beneficial result of the past. Any spirituality demanding retreat from historical and political responsibility would have to be critically analyzed. The event would become the tool that interprets the text. Tracy has urged that Catholics return to history and the world, a position which was mandated by Vatican II as well as by such earlier commentators as Friedrich Heer. Such a return has in fact provided the speculative foundation for political and liberation theologians who have been analyzing contemporary society through this hermeneutics of suspicion, which has allowed them to introduce the Christian message of salvation into the real context of "this" world, which they are continually creating.[32] Such an approach to systematic theology could suggest a methodology useful to those engaged in biblical research as well.

Tracy and others engaged in this hermeneutical enterprise have noted the anti-Jewish polemics of the Christian Scriptures but have stressed that such vituperations erupted from local circumstances and were not the gospel message. The historical acts of forming identities led to a rivalry between church and synagogue. Should such historical encrustations be removed? Rather than excising such biased scriptural statements, such elements could be the subjects of homilies whenever they have to be used in liturgical settings. Certainly, the bias and its historical environment should be elucidated in commentaries on the Scriptures so that Christians as a group can become theologically more sophisticated when dealing with historical contextualization. In fact, the antisemitic texts could serve as an object lesson to illustrate the insidious effect of how prejudicial comments launched in one era historically have assumed lives of their own. Anti-Jewish statements, it now seems clear, can bear *no* authoritative status in Christianity. The meaning of the Christian Scriptures — the God who is love — should provide the critical insight that allows us to extirpate through scholarly exegesis the baneful significance of these hateful statements that were included in the Christian canon.[33]

The positive, critical, and retrieval role of Tracy's hermeneutic can be used to help us also understand the meaning of the early Christian eschatology. The crux of the matter does not concern accommodating Christian to Jewish claims or vice versa. The Christian Testament has a duty to proclaim its own message and not be viewed as the fulfillment of the Hebrew Bible. In no fashion should Judaism be authenticated or legitimated only because Christians may see its value as they fashion their own identity. From a historical point of view, the contempt for Judaism during the patristic era did not automatically follow from the divinity claim of Jesus Christ but rather arose because Christians were engaging in the normal human activity of sculpting their identity. Crucial for the contempt was the historically constructed, and in hindsight warped, understanding of the messianic claim, which ultimately subsumed many earlier religious initiatives into itself.[34] The mistakes of our scholarly forbears need not be replicated if they can be challenged vigorously.

Tracy has attempted to retrieve the authentic proleptic (anticipatory) Christology that Ruether had initially suggested. Affirming faith in Jesus would mean proclaiming the belief that in his life, Crucifixion, and Resurrection the decisive manifestation of the future reign of God exists in proleptic form. From this stance Christianity could affirm that the Jews are God's chosen covenanted people and need no validation by the Christian faith. This faith tied to

Israel's expectancy of the messianic times can suggest Christian proleptic belief as well.[35] God's revelation would be seen as a unified
fabric.

Based on this Christian rethinking of the end times, both Jews and
Christians can view proleptically the eschaton, but neither can claim to
be the sole custodian of the messianic kingdom. Even here, Christian
thinkers must keep in mind that their Jewish counterparts have
absolutely no obligation to join in the dialogue. They may find the
discussion useful, but they also may not. Ruether as well has insisted
that the historically discordant defect seems to be the myopic and
triumphalist Christian insistence that the messianic kingdom will only
be reached through faith in the Resurrection. For Ruether, Christians
are able to articulate only in an anticipatory fashion and not as a
completed reality their faith in Jesus as the Christ. A proleptic
understanding of Jesus' messianic identity can be useful for scriptural
exegesis and could become foundational to liberation theologies, given
that these latter seem to demand a critical dissection of our
contemporary social, political, and economic environment. Jesus'
living and proleptic message is not the final spiritualized fulfillment
that has frequently been institutionalized in historical Christianity.[36]
Within the context of God's revelation to Jews and Christians, both
continue to have an ongoing role in creating the Kingdom of God.

Such an intersection of the Jewish and Christian horizons can be
made immediately relevant through a theological discourse concerning
the meaning of the Republic of Israel. A. Roy Eckardt has insisted that
the Republic of Israel may be taken as a sign that God has continued
to choose and protect human beings apart from Jesus' Resurrection.
Thus, the Republic of Israel can be viewed as a liberating event for the
Jewish people. From her analyses of Jewish-Christian relations and the
revelatory meaning of the Republic of Israel, Alice Eckardt has
concluded that a Christian triumphalistic ethic of love that excludes
Jews can no longer be acceptable. She has also asserted that the
exaltation of suffering as redemptive has to be replaced with a
dedication to end suffering and to an empowerment of the oppressed.
In her opinion, the Republic of Israel ensures the covenant's
preservation, helps make Jews less vulnerable, and heightens our
understanding of hope. All of these have been traditional components
of Jewish reflection. Through the Republic of Israel, God has provided

a sign and witness of his persistence in accepting human beings totally apart from the Resurrection of Jesus. Today's Israel may well be in a sense sacramental for Christians, who can come to an understanding that their victimization of Jews is not really necessary to God's acceptance of them or to their own process of self-identity.[37]

Recent biblical studies, therefore, have helped clarify the sense of Jesus' announcement of the Kingdom to come. We can now understand more clearly the early church's teachings *about* Jesus, why some potentially dangerous ideas have emerged, and what course the remedies may have to take. A healthy sense of progress, at least in clarifying the questions that need to be addressed, has been the fruit of this dialogue, in which the Scriptures are being allowed to speak. The Shoah experience has demanded a thorough reappraisal of the initial contacts between the followers of Jesus and their Jewish contemporaries to discover whether Christianity is antisemitic. Several elements can be shared in common and can help us understand the identity of the Christian and Jewish experiences. Both initially had a mutual respect for the faith of Abraham and of the patriarchs in God as the one who chose Israel with an irrevocable love. Both communities have focused on the necessity for the "conversion" of the heart as they venerate God's revelation and adhere to the moral law promulgated in the Ten Commandments. Both traditions have at times committed themselves to peace and to the good of all humanity without discrimination. But there also are differences in their orientations. Judaism has tended to be communally oriented, and so relationships are socially based. Christianity has stressed personal responsibility and individualism, although in the postmodern era, including Vatican II, Catholics have begun to question individualism as a fundamental cultural value unless it can be created and nurtured in the social organism. As we will see, these orientations, if properly concretized, can actually become the basis for societal safeguards to combat genocide, a radical solution to sociopolitical problems.

This Jewish-Christian dialogue, focusing on common faith-experiences, is particularly crucial because such interreligious relationships can have a profound social effect as values are reconfigured and religious symbols are used in political discourse. Jews and Christians may well be crafting a sense of mutual identity and rootedness. Such mutual appreciation of what is similar and different in their traditions has put these faith groups into a secular civilization that can today be viewed as a very real threat posed to both Judaism and Christianity. Hitler's Holocaust has taught us that. Both religious communities seem aware that they must reject any doctrinaire claim that an affirmation of the secular realm is necessary for the support of our enduring values.[38] Hence, the religious dialogue focusing on the meaning of the Christian testament in light of its Jewish forbears can have a transformative function by orienting us toward God and ultimately can be seen as supportive of sociopolitical change.[39] Biblical scholarship has prepared the way for some much-needed revisions in theological speculation by reexamining the origins of Christianity in its Jewish culture where Judaism and Christianity can both be seen as basically moral revolutions with a common moral core.[40] The first step in reaching this core is to understand the original faith-experiences present at the intersection of these faith communities. For this, Christian theology has to be critically informed by all of Scripture. Only a fraction of the spectrum has been offered here.

Notes

1. Eugene Fisher, "The Impact of the Christian-Jewish Dialogue on Biblical Studies," in Richard Rousseau, ed., *Christianity and Judaism: The Deepening Dialogue* (Montrose, PA: Ridge Row Press, 1983), 118-38.

2. Samson H. Levy, *The Messiah: An Aramaic Interpretation; the Messianic Exegesis of the Targum* (Cincinnati: Hebrew Union College, 1974); Martin McNamara, *Targum and Testament: Aramaic Paraphrases of the Hebrew Bible: A Light on the New Testament* (Shannon: Irish University Press, 1972); E.P. Sanders, *Paul and Palestinian Judaism: A Comparison of Patterns of Religion* (Philadelphia: Fortress Press, 1977); Daniel Harrington, *God's People in Christ: New Testament Perspectives on the Church and Judaism* (Philadelphia: Fortress Press, 1980); Sean Freyne, *The World of the New Testament* (Wilmington: Michael Galzier, 1980). For an excellent review of the literature on the issue of Jewish-Christian relationships in the first two centuries, see Anthony Saldarini, "Jews and Christians in the First Two Centuries: The Changing Paradigm," *Shofar* 10 (1992): 16ff.

3. On the Pharisees, see Anthony Saldarini, *Pharisees, Scribes and Sadducees in Palestinian Society: A Sociological Approach* (Wilmington: M. Glazier, 1988); Jacob Neusner, *The Rabbinic Tradition*

about the Pharisees before 70, 3 vols. (Leiden: E.J. Brill, 1971); Ellis Rivkin, *A Hidden Revolution* (Nashville: Abingdon, 1978); Michael Cook, "Jesus and the Pharisees: The Problem as It Stands Today," *Journal of Ecumenical Studies* 15 (1978): 441-60; Thoma, *A Christian Theology of Judaism*. For recent studies on Paul, see E. Randolph Richards, *The Secretary in the Letters of Paul* (Tübingen: J.C.B. Mohr, 1991); Karl Olav Sandnes, *Paul—One of the Prophets? A Contribution to the Apostle's Self-Understanding* (Tübingen: J.C.B. Mohr, 1991); George Howard, *Paul: Crisis in Galatia*, 2nd ed. (New York: Cambridge University Press, 1989); Anthony Saldarini, "Delegitimation of Leaders in Matthew 23," *Catholic Biblical Quarterly* 54 (1992): 659-80.

4. Joseph Fitzmyer, "Antisemitism and the Cry of all the People (Matt. 27: 25)," *Theological Studies* 26 (1965): 667-71; Joseph Fitzmyer, "Jesus the Lord," *Chicago Studies* 17 (1978): 87-90; Joseph Fitzmyer, *Paul and His Theology: A Brief Sketch*, 2nd ed. (Englewood Cliffs, NJ: Prentice Hall, 1989). For comprehensive, even if sometimes flawed, analyses of the New Testament and its relation to Judaism, see Thoma, *A Christian Theology of Judaism*; Mussner, *Tractate*, which unfortunately defines Judaism in relation to Christianity rather than in and of itself, a fairly common and difficult error to avoid; Peter von der Osten-Sacken, *Christian-Jewish Dialogue: Theological Foundation* (Philadelphia: Fortress Press, 1986), 15. For a current incisive analysis of John, see Leibig, "John and 'the Jews'": 209-34.

5. Croner, *Stepping-Stones;* "Guidelines and Suggestions for Implementing the Conciliar Declaration, *Nostra Aetate* #4 (1974); Jorge Mejia, "A Christian View of Bible Interpretation," in Lawrence Boadt et al., eds., *Biblical Studies: Meeting Ground of Jews and Christians* (New York: Paulist Press, 1980), 45-72; Johannes Cardinal Willibrands, "The Church and Modern Antisemitism," in Willebrands, *Church and Jewish People*, 125.

6. John Paul II, Address to the American Jewish Committee Representatives, 15 February 1985.

7. Katz, "Issues": 43-76. For studies focused on antisemitism in early Christianity, see Gager, *The Origins of Anti-Semitism*; Wilken, *John Chrysostum and the Jews*, 164; Gerard Stephen Sloyan, *Jesus on Trial: The Development of the Passion Narratives and Their Historical and Ecumenical Implications* (Philadelphia: Fortress Press, 1973); John T. Townsend, "The Gospel of John and the Jews: The Story of a Religious Divorce," in Davies, *Antisemitism and the Foundations of Christianity*, 72-97.

8. Eugene Fisher, "The Impact of the Christian-Jewish Dialogue on Biblical Studies," in Rousseau, *Christianity and Judaism*, 121.

9. For Black's essay in *The Interpreter's Dictionary of the Bible* (3: 778-81), see the comments of Samuel Sandmel, *Two Living Traditions: Essays on Religion and the Bible* (Detroit: Wayne State University, 1972), 291-304; Samuel Sandmel, *The First Century in Judaism and Christianity: Certainties and Uncertainties* (New York: Oxford University Press, 1969), 66, 101ff.
10. Sanders, *Paul and Palestinian Judaism*, 35, 57.
11. Raymond Brown et al., eds., *Mary and the New Testament* (Philadelphia: Fortress Press, 1978) and *Peter in the New Testament* (New York: Paulist Press, 1973). For journals that deal intensively with the Jewish-Christian dialogue, see *SIDIC, Journal of Ecumenical Studies, Christian-Jewish Relations, Freiburger Rundbrief,* and *Face to Face: An Interreligious Bulletin*.
12. van Buren, *Discerning the Way*. For an analysis of the Hebrew Bible as the spiritual antecedent for both Rabbinic Judaism and Christianity, see Nancy Fuchs-Kreimer, "Christian Old Testament Theology: A Time for New Beginnings," *Journal of Ecumenical Studies* 18 (1981): 90-92.
13. Baum, *Is the New Testament Anti-Semitic?*; Bruce Vawter, "Are the Gospels Anti-Semitic?" *Journal of Ecumenical Studies* 5 (1968): 473-87.
14. See Gregory Baum's "Introduction" in Ruether, *Faith and Fratricide*, 2-4. As another example, similar to Ruether's, of a linear development that omits contextual complexities, see Hyam Maccoby, "The Origins of Anti-Semitism," in Braham, *The Origins of the Holocaust*, 1-14. For a response, see Eugene Fisher, "The Origins of Anti-Semitism in Christian Theology: A Reaction and Critique," in Braham, *The Origins of the Holocaust*, 17-29.
15. Sandmel, *Anti Semitism*, has discussed which term — antisemitism, anti-Judaism, anti-Jewish — should be used and has concluded that in early Christianity "antisemitism" is probably wrong to use, but that really has not stopped anyone. See also, Fisher, *Faith without Prejudice*, 54-75; John Pawlikowski, *The Challenge of the Holocaust for Christian Theology* (New York: Center for Studies on the Holocaust, 1978); John Pawlikowski, *What Are They Saying about Christian-Jewish Relations* (New York: Paulist Press, 1980).
16. Several works have proven useful in explicating the history of Jewish-Christian relations; see, for example, John Edwards, *The Jews in Christian Europe, 1400-1700* (London: Routledge, 1988); Schmuel Almog, ed., *Antisemitism through the Ages* (Oxford: Pergamon Press, 1988); Flannery, *The Anguish of the Jews* (1985), although it is somewhat biased by interpreting Judaism through Christian glasses; Solomon Grayzel, *The Church and the Jews in the XIIIth Century, vol. 2,*

1254-1314 (Detroit: Wayne State University Press, 1989); Hans Küng, *Judaism between Yesterday and Tomorrow* (New York: Crossroad, 1992).

17. Yosef Hayim Yerushalmi, "Response to Rosemary Ruether," in Fleischner, *Auschwitz: Beginning of a New Era?*, 103.

18. For a good analysis, although somewhat superseded by subsequent research, see the essays in Davies, *Antisemitism and the Foundations of Christianity*; see also Leibig, "John and 'the Jews'": 226-27.

19. Eugene Fisher, "The Impact of the Christian-Jewish Dialogue on Biblical Studies," in Rousseau, *Christianity and Judaism*, 124; Robert Osborn, "The Christian Blasphemy," *Journal of the American Academy of Religion* 53 (1985): 339-63.

20. This statement from the bishops can be found in Fisher, *Faith without Prejudice*, 164-65. Reinforcing this point, see Mejia, "A Christian View of Bible Interpretation," in Boadt, *Biblical Studies*, 60, 71. For analyses of Pauline ambivalence, see Paul van Buren, "The Church and Israel: Romans 9-11," Opening Address, Third Frederick Neumann Symposium on Theological Interpretation of Scripture, Princeton Theological Seminary, 13-16 October 1989.

21. Davies, *Antisemitism and the Foundations of Christianity*, xv.

22. J. Blenkinsopp, "Tanakh and New Testament: A Christian Perspective," in Boadt, *Biblical Studies*, 96-119, and A. LaCocque, "The 'Old Testament' in Protestant Tradition," in Boadt, *Biblical Studies*, 120-46.

23. Eugene Fisher, "Continuity and Discontinuity in the Scripture Readings," *Liturgy* (May 1978): 30-37; J. Blenkinsopp, "Tanakh and New Testament: A Christian Perspective," in Boadt, *Biblical Studies*, 113; Bernardin, "Emerging Catholic Attitudes": 432-46.

24. J. Blenkinsopp, "Tanakh and New Testament: A Christian Perspective," in Boadt, *Biblical Studies*, 110.

25. Ibid., 100-3; William Scott Green, "Introduction: Messiah in Judaism: Rethinking the Question," in Jacob Neusner et al., eds., *Judaisms and Their Messiahs at the Turn of the Christian Era* (Cambridge: Cambridge University Press, 1987), 5; Pelikan, *The Emergence*, part 1, 14.

26. J. Blenkinsopp, "Tanakh and New Testament: A Christian Perspective," in Boadt, *Biblical Studies*, 100; Julius Wellhausen, *Prolegomena to the History of Ancient Israel* (New York: Meridian Books, 1957), 512.

27. A. LaCocque, "The 'Old Testament' in Protestant Tradition," in Boadt, *Biblical Studies*, 138. For subsequent studies on this issue, *Christian-Jewish Relations*, for example, provides articles and notes dealing with the ongoing dialogue as well as good reviews of the literature at regular intervals; see, for example, Karl-Josef Kuschel, "Ecumenical Consensus

on Judaism in Germany? A Theological Analysis of Recent Catholic and Protestant Statements on the Jewish Question," *Christian-Jewish Relations* 17 (1984): 3-20; Bronfman, "Catholic-Jewish Relations": 26-38; Pawlikowski, "Christian Ethics": 649-69.

28. Fisher, *Faith without Prejudice*, 154-55.

29. John Pawlikowski, *Christ in the Light of the Christian-Jewish Dialogue* (New York: Paulist Press, 1982); John McKenzie, *A Theology of the Old Testament* (Garden City, NJ: Doubleday, 1974), 113, 119. For a comprehensive analysis of political and liberation theology, see Matthew Lamb, *Solidarity with Victims: Toward a Theology of Social Transformation* (New York: Crossroad, 1982). Several prominent Protestant scholars have devoted a major portion of their scholarly pursuit to delineating the issue of Jewish-Christian relations; see, for example, Eckardt, *Jews and Christians*; Franklin H. Littell et al. eds., *In Answer: The Holocaust: Is the Story True? Why Did the World Community Not Respond? What are the Lessons?* (West Chester, PA: Sylvan, 1988).

30. George Mac Rae, "Messiah and Gospel," in Neusner, *Judaisms and Their Messiahs*, 173-74, 184.

31. The controversy around such notions as "covenant" and "Messiah" still need to be delineated before a sound resolution can be achieved. Some works that help establish the parameters are: Gershom Gerhard Scholem, *The Messianic Idea in Judaism and Other Essays on Jewish Spirituality* (New York: Schocken Books, 1971); Gavin D'Costa, *Theology and Religious Pluralism: The Challenge of Other Religions* (Oxford: Blackwell, 1986), chap. 5; Arnulf Camps, *Partners in Dialogue: Christianity and Other World Religions* (Maryknoll, NY: Orbis Books, 1983). D'Costa suggests that there is only one normative covenant and within it are to be found many further legitimate covenants. This situation arises because there is only one God, who discloses himself in many ways, but for discerning or analyzing these ways there is only one set of criteria available to Christians — a christocentric Trinitarianism. Issues swirling around the issue of the meaning of "covenant" continue. For D'Costa's current views, see his paper "Jews and Christians: Reflections on 'Covenant' and 'Fulfillment' towards a Theology of Christian-Jewish Relations," presented at Harvard, October 1989.

32. Friedrich Heer, *Offener Humanismus* (Bern: Scherz, 1962), 232; McKenzie, *A Theology*, 31-32; David Tracy, "Religious Values after the Holocaust: A Catholic View," in Abraham Peck, ed., *Jews and Christians after the Holocaust* (Philadelphia: Fortress Press, 1982), 96-97; Harrington, *God's People*.

33. In the view of Willebrands, absolute hatred of the Jews, as this appears in the Nazi persecution and ideology, argues for a continuous and serious inquiry into Christian history and culture in order to eradicate anti-Jewish prejudices with erroneous theological motivations; see Johannes Cardinal Willebrands, "Is Christianity Antisemitic?" *Christian-Jewish Relations* 18 (1985): 8-20. Cardinal Bea's early views opposing racism can be found in Augustin Bea, "Antisemitismus, Rassentheorie, und Altes Testament," *Stimmen der Zeit* 100 (1920): 171-83; David Tracy, "Religious Values after the Holocaust: A Catholic View," in Peck, *Jews and Christians,* 94. On the meaning of revelation as a source of new life and so the need to correct scripture and tradition, see Gregory Baum, "Catholic Dogma after Auschwitz," in Davies, *Antisemitism and the Foundations of Christianity,* 140-41.

34. Monika Hellwig, "From the Jesus Story to the Christ of Dogma," in Davies, *Antisemitism and the Foundations of Christianity,* 122.

35. David Tracy, "Religious Values after the Holocaust: A Catholic View," in Peck, *Jews and Christians,* 100.

36. Rosemary Ruether, "Christology and Jewish-Christian Relations," in Peck, *Jews and Christians,* 37; Pawlikowski, "Toward a Theology": 138-53.

37. A. Roy Eckardt, "Is There a Way Out of the Christian Crime? The Philosophic Question of the Holocaust," *Holocaust and Genocide Studies* 1 (1986): 121; Alice Eckardt, "Post-Holocaust Theology: A Journey Out of the Kingdom of Night," *Holocaust and Genocide Studies* 1 (1986): 229; Charlesworth, *Jews and Christians.* On the romanticization of suffering victims, see Gudorf, *Victimization,* 54-74.

38. Peter Haas, *Morality after Auschwitz: The Radical Challenge of the Nazi Ethic* (Philadelphia: Fortress Press, 1988), 1-9.

39. Willebrands, *Church and Jewish People*; Maurice Wiles, *Christian Theology and Interreligious Dialogue* (Philadelphia: Trinity Press International, 1992); Leonard Swidler et al., *Death or Dialogue? From the Age of Monologue to the Age of Dialogue* (Philadelphia: Trinity Press International, 1992). Most works on the issue of dialogue suggest that interaction and discussion will lead to understanding. Jacob Neusner, however, explores the theme that the idea of a common Judeo-Christian tradition is a myth. Both religions comprise different people talking about different things. Ignoring this axiom will lead to misunderstanding. See Jacob Neusner, *Jews and Christians: The Myth of a Common Tradition* (Philadelphia: Trinity Press International, 1991).

40. Daniel Maguire, *The Moral Core of Judaism and Christianity: Reclaiming the Revolution* (Minneapolis: Fortress Press, 1993).

4

Theology and the Christian-Jewish Dialogue: The Spectrum of Issues

After being sensitized to the fusion of antisemitism into our culture, surveying selected institutional responses, and analyzing what effect instituting a biblical dialogue between Christians and Jews can begin having in clarifying our heritage, theologians have been able to start developing the tools and the rationale that could allow them to reconfigure Christian theology. Historically, Christian theologians have helped proclaim and then have systematically articulated the values that have helped shape European civilization. To introduce a modification in or transformation of this pattern of values would seem to require even today the contribution of theologians to help articulate a moral architecture that can help support society poised between God and brutalization. Value formation extends across societal groups, and so those representing religion have a very particular role in reorienting society after the Holocaust, which in part was caused by a theology of contempt. This chapter will briefly survey some of the theological themes that have emerged in the discourse that has occurred over the last twenty-five years in order to assess the current state of the question. The issues that seem to be controlling the discussion have been labeled: fulfillment, continuity/discontinuity, triumphalism, and supersessionism. Because of an increased sensitivity to the importance of the concrete event, historically grounded theological speculation has also gained in favor over abstract, ahistorical systematization. This survey chapter of theological reflection will help set the tone and establish the context needed to understand the state of the research, will help serve to introduce some of the issues, and will help create the environment for the more careful consideration of Christology that follows in chapter 5, given that this latter point seems to be the keystone of the antisemitic edifice.

Christian Theology and Judaism

Responding to *Nostra Aetate* as well as the other initiatives from the Christian churches, such scholars as Clemens Thoma and Franz Mussner have developed what they label as a "Christian theology of Judaism." Mussner's Tractate on the Jews has attempted to critique previous historical tractates *against* the Jews and to dissociate "real" Christianity from its tawdry past by claiming that some Christian traditions have very clearly gone awry. Reflecting on past Christian interpretations, both Mussner and Thoma have tried to offer scholarly analyses that they hope can help delineate Jewish-Christian relationships in a manner that is "true" to the tradition of both religions.[1] One issue, however, that is not dealt with adequately is that of the meaning of the Republic of Israel, which now, as we have seen, has become a factor in any theological dialogue and part of the environment within which terms are defined and horizons delineated. The Jewish people have had a history and are still making history. Treating this issue serves to recall that for the Jewish people history is crucial for their social and religious self-consciousness. Christian, and especially Catholic, theologians, have tended to deal with abstractions which until recently have not been clearly tethered to the real world. If this century has taught us anything, it has illuminated the dangers that lie in abstractions disconnected from real people. For some, the emergence of the Israeli state indicates God's continuing care of his people. Thus, "a theology of Judaism" could set the wrong tone because the Jewish experience becomes an object of study and not something rooted in a still-living faith community.

Among earlier theologians there was a tendency to forget the intimate relationship that religious Jews have had and still have with God and especially to ignore that so much of their mutual experience was related to the land of Israel. The present Republic of Israel helps recall that relationship, and, despite their focus on "Judaism as a religion," Mussner and Thoma do well to include some reflections on this fact. Focusing wholly on such an abstraction as "Judaism," they seem to realize, can make it more easily possible for Christians to ignore the real lives of those who have constructed Israel's unique history and present political life, which is for some the authentic community of the Jewish people. Some Christian theologians have even suggested that the existence of Israel affirms God's continuing favor and adds a different perspective on the covenant today. In his sensitive introduction to Thoma's study, David Flusser, for example, frequently refers to the living Israel, meaning the people, rather than Judaism. He insists that in studying Judaism, Christian theologians have to accept the Jewish view that "it was not a religion that was chosen but a group of human beings, not the Jewish religion, but Israel." Flusser's observation seems to reflect some of the ambivalence concerning the role of Israel as a nation-state, which stimulated the debate that swirled around Vatican-Israel negotiations. He has maintained that a Christian theology of Judaism that ignores the divinely willed connection between Israel and the Land is impracticable today in light of the Holocaust and the foundation of the Republic of Israel.[2] For some, the concrete word "Israel" is preferable to the abstraction "Judaism" and drives to the heart of the issue. But Judaism can be a valid term as long as the history of the people is accepted as still an open-ended enterprise reflecting the ongoing vitality of the Jewish faith.

As a theologian reflecting on the Jewish faith-experience in terms of Christianity, Thoma, unfortunately, initially asserts everything that Israel is *not*, which does not help in constructing an unencumbered openness to Jewish integrity. More positively, he does maintain that Israel should be accepted as a state. Mussner treats the subject of Israel and its land empathetically and also perceives Israel theologically as a sign that God has continued guiding the Jews. In this sense, Israel as a political state has become a sign of hope for both Israel and the church. As a people, Israel continues the revelation of God.[3]

Do the Jewish people as such include more than the Republic of Israel, given that in contemporary usage it is usually only the political state that is associated with the name Israel? Also, how does Christianity take its bearings from such a phenomenon? Some in the Republic of Israel do not feel themselves separated from the Jewish Diaspora because every Jew, they maintain, is potentially a citizen of that state and by law can take up residence there. Many Jews in the Diaspora also feel living connections to the land of Abraham, modern Israel. They view themselves as citizens of their own particular countries and simultaneously feel a special relationship to Israel as a state. The issue is complex, but it serves to remind us that use of the term "Judaism" has to be sensitive to all the historical strata and contemporary nuances. A Christian theology that glosses over the complex religious and geopolitical fact of Israel by only using the term "Judaism" in an imprecise or abstract way and ignoring the historical reality that gives life to the Jewish faith community would constitute an obstruction to any meaningful dialogue with the Jewish people.[4] Recalling the significance of the Republic of Israel does serve to remind us also that the Jewish people and their connection with the God-of-history is a living relationship. This as much as anything should counter supersessionism and should help set the tone for discussions revolving around the continuity/discontinuity challenge.

A "Christian theology of Judaism," if not understood with its complexities, however, would be conceptually weak because it would be considered only the subject of a specific "religious studies" category. Judaism cannot be defined through the lens of Christian theology. From past experience, Jews finding an identity through Christian experiences can and have been placed in a very vulnerable position. Ultimately, the complex systems that Thoma and Mussner have elaborated tend more to be seen as "Judaism from the viewpoint of Christian theology." Even so, their attempts to probe into the root issues can be applauded as long as we remember that they have examined the Jewish experience through a Christian lens, and that both men have taken some very important initial steps in isolating the issues of concern. Both have struggled to implement concretely Vatican II's *Nostra Aetate* and to interpret the experience of the

Jewish people theologically as a positive contribution to Christian reflections. In attacking the "teaching of contempt," Thoma and Mussner have aligned themselves with the necessary corrective to the dismal and negative meaning that consigned the Jewish people historically to a role as a "remnant" in Christian theology. That in itself is a significant accomplishment.[5] Their studies, however, have also reminded us of the traditional perspective wherein Israel's significance still seems to subsist within the framework of Christian theology without redefining or totally restructuring that theology. Both studies exude strong apologetic tendencies as they attempt to diagnose such key issues as the "anti-Judaism" in the Christian Testament. Both scholars perceive that wrongs have been done, but they cannot see that radical steps may have to be taken to remedy past perspectives that have interpreted the Jewish phenomenon from the standpoint of the Christian.

Thoma underestimates whenever possible what he refers to as the "possible anti-Judaism in the New Testament." He explicates the meaning of this "Theology of Judaism." "If one wishes by any means to subsume the New Testament under anti-Jewish literature, then the Hebrew Scriptures should be called even more anti-semitic," presumably because of the frequent diatribes against Jews unfaithful to the covenant as well as because of the emphasis on the Jewish people as chosen and "different" from others. Such an apologetic fails to take into account the historical environment that produced the two testaments. None of the cited Hebrew Bible texts, for example, was created within a religious community of Jews and religious Gentiles, even though the Jewish people are portrayed as the "light of the nations." But this pluralistic mixture is a dominating issue for *all* of the Christian texts. Thus, it is impossible really to compare rigorously the polemic of the Hebrew with that of the Christian texts in light of the intensive scriptural research available.[6] Thoma is comparing apples and oranges or, perhaps even worse, is suggesting a continuity running through both revelations.

In Mussner's work, apologetic tendencies have been placed in the forefront. He discusses the "anti-Judaism in the Gospels and in the entire New Testament," "distortions of Judaism," and "hostile images even in the time of the primitive church." He also candidly concedes what the Pauline doctrine of justification by faith in Jesus Christ has historically meant over the centuries. This resultant view of justification has meant that the life of the Jew has had minimal value in Christian society. Mussner insisted that for Paul the Law derived its meaning from his own Jewish culture. Thus, exegetically it seemed that it would make no sense to see Paul's teaching of the Law and justification as stemming from an alleged anti-Judaism. Mussner has asserted, therefore, that it was Christian theology after Paul that misused the apostle's statements and initiated the ongoing defective tradition. In Mussner's view, therefore, Auschwitz can exercise a hermeneutical function that will compel a rethinking of the revelatory texts that can lead to a new understanding. Several of his suggestions can be profitably pursued:

1.   The Hebrew Scriptures compose an ongoing source for the faith of Israel.
2.   Israel is the enduring "root" of the church.
3.   The covenant of God with his people Israel, whom he has chosen for himself, still continues.
4.   The "land" has a special role in the thought of Israel.

The Jewish people have a significant and comprehensive salvific function in the world both before and after Christ and so can help Christians find an identity given that Israel is the root of Christianity.[7] Christians, therefore, are not needed for Jewish identity and have merely been a force negatively in shaping the reflection of the people Israel.

Thoma and Mussner have offered post-Holocaust interpretations steeped in apologetics. In Thoma's problematic theological view, a believing Christian is asked to focus on interpreting the Jewish experiences in the Third Reich from the standpoint of Christian theodicies. By this time such a conceptual hermeneutic should probably have been expunged because it would suggest that extermination was to be seen as part of God's plan and so would somehow relieve Christians of responsibility. Thoma also has asserted that Christians should focus on Christ to understand the Shoah because the Jewish victims of the Holocaust seem to resemble Jesus in sorrow and death. For Thoma, Auschwitz seems to be a monumental sign that should be able to help humanity comprehend the intimate bond and unity between the exterminated Jewish martyrs, representing all the Jewish people, and the crucified Christ. Despite all the misunderstandings and persecutions leading to 1945, the Holocaust has been transformed by Thoma into a milestone communicating to Christians a comprehension of the inviolable oneness that cements Judaism and Christianity after Christ's Crucifixion. Thus, for Thoma, both religions have been legitimized through victims. The suffering of Jesus should help us understand the sufferings inflicted by the Nazis. According to Thoma, Jewish identity was at least partially tied to the Crucifixion. Despite Thoma's good will, the connections do not incite real dialogue. Thoma states that all the witnesses to the faith of Christians and non-Christians are by definition the people of Christ. Taking a different approach, Mussner has insisted that the Christian, facing the total sacrifice of the Jews in Auschwitz, must openly admit to complicity in antisemitism. After such an admission, how can Auschwitz be connected to Golgotha? Even though sensitive to historical Christian antisemitism, however, Mussner cannot seem to accept the meaning of this Jewish experience unless he can attach the brutalities of Auschwitz to Christ's now glorified Crucifixion.[8]

The cure for our cultural, antisemitic malady cannot be the connection of Jewish suffering to the death of Jesus. That would identify the Jewish experience with the Christian faith community and could suggest that the Jewish suffering is somehow good. Christians do not have the right to make such statements. The victim becomes romanticized. It is also particularly difficult to justify the use of the word "sacrifice" in the context of the Holocaust because "sacrifice" is rooted in freedom. No one can believe that the Jews freely embraced Hitler's murderous plan. Even though both scholars seem aware of the issues at stake, neither seems able to escape the coils of the need apparently to connect somehow the Jewish experience to Christianity. The Carmelite Convent issue of recent memory should illuminate the ramifications of this perspective.

Mussner's interpretation has portrayed Israel as the servant suffering for the sins of the world (Col. 1:24), which in his view can complement the atoning sufferings of Jesus Christ. Using this approach, such an interpretation would avoid locating the murder of the Jewish people solely in a Christian theological context. A more appropriate response might be that the Holocaust has a significance for the Jewish people that would not depend on Christian revelation. Mussner could have deflected some of the criticism attending his views by extending his theological conclusions. He could have asserted, for example, that the Jews enmeshed in the Final Solution had died vicariously for the whole world, including the Christians as well, but the issue of freedom of choice would still not be resolved. Such an extension, however, might help move the dialogue along because the Jewish extermination could then be seen to have had a universally salvific mission similar to that of Christ's, but we would still be defining this massacre in terms of Christian theodicy. The Jewish experience could still be seen as the "light to all nations." Even with its limitations, the carefully delineated soteriological and christological conclusions in Mussner's interpretation have stimulated more sensitive analyses that have helped ensure that this horrific Jewish experience cannot gain significance only through Christian perspectives. Mussner's work is a major contribution, even though he has not fully responded to the call of *Nostra Aetate*. To say the least, his perspective requires substantial amplification in light of where the Jewish-Christian dialogue has been and seems to be going because he seems constrained from following fully the logic of his assertions. His approach does remind us, however, of the pitfalls of anything but a thorough reexamination of Christian theology and the universal questions posed by theodicy issues.

The Jewish intellectual Emil Fackenheim, for example, has wondered whether an answer can ever be given even in messianic times for the death of even one child. Fackenheim has labeled as blasphemy any attempt to find a religious meaning in the Holocaust because presumably the covenant should not demand that people die. These and similar soul-wrenching questions suggest how difficult it has been even to agree where to look for meaning in these events. Still, the tradition of both Jews and Christians has been to try to uncover God's words in historical events. Perhaps Auschwitz only has the meaning that can be derived from its impact on post-1945 Christians and Jews as they probe the mystery of God. Rooted in a more conservative tradition, neither Thoma nor Mussner seem prepared to accept fully the challenge formulated by Johannes Baptist Metz: "No longer to pursue any theology that is so conceived that it remains untouched by Auschwitz or could remain untouched by it."[9] At the essence of pluralistic postmodernism would seem to be that all groups have a right to speak for themselves in their own authentic and legitimate voices. Jewish experiences cannot be read through the lens of the Christian faith without harming both.

Christian Identity and the Jewish Revelatory Experience

An early proponent of this more realistic dialogical approach, J. Coert Rylaarsdam, has suggested that the historical Christian-Jewish encounter has been significantly metamorphosed through the horrors of the Final Solution. The past persecutions and pogroms, and especially the policies followed in Nazi Germany, demand that persons having freedom also have a duty to assume a responsibility that can help to ensure that such an event will not recur. The Shoah can teach that we have a responsibility when we theologize for and against others. In particular, Rylaarsdam seems to focus on the need for a sensitivity and mobility in dialogue that he has modeled on the pre-1933 works of Franz Rosenzweig and Martin Buber.[10] The interaction among Holocaust theologians has been intense, perhaps in part because our pluralistic culture virtually demands arguments against exclusion. In both Europe and the United States, the insistent demand for an essential theological transformation and a restructuring of the Christian relationship to the Jewish people has become part of the ongoing dialogue. This dialogue seems to be necessary for the people of both faiths because more is really at stake than just ecumenical relations. Issues posed in Auschwitz go to the essence of the human condition. Faced with what Jews have suffered under Christians, for example, Irving Greenberg has suggested that we may be tempted to conclude that it would have been better had Jesus not lived. From the perspective of two millennia of suffering inflicted by Christians, Greenberg posits Christianity at a real crossroads where its choice of direction is contingent on whether it can overcome its earlier contempt for the Jewish people that has incubated in our civilization. In light of the Holocaust, he has suggested that Christianity may have to "die" as a prelude to receiving new life. If Christianity continues unaffected and does not rethink itself in its search for its authentic identity, he has asserted, then it will die to both God and humanity.[11] The fundamental issue is how to relate Jewish and Christian experiences in such a way that both retain their integrity and lead to a new level of reflection on their faith-experiences. Catholic leaders have suggested that the hatred of the Jewish people, which has marked our culture for nearly two millennia, was not an expression of true Christianity but rather a deformation that has to be eliminated. Some Christian theologians have insisted that we have to admit finally that contemptuous passages in the Scriptures have to be condemned as not in line with the Christian message. Thus, those interacting in the first centuries of the Christian tradition made mistakes. A commitment to interactive theological dialogue may demand a radical hermeneutic that can help support this emerging religious reexamination, which in turn could help reinforce a new social ethic.

Insightful and path-breaking studies on interfaith relations have been done by the Protestant theologians A. Roy Eckardt and Franklin Littell, who have helped institutionalize this desirable Jewish-Christian dialogue into associations and journals. The works of both theologians seem to foreshadow a new understanding of historical revelation as an event and the theological hermeneutic as a cognitive approach tied to historicity. Both have found an impetus for the reexamination of Christian theology in the near annihilation of the Jewish people in Europe and its rebirth in the Republic of Israel. Paul van Buren has also elaborated a more nuanced relationship that could exist between Christians and Jews, if careful analyses of the Scriptures were made. Even if one might disagree with the specifics, his three-volume study of the ongoing Jewish-Christian conversation, which tends to mute some traditional Christian doctrines, has provided an impetus for future dialogue. All of these theologians have begun sketching systemic outlines that go to the heart of the matter. How can both faiths maintain their doctrinal integrity in the post-Shoah world? These scholars emotionally project a more sensitive reflection on Judaism and the Jewish people and have established the parameters for the dialogue along lines similar to those suggested by the Catholic theologian, Metz, for whom the event has to become the directing agent for theologizing. In essence, they have been engaged in an ongoing project of rethinking Christian theology in light of the Holocaust perpetrated by Christians. Theologians have also begun reformulating traditional Christian doctrines in order that they may be rooted more definitively in the original Christian message.

In Eckardt's early work, the position taken seems to be almost identical to the view adumbrated by the German Protestant Church of the Rhineland in its "On the Renewal of the Relationship between Christians and Jews" (1980). This document stated that a Christian theology of the Jewish-Christian relationship could profit from Franz Rosenzweig's earlier assertions. Rosenzweig had observed that if Judaism were the "star of redemption," then Christianity could be seen as the rays of that star. Thus, Christianity could be affirmed as the successor of Israel only by the fact that it carried outwardly the power of the Jewish faith-experience. From the analogy a very important determination may be made. To eliminate the star would be to eliminate the rays. In essence, with the Christian gospel, any division between Jew and Gentile could be expunged once and for all because the eternally abiding covenant with Israel could now definitively be opened to the world in a way that the Jewish faith could not provide. Christianity could be seen as designed for disseminating the revelation that had been lodged in Israel. This approach has its problems, but it does offer some provocative insights. All Jews, of course, could not assent to Rosenzweig's contention that the gentile world could come to God only through Jesus Christ, because a limited reading of this could lead to supersessionism. Christians could applaud Rosenzweig's insight only from the problematic standpoint of their own christological persuasions, which would stress that even if there were continuity on one level, discontinuity simultaneously may exist on another. This issue of continuity/discontinuity not surprisingly seems to pervade any dialogue on the Jewish-Christian relationship. An acceptance of continuity at some level, however, seems crucial in order to obviate the "teaching of contempt." In being nurtured by Israel's sacred role, Christianity could avoid annulling the role of original Israel and most certainly could not take the place of Israel. In this model, historical Israel would perdure as God's people. Israel "is to sanctify the name of the Lord, to adore the God who is superior to idols, and to obey joyfully the Torah while awaiting the messianic kingdom."[12] Christians are tied to this task, but in a distinctively different way. The Jewish-Christian dialogue has again and again examined the discontinuity/continuity models and focused its energies on the companion theodicy issue because following both lines of thought plunges us into Christian mysteries.

Because of the Shoah, we have to concentrate on the questions that this mass murder has posed to a humanity created in God's image.

Reflections on theodicy, which lend an emotional backdrop to discussions on supersessionism, have also been given a cutting poignancy as the Jewish people have religiously speculated on what transpired. Greenberg, for example, has suggested that after the Holocaust the only relation of man to God may be one of anger and conflict. Eliezer Berkovits has similarly insisted that nothing could excuse God from the sufferings inflicted on the innocent because he has to be made to assume responsibility for creating a world in which humans freely engage in sanctioned murder. Eckardt has also reflected theologically on what these and other writers have said about the theodicy question[13] by demanding that revelation be reinterpreted as it has often been refracted through the Shoah. This theodicy issue has generated a heat that has driven theologians into the texts and faiths of both religions and has sharply posed the continuity/discontinuity dichotomy. Theodicy asks questions of God and humanity that demand answers, and some have been forthcoming. Basically, theodicy calls for reflections on what God and humans have freely done and why; it also calls for a questioning stance on continuity/discontinuity as theological models, given that discontinuity can help justify the Holocaust.

Littell has maintained that supersessionistic theology is one of the principle intellectual reasons that could be used to support the annihilation of the Jewish people in Europe. He has suggested that theological concepts based on such Christian "truths" as the Crucifixion and Resurrection may well have to be considered only the cognitive categories that aided earlier Christians in understanding the significance of the faith event that was Christ. As such they have to be susceptible to change. From this perspective, a Christian culture counter to the Holocaust would have as its duty a rethinking of a theology that could oppose totalitarian systems as well as the value-free trends of modern societies. Sources of value and the meaning of revelation will have to be explored in the process. This "counterculture," he maintains, can only be shaped through ties of commitment to the Jewish people, the original purveyors of God's revelation. The absence of this connection to the freedom originally offered by God helped produce the domineering political culture rooted in interwar Europe and seems to have been instrumental in paving the way to Auschwitz. In Littell's view, just as today's Christians are linked in "the communion of saints" to past martyrs, so too are they connected in a solidarity of guilt to those who sustained the Christian antisemitism that fostered the rebellion against the God of Abraham and Moses. Christians, he has remarked, should begin assessing their own religion by affirming that in their betrayal of God's love, the most recent martyrs to Christian supersessionism were the Jews of Europe. As God's people, the Jews seemed to adhere to God's historical plan that the Christians were abandoning. Thus, the sterility of a messianic religion, he observes quite correctly, in which nothing significant seems to have occurred between the Ascension and the Second Coming, has become clear through the Holocaust.[14]

Adhering to a similar line of reasoning, which stresses ongoing continuity and interaction and vigorously sublimates the doctrinal distinctiveness separating the Christian and Jewish faiths, van Buren has isolated the biblical concept of "Way" as a useful metaphor that can help describe more intimately the reality of the Christian-Jewish relationship. This Way is the thoroughfare through the history of Israel that was carved by the God of Abraham, Isaac, and Jacob as well as now by Jesus Christ, who can be seen as the specific revelation of the God of Israel to the Gentiles. The Christ-event, therefore, could be seen as a new step taken by God and his creation. But van Buren stresses that this does not abrogate any commitment to Israel, the original and continuing people of God, because the christological revelation was directed primarily toward the Gentiles. Relying on this approval, van Buren hopes to succeed in highlighting the full significance of the church's traditional Christology, rooted in the Trinitarian concept of God, and would not really infringe on the authenticity of Israel's relationship to Jahweh. In van Buren's approach, the Son revealed God in a fashion significantly different from prior events by announcing what God now wants for gentile humanity. Van Buren has offered a unique approach to the issues that theodicy poses. God, according to van Buren, has allowed humanity the freedom to work his will, and therein lies the power of his own infinite freedom. From this vantage point, therefore, God is free to "step back" to allow us to exercise the freedom that we have received, even if it would mean implementing murderous policies. Similar to Bonhoeffer, van Buren holds that it is God's will that humans live *before him* as though he were not present, and so humanity would have a grave responsibility to do God's will.[15] In van Buren's reflection, however, making Sinai *the* controlling event could create a very real problem. Losing his distinctive role, which is a key to the Christian understanding, Christ would then merely become the entry point for non-Jews into this ongoing covenant. Sinai certainly would continue to have its importance, but van Buren's theology as determinedly based on this Christ-event may not be powerful enough for the construction of a theology of the Christian-Jewish relationship, in which two equal partners are seen as coexisting with all of their integrity intact. In his system, such controlling events as the Jesus and Sinai events lose their idiosyncratic potency through van Buren's sublimation process.

Rather than just suggesting that the Holocaust is a unique source of revelation comparable to the Scriptures, some Christian theologians have sought to redefine religious life in the context of the freedom and responsibility of humanity, which have been given a new poignancy by the sanctioned murder of God's people. Eckardt, Littell, van Buren, and Abraham Heschel have contributed responses. From their very provocative perspective, it is not only human beings who need God; God also needs human beings to shape and empower creation. Within this context, Greenberg has also suggested that humans should take greater responsibility for the accomplishment of covenantal goals. They should assume power and restore the image of God to humankind, which could help lead to the removal of the sources of stereotypic hatred.[16] The Shoah has made this conclusion inescapable.

In light of the Holocaust and of this connection between God as creator and humans as responsible agents, the Jewish and Christian faith-experiences have assumed a seminal position as we reexamine our culture.[17] The theologians briefly discussed above illustrate some of the issues involved. No matter what approach they take, almost inevitably they seem to return to those original Christian communities and ask if Christianity is by its very nature antisemitic or if the fault lies in its subsequent trajectories. How can both Christianity and Judaism exist concurrently as authentic revelation experiences? In general, much of the creative post-Holocaust work has consciously rejected an indictment of Christ's message in favor of blaming human interpretations made in specific contexts. The problem, however, is not just to reject supersessionism but more positively to maintain each tradition with its unique integrity, a problem that is made more difficult because Christianity owes its origins to the fact that Jesus was Jewish, while historically Christians have tried to delineate their identity at the expense of the Jews.

The deep probing of this issue, as we have seen, has demanded delving into the New Testament traditions to uncover antisemitism and the reasons for its existence. Such efforts can provide theologians with the tools to develop a healthy skepticism and a more realistic relationship between Christians and Jews, free from destructive Christian absolutism, which in turn can help resolve the continuity/discontinuity issue. This necessary transformation in understanding has begun to emerge from a healthy understanding of the New Testament contexts as it is from these writings that the structural elements and the content of religious antisemitism derived their legitimacy. The Holocaust event has challenged Christian theology today to reappropriate its own tradition, which would not be supportive of inhumanity. When the Jews were being persecuted, they were helped by individuals and groups in Christian Europe, but the churches were silent due in part to their traditional theology.[18] The Final Solution was implemented by at least nominal Christians in a Christian civilization that had nurtured the virulent antisemitism manifest within political agendas. Re-creating a viable theology in our post-Holocaust culture should be able to assist us materially to articulate values to sustain our political communities.

Few could dispute that the Christian churches and theologies have almost unceasingly incited and encouraged attitudes hostile to and contemptuous of the Jews and that they have searched for evidentiary support in Scripture. One theological assertion that has been lethally potent has been that of triumphalistic fulfillment. How can Christianity be blamed and yet not be held responsible in its essence? Even when the churches did not oppress Jewish communities in the physical sense, they contributed to a culturally rooted, latent antisemitism that would historically make it difficult to resist or protest prejudice and assault. The active and passive betrayal of the Jewish people during the Third Reich was fertilized in ground tilled theologically by Christians for centuries. Destroying Nazi hegemony did not automatically annihilate this antisemitism, which some have perceived as present in the essence of Christianity and its triumphalism. Such bias, they feel, has resulted in the theological denial of the Jewish people's right to exist as God's people adhering to the Torah.[19] Theological reflection rooted in scriptural research can act as a counterweight to this supersessionism.

Historically, theological contempt toward the Jews as superseded by Christianity helped lead to ghettos and pogroms.[20] Uriel Tal has correctly asserted that traditional Christianity and racial antisemitism, although originating with different goals in mind and not necessarily related, were both impelled toward resolving the "Jewish problem." The former opted for conversion; the latter could, and in one case did, end in extermination. By century after century insisting that there was a "Jewish problem," Christian theology helped reinforce the patterns of prejudice, hatred, and calumny in our civilization, and so helped offer a rationale justifying organized violence. The anti-Christian elements of racial antisemitism were interpreted in such a way that the traditional theological concepts of Christianity could be fused to the secular racist ideology to provide a moral underpinning for destruction. At least theologically, traditional Christians viewed the Jewish religion as an anachronism, for the Incarnation and the "new covenant" had made it superfluous and robbed the Jewish community of its reason for existence, except as the Augustinian remnant people useful for Christian pedagogical purposes.[21] Those engaged in rethinking the Christian faith message, which has in the past wreaked so much havoc, also have to be engaged in strengthening Christianity in the secular culture by historically allying with those intellectual elements that supported oppression.

Until this postwar era, the supersessionist error at the base of so much antisemitism had been reinforced for almost two millennia. Even until recently such theologians as Ernst Käsemann could still reiterate that through Jesus Christ the Torah as such was abolished and that Jesus restored the real sense of the Mosaic Torah, which had been perverted by the Jews. Fortunately, such perverse renderings are dwindling, but some of the theological convolutions designed to handle the supersessionist issue are almost as bad because they have developed terminology that only nominally solves the problem, or because they have redefined Christianity almost out of existence as a unique revelation by locating it amorphously in the mutual experiences of the Judeo-Christian communities of the classical common era.[22] In a very real sense, to obscure legitimate distinctions does justice to neither faith.

Christian theology is clearly anti-Jewish when it perceives the life of the Jewish people solely under the aegis of interpreting God's promise to the Jewish people as finished. Such theological thinking was formerly almost prototypical in the history of Christianity, and it ended by developing a life of its own. Any theology formulated within this antisemitic context has to be questioned because it has contributed to the anti-Jewish, Christian theology that emerged through historical conflict. Over the last few decades, theologians have been seeking to design fundamental necessary transformations in Christian theology, particularly as it has been described in the New Testament. Recalling the historical context within which the New Testament developed can help define the central function of a theology that calls for "repentance and renewal" and is conducive to understanding the meaning of the Holocaust.[23] No matter where theologians begin their journey, they invariably gravitate to the first Christian communities that were embedded in Jewish religious and cultural life and to the subsequent triumphalism that emerged.

In recent decades, an array of scholars has begun to define anew the relationship between the church and the synagogue in order to root out supersessionism. This dialogue between Jews and Christians has become the intellectual environment within which theologians presumably have to operate as they rethink theology and tradition. Nurtured by the ongoing conversation, this dialogue has been shaped into a listening and questioning posture rather than one that is proclaiming "truth." With this type of dialogue, theologians have found that they can no longer proceed from the traditional comfort of a dogma that purportedly defines what Israel and the Jewish people are supposed to mean in light of what some elements in later Christianity have thought. Rather, diagnosing the anti-Judaism in this tradition, theologians have been engaged in formulating their analyses in a way consonant with the essential aspects of Jewish self-understanding. This theological reflection on the Jewish experience, which can be contrasted to early Christian reactions, has been found useful in relating the Torah and the gospel. For Christians this has involved a double learning process from the very outset because Jews do not need Christians to define their own religious experience. Theologians are currently engaged in reconfiguring their formulations about the life of the Christian church standing before God *and* in the context of this church's relationship to God's people of Sinai.[24]

From this perspective, the Christian Testament is now being viewed as a document written and compiled by Jews who believed in and adhered to Jesus as they shaped their identity, although they were probably not initially conscious of any irremediable separation. Along with other groups within the Jewish faith community, this early group of "Jesus followers" intensified its disagreements with elements present in the common religious culture. It formulated an implicit and explicit structure that was responsible for molding the Christian canon. A sensitive concern related to the Christian Scriptures almost necessarily seems to demand that structural aspects of the emerging canon and the relationship of the Christian and the Jewish faith experiences have had to be reexamined, and we have seen some of the results in the preceding chapter. The most enduring component of the disastrous animosity cemented into Christian and Jewish relations was the uncritical historical retrojection of such elements as fulfillment into the early disputes that revolved around specific individual Jewish groups or laws. Here can be seen a classic case of how very specific historical attitudes and behavior can be universalized into subsequent centuries. [25]

Such ancient hostility will not evaporate by ignoring, denying, or trivializing it. Theologians have to focus on reconstructing a horizon that can allow us to avoid a recurrence of the Holocaust. Hence, Christian theology can fundamentally *only* be legitimate theology as a result of Christian-Jewish dialogue conducted in a spirit stripped of former encrustations. This continuing Christian-Jewish encounter should have the primarily heuristic function of transforming and releasing theology, proclamation, and instruction from its historically conditioned anti-Jewish forms. [26]

How have well-intentioned Christians excised latent, and sometimes even unconscious, antisemitism from their tradition? Some have reassessed early Christian documents and traditions for alternate meanings and perhaps for strands that were lost as one portion of the tradition became dominant over others. Attuned to Jewish history, Christian theologians have been engaged in deepening their appreciation of Israel's ongoing identity as God's people. Following this consciousness-raising activity, scholars have begun developing a more theologically authentic relationship to God's first people, the Jews. The faith event encased in primitive Christianity has to be studied, they feel, with an eye to the indissoluble tension between the deeds of Jesus as a member of the Jewish community and the acts of the Christian churches that were organized in an environment rooted in their struggle to define the church's identity in the pre-Constantinian era. In a fascinating reversal, the writings of those who lost the struggle are again being analyzed from the existing records that have survived to see if another path could have been followed. Such an approach is a particularly important initiative. After the ascendancy of orthodox Christianity, alternative forms of community life were neglected and the rich diversity of second- and third-century Christianity was lost, with only some traces remaining.[27] In combating such problematic attitudes as supersessionism, it is helpful to know that there once existed other traditions that were not so myopic.

Since the paths of Jews and Christians separated after a few decades, theologians and biblical scholars have gone back to the initial testimonies and to the original meaning of the canon in order to develop a theology that can affirm Israel as God's people. Chapters 9-11 of Romans, for example, has become of fundamental importance. Karl Ludwig Schmidt, Karl Barth, Paul van Buren, and Franz Mussner have all stressed the relevance of this text[28] and have tried to understand what Paul meant in his often contradictory and nuanced statements.

For Paul, Israel had a positive function in past as well as future salvation history. Israel's protological election by God was to be confirmed by Israel's eschatological salvation, and three very explicit reasons can be offered.

1. No eschatological deliverance of the world could occur without the salvation of all Israel (Rom. 11: 25-26).
2. The gentile church would have no authenticity or identity in the absence of realizing that it had been "grafted, contrary to nature, into a cultivated olive tree," i.e., into Israel, "beloved for the sake of their forefathers" (Rom. 11: 24, 28).
3. God's promises to the Gentiles would become null and void unless his promises toward Israel were in the process of being realized.

The Gospels, therefore, cannot have any authentic validity or legitimation apart from Israel because the theological issue of God's faithfulness and righteousness toward Israel has to determine the truth of the gospel (Rom. 3:3).

How could Christians trust a God who could abandon Israel? The priority of Israel and the universality of the gospel can be maintained simultaneously, it seems increasingly to be realized, because they both have a theocentric foundation. The Christ-event, according to Paul, makes clear that Israel's priority does not stem solely from its empirical achievement of "covenant keeping" but rather also in God's faithfulness to his own promises of grace. Although his letters may well create some confusion, Paul does manage to unpack the hope that Israel and Christianity, albeit in separate ways, will yet rejoice together in the God of their destiny.

Paul delineated Israel's position before God christologically, and unfortunately for subsequent Jewish communities this was dogmatically elaborated down through the centuries. Paul described Israel's understanding of itself accurately, but, given his own needs, he unfortunately highlighted the spirit/Law and cultic/ethical dichotomies. He skewed for future generations in Christian minds Israel's continuing vibrant relationship to the Torah. Scholars have reminded us that Paul's letters were being written to living people with specific questions and problems. Thus, the context is important. The Jewish people thrived after the emergence of the early Christian communities and after 70 C.E. (destruction of the Temple) entered a phase of their history that the apostle Paul did not personally experience. The tacit and long-dominant assumption of many that over time Paul would have developed an immutable theology is a historically untenable supposition and theologically highly problematic because of Paul's own personality and unclear sense of mission. Paul's letters suggest a vibrant intellect constantly wrestling with challenges during this first era of Christian self-definition. One thrust of Pauline theology was, for example, the expectation of the imminent Parousia. His theology does not universally suggest that he was prepared for a two-thousand-year delay, even though other portions of the canonical Scriptures do not preclude that possibility.[29]

Surely one of the crucial statements in chapters 9-11 of Romans is the promise that Israel was receiving mercy *in Paul's era* even without the help of the church during what Paul seemed to foresee as the imminent consummation of the world. God's mercy to Israel, then, did not seem conditioned by conversion. Theologians are now trying to express Paul's testimony without reference to his often highlighted eschatological presupposition. Israel's own testimony stresses that God's loving commitment to his people is a continuously unfolding event, particularly relevant after 1945.[30]

Today's theological goal may be simultaneously to affirm Jesus and to end the theological rejection of Israel as God's people. This dual mission seems to be coupled with humanizing and historicizing theology. Both the traditions and the currently living testimony of Jews and Christians should be equally appreciated. Confinement to *either* the Jewish *or* the Christian tradition now seems to indicate a disturbing lack of biblical orientation for a theologian. The command to love one's neighbor is a maxim that should become the yardstick for Christian hermeneutics as theologians grapple with this issue.[31] Christian theologians, of course, have no right to demand that Jews enter into this dialogue, but certainly they should try to be sensitive to the Jewish perspective on Israel as God's people. The meaning derived from the Jewish outlook could help Christians, who are trying to diagnose the meaning of the Hebrew Bible for Christianity.

The Formation of Christian Identity

The Jewish-Christian dialogue is currently reshaping Christian identity because it has demanded that theologians go back to the basics. In all likelihood, however, there probably would have been precious little interaction if the horrors of 1933-45 had not elevated the issue to a theologically imperative plateau. The Holocaust has become part of the Jewish and Christian historical intersection and seems to demand an ongoing exploration of Christian theological roots. The Shoah has become the historical and hermeneutical starting point for any theological work that seeks to define the relationship between Christians and Jews as historical victimizers and victims. Interest in the connection between theology and victimization has also reinforced such directions as those pursued in liberation theology and feminist theology, which are responding to the needs of marginal groups. The Shoah has compelled theologians to realize that ideas have consequences. But the dialogue should not conclude with some kind of vague theology that glosses over crucial as well as perhaps insoluble theological concerns and should not be read as an esoteric exercise that avoids the rancorous issues. Jews and Christians have to preserve their own identity, but there can be a link, at least from the Christian perspective, that can help create a constructive relationship that would exclude contempt, enmity, or condemnation. This path shared by Christians, and by those Jews who volunteered to assume this burden, could result in the preservation of the identity of both, albeit in a creative tension.[32] Theology has a task unmatched since the early days of the church. What has to be done?

Christian theologians have to identify the unique initiatives that have yielded the attitudes and behaviors of historically conditioned antagonism and estrangement as they isolate what can promote a new relationship. Christian theologians and biblical scholars, as we have seen, are currently looking for ways to access Israel's understanding of salvation that would allow them to begin constructing a revised approach to such systematic organizing principles as those of Christology and eschatology. On the Christian side,[33] the traditionally derogatory view of the Torah and Israel has been intrinsically connected to an interpretation of Jesus Christ as "superseding the Jewish covenant." In the context of a revised Christian-Jewish relationship, therefore, a central task for theology would be to devise a Christology that can help obliterate anti-Judaism in Christian theology. This massive undertaking, as the next chapter suggests, will be achieved in all likelihood only incrementally.

What must be included to re-form Christian theology after Auschwitz? As a first step, such a theology should be guided by the insight that Christians can achieve their identity only in positive connectedness to their Jewish antecedents and not in confrontation with an abstract "Judaism." Christianity has to be constructed in a living faith relation to the Jewish people as God's people. Christian theologians should not automatically expect any reciprocity from the Jewish people because it is not the problem of the Jews. It is necessary here to avoid a terminology that ignores concrete human persons. Greenberg has already so graphically suggested such an approach by maintaining that theological discussions are only aiming at truth when they can be uttered in the presence of burning children.[34] While not a suggestion that can be implemented, its meaning is clear.

Unfortunately, in the past, Judaism has been objectified as an outdated precursor of Christianity. In response to this, for example, Metz has opposed the use of "system concepts" or such unanchored abstractions as a theology of Judaism. Because of Auschwitz, such a statement as "Christians can only form and appropriately understand their identity in the face of the Jews" may have to be sharpened and refocused as follows: "Christians can protect their identity only in front of and together with the history and beliefs of the Jews." Post-Auschwitz Christian theology has to renew its commitment to the Jewish dimension in Christian faith and has to avoid excluding the Jewish heritage from Christianity. For its own ecumenical perspectives, such a Christian theology should regain from Judaism the biblical-messianic concepts that are rooted in its own earliest experiences.[35]

To analyze the Christian Scriptures, in which the major figures are Jewish, requires a knowledge of the history of the period and an understanding of scriptural hermeneutics to resolve the issues that Paul, for example, raised as he tried to resolve the tensions that were manifested in the communities that concerned him. Otherwise, when Paul states that the Law has come to an end, we might not realize that he meant it solely for gentile converts to Christianity, not for Jews, and that he did not believe that God had abandoned the Jewish people who had remained faithful to the Law.[36] The arguments of Ruether, Stendahl, Gager, and others clearly have shown that in a kind of misdevelopment, anti-Judaism was rooted in the faith community as it developed its identity from the beginning and that, even though unintentionally, Christianity did prepare the ground for racial antisemitism in the nineteenth and twentieth centuries. The reason for this early anti-Judaism seems to be the Christian search for a conscious self identity, and not due to the original faith-experience, in which the participants were in fact Jewish. The post-1945 theological arguments may defend the Christian faith by now searching for its real meaning, but its past cannot be altered. Insofar as the arguments are historical rather than theological, subtle theological arguments cannot cleanse Christianity as an institution of its responsibility in the Holocaust and for nurturing historical antisemitism.

The problem with ahistorical theological arguments is that they cannot deal with Jesus and authentic Christianity as well as historical anti-Judaism. They fail to demonstrate the desired differentiation in an empirically, historically rooted, and satisfactory fashion. A more fruitful approach might be to accept the historical corollary that the emergence of the Christian faith with its desire for a well-defined identity, along with the continuation of the Judaic faith, led to Christian antisemitism. This latter resulted in a rejection of Judaism that has varied in intensity and that has been accompanied for nearly two thousand years by an often extreme hostility toward Jews on the part of Christians. After accepting that position, the crucial next step would then be to distinguish early antisemitism from later antisemitism and to demonstrate that even though Christian beliefs prepared the way for this frightening bias, they were not originally designed to teach a universalized contempt. The historical connections, however, should alert us to the dangers of using prejudice for self-definition. Christianity created an environment that nurtured the terminology and models, which could be subsequently used by others who had social, political, and biological/racial motives. Why did the original Christians, who were Jews, have to seek their own identity?

The Jews who initially followed Jesus began to establish a new communal society responsive to a new authority that emphasized interpersonal conduct and disobeyed the social prescriptions of the established Jewish authorities. This nascent religion was less exclusivistic and could be more readily adapted to the cosmopolitan Roman Empire. Early Christians also had a unique notion of a universality that separated them from some contemporary Jewish communities. Additionally, with Paul and his gentile converts, obedience to many prescriptions of Judaic law and attendance at synagogue were deemphasized, and many early Christians as they intermarried soon had no significant familial and social ties with those adhering to Judaism. The salvation promised in Pauline Christianity did not require membership in any particular people or society except that linked to the apostles.[37] Since Christianity's proponents rejected the authorities of Judaism and gradually established new ones, they ultimately ushered in a new religion with a distinctive society, despite, perhaps, their original intention.

With the extension of Pauline Christianity, which could easily adapt to other cultures, Christianity emerged with a distinctive form.[38] To understand Christian anti-Judaism as necessary for modern antisemitism is reasonable, but it may be indefensible to say that antisemitism was the logical result of faith in Jesus of Nazareth and so was the perverse result of that faith. The problem for scholars continues to be to uncover a method of distinguishing reactions against the Jews, which emerged in this identity-seeking process as psychologically unavoidable consequences of faith in the Christ-event, from later antisemitic hatred and still maintain a theology true to its roots. Langmuir's reexamination of antisemitism, for example, moves this bias out of Jewish-Christian interaction for about a millennium. His approach suggests that anti-Judaism could be seen as a tool useful for the development of a Christian identity, whereas antisemitism was an irrational explosion of hatred beginning with the Crusades.[39] But could such an explosion have occurred without its precursors in theology? Does Langmuir's definition, which discriminates between anti-Judaism and antisemitism, make Christian theology any less culpable? Nominal distinctions do not erase the contempt that became structurally and at a very early time a part of our civilization. Without the construction of a "theology after Auschwitz," therefore, Christian antisemitism cannot be dismantled.

This chapter has touched upon several of the pertinent, post-Holocaust, theological issues, has suggested what theologians are discussing, and has isolated such theological perspectives as those revolving around fulfillment, continuity/discontinuity, and covenant, which have caused such contentious debates. How can Christians maintain faith in Jesus and simultaneously continue the role of the Jewish people in God's revelatory plan? What was irresponsible about the theological doctrine that was developed to instruct? Theology and the churches can only evade these questions if they pay the price of surrendering a viable identity in a pluralistic world where Christianity has played a role in this mass destruction. The task of the Christian theologian with respect to "the Jewish question" is foundational and can be helpful in understanding the meaning of both divine and human freedom. To critique Christian tradition in terms of its response to the Jewish faith-experience virtually means that we cannot exempt the Christian reflection from a scholarly assessment designed to evaluate the anti-Jewish statements in this testament. Such an ideology critique can best and most briefly for our purposes be accomplished through a reflection on Christology with all its implications for the meaning of covenant.

Notes

1.   Thoma, *A Christian Theology of Judaism*, 23; Mussner, *Tractate*; Osborn, "The Christian Blasphemy": 339-63; Williamson, "The *Adversus Judaeos* Tradition": 273-96. Several recent works have focused on "theology after Auschwitz": Johanne Kohn, *Haschoah, Christlich-jüdische Verstandigung nach Auschwitz* (München: Kaiser, 1986); Friedrich W. Marquardt, *Von Elend und Heimsuchung der Theologie: Prologemena zur Dogmatik* (München: Kaiser, 1988); Friedrich W. Marquardt, *Das christliche Bekenntnis zu Jesus, dem Juden: Eine Christologie*, 2 vols. (München: Kaiser, 1990).

2.   David Flusser, "Reflections of a Jew on a Christian Theology of Judaism," in Thoma, *A Christian Theology of Judaism*, 4-5, 9-10, 18. For a spirited discussion of Israel as a nation-state, see Herman and Rosemary Ruether, *The Wrath of Jonah: The Crisis of Religious Nationalism in the Israeli-Palestinian Conflict* (San Francisco: Harper & Row, 1989). For responses, see John K. Roth, "The Ruethers Wrath of Jonah: An Essay Review," *Continuum* 1 (1990): 105-15 and Mary Boys et al., "Symposium: Why do the Ruethers so Furiously Rage? Christian Critiques," *Continuum* 1 (1990): 116-27.

3.   Thoma, *A Christian Theology of Judaism*, 176; Mussner, *Tractate*, 16.

4.   S. Talmon, "'Exil' und 'Rückkehr' in der Ideenwelt des Alten Testaments," in Rudolf Mosis, ed., *Exil, Diaspora, Rückkehr: Zum theologischen Gespräch zwischen Juden und Christen* (Düsseldorf: Patmos-Verlag, 1978), 54; Mussner, *Tractate*, 45ff.; Friedrich W. Marquardt, "'Feinde um unsretwillen': Das jüdische Nein und die christliche Theologie," in Friedrich W. Marquardt, *Verwegenheiten: Theologische Stücke aus Berlin* (München: Kaiser, 1981), 331, 334ff.; Hans J. Kraus, *Reich Gottes, Reich der Freiheit: Grundriss Systematischer Theologie* (Neukirchener: Neukirchener Verlag, 1975), 75-76; A. Altmann, "'Exil' und 'Rückkehr' in heutigier jüdischer Sicht," in Mosis, *Exil, Diaspora, Rückkehr*, 95-110.

5.   See the title of another contribution of Clemens Thoma to this subject: Clemens Thoma, *Jüdische und christliche Exilserfahrungen und Exilstheologien: Deutung des nachbiblischen Judentums aus christlich-theologischer Sicht* in Mosis, *Exil, Diaspora, Rückkehr*, 81-94.

6.   Thoma, *A Christian Theology of Judaism*, 157-58, 160; von der Osten-Sacken, *Christian-Jewish Dialogue*, 51-56. For the environment within which these documents were created, see Wayne Λ. Meeks, *The First Urban Christians: The Social World of the Apostle Paul* (New Haven:

Yale University Press, 1983); Peter Brown, *The World of Late Antiquity, AD 150-750* (New York: Harcourt Brace Jovanovich, 1971).

7. Mussner, *Tractate*, 4, 51, 144, 158, 161-62.

8. Ibid., 44-45; Thoma, *A Christian Theology of Judaism*, 159.

9. Mussner, *Tractate*, 254; Fackenheim, *God's Presence*, 40; Y. Amir, "Jüdisch-theologische Positionen nach Auschwitz," in Günther B. Ginzel, ed., *Auschwitz als Herausforderung für Juden und Christen* (Heidelberg: L. Schneider, 1980), 453; Johannes Baptist Metz, "Ökumene nach Auschwitz: Zum Verhältnis von Christen und Juden in Deutschland," in E. Kogon et al., *Gott nach Auschwitz: Dimensionen des Massenmords am jüdischen Volk* (Freiburg: Herder, 1979), 138.

10. J. Coert Rylaarsdam, "Common Ground and Difference," *Journal of Religion* 43 (1963): 264. For an incisive study of modern Jewish thought, including chapters on Buber and an analysis of Rosenzweig's impact on such scholars as Berkovits, Fackenheim, and Rubenstein, see Steven Katz, *Post-Holocaust Dialogues: Critical Studies in Modern Jewish Thought* (New York: New York University Press, 1985).

11. Irving Greenberg, "Cloud of Smoke, Pillar of Fire: Judaism, Christianity, and Modernity after the Holocaust," in Fleischner, *Auschwitz: Beginning of a New Era?*, 13, 36.

12. A. Roy Eckardt, *Elder and Younger Brothers: The Encounter of Jews and Christians* (New York: Schocken Books, 1973), 160; Littell, *The Crucifixion*. For a journal devoted to analyzing the Holocaust from a variety of perspectives, see *Holocaust and Genocide Studies*. The annual Scholars Conference has met for years to reflect on Holocaust issues through a perspective of church history. Paul van Buren, *A Theology of the Jewish-Christian Reality: Part I: Discerning the Way; Part II. A Christian Theology of the People of Israel; Part III. Christ in Context* (New York: Seabury Press, 1980-88). For a comprehensive review of the literature focusing on this issue until 1980, see A. Roy Eckardt, "Recent Literature on Christian-Jewish Relations," *Journal of the American Academy of Religion* 49 (1981): 99-111.

13. Irving Greenberg, "Cloud of Smoke, Pillar of Fire: Judaism, Christianity, and Modernity after the Holocaust," in Fleischner, *Auschwitz: Beginning of a New Era?*, 40; Eliezer Berkovits, *Faith after the Holocaust* (New York: KTAV Pub. House, 1973), 99, 131. For other insights into the Holocaust's meaning, see Helmut Starck and Bertold von Klappert, eds., *Umkehr und Erneuerung: Erläuterungen zum Synodalbeschluss der Rheinischen Landessynode 1980 "Zur Erneuerung des Verhältnisses von Christen und Juden"* (Neukirchener: Neukirchener Verlag, 1980); Michael Brocke and Herbert Jochum, eds., *Wolkensäule und*

Feuerschein: Jüdische Theologie des Holocaust (München: Kaiser, 1982); A. Roy Eckardt, "Christians and Jews: Along a Theological Frontier," *Encounter* 40 (1979): 116.

14. Littell, *The Crucifixion*, 15ff, 79-80, 96; Irving Greenberg, "Cloud of Smoke, Pillar of Fire: Judaism, Christianity, and Modernity after the Holocaust," in Fleischner, *Auschwitz: Beginning of a New Era?*, 36ff.

15. van Buren, *Discerning the Way*, 116-17; Pawlikowski, "Toward a Theology": 138-59; van Buren, *A Christian Theology*; Paul van Buren, *Christ in Context* (New York: Harper & Row, 1988).

16. Uriel Tal, "On the Study of the Holocaust and Genocide," *Yad Vashem Studies* 13 (1979): 7-52; Alice and A. Roy Eckardt, "The Holocaust and the Enigma of Uniqueness: A Philosophical Effort at Practical Clarification," *Annals of the American Academy of Political and Social Science* no. 450 (1980): 165-78; Abraham Joshua Heschel, *God in Search of Man: A Philosophy of Judaism* (New York: Farrar, Strauss, and Cudahy, 1955), 68, 156, 196, 291; Y. Amir, *Deraschot: Jüdische Predigten* (Berlin: Institut Kirche und Judentum, 1983), 454; Pawlikowski, "Christian Ethics": 649-69; Irving Greenberg, "History, Holocaust and Covenant," *Holocaust and Genocide Studies* 5 (1990): 1. Stephen Haynes' *Prospects for Post-Holocaust Theology: "Israel" in the Theologies of Karl Barth, Jürgen Moltmann, and Paul van Buren* (Atlanta: Scholars Press, 1991) distinguishes Moltmann and van Buren from the movement known as Holocaust theology and places their work in the light of both the reformed tradition and the revision of Christian doctrine after Auschwitz.

17. Thoma, *A Christian Theology of Judaism*, 152ff. Paul van Buren's *A Christian Theology of the People of Israel* avoids the creation of a "Christian theology of Judaism" and the consequent problem of Judaism's finding its identity in Christianity.

18. For a recent study of the evolution of antisemitism, see Gavin Langmuir, *History, Religion and Antisemitism* (Berkeley: University of California Press, 1990); he has suggested (39-40) that a fruitful approach for those trying to decouple Jesus and his followers from Christian antisemitism, which he feels really occurred in the eleventh through thirteenth centuries as an ideological development, might be to accept the historical corollary of the emergence of the Christian faith and the continuance of Judaic faith, which led to Christian anti-Judaism. Such an interpretation would allow us to move antisemitism as a cause of the Holocaust to the High Middle Ages and to preserve the early Christians from this charge. But such an approach fails to see the continuing importance of theology as defining the Christian attitude toward the Jewish people and seems to

be only a nominal solution to preserve the early Christians from the charge of antisemitism. For critical works somewhat sympathetic to the struggles of Christians facing the Third Reich, see Vincent Lapomarda, *The Jesuits and the Third Reich* (Lewiston: E. Mellen Press, 1989); Dietrich, *Catholic Citizens*. For negative analyses of ecclesial institutions that can help explain the role of Christians in the Third Reich, see John Conway, *The Nazi Persecution of the Churches, 1933-1945* (New York: Basic Books, 1968); Guenther Lewy, *The Catholic Church and Nazi Germany* (New York: McGraw-Hill, 1964).

19. For a recent analysis of the decision-making process leading to Hitler's Final Solution, see Christopher Browning, "The Decision Concerning the Final Solution," in Furet, *Unanswered Questions*. For classic analyses of theological antisemitism, see Parkes, *The Conflict;* Jules Isaac, *Genèse de l'antisémitisme: Essai historique* (Paris: Calmann-Lévy, 1956); Poliakov, *The History of Anti-Semitism*; Ruether, *Faith and Fratricide*. These and other works illustrate how Christianity prepared the ground for the antisemitism of modern times by offering instruction in despising the Jews and by systematically degrading the Jewish people.

20. Kornelis Heiko Miskotte, *When the Gods Are Silent* (London: Collins, 1967).

21. Tal, *Christians and Jews in Germany*, 292-93, 304.

22. Ernst Käsemann, *Commentary on Romans* (Grand Rapids: Eerdmans, 1980); Ernst Käsemann, *Perspectives on Paul* (Philadelphia: Fortress Press, 1971), 146-47, 151, 154; Hans Hübner, *Das Gesetz bei Paulus* (Göttingen: Vandenhoeck und Ruprecht, 1978), 115, 124, 126, 128. On the problems resulting when interpreting Jesus Christ as the "end of the Law," see, for example, Markus Barth, "Das Volk Gottes: Juden und Christen in der Botschaft Paulus," in Markus Barth et al., *Paulus— Apostat oder Apostle? Jüdische und christliche Antworten* (Regensburg: Pustet, 1977), 133; Kraus, *Reich Gottes, Reich der Freiheit*, 75; Pierre Lenhardt, *Auftrag und Unmöglichkeit eines legitimen christlichen Zeugnisses gegenüber den Juden: Eine Untersuchung zum theologischen Stand des Verhältnisses von Kirche und jüdischen Volk* (Berlin: Selbstverlag Institut Kirche und Judentum, 1980), 41-42. The results can be controlled if something more positive than talk about "the end" can be included; see Mussner, *Tractate*, 138. In their works, van Buren and the Eckardts have struggled with this issue. For a recent interpretation that gets to the heart of supersessionism, see Gavin D'Costa, "Jews and Christians: Reflections on 'Covenant' and 'Fulfillment': Towards a Theology of Christian-Jewish Relations," paper presented at Harvard, October 1989.

23. Charlotte Klein, *Theologie und Anti-Judaismus: Eine Studie zur deutschen theologischen Literatur der Gegenwart* (München: Kaiser, 1975); Friedrich W. Marquardt, "Hermeneutik des christlich-jüdischen Verhältnisses: Über Helmut Gollwitzer's Arbeit an der Judenfrage," in Andreas Baudis et al., eds., *Richte unsere Füsse auf den Weg des Friedens: H. Gollwitzer zum 70. Geburtstag* (München: Kaiser, 1979), 145; T. Filthaut, *Israel in der christlichen Unterweisung* (München: Kösel-Verlag, 1963); Herbert Jochum and Heinz Kremers, eds., *Juden, Judentum und Staat Israel in christlichen Religionsunterricht in der Bundesrepublik Deutschland* (Paderborn: Schöningh, 1980); Peter Fiedler, *Das Judentum im katholischen Religionsunterricht* (Düsseldorf: Patmos-Verlag, 1980).

24. On the difficulties involved in genuine dialogue given the historical framework of the Christian-Jewish relationship, see Lenhardt, *Auftrag und Unmöglichkeit eines legitimen christlichen Zeugnisses gegenüber den Juden*, 16ff., and Pawlikowski, "Toward a Theology": 138-53.

25. von der Osten-Sacken, *Christian-Jewish Dialogue*, 16.

26. Ibid., 119-24. In the encounter, only Jews can explain what the dialogue means for them. Christians also have their own agenda in the dialogue; see Franklin Littell, "A Milestone in Post-Holocaust Church Thinking: Reflection on the Declaration by the Protestant Church of the Rhineland Regarding Christian-Jewish Relations," *Christian News from Israel* 27 (1980): 113-16; "Christen und Juden: Eine Schwerpunkt-Tagung der Landessynode der Evangelischen Landeskirche in Baden. 10.-11. November 1980," in *Bad Herrenalb: Referate, Diskussionen, Bekenntnisse, Konsequenzen* (Karlsruhe, 1981), 184-85. For a sample of a resolution, see "Orientierungspunkte zum Themen 'Christen und Juden,'" *Berliner Theologische Zeitschrift* 1 (1984): 370-72.

27. von der Osten-Sacken, *Christian-Jewish Dialogue*, 17; Gager, *The Origins of Anti-Semitism*. For the classic affirmation of diversity, see Walter Bauer, *Orthodoxy and Heresy in Earliest Christianity* (Philadelphia: Fortress Press, 1971); Jack Lightstone, "Christian Anti-Judaism in Its Judaic Mirror: The Judaic Context of Early Christianity Revised," in Peter Richardson, ed., *Anti-Judaism in Early Christianity*, vol. 2, *Separation and Polemic* (Waterloo, Ontario: Wilfrid Laurier University Press, 1986), 103-32.

28. Karl Ludwig Schmidt, *Die Judenfrage im Lichte der Kapital 9-11 Römerbriefes* (Zurich: Evangelischer Verlag, 1943); Friedrich Marquardt, *Die Wiederentdeckung des Judentums für die christliche Theologie. Israel im Denken Karl Barths* (München: Kaiser, 1967); L. Steiger, "Die Theologie vor der 'Judenfrage': Karl Barth als Beispiel" in Rolf Rendtorff and Ekke-

hard Stegemann, eds., *Auschwitz—Krise der christlichen Theologie: Eine Vortragsreihe* (München: Kaiser, 1980): 82-98; Mussner, *Tractate*, 36.

29. Andreas Lindemann, *Paulus im ältesten Christentum* (Tübingen: Mohr, 1979); Ekkehard Stegemann, "Alt und Neu bei Paulus und in den Deutero-Pauliner (Kol/Eph)," *Evangelische Theologie* 37 (1977): 508-36; Peter von der Osten-Sacken, "Die paulinische Theologia Crucis als Form apokalyptischer Theologie," *Evangelische Theologie* 39 (1979): 477-96. The quantity of scholarly work appearing on Paul is nearly overwhelming. For a view of Paul, who, like Jesus, is Jewish, see William David Davies, *Jewish and Pauline Studies* (Philadelphia: Fortress Press, 1984) and J. Christian Beker, *Paul the Apostle* (Philadelphia: Fortress Press, 1984); Richards, *The Secretary*, explores when and how Paul used a secretary to help write his letters and how using a secretary affected them; Sandnes, *Paul—One of the Prophets?*, contributes to the discussion of Pauline apostleship as well as prophecy in the Early Church. Other by now more standard works include Sanders, *Paul*; Stendahl, *Paul among the Jews*; Lloyd Gaston, *Paul and the Torah* (Vancouver: University of British Columbia Press, 1987). On the controversial Romans 9-11, see Joseph Fitzmyer, "The Letter to the Romans," in Raymond Brown, ed., *The New Jerome Biblical Commentary* (Englewood Cliffs, NJ: Prentice-Hall, 1990); Heikki Raisanen, "Paul, God and Israel: Romans 9-11 in Recent Research," in Jacob Neusner et al., eds., *The Social World of Formative Christianity and Judaism: Essays in Tribute to Howard Clark Kee* (Philadelphia: Fortress Press, 1988); Paul van Buren, "The Church and Israel: Romans 9-11," opening address at the Third Frederick Neumann Symposium, Princeton Theological Seminary, 13-16 October 1989.

30. Hermann Adler, *Vater ... vergib! Gedichte aus dem Ghetto* (Berlin: Im Christian-Verlag, 1950); Alan Segal, *Paul the Convert: The Apostolate and Apostasy of Saul the Pharisee* (New Haven: Yale University Press, 1990). Using research on the sociology of conversion, Segal has analyzed Paul as part of Jewish history. Though Paul may have regarded himself as still within Judaism, his insistence on transformation in Christ for both Jews and Gentiles led to the perception of Pauline Christianity as a new religion. In Segal's view, Paul did not propose distinct ways to God for Jews and Gentiles. What surprised people in the first century, Segal maintains, was Paul's claim that Jews and Gentiles could form a single community, leaving some Jews to regard Paul as an apostate.

31. J. Maier, "Jesus von Nazareth und sein Verhältnis zum Judentum: Aus der Sicht eines Judaisten," in Willchad Paul Eckert and Hans Hermann Henrix, eds., *Jesus Jude—Sein als Zugang zum Judentum: Eine*

Handreichung für Religionsunterricht und Erwachsenenbildung (Aachen: Einhard-Verlag, 1976), 112: "The Christian claim becomes unconvincing if its presentation is linked with a more or less extensive polemical distortion and defamation of Judaism, and hence with a self-corruption of the Christian ethos." H. Stroh, "Gibt es eine Verständigung zwischen Juden und Christen?" *Zeitschrift für Theologie und Kirche* 71 (1974): 227-38.

32. Amir, *Deraschot: Jüdische Predigten*, 60; Peter von der Osten-Sacken, "Auf dem Weg zum jüdischen Volk: Eine Einführung in Günther Harders Sicht des christlich-jüdischen Verhältnis," in Günther Harder, ed., *Kirche und Israel: Arbeiten zum christlich-jüdischen Verhältnis* (Berlin: Institut Kirche und Judentum, 1986), 8ff.; Peter von der Osten-Sacken, "Die Entwicklung des christlich-jüdischen Dialogs auf dem Felde der kirchlichen Theologie: Die Aufgaben der nächsten Generation," in Deutscher Koordinierungsrat der Gesellschaften für christlich-jüdische Zusammenarbeit e. V., ed., *Im Blick auf Morgan: Juden und Christen in der Verantwortung*, unpublished manuscript, Frankfurt, 1985: 16-27. In her recently published *Victimization: Examining Christian Complicity*, Christine Gudorf explores how well-meaning but frequently used scriptural passages teach preferential option and do political advocacy in a manner that contributes to the very types of sinful victimization they oppose.

33. See Ruether, *Faith and Fratricide* and Hyam Maccoby, *The Mythmaker: Paul and the Invention of Christianity* (New York: Harper & Row, 1986).

34. Gregory Baum, "The Holocaust and Political Theology," in Elisabeth Schüssler Fiorenza and David Tracy, *The Holocaust as Interruption* (Edinburgh: T&T Clark, 1984), 34-42. For the view that sensitivity to the Holocaust and genocide should impact on social science analyses of state power and its effect on individual freedom, see Horowitz, *Taking Lives*.

35. Johannes Baptist Metz, "Facing the Jews: Christian Theology after Auschwitz," in Fiorenza and Tracy, *The Holocaust as Interruption*, 27-28, 31, 33.

36. Stendahl, *Paul among the Jews;* Gager, *The Origins of Anti-Semitism*; Gaston, *Paul and the Torah*. For an analytically refined treatment of the emergence of antisemitism in Christianity, see Langmuir, *History*; Gavin Langmuir, *Toward a Definition of Antisemitism* (Berkeley: University of California Press, 1990). For a recent collection of essays on the Jewishness of Jesus and the earliest Christians, see James Charlesworth, ed., *Jesus' Jewishness: Exploring the Place of Jesus within Early Judaism* (Philadelphia: American Interfaith Institute, 1991).

37. Meeks, *The First Urban Christians*.
38. Brown, *The World of Late Antiquity*, 82.
39. Langmuir, *History*, 297; Cohen, *The Friars and the Jew*; Robert Chazan, *Daggers of Faith: Thirteenth-Century Missionizing and Jewish Response* (Berkeley: University of California Press, 1988).

5

Christology and Antisemitism

For centuries, Christianity did not effectively deal with the implications of the historical fact that Jesus was a Jew. Since 1945, theologians have tried to delineate a more appropriate and historically sensitive relationship between Christianity and the Jewish people.[1] Virtually every official statement has not underscored the significant fact that Jesus was Jewish and that he lived in and interacted within a Jewish milieu. Although some ecclesial statements may still mention that Jesus somehow *fulfilled* the Hebrew Bible prophecies and *realized* Israel's hope for a messiah, the more sensitive interpretations, as we will see, have stressed only an initial glimpse of fulfillment in Jesus and a complete fulfillment only in the end times. Such an approach presumably can enclose both Christian and Jewish messianic hopes. In one way, of course, this thematic line merely postpones the issue of fulfillment, but it at least opens up the issue for discussion. Although ambivalent, the early Christian documents can help support rethinking Jewish-Christian relations. None of the official credal statements unequivocally asserted a definitive break that would negate Judaism, even though they did see in Jesus a new beginning, which by implication suggested over time that the bond had been severed.

Increasingly, most theologians seem convinced that the Christ-event did not abrogate the initial covenantal experience(s) but did mean in the eyes of earlier commentators that Christianity had to some extent superseded and gone beyond the initial covenant.

References to the Resurrection as central to this Jesus experience, therefore, have been increasingly minimized in theological reflections. By the late 1970s, a conscious effort to avoid supersessionist language was the order of the day. Catholic scholars, who were engaged in Jewish-Christian discussion, for example, tended to underemphasize christological claims in their encounters and stand opposed to the absolutist impediments proclaimed in earlier Catholic documents that seem to ignore all connections with Judaism.[2] The Second Vatican Council's position on ecumenism and on missionary activity, for example, insisted that God's message has been communicated in a variety of religious forms. Those sensitive to an ecumenical focus, therefore, have attempted to construct a *Weltanschauung* that could reflect the theological reality introduced by the Holocaust as a controlling historical event. But for the Christian, Jesus has a special significance and is not just another instrument of God's message, and therein lies the crucial problem.

Formal dialogues have occurred but not yet yielded institutional statements that can extinguish dissonance. On the Jewish side, the response to such conversations has been ambivalent. Many conservative and nearly all orthodox Jews have understandably opted to refrain from such encounters because they do not wish their definition of Jewish experiences to be made contingent upon Christian reflections. Suspicious of historical Christian missionizing efforts, some Jews have wanted to know why Christians want to engage in any dialogue. Is this yet another attempt to convert through assimilation? Their suspicion is certainly warranted because it has only been in relatively recent times that the Christian churches have methodically sought to engage Judaism as a still-living faith and so have tried to establish a posture conducive to dialogue. Initially, the churches delineated official positions on Jewish-Christian relations for their own members, which meant placing dialogues into formal surroundings that did not lead to candid discussion, but did create an opening.

In 1973, for example, the National Catholic-Protestant Theological Dialogue issued a position paper entitled "Israel: Land, People, State."

Those involved in the drafting portrayed the Christian church as embedded into the life of the people of Israel. From this perspective, Abraham was viewed as the spiritual ancestor and father of Christianity. Jesus' ministry and the vibrant life of the early Christian community had emerged within the Judaic environment of the era, particularly within the sociological strata composed of the Pharisees. To promote linkage outside of the Jewish communities, the document continued, Christ enabled the Gentiles to be assimilated as Abraham's spiritual "offspring" and so as heirs to God's promise. The drafters recognized that, tragically, Jesus as the bond of unity between Gentile and Jew had frequently become the source of division and bitterness as Christians organized their identity with a christological focus. The very survival of the Jewish religion, according to the authors of the document, should be taken as a sign of God's continuing fidelity to his people. God's love had mandated the continuity of Judaism. This continuity was to demonstrate the abiding validity and life of Jewish worship as an authentic response to the true God.[3]

Most subsequent official documents have sought to root the Christian faith in its Jewish antecedents. But how can it be done while maintaining the truth, value, and integrity of both traditions? Some scholars have suggested that the Jewish-Christian experiences form at base one tradition. Some have denied any single Judeo-Christian tradition and have insisted that both have helped mold Western culture. No matter which approach has been taken, the Jewishness of Jesus has now become a base fact, although Christians have generally maintained that he also transcended history, even his own. Such an approach would explicitly repudiate supersessionist doctrine and yet sustain the uniqueness of Jesus. To continue the dialogue, most have included demands that the Jewish covenant never be considered invalidated. But what happens to the so-called Christian or "new" covenant? Apparently afraid of moving too rapidly, this 1973 document frames the issue in an awkward fashion. The Christian faith does not mean that God has abandoned the Jews, because he has not ceased responding to Jewish worship as a reaction to his blessing.[4] Among others, Catholics have found it particularly difficult to deal with bringing the two faith traditions into real dialogue.

In the United States, groups in the Lutheran Church have also tried to foster dialogue as a way slowly to raise consciousness. But some early declarations reduced constructive interchange. In 1954, for example, "The Evanston Report" viewed Jesus Christ as the Savior of all mankind and concluded that Jews should become Christians.[5] Only after the early 1960s did a systematically more radical critique of standard positions occur on the official level. Behind the official proclamations and meetings, the theological activity has been staggering, especially since the 1960s. Progress toward meaningful interchange can be measured by mentioning a few of the past *discontinuous* theologies that have been offered, because these have been supportive of the traditional supersessionism that held that the Jewish covenant ceased with the beginning of Christianity.

Discontinuity and Covenants

Historically, the fact of continued Jewish existence did not seem to question traditional Christian theological positions or presuppositions that tended to be universalistic. Christ's call referred without discrimination to all non-Christian peoples. As a result, antisemitism was viewed only as one expression of sinful man's failure to respond to God, and not as something structurally or institutionally dangerous. Such twentieth-century apologetic theologies of discontinuity appeared in the works of Karl Barth and Rudolf Bultmann, who influenced succeeding Christian thinkers.[6] In essence, the existence of antisemitism seemed to have no impact on the message of Christianity because earlier theologians found the prejudice acceptable and justified. A theology of discontinuity supported their viewpoints.

Following the Holocaust, Jacob Jocz claimed that the chasm between Christianity and Judaism could be located in Christology. Jocz critiqued the tendency of Christian theologians, who sought better relations with the Jews, to view messianic claims only in terms of eschatological fulfillment. From this perspective, Christ was the messiah who contradicted existential Jewish messianic hopes and who became the controlling force for subsequent imperialistic, missionary activities. For Jocz, Jesus had to be seen as someone who transformed rather than merely fulfilled the Jewish concept of Messiah. Seen in this context, Judaism was still viewed as preparatory for Christianity.[7] Jews, he insisted, did not yet believe in Jesus, but they would in the end time.

Echoing his emphasis on the fulfillment of the earlier prophecies in Jesus, Jean Danielou, a Catholic theologian, described the relation between Judaism and Christianity as follows: "The offense of Israel is not that they crucified Jesus; it is that they did not believe in the risen Christ.... The true Israel continued in a small group of Jews who believed in the risen Christ."[8] He maintained that accepting Jesus as God-man should not result in a problem because the Jewish people have lived a history in relation to the personal God of both and should be able to adapt. Danielou did not opt for two covenants but for an enlarged one that was to include all peoples in Christ, the total realization of all messianic prophecies. Christian conversion missions should continue until this goal had been reached. Although Danielou seemed intransigent in his absolute christological claims, he continued to urge dialogue as the selected mode to conversion.[9] The goal of the Christian missionizing activity remained the same; only the means had really changed. The Catholic theologian Hans Urs von Balthasar also focused on the "reprobation of Israel" even though, as he recognized, the Jewish people originally funneled salvation into the gentile world. For him, the relation between Israel and the church became one of promise and fulfillment. From this "discontinuous" standpoint, modern Judaism had lost its "historical mission to fulfill mankind, which has now been assumed by the Church."[10]

In a similar vein, the Lutheran scholar, Johannes Aagard, has also asserted that either Jesus fulfilled the Old Testament messianic prophecies or he corrupted them. For Aagard, the Christian church, stemming from the new covenant and the new people of election, has become the eschatological reality. No longer could the Jews be considered the covenanted elect. Still, the result was not as harsh as might be imagined. The Jews would not have lost God's love, which is unchanging, even though their exclusive election as such might change. Aagard seems to want the best of both worlds. In Christ, Israel's mission was fulfilled and the Kingdom has already begun because the church is the new and sole Israel. Following the Resurrection, the nation Israel became secularized, and it assumed, according to Aagard, a duty similar to that of other nations, which was to recognize Jesus, the Messiah.[11]

Kurt Hruby, a French Catholic scholar, has also asserted that, as originally covenanted, the Jewish people should now accept Christ as the fulfillment of Israel's election. In his opinion, the chosen people cannot be considered a specific ethnic group but rather are all of those who believe and are united in Christ. The chosen people now include more than the Jewish people. In the light of this supersessionist Christology, election meant that Israel was merely a preparation for Christianity that was viewed as the fulfillment of all the messianic prophecies. To a Jew who came to accept Christ as the Messiah, Hruby would not apply the word "conversion" to suggest that something had been abandoned, but would stress that fulfillment meant a Jewish awareness of and fidelity to all the authentic Judaic values, which had now been raised to a newly elevated level in Jesus,[12] who was viewed as having completed the Jewish mission.

Common among the discontinuous Christologies is their stress on the universal salvific efficacy of Christ as the total fulfillment of the messianic prophecies in the Hebrew Scriptures. Without analytically delineating the essence and historical function of Israel's messianic hopes, sweeping statements related to the fulfillment in Jesus have been made. In cases where pre-Vatican II Catholic thinkers were forced to admit that Jesus did not exactly embody Israel's hopes, they asserted that Jesus had actually *transformed* the Jewish messianic expectation and had really offered more than Israel could have hoped to expect. In brief, Israel's election was fulfilled, and Christians were the new elect of God. Christ's church became the new people of God, and its place in God's plan was derived from the nature of kerygma.[13]

In general, theologians of discontinuity cannot easily handle the religious significance of contemporary Judaism. Even though pre-Christian Israel faithfully adhered to the covenant, that mission of Judaism was now seen by these theologians as passed on to the Christian church. To counteract the antisemitism which seems to issue logically from such a christological position, these theologians generally conclude by exhorting Christians to love and respect persons of all religions. In the explication of their theologies, however, they create a situation in which love and respect are difficult to attain because they have organized an "us-them" dichotomy. Such an altruistic initiative would probably not prove efficacious because it would be difficult to counteract the almost normal human proclivity to dislike or fear what is distinct. Israel would be seen as special only because of its preparatory mission, which was necessary in the mystery of God's plan. Israel would be seen as an archaic relic of God's love, but after the appearance of Jesus as Messiah, it would be seen as losing its positive meaning in God's salvific plan. All of these theologians of discontinuity have deplored the disrespectful proselytization tactics used over the past centuries and have tried to interact with Jewish thinkers within the context of dialogue or "witness" rather than argument or persuasion. This has softened their approach to an extent. Ultimately, however, they cannot drop their own absolutist claims because they assert that the Jewish people have failed to understand their own Scriptures, which, they insist, should be read from a christological perspective. From the 1960s, however, a plethora of scholarship has begun to undermine this discontinuity hypothesis. For most commentators, the doctrine that Israel was rejected, while Christianity was selected to be a new people of God, has shown itself as lethal.[14] The critical theological issue was joined, then, around the true meaning of fulfillment, Messiah, election, and covenant. Part of this process of rethinking traditional formulae was the increasing realization that God did not promise when fulfillment would occur. When dealing with God, promise does demand fulfillment. It would be difficult, therefore, to see the loss of Israel's integrity as its fulfillment. How have Christian theologians handled this issue, if discontinuity is not viable?

Rethinking the Discontinuity Thesis

Theologians focusing on the improvement of Christian-Jewish relations have aggressively sought to reconfigure their theological positions. Disturbed by the historical divergence between the Jewish and Christian traditions, these theologians have insisted that there can be no strictly cognitive theology that merely manipulates terms and concepts to "paper over" the fissures. Such a superficial process of deploring antisemitism and of encouraging Christians to appreciate their Jewish heritage would not intrude into the essential issues. Such a theology would very clearly and essentially still rest on theological discontinuity and semantic continuity while condemning antisemitic hostility. A group of these theologians has constructed a "bridge theology" that presumes as a given the theological integrity and validity of both traditions. Such theologians as James Parkes, Peter

Chirico, Gregory Baum, and Rosemary Reuther have insisted that both
traditions possess a valid theological integrity and validity. Their
emphases vary as they introduce new and unique approaches, but
virtually all claim that the keystone of a proper Jewish-Christian
relation will have to rest on a new analysis of revelation, covenant,
election, and messiahship. [15] Theologians have selected various focal
points in order to unpack the issue.

A. Roy Eckardt and others, for example, have described theologies
of continuity and discontinuity and have indicated the implications
that each has in redefining the dialogue between Christians and Jews.
Rooted deeply in the Christian theological tradition, *discontinuity*
would stress the uniqueness of Christ, his universal mediative role in
the drama of salvation, and his fulfillment of Jewish hopes and
prophecies. The theology of *continuity* would stress that Christianity
still supports Israel's covenant, which was not abrogated by Christ's
opening to the gentile world. Jesus of Nazareth, therefore, represented
and embodied the great religious ideas of Israel, which had been
codified and systematized in the Hebrew Bible and continued existing
in the living Jewish tradition. Jesus' teachings, obedience to God's
will, and adherence to the concepts of covenant and of eschatology,
for example, could be seen as consistent with his Jewish roots as he
mediated Israel's heritage to all nations. Such a Christology insists
that the covenant with Israel has perdured but now has to be coupled
with the *positive* witness of the Jewish "no" to Jesus and to the
acknowledgment of the unredeemed character of the world. Stressing
continuity, Jesus could be seen as the *partial* fulfillment of Jewish
messianic prophecies prior to the eschatological unification of all
God's peoples. [16] Here is a very provocative attempt to bridge the gap
between the continuity/discontinuity thesis. Recalling that Jesus was
Jewish and attempting to deal creatively with the discontinuity issue
so crucial to antisemitism, Eckardt and others have creatively
responded to the older "discontinuity" tradition.

Christian theologians, who assert the continuing validity of
Judaism, have tried to introduce a Christology designed to avoid
absolutism as well as stark relativism. Supporting a model of
"continuity," such theologians as John Pawlikowski in 1974 took a
position that traditional christological models should be revisited. The
goal would be to define what a faithful adherence to Jesus means

when the legitimacy of the Jewish experience is also maintained. For such theologians, Christianity need not necessarily replace the Jews as God's people. Avoiding supersessionism, they have asserted that Christ's advent did not automatically negate the election and the love of God for Israel. Some theologians of continuity have even viewed the Jewish "no" to Jesus as a positive contribution because the response has forced us all into a more penetrating review of the relationship between God and humanity. The Jewish people have continued adhering to their historical relationship to God and are to be commended.[17]

The meaning of "covenant" is also vital in the continuity model where clear boundary delineations are not welcomed, so that christological supersessionism can be avoided. Some Christologies of continuity perceive Judaism and Christianity as participants in a dual covenant because of their shared biblical roots. Others prefer a single covenant, and still others hypothesize a multitude of covenants. The dual-, single-, and multiple-covenant theories have opened up several avenues that can be followed to counter supersessionism.[18]

Laying the basis for the movement toward dialogue, James Parkes had suggested that Judaism and Christianity have offered distinct, yet complementary, perspectives on the single revelatory message of God, which addresses the perennial tension in our culture between the community and the individual. More explicitly, the distinction between the two revelations (Judaism and Christianity) exists in their complementary, not contradictory, reflections on the relation between the individual and the community. For Christians, the risen Christ makes new persons of "Jew and Greek, bound and free." That divine power with its origin in the Incarnation has served as a motivating force for those accepting the will of God as a direction for life. The purpose of God, which Sinai revealed to the Jewish community, has been revealed by Calvary to persons as individuals.[19]

The Sinai experience for Parkes and others was fundamentally communal, while Calvary illuminated the individual's link with God. The revelation given through Jesus in no way replaced that given through Moses. Historically, Jesus lived during a complex period when older ideas were gradually dissolving into an outlook that could help order the cosmopolitan Roman world. Jesus' abiding concern with the individual as person, for example, was culturally conditioned by his pharisaic milieu and did not in itself vitiate the Sinai revelation. Judaism and Christianity can be seen entwined as complementary equals. From this perspective, the tension that continues between Jews and Christians may merely reflect the perennial and inevitable tension that exists between persons as social beings in a community and as individuals with a unique value. The enduring bond between Christians and Jews may include this ongoing tension as well and may reflect the human condition. Parkes' model has proven suggestive in this entire dialogue.[20]

In his Christology, Parkes has emphasized the aspects of atonement and sacrifice. Thus, Christ's sacrifice on the cross has a universal application by reaffirming persons as individuals and as ends. In this context, Parkes viewed the traditional christocentric obsession as debilitating because it saw salvation only through Christ, who can only reflect one pole in this ongoing tension between the individual and the community. Parkes has suggested that a reassertion of the Trinity doctrine might help resolve the stress between person and community because this dogma encapsulates both the individual and a community. By using the word "channel" instead of "person" in the doctrine of the Trinity, Parkes also has suggested that God's life could be seen to flow through three distinct conduits. Each channel achieved its results at an appropriately historical moment. Just as each person has social and individual aspects, the grace flowing from the Incarnation could be seen in tension with that which flows from Sinai.[21] Thus, the salutary tension between the faiths perhaps was intended by God. Each faith would be valued as an incomplete revelation, and so each would contribute to the holistic proclamation. Christians could argue in this fashion but could never demand that Jews would have to make this concession, because the Holocaust and antisemitism were Christian problems.

Both Judaism and Christianity may have complementary roles and missions, at least from a Christian viewpoint, as witnesses that God has elected humanity as a group (Israel) as well as each individual (Christianity) to do his will. Repeatedly, Parkes insisted that his christological views could be widely accepted, but he deemphasized the issue of the messiahship of Jesus so that he could stress a messianic age for which Jews waited rather than a personal messiah. A similarly ambiguous transformation has emerged around the notion of covenant. Within this model of revelatory tension, Judaism and Christianity would become complementary expressions of God's plan. Such theologians as Parkes and subsequently Rylaarsdam have argued for a dual-covenant position. Their nuanced reflections would view the Christian and Jewish traditions as distinct and complementary covenants. Jews are being faithful to their covenant with God, the identical God who grafted Gentiles onto God's revelatory gift. Neither negates the other, and the mission to the Jews could be terminated.[22] Other possibilities of dealing with supersessionistic issues have been offered and should be reviewed to further open the richness of reflection on this seminal religious issue.

Attempting to connect Judaism and Christianity, Peter Chirico,[23] for example, has suggested that the ultimate nature of revelation has not been understood clearly and has left Christians with a less than clear understanding of fulfillment. Chirico seems to feel that Christians probably cannot totally abolish fulfillment theology because it is so deeply ingrained in their tradition. Fulfillment has been accepted in terms of *past* fulfillment in Jesus and now contemporary fulfillment in the church. Historically, fulfillment has become the basis of mission rather than a state to be achieved through continuing historical development. For Chirico, one revelation was manifested in Christ, who as truly human, was God's manifestation in creation. Both Chirico and Karl Rahner have maintained that the Christian can believe that whenever messianic prophecies are fulfilled, Christ as the revelatory messenger is the active agent. "Anonymous Christians" have been at work since the time of Christ. The Jewish people, therefore, would seem to be awaiting the future messianic times along with the Christian people, even though the latter may claim to know the Messiah's identity. Jesus' identity may be clear to Christians, but the messianic era in its most complete dimension has not been revealed to Christians or Jews. Until the eschaton, the Christian duty is to respect other bearers of revelation. This posture of nonmissionary humility would seem to suggest that the Christian can recognize that God's design has not been fully revealed. This may be fine to say to clarify the Christian identity, but it does threaten Jewish integrity.

Chirico has introduced an important thematic change of direction. By emphasizing an incarnational dimension, he can avoid embracing traditional Christology, which coupled belief in Jesus with the fullness of revelation. But Chirico's solution also has established a tension difficult to resolve. Christians have historically been virtually unable to see their faith as incomplete. After the Shoah, however, Christians have increasingly come to realize that the present, concrete Jewish community can illuminate aspects of the revelation that Christians fail to manifest. Essentially, the same criticisms might be leveled at both Chirico's and Rahner's approaches because both root religious validity in the Christian message that can be promulgated by non-Christians as well. Still, Rahner's and Chirico's approaches signify an advance since they are not designed to promote conversion. Christians can understand the roles of other religious forms while validating the other as a legitimate bearer of revelation and not only as a preparation for Christianity. Unfortunately, the other's identity is still defined in terms of Christianity. Similar to the theologians supporting models of discontinuity, Chirico has reoriented the notion of completion so that he can metamorphose the understanding of fulfillment and go beyond earlier limitations. *Accomplished* fulfillment would be a thing of the future. Jews and Christians would thereby both be obliged to realize messianic promises in the present and simultaneously work to complete God's plan in the future.

To establish a Christology that clears space for the ongoing validity of Judaism, while accepting the perennial tension between Jews and Christians, such scholars as Eva Fleischner have insisted that the multiple New Testament Christologies could help legitimize theological pluralism. She has rejected the use of "implicit Christianity" or anonymous Christianity because such a frame of reference would basically deny Jewish identity by imposing on the Jewish people the Christian vision of the truth.[24]

The heart of the christological tension for Fleischner is the Christian claim that in Jesus the Kingdom of God has fully come to humanity. Unable to abandon this problematic, Fleischner reinforces the Christian claim by asserting that ultimately all peoples will be brought to Christ. Care must be taken, she insists, against using Judaism as a means for Christianity's perfection. She is unwilling to compromise Judaism's validity and does not want to surrender belief in Christ. Thus, she urges an open dialogue that would permit Christians to rethink Christology along with its historical ramifications while they amplify their own dogmatic formulations.[25] It is difficult to see the outcome of this dialogical process because Christology drives to the very essence of the Christian faith-experience and cannot simply be bracketed as one hopes for the best. Christological models may be more easily refined and appreciated for their contributions if the meaning of covenant in all its dimensions could be examined.

Varied scholars have offered an array of two-covenant theories and they have generally found the exclusive origin of the second in Jesus. But this may be an ossified position. Rylaarsdam, for example, has insisted that two covenants may be found in Hebrew Scripture: the covenant with Israel on Sinai and that with David, which could imply that there can be many covenants. The dilemmas of Christology have been created by the challenges posed by those speculating on the ultimate meaning of history and eschatology. How can Christianity be both eschatological and historical? Traditionally, Jesus has been viewed within an eschatological frame of reference. Only rarely have Christians seemed concerned with the ongoing development into the messianic age. This is not surprising because the Christian Scriptures have usually been seen as the expression of an eschatological interpretation of the Hebrew Bible, but rarely do they offer meaningful support in analyzing the historical emergence of the eschaton. Rylaarsdam has reminded us that the eschatological understanding of the day of triumph was actually rooted in the covenant with David, and that this idea was subsumed by the New Testament. If the "covenant with Israel" model could be used because it is more historically grounded, then Jesus could more easily be accepted as a historical God intervening in a normal fashion in human history. Among the features that stand out in the "covenant with Israel" model would be the renewal ceremonies, the societal communalism at work in God's people, and the ongoing sequential advance *toward* the fulfillment of the promise.[26] The emphasis is on process and not stasis.

The varied covenants with Israel, as Rylaarsdam describes them, focused on God's intimately personal union with this specific historical community. At the very core of this ongoing relationship was a mutual pact of faithfulness and responsibility between God and the Jewish people. Since the spiritual presupposition of this covenant could not reinforce the eschatological proclamations rooted in the

Christ-event, this covenant was basically ignored by the early Christian writers in favor of the Davidic covenant and its stress on the eschaton. This Davidic covenant celebrated God as the king of creation as well as of the nation and so muted the earlier stress on the historically emerging people. Tension between those who favored each covenant led to the growth in Israel of dynamic sectarian groups, and these fissures became part of the early Christian experiences. The eschatologically oriented Christian church focused on Jesus' preaching with its Davidic root, and this overpowered other possible options. The Christian dynamic, however, did not originally illustrate chronologically successive covenants, which might imply development. Both covenantal experiences appear in the Hebrew Bible and Christian Scriptures, although with varying importance. If both Judaism and Christianity were sensitive to these two covenants, which seem to be paradoxically related to one another, then the historical church-synagogue relation could be one of mutual interdependence rather than supersessionism.[27] Such a church-synagogue relationship may even reflect the earlier sectarian groupings in Israel. The Hebrew Bible would no longer be considered an inferior preparation for the Christian Testament. Each of the covenants could serve to remind the faithful of the obscured elements in the streams of tradition. Rylaarsdam perceives that this realization would help ensure the interdependence of Judaism and Christianity as well as the validity of both. His work has helped illuminate how the Davidic covenant became the dominant model of the early church. Other perspectives on the covenant issue are equally as provocative.[28]

Revisiting the church's classic displacement theology, Baum has articulated the two cardinal axioms that he sees as essential to relate Judaism positively to Christian theology.

1. Judaism was not condemned to disappear after Christ's coming because it has continued to play a role that can help complete God's salvific plan at the end of time.
2. Jesus is not the sole mediator of salvation.

Even though open to the Jewish faith-experience, Baum also appreciated the central significance of the Christ-event. This event goes beyond the mere gentile appropriation of or adherence to the ongoing Jewish covenant as Van Buren has proposed. What emerged from the Christ-event was that initially Jews and subsequently Gentiles were assured of God's full victory. Jesus would become the Christ only at the eschaton. Baum has very carefully created a theological space for Judaism and has shown how the displacement model could be moved to the onset of the eschatological era. This may solve a current problem, but it only delays resolution of the issue.[29]

Although Baum's Christology is similar to that of Rosemary Ruether, he has introduced a somewhat divergent thrust. Several points seem to be emerging from the attempts at dialogue that could lead to the formulation of a legitimate Christology in the face of the Jewish-Christian encounter after Auschwitz:

1. Christianity should avoid considering itself the successor of Israel, the original, but not "obsolete," people of God;
2. Judaism has its own integrity and is not just the prelude for Christianity;
3. Christianity should accept that its reading of the Hebrew Bible may offer only one dimension and that both Christians and Jews can reflect equally on God's revelation;
4. the traditional claim that without Jesus there is no salvation should be reinterpreted;
5. Christianity should revisit the notion of the "absolute and universal significance" of Jesus and see it as offering a relevant critique applicable to Christianity;
6. Christians could see Jesus as the pivotal point for themselves in history and as their insurance of God's final victory, but not necessarily as the person who has already fulfilled the promises for all people; and
7. Christianity may want to proclaim the redemption brought by Jesus as the beginning of fulfillment, which can empower believers to pray and struggle to do God's will on earth while awaiting the final coming.[30]

In Baum's view, Jesus is the Christ, fully realized only in the eschaton, but at this juncture in time only in a proleptic or anticipatory fashion because he has extended the grace that has stimulated humanity to yearn for fulfillment, and so Judaism would continue with its abiding validity. A solution resting on a proleptic dimension may be too subtle for some and may even suggest using "smoke and mirrors" to gain its effect. Are there substantial differences in saying (a) that the Jews are not currently summoned to recognize Jesus as

Messiah either historically fulfilled or even as eschatologically proleptic, (b) that he is working in them unrecognized, or (c) that in the end time all will be reconciled in Christ? Any choice seems to depend on a theological level of comfort and on a praiseworthy desire for accommodation.[31] Such an improvement in the theological climate, however, is welcome, but it is only a beginning step for a lasting and fruitful Jewish-Christian interchange. Both Baum and Ruether have adopted this concept of prolepsis and have pursued this notion of covenantal reconfiguration relentlessly. Ruether's work has virtually driven the scholarly debate on whether Christianity in its very essence is antisemitic, by portraying antisemitism as the left hand of Christology. Her work raises profound questions for Christians who are determined to uphold the axioms of their faith and also engage in interfaith dialogue.

Probably the leading provocateur in this theological exploration, Ruether has found the christological hermeneutic rooted in a bifurcated vision of the Hebrew Bible. Christians, she has insisted, seemed to see Jesus as fulfilling the prophecies. By "historicizing the eschatological," she has insisted they interpreted the church as the beginning of the Kingdom's establishment, which superseded the chosen people. Simultaneously, they "spiritualized the eschatological" by making the end time of the messianic era the result of internal, undetectable transformations rather than concrete events that led toward an undefined future. Both perspectives gained sustenance by Christ's nonappearance in a historical messianic victory immediately after the Resurrection. A radical reinterpretation of the Hebrew messianic prophecies with their fulfillment in Jesus seemed to be demanded, especially since the concrete messianic era did not materialize. This Christian reformulation of the prophecy/fulfillment model, which appeared in the Hebrew Bible historically, resulted in attributing absolute finality to Jesus and his church. The result, even if not initially intended, served as a source of antisemitism. To avoid this, Ruether has suggested that we should see the messianic meaning of Jesus' life as paradigmatic and proleptic in nature.[32] Closure could, therefore, be avoided.

Equally as devastating for her, early Christian writers, including the Evangelists, used Jewish texts to validate the separation between synagogue and church. These Christian authors extracted prophecies in the Hebrew Bible about blindness, reprobation, and infidelity that they felt could illustrate the "Jewish infidelity" foretold in their own Scriptures. This "left hand of Christology" served as the basis for the *Adversus Judaeos* tradition. The remedy for the misinterpretation of promise/fulfillment would seem to demand that any Christology allow an affirmation of the abiding validity of Judaism. A little too dramatically, perhaps, Ruether has suggested that such a proleptic understanding would parallel the Exodus experience, with Easter reinforcing this Jewish event. [33]

Ruether has elaborated Jewish messianic hopes and has situated Jesus within the historically developed notion of sacred kingship. Jesus' own self-consciousness could now be seen from this perspective. His and his contemporaries' messianic understanding, with its hope for fulfillment, almost had to be revolutionary. But the New Testament writers, according to Ruether, "suppressed the confrontationist content of Messianic faith and spiritualized and depoliticized its purpose." In her opinion, the historicopolitical development of Christian theology led to a universal religion that was depoliticized. Such roles as that of the eschatological judge, originally part of the Jewish apocalyptic tradition, were divorced from Jesus' historical career and propelled into the future. Early Christian commentators stressed that Jesus would one day return to exercise these messianic prerogatives. They failed to observe the messianic dimension in the living Jesus as a proleptic reality. Ultimately, both the historical and the eschatological role were configured in such a way that Jesus was already the future Messiah because he was the original manifestation of God to humanity. [34]

Rejecting the more traditional Christologies of Bultmann, Pannenberg, and Moltmann, Ruether would prefer seeing Jesus as the *not yet* Christ who can represent that unification of humanity with his destiny that has still not come. The Exodus story highlights for Jews the "hoping man." For Christians, the Resurrection seems to vindicate this hoping man and can offer us the proleptic preview of human fulfillment. The reactions to her book have been vigorous and have suggested that Ruether may have partially truncated, if not wholly obviated, the Christian message for many. Focusing on Jesus as a paradigm may be clarifying for speculative theologians, but as an abstraction it may be useful to only a few. Legitimate dialogue with the Jewish faith seems to require an authentic, and not necessarily speculative, Christianity true to its transformative elements maintaining Jewish integrity. She has opened some very provocative directions. To create dialogue with Jewish scholars, such Christian thinkers as Ruether have urged the abandonment of the supersessionistic Christian meaning of the Resurrection, at least as it is traditionally expressed. This triumphalistic anti-Judaism can be rooted in early reflection on this event, but it may have been only one stream in early Christianity. For her, Jesus at times seems to be merely a Jew who hoped for the Kingdom of God and died for that hope.[35] Such an approach may reduce the significance of the event and make it more human than divine. She has reconfigured Christianity very creatively by moving beyond the dual covenant; but has she remained true to the integrity of the Christian message?

In a very innovative fashion, Ruether has proposed a multicovenantal model so that Sinai and the Christ-event represent only two messianic experiences of an indeterminate number. She apparently feels that no new positive theology of Judaism can be possible if there does not occur in Christianity a metamorphosis of traditional Christology and the destruction of old forms. The anti-Jewish Christologies in the patristic era, which seem to be derived from the Christian Testament, need to be bypassed through an interpretation that rests on a genuine and historically rooted theological outlook to originate a creative Jewish-Christian relationship. Thus, the church should abandon its claims about Christ launching the messianic age in any form. For Ruether, Jesus would not be the Jewish messiah but a Jew who voiced his hopes for the Kingdom of God. Jesus would represent the unification of the human community with its ultimate destiny, which can now be known more clearly, even though still not fulfilled. The Christ-event, therefore, would constitute one authentic eschatological paradigm, but only for Christians. Such alternative paradigms as the Exodus, which result from central historical experiences, have informed the Jewish people, who cannot be viewed as unredeemed.[36]

Each event, therefore, would speak validly to a different group. In the final analysis, it might be better to speak of one normative covenant within which there can be other legitimate covenants because the one God has disclosed himself in varied historical eras. For

Christians, one set of defining characteristics seems pertinent, and this perspective can be summarized as christocentric Trinitarianism. Perhaps now is an opportune time for theologians to add further dimensions to the covenant formation as the encounter and dialogue mature. In any event, a general reference to a single Judeo-Christian tradition would for Ruether and others distort reality because disparate groups have been involved in contributing, both positively and negatively, to our mainstream culture.

The Christ-event and Human Dignity

Critics have suggested that Ruether excessively has relativized the Christ-event. Perhaps, for example, the Exodus and the Christ-event may be complementary to one another and not just points on a line between her radical surgery — some would say amputation — and the mere affirmation of the traditional claims in toto. For Christians, Jesus increasingly is seen as uniting traditions and religious dimensions in a unique way that has helped open some very fruitful speculative approaches to understanding God and the human condition. A leading Catholic scholar, John Pawlikowski two decades ago followed her lead and has asserted that Jesus did not fulfill messianic hopes and prophecies. Hence, the real mission of authentic Christianity may be to "explicate the uniqueness and mystery of the Christ-Event." Pawlikowski has posited that an essential relationship exists between Christianity and the pharisaic revolution within Judaism of the Second Temple period. This revolutionary perspective in Judaism was designed to highlight the new intimacy of the God-man relationship and stressed a heightened respect for the human person. Pawlikowski has suggested that an understanding of the pharisaic basis of Christology could help reduce the gulf between Judaism and Christianity by pointing to their relationship.[37]

Refining the image of the Pharisees in Christian teaching could also serve to remove a source of continuing prejudice against Judaism by elucidating the authentic meaning of the Christ-event. The pharisaic movement of that period maintained that the God-of-revelation was the Father of each person no matter what the social status. As the Pharisees advanced the concept of each individual's value, Jesus fused with this the important concept of community, an integral component of the Jewish tradition. Maintaining the ongoing community/individual dialectic was to be the task delegated to Jesus' followers, who subsequently ignored this important Jewish initiative.[38] Since this dialectical tension is a perennial issue, the Christ-event could help illuminate our own efforts at reconciliation.

What Christianity has contributed has been a new perspective on how profoundly integral humanity has to be to correspond to the self-definition of God. Some Scripture scholars have even suggested that humanity already existed in the Godhead from eternity. Rather than the Resurrection, it may really be in the Incarnation where Judaism and Christianity diverged because here the human personality was mysteriously identified with God. The tragedy was that Christianity emphatically stressed this incarnational vision but ignored Jesus' own adherence to Torah Judaism. Since Vatican II, Christians have tried to reappropriate the Jewish Jesus and early Christianity.[39]

Following the Resurrection, the familiar categories of the Jewish messianic titles were used to describe Jesus. Since the messianic era did not historically appear, the infant Christian community transformed categories from historical manifestations to interior qualities so that each person could now be seen as sharing in the divinity of God. Humanity could exist in the Godhead in some fashion. But the Resurrection was not the first moment of "sharing" in the Christian tradition. The ultimate meaning of the infancy narratives can suggest that God always was man in some mysterious dimension. For Pawlikowski, an incarnational Christology would allow this reality to become more clearly apparent.[40]

According to Pawlikowski, Jesus can be viewed as the fulfillment of the growing sense of human dignity. The viewpoint that men and women are saved in community is a Jewish message that Christianity could now reappropriate to counterbalance the radical individualism powering the earlier Christianity and then reinforced in the Enlightenment. The Jewish concern with concrete history also can serve as a corrective to the traditional Christian temptation that promotes the spiritual Kingdom. To await the spiritual eschaton has served in the past to justify the abandonment of the responsibility of being a cocreator of the world. Pawlikowski's suggestion of mutually enhancing and corrective covenants is reminiscent of Buber's allusion to the two dimensions of faith.[41]

Relying on a biblically based version of the dual covenant, Thoma also has rejected an adherence to the earlier tension between the church and Israel, which was rooted in the presumed need to accept or reject Jesus. Ideas of a subsequent messiah during the first century were not as clear then as they have seemed to Christians through the ages. In Thoma's view, the uniqueness of Jesus for Christians seems located in connecting the coming Kingdom of God to his own Jewish person, which reflects Jewish apocalyptic writings as well. His sense of intimacy, however, exceeded what Judaism normally could acknowledge, and this helped reinforce the cleavage between Judaism and early Christianity.[42]

Ignoring the "messiah issue," Mussner has also focused on Jesus' deep links to the Jewish tradition. The uniqueness of the Christ-event can historically be found in the complete identity of the actions of Jesus with the works of God. Jesus' deeds have allowed the Christian Scriptures to speak about God with an anthropomorphic boldness absent in the Hebrew Bible. A congruence of Jesus with God can be found in the Christian writings.[43] The most distinctive feature of Christianity, at least when contrasted to Judaism, however, may be its reliance on the Incarnation and not on the fulfillment of the messianic prophecies, although other paths have also been opened. Mussner has amplified his model by delineating what he has called "prophet Christology" and "Son Christology," which was a later or post-Jesus development. In this context, Jesus belonged to the line of prophets who were illuminating and clearing paths to God. Christianity never completely abandoned this prophet Christology, even in the Gospel of John, which was characterized by a dominant Son Christology. Unfortunately, the Son Christology can accentuate the differences between the Christian and Jewish faith-experiences in a more pronounced way by highlighting what the Christians see as the superiority of Jesus.

Varied strata, dimensions, and agendas that have been embedded in Christian writing become apparent as one analyzes the development of Christology during the first centuries of Christianity.[44] Raymond Brown has suggested, for example, that early christological development was associated with liturgical experiences and so may not necessarily be an essential element in the Christian faith-experience today.[45] In other words, "Christology" can be a dominant element or not. If Ruether has correctly connected antisemitism and Christology, the approach outlined by Brown and others would suggest that antisemitism is certainly not necessarily indigenous to Christianity because a single Christology is not essential to the faith. Each expression in the Christian Scriptures does not have equal value for contemporary faith expressions. Hence, the "Son" or "consciousness" Christology has suggested the possibility of deemphasizing one of the early Christian proclamations that has birthed a fulfillment mentality that seems to submerge the salvific role of the Jewish people.

Affirming the fundamentally ongoing nature of revelation also seems necessary to shatter the notion that antisemitism is the obverse side of Christianity. Subsequent revelations through such historical experiences as the Holocaust can serve to convince the Christian community of the weakness of the fulfillment claims that have supported the "teaching of contempt." Vatican II has also reinforced the commitment to the positive affirmation of religious pluralism that can help eliminate "spiritual monism." The Christ-event, therefore, can profitably be diagnosed from perspectives other than that of messianic fulfillment if we hope to renew the Christian connection to its Jewish heritage, given that Jesus is not the completion of all of the Jewish messianic prophecies.[46] For all of their interest in furthering dialogue, according to Pawlikowski, Thoma and Mussner have failed to develop a theology of what Judaism *still* has to offer Christianity.[47] Perhaps the most outstanding Catholic theologian to deal directly with this issue has been Johannes Baptist Metz.

Although Metz has not written extensively on the Shoah, he has insisted that such sanctioned murder demands that any Christology, which obviates the continuing role of the Jewish people in salvation, has to be labeled totally immoral. He has insisted that an authentic theology has to be informed by the realization that Christians can only grasp their own identity through a focus on their Jewish origins. Jewish history is not merely Christian prehistory because it has an ongoing integrity of its own. In terms of both its own unique formulation and content, Jewish historical belief and tradition seem to demand a central position in the Christian faith expression. For Metz, the critical theological fact at the beginning of any inquiry has to be the presence or absence of God. Christians have to be cognizant of contemporary Jewish reflections on God. It was the Jews, after all, who were at the very root of Christian reflections, who still contribute from their own living tradition, and who were nearly communally extinguished as a result of the Holocaust.[48]

Metz favors the double-covenant approach that would stress a new revelation in Christ, which would allow the Gentiles entrance into revelation but would not rely on the Sinai covenant. He has reflected on the two modes of believing contained in the Christian Testament. One, the Pauline or Hellenistic mode, highlights philosophical distinctions and has dominated Christianity. The other, the synoptic mode, can be found in the tradition nourished by the Hebrew Bible and proved to be a source of sustenance for the early Christian communities. What historically seems to have happened is that those Christian theological trends that were fortified by Paul's aggressive reflections, forced the Jewish contributions to the fringes of Christian consciousness. To deal simultaneously with Christology and Judaism today, therefore, the church may have to recapture the Hebraic mode of belief, which would help extinguish the "victorious" Christology that has ended in marginalizing the Jewish people. Such an expansive approach could result in an open-ended Christology. Such a Christology would envision an eschatological role for the Jewish people that would not demand Jewish conversion as the premise for the end times. A Jewish-Christian partnership, fostering dialogue with other world religions, might even assist the eschatological reign of God fully to emerge.[49] In recent years, theologians have expansively broadened theological reflections on the meaning of covenant, which is so intimately tied to christological fulfillment.

Several theologians have suggested that the Christ-event brings to the forefront a new sense of intimacy between God and humanity. These scholars have insisted that contemporaries of Jesus caught a new vision of the God-humanity relation. To ignore a holistic analysis of the unity of God's revelation would make Jesus into a barrier and not a link between Jews and Christians. From another angle, of course, the double or multicovenant approach can be observed as a way to postpone the Christian eschatological notions of fulfillment/displacement in order to avoid the cleavage that in the past has characterized the meaning of the Jewish-Christian relationship. The varied avenues of speculation are opening up new avenues that have helped fructify the dialogue.

The Single Covenant and the Eclipse of Fulfillment

Another way suggested out of the historical antisemitic imbroglio might be through single-covenant Christologies. Monika Hellwig, for example, has suggested that Judaism and Christianity in a complementary fashion seem to be finding the meaning of God and creation within one covenant. With unfortunate results, Christians have frequently dwelt on the messianic rather than the covenantal theme in the Hebrew Bible. Inspired by Ruether's lead, Hellwig has suggested that the Christian absolutizing of Jesus may stem from simultaneously spiritualizing and historicizing for very different contextual reasons the eschatological dimension, which early Christians saw as embodied in the person of Jesus. Hellwig has asserted that messiahship could be conceptualized as a mission for both Christians and Jews to realize jointly in history and so remove completely its christological aspect. Her scenario is creative. One could see the Jews as initially offering witness to the transcendent unity of God. Election would then merely become a graphic way of asserting that God conversed first with the Jews, who were then joined by the Christians. The post-Resurrection covenant would then be "new," since it now would include more people. Christians would no longer have to focus on the fulfillment of the messiahship in Jesus. Now future-oriented Christians could see a glimpse of the anticipated eschatological fulfillment in Jesus, and this could lead to a more profound reflection on the meaning of Jesus' divinity. Hellwig's phenomenological interpretation finds Jesus as the locus where humanity encounters the transcendent God, which for the Jews and Gentiles could be central to human existence.[50] Thus, God continues the revealing process in contemporary Jewish and Christian experiences. The 1985 Vatican "Notes" has also declared a preference for a unitary covenantal model.

One of the most forceful affirmations of the Jewish-Christian bond was offered by the Synod of the Protestant Church of the Rhineland in 1980. The statement encouraged confessing that the Jewish Jesus is the messiah of the Jews as well as the savior of the world. The affirmation attempted to adhere to a singular covenantal model, but it really means that Christians are seizing the initiative to define the meaning of Judaism. The document served to remind its readers that the Jewish people have been permanently elected, and pointed out that through Jesus Christ the church had been invited into this covenant. Along these lines, such scholars as Paul van Buren have tried to remind us that the function of binding the Gentiles to the Jewish people cannot be construed as part of Jewish messianism.[51]

Van Buren and others have indicated that the Holocaust has illustrated the impoverishment of a Christian tradition that has ignored its Jewish roots. Such a flawed Christianity created a tradition that featured a metahistorical realm of messianic fulfillment that faith could accept but that could not be validated through concrete history. In this fulfillment tradition, the Easter mystery was proclaimed as an unqualified triumph of faith that excluded the continuing significance of the Jewish people. Van Buren has insisted that the church would not have to abandon its foundational belief in Jesus as the Christ and Son of God. But this did not necessarily mean that he was the long-awaited Jewish messiah. This position would mean that post-Easter Judaism as a living entity could still sustain its legitimate messianic hope. The Christ-event as the manifestation of God's will means for van Buren that the Gentiles have been invited to commune with God. In line with viewing God's revelation as continuous, Christians are not to bypass the Jewish people who are connected to the God of Abraham, who has now again revealed himself through the person of the Jewish Jesus. Thus, the classical christological claims could be modified by a revised understanding of Jesus, a member of the Jewish community, by the occurrence of the Shoah, and by the Jewish people's construction of the modern Republic of Israel. Christian discipleship might begin to mean adherence to the cause of God through love for the weak and oppressed. This original message of Christianity opposed dehumanization and marginalization techniques.[52] By developing an "Israel-affirming Christology" to replace the old displacement theology, the *ecclesia semper reformanda*, according to van Buren, would be reversing its historical direction of working against God's people, Israel.

John Paul II's single-covenantal statements have also recognized the intimate bond connecting the church and the Jewish people, which have been "linked" in their specific identities. The pope has stated:

> It is this link that is the real foundation for our relation with the Jewish people, a relation which could well be called a real parentage and which

we have with that religious community alone, notwithstanding our many connections with other world religions.... This link can be called a sacred one, stemming as it does from the mysterious will of God.[53]

The Christ-event would seem to be a proleptic glimpse of the messianic hope that partially depends on human efforts for completion. Such an approach would offer a very creative solution to understand the identities of both Christians and Jews, but it is not consistent with other Vatican supersessionist statements. The church's contradictory statements reflect a tension temporarily within the institution. The single-covenant theory fuses the two religious groups together, but it also incorporates a tendency to identify one in terms of the other. The only solution may be to accept the tension as a positive result and not necessarily a phenomenon that has to be surmounted.

Affirming that Jesus opened salvation to the Gentiles, A. Roy Eckardt has suggested that messianic fulfillment occurred in Jesus to the extent that a basic evil or deprivation was overcome by saving pagans. The redemption of humanity was progressing, and Jesus was a historical figure with eschatological implications. Jesus seems to become the second Abraham opening salvation to the Gentiles. The Jewish nonacceptance of Jesus as the Christ could be an affirmative act that signified their faithfulness to the God of the covenant. Jesus partially fulfilled Jewish messianic expectations and opened salvation to the pagans, but he did not claim that he was the messiah and Lord — his followers did that. This unitary-covenant model also necessarily demands an ongoing dialectical tension between Judaism and Christianity.[54] Each is to proclaim the revelation that God has given to its respective group and in so doing can reveal God to the fullest extent possible.

In Eckardt's creative view, God's plan called for a significant number of his chosen people to respond negatively to the Christ-event so that the integrity of Judaism could be preserved. Neither Christians nor Jews are to exalt in their gifts. Fulfillment would now take on a new meaning as an event that finally shattered the wall between Jews and Gentiles. Christianity would no longer be seen as Israel's replacement, and so the two communities could now go their respective ways in a carefully fused relationship of mutual love and respect. Fearing the sublimation of one partner, Eckardt has wisely opposed any kind of "intimate identity," which official Catholic or Protestant documents seem to prefer. Attempts at unity or identity have resulted in tragedy, and so other nonmissionary modes of independent relationship might prove more viable. Even the meaning of "resurrection" may have to be reexamined. A revised depiction of the future resurrection in Jesus could make it possible for the Gentiles to enter into the ongoing covenant with Israel. Similarly, the future resurrection of Moses and Abraham could assume distinctive implications for Jews in their eschatological community. Both Jews and Christians have made independent contributions.[55]

In his recent works, Eckardt has rejected the traditional meaning of the Resurrection doctrine by locating it in both the Jewish and the Christian traditions. Such a controversial step may be critical if we genuinely want to develop a new theological model for the Jewish-Christian relationship. Triumphalism may be bankrupt, but the Resurrection is crucial for Christian integrity. Eckardt's commendable effort may not be accepted by more conservative Christian theologians. The Resurrection, according to Eckardt and others, should only have a spiritually living meaning and should not have been allowed to structure historical Jewish-Christian relations. The eschaton should not be normative for our ongoing contingent relations. Eckardt states:

> The Jewish man from Galilee sleeps now. He sleeps with the other Jewish dead, with all the disconsolate and the scattered ones of the murder camps.... But Jesus of Nazareth shall be raised. So too shall the small Hungarian children who were burned alive at Auschwitz.[56]

To accept Eckardt's viewpoint may prove difficult for those Christian commentators who insist on the centrality of the historical Resurrection.

John Pawlikowski has also tried to modify the traditional triumphalistic perspective by stressing that a concept of the Resurrection was already being developed by the Pharisees, and so it is not an explicitly and exclusively Christian notion. Pawlikowski has noted that the pharisaic notion of the Resurrection seems to be rooted in an intensified consciousness of the divine-human intimacy that resulted from their reflection on God as Father. The Christian notion of the Resurrection, therefore, could be viewed from an incarnational vantage point and need not necessarily be seen as an eschatological phenomenon. From this perspective, Jesus *had* to rise to validate humanity as an ongoing dimension of divinity and to clarify God's meaning for humanity. Pawlikowski views the Resurrection as one event in a theology that could actively articulate Judaism's continuing role. For Pawlikowski, the Incarnation/Resurrection would be seen, then, as an integral part of the more complete revelation that would also include the Jewish covenant as a component of God's message.[57]

Since this incarnational development remains incomplete, according to Eckardt, the Resurrection would become a future promise and not a finished reality. Here again we see that the Jewish communal perspective could be introduced with profit. An individual person may not be able to experience the Resurrection until the full human community reaches the messianic end time. The fact that Christianity might embody a unique revelation because of the Christ-event would not automatically lead to a triumphalistic attitude as long as the enduring insights of the Jewish covenant would be continuously reappropriated. A Christian standing before God's message could never have the same self-definition as a Jew might have. This diversity can be useful, however, because it can help amplify a richer meaning of revelation.[58]

Cornelius A. Rijk, former head of the Vatican's office on Catholic-Jewish relations, has also observed that the ongoing tension between Christians and Jews on this messiah issue can be potentially fruitful. The eschaton has not arrived, he has reminded us, but has been only partially glimpsed in Jesus. This increased consciousness of the covenant appearing in Jesus would not necessitate a second covenant as such because it could be seen as merely amplifying the original covenant. The Jewish people have maintained faith in their covenant's *not* accepting Jesus as its fulfillment. Rijk, Eckardt, and others have reflected on both the continuity and the discontinuity characterizing the Jewish-Christian relations that express the "already" and "not yet" of the messianic age.[59] This single-covenant approach presumes a healthy tension between the Christ-event and Israel as a people. Such issues as the tension between individual and society and the relationship between Incarnation and Resurrection can be viewed positively in the single-covenant approach, which presupposes that

Jews and Christians have been and still are the recipients of God's revelatory message.

Pluralism and Complementarity

In their catechesis and popular preaching, Christians have continued reevaluating their attitude toward historical Jewish experiences.[60] They have begun stressing the abiding validity of Judaism as well as its impact on Christian theology as the latter has closed or opened itself to God's revelation to his first people. Common themes have emerged and begun to sharpen the ongoing christological reflection. A pluralism of Christologies seems to exist within the Christian Testament as well as in postapostolic times. Such viable theological reflections that are rooted in an array of Christologies may engage theologians as they test the boundaries of revelatory transmissions beyond a supersessionistic approach. In considering doctrinal pluralism, for example, Bernard Lonergan has insisted that philosophies and theologies make sense only within a specific historical environment that stimulates theological horizons to emerge. Since historical contexts change, the possibility of theological metamorphoses could induce for some a fear of any substantive understanding.[61] Certainly religious institutions prefer dogmatic consistency because it undergirds their need to control. To break theological molds could suggest errors in the past, but more optimistically could also be an acknowledgment that human error is rooted in our human condition tarnished with sin. Before anything, we would have to accept the fact that we are a sinful humanity that has made mistakes and that theologies are connected to historical consciousness.

Religious pluralism, however, is a fact of life that Christians have been struggling to handle in the context of their belief in the universal salvific mission of Christ. Facing the fact of historical pluralism, Logos-Christology may be a fruitful way for Christians to affirm the religious validity of others. Karl Rahner, for example, has suggested that Logos-Christology does not portray Judaism as merely preparatory to Christianity. Judaism can be seen as one of God's ways of speaking to humanity through his ongoing election of the Jewish people as one of the diverse forms that Christians can comprehend.[62]

Such speculative insights as those of Rahner and Lonergan seem to recognize that deleterious effects follow from merely an intellectual understanding of revelation without a grounding in human history. Such a realization may offer to theologians the tool or incentive, which could be useful in reexamining their past reflections, pronouncements, and systematizations, which they will have to review in light of their historical impact.

In the context of pluralism, a growing number of Protestant and Catholic theologians clearly have begun seeking ways for envisioning the linkage between Jews and Christians by modifying in a more positive fashion the classical Christian claims that end with fulfillment in and through the Christ-event. They have been rethinking their faith in its deepest meanings. Along with John Paul II, the single-covenant theologians have done justice to the unique and distinctive contributions of both Christianity and Judaism. In the single-covenant approach, of course, Christianity can tend to be, as Pawlikowski and others have suggested, Judaism for Gentiles. But it is more than just that because both have to have their own integrity.[63] To opt for a dual covenant would seem to restrict God's own covenant-making ability by ignoring other Judaic experiences and by, at least implicitly, assuming that the future is closed. Beyond the single and dual covenants, Ruether, among others, has suggested that Sinai and the Christ-event are only two of a multiplicity of messianic experiences, but the same possibility exists in the single-covenant model if one accepts a variety of divine manifestations as one revelation. This seemingly unstoppable array of perspectives may ultimately help suggest the unfathomable richness of revelation.

The Christian vision of truth, most seem to agree, should include the validity and value of the Jewish faith in itself and of the Hebrew Bible in itself, and not as merely preparing faith in Christ for the Gentiles. To eliminate the preparatory character would lead to an understanding of the Hebrew Bible whereby it would lose its role as solely an anchor that is needed to provide Christianity with its own historically grounded validity. Removal of this traditional viewpoint could tempt Christianity to an ahistorical grounding or might even suggest its creation by spontaneous intervention. Hence, a theological pluralism within the framework of nonsupersessionistic covenantal and/or Logos-Christology, which can explain the role of Jesus along with the abiding validity of the Jewish tradition, could serve to inspire rapprochement between Jew and Christian. Such a theological pluralism could help more clearly illuminate God's way of communication, which none of us knows with absolute certainty.

Within the pharisaic environment of his time, according to Pawlikowski, Jesus began constructing a community on a foundation that highlighted the utter dignity of each individual. Each individual was to be anchored in the social group that was needed to enrich personal dignity. Perhaps here is a view into the intimate and dialectical relationship that can form the basis for an authentic Jewish-Christian relationship. Grounding religious faith in the solemn commitment to community, Judaism has historically found it difficult to relate to the "outsider" in its midst. For its part, Christianity has labored to sustain personal dignity but has in the process historically become hostage to excessive individualism. Both Christian and Jew, then, are challenged by the perennial question of balancing the individual and society, which has obsessed virtually all of our outstanding philosophers as well. Any reference, therefore, to a single Judeo-Christian cultural strand could represent a distortion of the human condition, which each tradition has plumbed in a distinct manner.[64] Indeed, to gain an understanding of the Jewish-Christian relation may offer an insight into issues that have exercised political philosophies since virtually the dawn of our civilization.

Like the Christian meaning, Christology also has to be subject to reexamination. Since revelation is before as well as behind humanity, Christian and Jewish excavations into God's mystery continue existing within an ever-widening and unending horizon. To alleviate fear about tampering with historical doctrines and viewpoints, theologians have to realize that the God of Abraham, who is the God of Jesus, is the same God speaking to all people. Christians,[65] therefore, may continue to announce the good news but should come to a more complete understanding of their own process of conversion. The encounter between Christian and Jew should not be merely humanitarian but should probe the theological dimension where ultimate issues can be explored. Missionizing should be conceptually as well as literally obliterated, and the stress should be on understanding, mutual assistance, and collaboration. In light of this, the Jewish theological reactions to the Holocaust can add a dimension to the reflection on the human condition and help suggest values that could aid us in reconfiguring our culture so that sanctioned massacres can be avoided. Both the Christian and Jewish theologians have those symbols and doctrines that potentially can help inform our political and ethical discussions.

Notes

1. McGarry, *Christology after Auschwitz*; Fleischner, *Judaism in German Christian Theology*; Gabriel Fackre, "The Place of Israel in Christian Faith," in Markus Bockmuehl and Helmut Burkhardt, eds., *Gott Lieber und seine Gebote Halten* (Giessen: Brunnen Verlag, 1991), 21-38; A. Roy Eckardt, *Reclaiming the Jesus of History: Christology Today* (Minneapolis: Fortress Press, 1992).
2. Horacio Simian-Yofre, SJ, "Old and New Testament: Participation and Analogy," in Rene Latourelle, ed., *Vatican II: Assessment and Perspectives. Twenty-Five Years After (1962-1987)* (New York: Paulist Press, 1988), 1: 292-93; Stanislas Lyonnet, SJ, "A Word on Chapters IV and VI of *Dei Verbum*: The Amazing Journey Involved in the Process of Drafting the Conciliar Text," in Latourelle, *Vatican II*, 1: 164.
3. Document produced through the Commission on Faith and Order of the National Council of Churches and the Secretariat for Catholic-Jewish Relations of the National Conference for Catholic Bishops and issued on 19 June 1973. See also 1987 General Assembly, Presbyterian Church (USA), *A Theological Understanding of the Relationship Between Christians and Jews* (A Paper Commended to the Church for Study and Reflection) (New York: Office of the General Assembly, 1987), 9.
4. McGarry, *Christology after Auschwitz*, 59
5. "The Evanston Report (1954)," *Lutheran World* 11 (1964): 358.
6. Eckardt, *Elder and Younger Brothers*, 52f., 58f.
7. Joseph Estes, "Jewish-Christian Dialogue as Mission," *Review and Exposition* 68 (1971): 9; Jocz, *Christians and Jews*, 40, 47; Jacob Jocz, *The Jewish People and Jesus Christ; A Study in the Controversy between Church and Synagogue* (London: SPCK., 1962), 264, 320-22; George A.F. Knight, "Beyond Dialogue," in George A.F. Knight, ed., *Jews and Christians: Preparation for Dialogue* (Philadelphia: Westminster Press, 1965), 175; George A.F. Knight, "The Mystery of Israel," in Knight, *Jews and Christians*, 48.
8. Jean Danielou, *The Theology of Jewish Christianity* (London: Darton, Longman, and Todd, 1964); Jean Danielou, *The Dead Sea Scrolls and*

Primitive Christianity (Baltimore: Helicon Press, 1958); Jean Danielou and André Chouraqui, *The Jews: Views and Counterviews—a Dialogue* (Westminster, MD: Newman Press, 1967); Jean Danielou, *Dialogue with Israel* (Baltimore: Helicon Press, 1966), 99.

9. Danielou and Chouraqui, *The Jews*, 25, 69-70; Jacob Bernard Agus, "Response to Father Danielou's *Dialogue with Israel* and Cardinal Bea's *The Church and the Jewish People*," in Jacob Bernard Agus, *Dialogue and Tradition: The Challenge of Contemporary Judaeo-Christian Thought* (London: Abelard-Schuman, 1971). Agus labels Danielou's position theological antisemitism (Bea, *The Church*, 96).

10. Hans Urs von Balthasar, *Church and World* (New York: Herder and Herder, 1967), 169-74.

11. R.L. Lindsey, "Salvation and the Jews," *International Review of Missions* 61 (1972): 20-37; Johannes Aagard, "The Church and the Jews in Eschatology," *Lutheran World* 11 (1964): 273-75; George Papademetriou, "Jewish Rite in the Christian Church: Ecumenical Possibility," *Scottish Journal of Theology* 26 (1973): 466-87.

12. Kurt Hruby, "Peoplehood in Judaism and Christianity," *Theology Digest* 22 (1974): 11; Kurt Hruby, "Reflections on the Dialogue," in John Oesterreicher, ed., *Brothers in Hope* (New York: Herder and Herder, 1970), 106-31; Kurt Hruby, "Jesus, Disciple of Moses: The True Relationship of Christianity and Judaism," *Encounter Today* 8 (1972): 6ff.; K. H. Rengstorf, "The Place of the Jew in the Theology of the Christian Mission," *Lutheran World* 11 (1964): 194ff.

13. Estes, "Jewish-Christian Dialogue": 9; George A.F. Knight, "Beyond Dialogue," in Knight, *Jews and Christians*, 172ff.; Vatican II, "Decree on the Missionary Activity of the Church," article 2, in Walter Abbott, ed., *The Documents of Vatican II* (New York: Herder and Herder, 1966), 585; Jocz, *Christians and Jews*, 47.

14. Nils A. Dahl, "Election and the People of God—Some Comments," in Paul Opsahl and Marc Tannenbaum, eds., *Speaking of God Today: Jews and Christians in Conversation* (Philadelphia: Fortress Press, 1974), 36; Robert Cushman, "Biblical Election as Sacred History: A Study in the Ancient History of Ecumenism," in John Deschner et al., eds., *Our Common History as Christians: Essays in Honor of Albert C. Outler* (New York: Oxford University Press, 1975): 179-216; S. Siegel, "Election and the People of God: A Jewish Perspective," *Lutheran Quarterly* 21 (1969): 437-50; Leonard Gappelt, "Israel and the Church in Today's Discussion and in Paul," *Lutheran World* 10 (1963): 364.

15. Peter Chirico, "Christian and Jew Today from a Theological Perspective," *Journal of Ecumenical Studies* 7 (1970): 37-51; J. Coert

Rylaarsdam, "Jewish-Christian Relationship: The Two Covenants and the Dilemmas of Christology," *Journal of Ecumenical Studies* 9 (1972): 249-70; Frank M. Cross, Jr., "A Christian Understanding of the Election of Israel," in Sanford Seltzer and Max Stackhouse, eds., *The Death of Dialogue and Beyond* (New York: Friendship Press, 1969): 72-85; Alan T. Davies, "The Jews in an Ecumenical Context," *Journal of Ecumenical Studies* 5 (1968): 496; James Parkes, *Prelude to Dialogue: Jewish-Christian Relationships* (New York: Schocken Books, 1969), 200; Rosemary Ruether, "An Invitation to Jewish-Christian Dialogue: In What Sense Can We Say that Jesus Was 'The Christ'?" *The Ecumenist* 10 (1972): 17-24; Gregory Baum, "The Jews' Faith and Ideology," *The Ecumenist* 10 (1971-72): 71-76.

16. Eckardt, *Elder and Younger Brothers*, 50ff. For a recent book focusing on the fact and significance of Jesus as Jew, see Charlesworth, *Jesus' Jewishness*, especially the essay of Daniel Harrington, "The Jewishness of Jesus: Facing Some Problems" (p. 124); Mussner, *Tractate*, 113; P. Lapide and U. Luz, *Jesus in Two Perspectives: A Jewish-Christian Dialogue* (Minneapolis: Augsburg Pub. House, 1985).

17. John Pawlikowski, "Christ and the Jewish-Christian Dialogue: An Evaluation of Contemporary Perspectives," paper presented at the American Academy of Religion, Washington, DC, 26 October 1974, p. 2.

18. Ibid., 2, 7; Gavin D'Costa, "Jews and Christians: Reflections on 'Covenant' and 'Fulfillment': Towards a Theology of Christian-Jewish Relations," paper presented at Harvard, October 1989; Nahum Glatzer, *Franz Rosenzweig: His Life and Thought* (New York: Farrar, Strauss, and Young, 1953), xxv; Eugen Rosenstock-Huessy, *Judaism Despite Christianity: The Letters on Christianity and Judaism between Eugen Rosenstock-Juessy and Franz Rosenzweig* (University: University of Alabama Press, 1969), 134ff.; Franz Rosenzweig, *The Star of Redemption* (New York: Holt, Rinehart, and Winston, 1971), 413-16; Eliezer Berkovits, *Major Themes in Modern Philosophies of Judaism* (New York: Holt, KTAV Pub. House, 1974), 43-46. For critiques of Rosenzweig's dual-covenant theory, see Samuel Berman, "Israel and the Oikoumene," in Raphael Loewe, ed., *Studies in Rationalism, Judaism, and Universalism* (London: Routledge and Kegan Paul, 1966), 61-63; Markus Barth, *Israel and the Church: Contributions to a Dialogue Vital for Peace* (Richmond: John Knox Press, 1969), 38ff.; Maurice Bowleen, "Rosenzweig on Judaism and Christianity—the Two Covenant Theory," *Judaism* 22 (1963): 475-81.

19. James Parkes, *The Foundations of Judaism and Christianity* (Chicago: Quadrangle Books, 1960), 132; James Parkes, *Judaism and Christianity*

(London: Victor Gollancz, 1948), 30; Martin Buber, *Two Types of Faith* (London: Portledge & Paul, 1951), 174; Langmuir, *History*, 27-34.

20. John Pawlikowski, *Jesus and the Theology of Israel* (Wilmington, DE: Michael Glazier, 1989), 32-33; John Paul II, "The 20th Anniversary of *Nostra Aetate*," *Origins* 5 December 1985, pp. 409-11.

21. John Pawlikowski, "The Church and Judaism: The Thought of James Parkes," *Journal of Ecumenical Studies* 6 (1969): 594; James Parkes, *Prelude to Dialogue: Jewish-Christian Relationships* (New York: Schocken Books, 1969), 200-10.

22. James Parkes, "Judaism and the Jewish People in Their World Setting at the End of 1973," pamphlet, distributed by the Canadian Council of Christians and Jews, Toronto, 1974; James Parkes, *Prelude to Dialogue: Jewish-Christian Relationships* (New York: Schockcn Books, 1969), 38, 55.

23. Peter Chirico, "Christian and Jew Today from a Theological Perspective," *Journal of Ecumenical Studies* 7 (1970), 761; Karl Rahner, "Anonymous Christians," in *Theological Investigations* (Baltimore: Helicon Press, 1969), 6: 393-95; Karl Rahner, "Observations on the Problem of the 'Anonymous Christian,'" in *Theological Investigations* (New York: Seabury, 1976), 14: 280-94; Fleischner, *Judaism in German Christian Theology*, 133; Gregory Baum, "Introduction," in Ruether, *Faith and Fratricide*, 16ff.; Karl Rahner and F.G. Friedmann, "Unbefangenheit und Ausbruch," *Stimmen der Zeit* 173 (1966): 81-97; Karl Rahner, "Christianity and Non-Christian Religions," in *Theological Investigations* (London: DLT, 1966), 5: 115-34.

24. Fleischner, *Judaism in German Christian Theology*, 133-36.

25. Ibid., 129, 143.

26. Rylaarsdam, "Common Ground": 261-70; J. Coert Rylaarsdam, "Jewish-Christian Relationship: The Two Covenants and the Dilemmas of Christology," *Journal of Ecumenical Studies* 9 (1972): 250, 262; Rosemary Ruether, "Theological Anti-Semitism in the New Testament," *The Christian Century* 85 (1968): 191-96; Monika Hellwig, "Christian Theology and the Covenant of Israel," *Journal of Ecumenical Studies* 7 (1970): 37-51. Ruether is concerned with what she labels the "spiritualizing of the eschatological" and the "historicizing of the eschatological," which could be mitigated if Rylaarsdam's suggestion is accurate, that is, if even within the Hebrew Bible there is a trend toward historicizing and spiritualizing the eschatological.

27. J. Coert Rylaarsdam, "Jewish-Christian Relationship: The Two Covenants and the Dilemmas of Christology," *Journal of Ecumenical Studies* 9 (1972): 239-60; Williamson, *Has God Rejected His People?*

28. McGarry, *Christology after Auschwitz*, 81.
29. Gregory Baum, "The Jews' Faith and Ideology," *The Ecumenist* 10 (1971-72): 71-76; Gregory Baum, "The Doctrinal Basis for Jewish-Christian Dialogue," *The Month* 224 (1967): 232-45; Gregory Baum, "Rethinking the Church's Mission after Auschwitz," in Fleischner, *Auschwitz: Beginning of a New Era?*, 113-28; Gregory Baum, "Catholic Dogma after Auschwitz," in Davies, *Antisemitism and the Foundations of Christianity*, 137-50.
30. McGarry, *Christology after Auschwitz*, 82; John Mahoney, *The Making of Moral Theology: A Study of the Roman Catholic Tradition* (Oxford: Clarendon Press, 1987), 100; Gregory Baum, "Introduction," in Ruether, *Faith and Fratricide*, 15f., 17f.; H. Berkhof, "Israel as a Theological Problem in the Christian Church," *Journal of Ecumenical Studies* 6 (1969): 329-47; Krister Stendahl, "Judaism and Christianity: Then and Now," in Sanford Seltzer and Max Stackhouse, eds., *The Death of Dialogue and Beyond* (New York: Friendship Press, 1969), 112ff; Sullivan, *Salvation Outside the Church?*
31. Manfred Vogel, "The Problem of Dialogue Between Judaism and Christianity," *Journal of Ecumenical Studies* 4 (1967): 684-99.
32. Ruether, *Faith and Fratricide*, 65, 72, 112, 116, 160, 248-49; Jürgen Moltmann, *The Crucified God: The Cross of Christ as the Foundation and Criticism of Christian Theology* (New York: Harper & Row, 1974), 101; Rosemary Ruether, "Theological Anti-Semitism in the New Testament," *The Christian Century* 85 (1968), 194ff; Mary Hembrow Snyder, *The Christology of Rosemary Radford Ruether: A Critical Introduction* (Mystic, CT: Twenty-Third Publications, 1988). Snyder has organized a coherent presentation of Ruether's Christology that has led this bold critique of male-dominated interpretations of Christ.
33. Gregory Baum, "Introduction," in Ruether, *Faith and Fratricide*, 18; Ruether, *Faith and Fratricide*, 250, 256.
34. Rosemary Ruether, "An Invitation to Jewish-Christian Dialogue: In What Sense Can We Say that Jesus Was 'The Christ'?" *The Ecumenist* 10 (1972): 17-24; McGarry, *Christology after Auschwitz*, 88-89; Rosemary Ruether, *Messiah of Israel and the Cosmic Christ: A Study of the Development of Christology in Judaism and Early Christianity*, unpublished manuscript, 1972, 162, 257, 278-80, 288, 289, 314.
35. Pawlikowski, *Jesus*, 80; Rosemary Ruether, "An Invitation to Jewish-Christian Dialogue: In What Sense Can We Say that Jesus Was 'The Christ'?" *The Ecumenist* 10 (1972): 17.
36. Ruether, *Faith and Fratricide*, n. 30; Rosemary Ruether, "An Invitation to Jewish-Christian Dialogue: In What Sense Can We Say that Jesus Was

'The Christ'?" *The Ecumenist* 10 (1972): 14-19; Paul Knitter, *No Other Name* (Maryknoll, NY: Orbis Books, 1985); Bernardin, "Emerging Catholic Attitudes": 437-46.

37. John Pawlikowski, "Christ and the Jewish-Christian Dialogue: An Evaluation of Contemporary Perspectives," paper presented at the American Academy of Religion, Washington, DC, 26 October 1974, pp. 10, 14, 17f.

38. Some perspectives on Pharisaism can be found in: Asher Finkel, *The Pharisees and the Teacher of Nazareth: A Study of Their Background, Their Halachic and Midrashic Teachings, the Similarities and Differences* (Leiden, Holland: E.J. Brill, 1964); Rivkin, *A Hidden Revolution*, 310; John Bowker, *Jesus and the Pharisees* (Cambridge: The University Press, 1973); Leonard Swidler, "The Pharisees in Recent Catholic Writing," *Horizons* 10 (1983): 267-87; James Parkes, *The Foundations of Judaism and Christianity* (Chicago: Quadrangle Books, 1960), 177; Pawlikowski, *Jesus*, 63; Saldarini, "Delegitimation of Leaders": 659-80.

39. Raymond Brown, "Does the New Testament Call Jesus God?" *Theological Studies* 26 (1965): 538-51; James A. Sanders, "An Apostle to the Gentiles," *Conservative Judaism* 25 (1973): 61-63; Fritz Rothschild, ed., *Between God and Man: An Interpretation of Judaism From the Writings of Abraham J. Heschel* (New York: Free Press, 1959), 25; Abraham Joshua Heschel, *The Prophets* (New York: Harper & Row, 1962).

40. John Pawlikowski, "Christ and the Jewish-Christian Dialogue: An Evaluation of Contemporary Perspectives," paper presented at the American Academy of Religion, Washington, DC, 26 October 1974, p. 17ff.

41. Ibid., 19; James Parkes, *The Foundations of Judaism and Christianity* (Chicago: Quadrangle Books, 1960), 132; James Parkes, *Judaism and Christianity* (London: Victor Gollancz, 1948), 30; Martin Buber, *Two Types of Faith* (London: Portledge & Paul, 1951), 174.

42. Thoma, *A Christian Theology of Judaism*.

43. Mussner, *Tractate*, 226; Franz Mussner, "From Jesus the 'Prophet' to Jesus the 'Son,'" in Aboldjavad Falaturi et al., eds., *Three Ways to One God: The Faith Experience in Judaism, Christianity and Islam* (New York: Crossroad, 1987), 76-85.

44. Pawlikowski, *Jesus*, 37-38.

45. Ibid., 44; Raymond Brown, "Does the New Testament Call Jesus God?" *Theological Studies* 26 (1965): 538-51.

46. David Hartman, "Jews and Christians in the World Tomorrow," *Immanuel* 6 (1976): 79; Gerald Anderson, "Response to Pietro Rossano,"

in Gerald H. Anderson and Thomas Stransky, eds., *Christ's Lordship and Religious Pluralism* (Maryknoll, NY: Orbis Books, 1981), 118-19; Raymond Brown, *The Community of the Beloved Disciple* (New York: Paulist Press, 1979).

47. Pawlikowski, *Jesus*, 85.

48. Johannes Metz, *The Emergent Church: The Future of Christianity in a Post-Bourgeois World* (New York: Crossroad, 1981); Johannes Baptist Metz, "Kirche nach Auschwitz," in Marcel Markus et al., eds., *Israel und Kirche Heute: Beiträge zum Christlich-jüdischen Dialog* (Freiburg: Herder, 1991), 110-22; Johannes Metz, "Facing the Jews: Christian Theology after Auschwitz," in Fiorenza and Tracy, *The Holocaust as Interruption*, 26.

49. Pawlikowski, *Jesus*, 38-39.

50. Monika Hellwig, "Proposal Towards a Theology of Israel as a Religious Community Contemporary with the Christian," Ph.D dissertation, Catholic University of America, 1968, 175ff., 181, 190-94; Monika Hellwig, "Christian Theology and the Covenant of Israel," *Journal of Ecumenical Studies* 7 (1970): 39, 44-51; Monika Hellwig, "Why We Still Can't Talk," in Robert Heyer, ed., *Jewish/Christian Relations* (New York: Paulist Press, 1975), 30ff.; Roland de Corneille, *Christians and Jews: The Tragic Past and the Hopeful Future* (Toronto: Longmans, 1966), 72ff.

51. Pawlikowski, *Jesus*, 30-31.

52. Paul van Buren, *The Burden of Freedom: Americans and the God of Israel* (New York: Seabury Press, 1976); van Buren, *Discerning the Way*; van Buren, *A Christian Theology*; van Buren, *Christ in Context*; Paul van Buren, "The Context of Jesus Christ: Israel," *Religion and Intellectual Life* 3 (1986): 31-50; Peter von der Osten-Sacken, *Grundzüge Einer Theologie im Christlich-Jüdischen Gesprach* (München: Kaiser, 1982).

53. "Important Declarations of John Paul II," *SIDIC* 15 (1982): 27; "Address to Rome's Chief Synagogue," *Origins* 15 (1986): 729, 731-33; "The 20th Anniversary of *Nostra Aetate*," *Origins* 15 (1985): 411; Fisher, "The Evolution of a Tradition": 42-43.

54. Eckardt, *Elder and Younger Brothers*, 159; A. Roy Eckardt, "Toward an Authentic Jewish-Christian Relationship," *Journal of Church and State* 13 (1971): 277; A. Roy Eckardt, "End to the Christian-Jewish Dialogue," *Christian Century* 83 (1966): 393-95.

55. Paul van Buren, "The Context of Jesus Christ: Israel," *Religion and Intellectual Life* 3 (1986), 50; Eckardt, *Elder and Younger Brothers*.

56. Eckardt, *Jews and Christians*; Eckardt, *Reclaiming the Jesus of History*; Pawlikowski, *Jesus*, 80-81.

57. A. Roy Eckardt, "The Resurrection and the Holocaust," paper presented at the Israel Study Group, New York, 4 March 1978; Pawlikowski, *Jesus*.

58. Eckardt, *Jews and Christians*, 145; Pinchas Lapide, *The Resurrection of Jesus: A Jewish Perspective* (Minneapolis: Augsburg Pub. House, 1983); Maccoby, *The Mythmaker*; Stuart Rosenberg, *The Christian Problem. A Jewish View* (Canada: Deneau, 1986).

59. Cornelius Rijk, "The Holy Year and the Reconciliation between Christians and Jews," *SIDIC* 7 (1974): 21-23; Cornelius Rijk, "Some Observations on a Christian Theology of Judaism," *SIDIC* 5 (1972): 3-17.

60. For examples of studies on Christian catecheses, see Claire Huchet Bishop, *How Catholics Look at Jews: Inquiries into Italian, Spanish, and French Teaching Materials* (New York: Paulist Press, 1974); Bruce Long, *Judaism and the Christian Seminary Curriculum* (Chicago: Loyola University Press, 1966); Bernhard Olson, *Faith and Prejudice: Intergroup Problems in Protestant Curricula* (New Haven: Yale University Press, 1963); John Pawlikowski, "Christian-Jewish Relations and Catholic Teaching Materials," *Catholic Library World* 45 (1973): 227-32; the many works of Eugene Fisher, executive secretary of the Secretariat for Catholic-Jewish Relations of the National Conference of Catholic Bishops since 1977, particularly, Fisher, "A New Maturity in Christian-Jewish Dialogue: An Annotated Bibliography, 1975-1978," *Shofar* 3 (1) (1985) 5-43. For a recent analysis of Judaism in Catholic religion textbooks, see Philip Cunningham, "A Content Analysis of the Presentation of Jews and Judaism in Current Roman Catholic Religion Textbooks," Ph.D. dissertation, Boston College, 1991.

61. John B. Cobb, *Christ in a Pluralistic Age* (Philadelphia: Westminster Press, 1975), 58ff.

62. Karl Rahner, "Current Problems in Christology," in Karl Rahner, ed. *Theological Investigations* (Baltimore: Helicon Press, 1961), 1: 149-54; Karl Rahner, "Theology of the Incarnation," in Karl Rahner, ed., *Theological Investigations* (London: DLT, 1966), 4: 105-20; McGarry, *Christology after Auschwitz*, 102; John B. Cobb, *Christ in a Pluralistic Age* (Philadelphia: Westminster Press, 1975), 31-94; David Tracy, *Blessed Rage for Order: The New Pluralism in Theology* (New York: Seabury Press, 1975), 204-6, 217, 225ff. For a Christology that opens up new ways to empowerment, see Roger Haight, SJ, "The Case for Spirit Christology," *Theological Studies* 53 (1992): 286.

63. Pawlikowski, *Jesus*, 84-85. For a discussion of this "theocentric model: many ways to the center," see Eckardt, *Reclaiming the Jesus of History*, 165.

64. Pawlikowski, *Jesus*, 86-89.
65. Hans Küng, "Christianity and Judaism," in Charlesworth, *Jesus' Jewishness*, 265; John Pawlikowski, "The Challenge of the Holocaust for Christian Theology," in Roger Gottlieb, ed., *Thinking the Unthinkable: Meanings of the Holocaust* (New York: Paulist Press, 1990), 240-70.

6

Jewish Faith After the Holocaust: The God-of-History

For Jews and Christians to engage in dialogue on common values, understanding some of the main issues that the Holocaust has raised for the Jewish people would seem essential. While Christians have placed their tradition under a microscope, Jewish scholars have also been reflecting on the deepest meaning of this tragedy, which questions the very nature of Israel's historical experience with God. "As a Jew," Elie Wiesel has written, "you will sooner or later be confronted with the enigma of God's action in history."[1] As we have seen, Christian antisemitism was not the sufficient condition for the Holocaust, but as a religious reinforcer it played a necessary role in marginalizing Jews socially and psychologically. Even if only nominally religious, Christians committed the crime and were reinforced by a historically developed pattern of belief. But Jewish scholars have approached the Holocaust with a different set of questions.

For some post-Auschwitz Jews, God, not genocide, has become inconceivable. How could a loving and just God break his covenant with his people? Surely, as the argument goes, two parties could not possibly agree freely to a covenant that resulted in such massive annihilation. God's benevolence and in some cases even existence have been questioned by commentators. In part, the Holocaust makes both Jewish and Christian affirmations of God's role and presence more difficult and problematic than they were before the event. If God's place in the cosmos has been challenged, so has that of humanity. After 1945,[2] previous Jewish religious experiences have been reexamined in light of the faith responses to the Shoah. The Nazi Holocaust and the reemergence of the Republic of Israel have together radically transformed Jewish responses to the God-of-history and to the meaning of the community of Israel. Is the traditional Jewish reaction to tragedy and evil still a viable option? Is the "faith" of past generations to be reexamined and judged anew?

Former "authentic" postures[3] for the "man of faith," who had to interpret disaster, seemed for some scholars no longer valid because they seemed to be insensitive to the real world, inauthentic, and historically naive. Israel's relationship with God has been dissected by Jewish scholars just as the essential meaning of the Christian message has had to be reappropriated by Christians. The Jewish scholars who have reacted directly to the Shoah's impact seem to feel that to live as if unaffected by the death camps or by the revolutionary impact of the creation of the Republic of Israel would ignore the hermeneutic of history with its bloody events that have related God and humanity. Historically for the Jewish people, God has been identified in and through the encounter with creation. The question of what it means to be a Jew today has mandated a focus on the dimensions of the Jewish post-Holocaust identity: What does it mean to be a Jew after Auschwitz? The Shoah has become a universal datum relevant to and crucial for virtually all Jewish reflection on the meaning and nature of the covenantal relation between God and humanity.

As a result, Holocaust issues[4] have assumed an unavoidable prominence because the event has demanded a radical reexamination of the three historical components of traditional Judaism: God, Torah, and the people of Israel. A horizon of potential responses can be listed because Jewish scholars have offered different perspectives as a result of their reflections. Katz has summarized the array as follows.

1.   Reminiscent of other tragedies, the Holocaust has illustrated the difficulty of constructing an embraceable theodicy.
2.   The classical Jewish theological doctrine of punishment for sins may help explain the Holocaust only if Auschwitz can be perceived as the retribution for Israel's sins. But what sins?
3.   In response to this conundrum, the Holocaust has been perceived as an act of vicarious atonement for others' sins.
4.   The Holocaust has also been categorized as a sacrifice similar to that of Isaac, which was designed as a test of faith.
5.   The Holocaust may mark a temporary "eclipse of God" in history, when for whatever reasons, he turned away his face.
6.   The Holocaust has for some affirmed that the traditional God is dead because presumably a God who cared would have prevented Auschwitz.
7.   The Shoah may be an example of human evil and the real price for human freedom when it ignores God's perfection.
8.   Some have seen the Holocaust as an instance of modern revelation that has commanded that Jews affirm survival.
9.   The Holocaust may be an inscrutable mystery that demands silent faith.

Some theologians have combined elements of the above in an attempt to organize an interpretation that includes as many dimensions as possible, because "truth" is seen as complex. From this ongoing debate and dialogue among Jewish thinkers, Richard Rubenstein, Emil Fackenheim, Ignaz Maybaum, and Eliezer Berkovits seem to be particularly important for our analysis. Each has his own unique perspective, characteristic arguments, and aims. Each has designed an original and provocative configuration of the "explanations" for the Holocaust, which have been suggested above. Each fashions his own reflective exegesis based on the radical facticity that is the Shoah.

Richard Rubenstein

Perhaps the most controversial thinker who has tried to come to grips with the Shoah has been Richard Rubenstein, who has formulated a Jewish "Death of God" theology. He hoped to address very directly the reality of evil in the death camps. His initial commentary was a stark confrontation that launched the conversation that eventually ameliorated his initial views. Ultimately, Rubenstein's comments may be most valuable for the questions that have to be answered. His comments illustrate the Jewish struggle to comprehend the meaning of this seminal experience. Forced by the singular and gruesome horror of Auschwitz, he has questioned the foundations of Judaism and has insisted that the viability of Jewish theology can now only be measured by the way the Shoah is handled. No Jewish theologian has educed more radical conclusions to a reflection on the theodicy problematic. Hitler's extermination policy has raised the ultimate theological question for Rubenstein. Since God has historically dialogued and interacted with Israel, his chosen people, what responsibility does God have for Auschwitz? Did God use the Nazis? If not, how could this horror unfold in God's presence? Reflecting phenomenologically on the Shoah, Rubenstein initially rejected God's presence at Auschwitz so that Hitler could not be seen as God's agent.[5] In his 1966 text, Rubenstein presented his radical solution, which has been discussed for twenty-five years. In light of the two and a half decades of conversation, at times rancorous, Rubenstein has modified his position by synthesizing other viewpoints into it. His original position, however, indicates the horror with which the Holocaust was viewed, because it impacted so massively on the Jewish people's relation to God.

The only honest response to the Shoah, Rubenstein felt, was to reject God acting in history. Such a position could imply the meaninglessness of a human existence, in which life ceased being planned or purposeful. Such murderous barbarity, which erupted in an apparently indifferent universe, could not possibly reflect God's concern. Rejecting past historical and religious illusions, Rubenstein asked that we now recognize that human life as such would have no essential value because no transcendental purpose seemed to be in control of the human condition. To hypothesize that Auschwitz was some type of revenge that meant that Israel's suffering was rooted in sins would blaspheme against both God and man. What sin of Israel, Rubenstein asked, could have been so monumental to call forth this retribution? Religious "rationalizations" explaining Auschwitz paled in light of such vast destruction. Rubenstein concluded by repudiating the traditional Jewish religious perspective when he insisted that there is no God or continuing covenant because the Holocaust cannot be interpreted through the faith-experiences of the Jewish people.[6]

From Rubenstein's perspective, humanity had to reject transcendental beliefs and look at its actual concrete situation. Inspired by twentieth-century existentialists, Rubenstein tried to deal with historical and religious nihilism. Humanity, he suggested, seems to be responsible to craft its own value, given that history seemed meaningless. Men and women were now being asked to create meaning. Faced with the apparent lack of religious purpose, Rubenstein insisted that humankind could only authentically act as if existence had a purpose. Hence, any viable telos demanded an exclusive connection to the human condition, which in a post-Auschwitz era seemed to be the only legitimate good remaining. Life no longer could be seen as reflecting God's will. In this new world, only humans could create value and the meaning of life. The thesis is not new except in the Jewish theological context that has traditionally been embedded in the interaction between God and human persons.[7]

Rubenstein's "death of God" theology certainly would have serious implications for the people, Israel. Some critics of Rubenstein suggested that denying God's covenantal relationship with Israel could well end Israel as it has historically existed. But Rubenstein has also unveiled a new plan for reflection by arguing that the "death of God" forced the existence of Israel as a community to assume even greater importance for Jews in the twentieth century. This "death of God" model, analogous to Nietzsche's approach, should not be understood as an actual event that has happened to God. Rubenstein made use of Jewish religious language to focus on secular humanity and culture. He hoped to direct attention to ourselves as keepers of the world of nature. Since God in this model no longer seemed to provide ultimate meaning, humans would need one another to give purpose to life. Because human existence would be without religious hope, and so would lack a transcendental perspective, the Jewish socioreligious community would consequently become vital. Classical Judaism would be "demythologized" by expunging all divine, normative claims that have given it a unique status. Paradoxically, the Jewish community would now assume greater status. "God is dead" would necessitate that the social community now define the meaning of Jewish existence. Conscious of our human condition, Jews would now need the "community" because any struggle for meaning and value would be centered in the temporal arena, devoid of God's presence.

Like others, Jews still would find themselves rooted in the past and present in this search for authenticity. As persons in the twentieth century, Jews have ultimately best expressed their aspirations by surviving personally and as a people during the Second World War.[8]

In his early work, Rubenstein critically reexamined classical Jewish values by testing their adaptability to the post-Holocaust era. By using psychoanalytic and existential categories, he reinterpreted the meaning of classical Judaism and advocated its retention, although he stripped such traditional forms of ritual as the bar mitzvah of their religious justification. Religious rituals now seem only to be useful as social and psychological supports.[9] Rubenstein's quest has been to delineate value-productive activity that can exist without God.

Coupled to this phenomenological and existential dimension in Rubenstein's work is a mystical paganism that mandates that the Jewish people shed all relationships with the God-of-history as they begin relying on the earlier cosmic rhythms of natural existence. Eschatological redemption, therefore, would cease to be the conquest of nature and become the sublimation of history by nature as men and women return to their primal origins. Rubenstein sees the rebuilding of Israel as reinforcing this return to nature. The Jewish people have been separated by historical necessity from these primal experiences for almost two thousand years. In this context, Rubenstein has suggested that the Jews can now finally escape from historical oppressions into the vitality of the self-liberation that can be introduced through a return to nature, wherein the Jewish people can connect with values that reflect the human condition. Rubenstein initially stressed that God was manifested through nature, which was probed by mystical religion. This mystical strain became increasingly dominant in his subsequent works as he began to realize the implications of the fact that most Jews were not in the Republic of Israel. The political goal of Jewish history, therefore, had not been and probably could not be reached. Rubenstein himself repudiated the biblical, activist version of the God-of-history because he realized that most religious Jews could not follow this path. The biblical vision would virtually demand that Auschwitz be seen as divine punishment.[10]

Rubenstein's approach tried to deal with the past and to suggest a viable future. He hoped to make possible Jewish renewal and spiritual reintegration by eradicating those elements that had added to the incendiary antisemitic mix culminating in the Holocaust. Antisemitism, he asserted, was birthed in the mythic structures at the very heart of Jewish and Christian theology. The Jewish claim of being a chosen people yielded disaster because it helped create the Christian myth of "chosenness." Early Christian commentators frequently viewed their church as the successor faith. Paradoxically, therefore, Israel managed to provide "both the incarnate deity and his murderers." To end historical antisemitism, Rubenstein has felt that the Jew has to renounce the self-image of a chosen people. This would be the initial step to normalizing relations with Christians. Such a renunciation could be made possible by casting aside the Jewish tradition of historical interaction with God and by returning to existential nature as the source of primal value. Christianity would have to demythologize its own portrayal of the Jewish people. Rubenstein has urged that the traditional theology that portrays Jesus as the promised one, the messiah who emerged from historical Israel, be expunged. Such a renunciation of supersessionism would go a long way toward precluding future disasters. [11]

An integral part of Judaism and Christianity in Rubenstein's opinion is the natural urge, at least according to psychoanalysis, toward vicarious atonement, which seems to demand a sacrificial victim. Freud has suggested that we always have a deep wish to kill God and be freed from the restraints of morality and virtue. Thus, the nature of the Crucifixion would allow Christians to project their own guilty desires onto the Jew, who has stood accused of killing God. Both Jesus and the Jews have seemingly ended in becoming sacrificial victims. [12] For Rubenstein, Auschwitz seems to signify that there is no meaning to history. The Final Solution would become a random, arbitrary series of events, unrelated to a transcendental order. In Rubenstein's words:

> When I say we live in the time of the death of God, I mean that the thread uniting God and man, heaven and earth, has been broken. We stand in a cold, silent, unfeeling cosmos, unaided by any purposeful powers beyond our own resources. After Auschwitz what else can a Jew say about God? ... I see no other way than the death of God position of expressing the void that confronts man where once God stood. [13]

Theologians through the centuries have exercised themselves in examining the "problem of evil" to respond to the popular assertion that physical evil is a punishment for sin or that suffering somehow proves love. In Rubenstein's mind, all of these theodicies have lost their meaning in the age of Auschwitz. Along with most, he cannot see the Shoah as a punishment for sin because it is difficult to see what kind of sin could be committed that could justify such punishment. How could a God of love wreak such misery on millions of people after thousands of years of loyal service? Given such brutality in World War II, Rubenstein has jettisoned the God of the covenant as the way to understand the God-human relationship. [14] For many Jews, however, this is more than a convenient myth, and critics have not been slow in responding.

Rubenstein may have focused too narrowly on the covenant, and he has ignored the pre- and post-Holocaust Jewish reality that can support distinct horizons. Some of his critics feel that the Holocaust cannot be isolated from the normal flow of Jewish tradition and ignored in trying to understand the meaning of historical Jewish existence. [15] The Republic of Israel, for example, has been seen as a seminal development for religious Judaism, although clearly such a political success could not really compensate for the horrors wreaked by the Shoah. Why did Rubenstein, moreover, need Auschwitz to deny the existence of God, given that inexplicable evils have always been part of the human story? Have the seeds of negation potentially always been there? And, if so, where? Rubenstein's readers are almost led to ask whether the historical Jewish faith has ever made religious sense. It would be difficult to sustain this state of dissonance. Since the Jewish faith for most Jews is legitimate, perhaps mere historical distance can put the faith and the Holocaust into perspective. For Rubenstein to develop more convincingly the "death of God" approach, the Holocaust would have to be seen as a unique instance of suffering, and past evils would simultaneously have to be obscured. The Holocaust, therefore, would end up as so unique that it would demand a reconsideration of all preceding Jewish history. Such a demand has been considered unrealistic.

Rubenstein's view and such "faith responses" as those of Emil Fackenheim, for example, depend on a shared affirmation that the Holocaust is unique and determinative, and this can be a problem for those who do not want to lose the universal dimension. For Rubenstein, the Holocaust would have to be perceived as uniquely, rather than just monstrously, evil in order to call God's relationship to humanity into question. Rubenstein has not satisfactorily proven that Auschwitz was unique, even though this would be a sine qua non for his entire theological enterprise. For the Holocaust to be uniquely monstrous, Israel as chosen and as a covenant partner would once again have to be placed at the forefront of reflection. Thus, the God-of-history would again become a focus of attention.[16] Rubenstein's rejection of the God-of-history would effectively strip historical Judaism of its role in history and would render meaningless the transformative significance of the Hebrew Bible. One could make a case that although adherence to the God-of-history has opened Israel to great suffering, faith has also given the Jewish people strength to endure physical and moral oppression.

Initially, Rubenstein supported pagan naturalism and urged Jews to reenter the cosmic rhythms of nature given that they should reappropriate normative ethical categories from naturalistic rather than historical experiences. Eschatologically, then, salvation would no longer be the conquest of nature by history but rather the reverse. Jews were urged to start anew to rediscover the sanctity of natural life and not consider this an unfortunate retrogression into a primitive past. In Rubenstein's naturalistic interpretation, contingent events would cease having a transcendental significance. The return to the soil of Zion would be a harbinger of this movement back to nature. Such a return would lead from the negativity of the historically grounded faith into freedom because Jews could now develop "real" relationships rooted in their natural community.[17] How does such a transformation begin and continue? Rubenstein has offered virtually no concrete program that would build on nature rather than on the historically covenantal community.

Rubenstein, the "deconstructionist," has rejected the biblical and historical God who has had a concrete relationship to his chosen people. This is an extraordinarily significant step for a Jewish theologian because it automatically meant calling into question historical Jewish identity. The elimination of historical Judaism's theological validation did not automatically eliminate for Rubenstein the psychological or sociological functions that religion can fulfill.

But, of course, presumably any religion could fulfill those functions. Why maintain Judaism? In response to critics, Rubenstein, especially since 1976, has agreed that expunging the historical faith could reinforce the assimilation of the Jewish people into the dominant cultures in which they are now living. Classical Judaism, therefore, may still be necessary for the ongoing and unique continuance of the Jewish people, even if "natural paganism" could be included as a response.

For Rubenstein, the Holocaust has proven the existential horrors of being permanent strangers in a modern society that lacks any universal sense of obligation that can be directed toward the survival of Judaism. Only those who can accept being marginalized in the Christian world would be likely to have the courage to remain in the classical Jewish tradition. To support this marginality of Jews in a Christian society, Rubenstein moved beyond his early position of the death of the God-of-history to a God who is viewed as the ground of existence and who can be comprehended in the Jewish mystical tradition. He has come to grips with the fact that to remain Jewish is to be an endangered stranger in dominantly Christian society, and to become an assimilated insider means to surrender the Jewish heritage and identity.[18] Mysticism rather than reliance on a historical covenant seems to him to offer a way to community integrity that does not rely on the God-of-history. Rubenstein has posed the issues raised by the Holocaust and has questioned the meaning of the God-human relationship. His initial approach has tried to avoid the marginalization possibility by urging Jewish men and women to surrender the meaning of their historical experiences and immerse themselves into the naturalistic community, where they would no longer be "the chosen people." This may not be a realistic possibility even if desirable. Through intermarriage and the adaptation to dominant societies, moreover, many Jews are indicating that their faith is not worth social or physical martyrdom. In his recent works, Rubenstein seems to maintain that, like others, the Jews have used their religion to help cope with their environments. For him, the existence of the Jewish people does not have any divinely bestowed significance. Rubenstein's final point is that the Holocaust has revealed the full dangers of being a "stranger" in the modern world. Rubenstein has tested the extreme limits of what it means to be Jewish in a post-

Holocaust world and has directed us to reexamine the human condition with an intent to re-create normative values that can deal with marginalization.

Emil Fackenheim

Having experienced Nazi rule himself, Fackenheim has focused on the overwhelming impact of the camps on the survivors to help him elicit the meaning of Shoah for contemporary Jews. Especially in his book *God's Presence in History* (1970), he has sought to avoid the absolute acceptance of the Shoah as God's will as well as to skirt the conviction of such commentators as the early Rubenstein, who seem to rely on the existential absurdity of history.[19] Fackenheim has insisted that neither the blasphemy of Hitler's victims nor the dissolution of the God of the victims can be permitted. The existential absurdity of history cannot be accepted. Somehow both the victims and God have to be united in a symbiosis after Auschwitz because neither can be devalued without distorting truth.

Most Jewish theologians have sought to retain and reinforce the continued union between God and Israel. As the exception, Rubenstein has responded to the Holocaust with a Jewish communal existence without the God of Judaism. This approach can be considered vacuous and unsatisfying to those who are loyal to a traditional covenantal Judaism. In Fackenheim's opinion, no theodicy can be formulated that would vindicate God's goodness in the midst of such evil. Auschwitz simply cannot be accepted as the result of a rational cosmic pattern. The Holocaust, therefore, would be devoid of explanation and significance as part of God's plan. Similar to Rubenstein, Fackenheim has also rejected an Auschwitz that resulted from Jewish sins. Selecting such a perspective would label the slaughter as vicarious suffering or martyrdom. Anyway, what sin could yield such suffering? The Shoah cannot be comprehended or justified because it moves beyond the traditional explanations of "normal" evil. Such brutal public policy demands that the God-of-history provide answers.[20]

Despite traditional theodicy's inability to grapple with the existentially absurd universe of the camps, Fackenheim has retained faith in God's relationship with Israel, because he was present in the camps. We now must find God's activity in Auschwitz. Why God allowed the carnage may be incomprehensible, but he was there. From the death camps, as from Sinai, God counsels and commands Israel.[21] But what has been the command in the midst of this unfathomable brutality?

Reappropriating the meaning of Judaism has assisted Fackenheim in developing his views and moving slowly but perceptibly from a liberal to a neo-orthodox outlook on Judaism. The classical liberal position, one bolstered by the Enlightenment, affirming the perfectibility of humanity and the transference of God's word into a moral ideal, was considered after the Holocaust as an inauthentic representation of Judaism's essence. Fackenheim seems certain that such a liberal perspective could not yield a truly comprehensive analysis of the human predicament, which was being voiced after being assaulted by the barbarity so prevalent in this century.[22]

Judaism cannot now be viewed as some kind of moral idealism rooted in the Enlightenment because this would rob it of its distinctive characteristics and dissolve its integrity. For Fackenheim, Judaism is not a philosophy but rather a way of faith that engages the living God pulsating through history. Judaism is the dynamic response to God's word. This existential faith in the reality of God and in his entrance into history is incarnated in specific persons or groups who have been summoned by their creator. Similar to Buber, Fackenheim has insisted that God acts in history through his personal encounter with Israel. Revelation as the God-human dialogue can happen anywhere and anytime. Fackenheim hears a "commanding voice from Auschwitz," which seems to ask him again to affirm the covenant.[23]

Jewish history for Fackenheim is a trail of "awesome" encounters. The Exodus experience and the Sinai Torah have established the religious identity of the Jewish people and can be labeled as "root experiences" that have such a formative character that they virtually program successive generations of the Jewish people. These crucial "root experiences," which help interpret faith-experiences, provide accessibility to God in the present. Today's Jewish believer, therefore, can be "assured that the saving God of the past saves still."[24]

Since not all the past major events in Jewish history, of course, appear as "root experiences," Fackenheim has formulated a category that can be labeled "epoch-making events." Such episodes have confronted the Jewish people with serious challenges, but are not formative and do not create the essentials of the Jewish faith. These unprecedented events pose situations that test the viability of the root experiences. In Fackenheim's opinion, the Holocaust was such an epoch-making event. The Jewish people met the challenge, and their faith continued connecting Israel with God. The Jewish people have historically been tested in other times, even if not with such brutality.[25] Fackenheim avoids positing the Shoah as a "root" event. By not having to judge the value of God for Israel, he has skirted the problem posed by Rubenstein. Each trial of the Jews has eventually yielded new resiliency and new insights into God's relationship with the human community. Each has led the Jewish people to affirm the saving and commanding Lord who has been with them since the Red Sea and Sinai. Can the Holocaust too be assimilated as an epochal event so that it fits the traditional challenge-response pattern?

In Fackenheim's opinion, the Nazi Final Solution is an epochal event asking that we understand how God is present to his people. Fackenheim was convinced that the Jewish people were called to continue affirming the ongoing proximity of God-in-history, even in the camps. Auschwitz demanded that the Jewish people again affirm the commanding God of Sinai, who continued living within the Holocaust. This almost unprecedented and astounding response to the severe crisis of faith was the essence of Fackenheim's response to Auschwitz. God was not to be rejected, because the Jewish people had experienced him as a living presence even in the gas chambers. In a daring move, Fackenheim has positively affirmed those disasters that have driven others to atheism or silence.[26]

Additionally, Fackenheim postulated a new command of God: "Jews are forbidden to hand Hitler posthumous victories."[27] Survival, he insists, has become obligatory and demands that the Jewish people continue their living relationship to God, whose injunction has forbidden despair of redemption or any cynical withdrawal from the world because either would abdicate responsibility for the world. To reject responsibility would ultimately mean transferring humankind to the control of such evils as Nazism, which sought to eradicate totally Judaism. What happened to the Jewish people should, moreover, warn us of the potential fate of humankind as a whole. To desert the God of Israel because of the Nazis would essentially be supporting Hitler's work of obliterating the Jewish historical role. The Jewish will for survival has been given a transcendental significance by Fackenheim because Hitler has now made Judaism a paradoxical necessity that performs a universal good for humankind. Saying "no" to Hitler serves to affirm the God of Sinai. [28]

The biblical God both commands and delivers his people, even though millions may be murdered. Fackenheim has focused on this commanding presence moving through Auschwitz. But where is the God of Exodus? To speak of a post-Auschwitz salvific God may be problematic because such a God should have extended in a more forthright fashion his saving kindness to those who were suffering. But who can fathom, one might respond, the mind of God? Who can know how many private "revelations" there were in the camps? Evidence from the survivors suggests that God was still alive for the prisoners and in the ghettos. The continued existence of the people of Israel has inspired Fackenheim to speak of redemptive hope. The Republic of Israel, for example, currently affirms the goodness of this God still present in history. Contemporary Jews can still reappropriate the root experience of God's presence to them in order to interpret epochal events. [29] The Shoah, according to Fackenheim, has not undermined the Jewish faith-experience but has led to a deepened understanding of the human condition and of God-in-history. Moreover, the Jewish experience can serve to remind us of the responsibility that humans have to make God present in the world and to re-form our communities.

Ignaz Maybaum

Ignaz Maybaum has denied the uniqueness of the Shoah and stressed its continuity with past oppression. He has "explained" the tragedy by suggesting that the victims, even though unknowingly, in some fashion accepted the concept of vicarious atonement. One problem with such an explanation becomes immediately clear. How can one unknowingly accept a situation of vicarious atonement? Maybaum has suggested that this type of reflection occurs after the act, although it is almost inconceivable that thousands of Jews somehow even implicitly had this in their minds as they tried to survive. Such theodicy themes can find a resonance in both Judaism and Christianity, as we can see in the "Suffering Servant" theme in Isaiah and in the account of the Passion of Jesus. In part, this may be a psychological tactic for those who reflect on suffering as they try to make sense out of acts which seem to have no rationale. Maybaum's adherence to this type of theodicy helps convey meaning for these many deaths.[30] Maybaum has anchored his theology in the dual acknowledgment of the historical God and of the uniqueness of the covenantal Israel that has witnessed God's purposeful existence in history. Because of being chosen, according to Maybaum, the Jew was unfortunately also singled out by Hitler for extermination. The Holocaust, therefore, conforms to God's will and reveals the blueprint for God's caring concern.[31]

What is the essential meaning of this divine pattern wherein even the Shoah has a role? What part does Israel play? For Maybaum the drama is designed to transform gentile nations into obedient servants of God's will. The Shoah seems also intended to incite the Jewish people to nurture their relationship with God. Israel's history, therefore, has been symbiotically related to the historical paths of the other nations. To accomplish God's transcendental task, Israel is to act in concert with other peoples as all engage in shaping the destiny designed by God, who has used the Holocaust as a means for "creative destruction" to highlight the communitarian emphasis that seems so vital for human survival. The Shoah can be observed as an event that has made restoration of the "old world" impossible by necessitating the creation of a new paradigm to support the existence of humankind.[32] Maybaum has no fundamental theological problem with God's allowing millions of innocents to suffer obscene deaths. But some might ask whether the introduction of this new paradigm is worth such a price. Maybaum hopes to ensure the continuing relevance of the God-of-revelation and to reinforce faith in the covenant as the means to save the human community.

Unlike Maybaum, many Jewish religious thinkers prefer to affirm the God-of-history by removing this God from Auschwitz and simply asserting that God's ways are "mysterious." Auschwitz was permitted to happen for unfathomable reasons. These theologians hope to avoid the very unpleasant dilemmas that arise when a beneficent God is juxtaposed with human horrors. To limit the biblical view of God could lead believers to ask why they should even participate in the covenant at the mercy of a God who permitted the Holocaust. To say that God is responsible for Auschwitz could lead the faithful to ask whether such a God can even demand loyalty.[33] God would seem to be perpetrating this heinous crime.

Given such a dilemma, it would be convenient, but may not be possible, to gloss over any connection between God and the Holocaust. Maybaum has managed to acknowledge positively the biblical God in light of the Holocaust by insisting that it is nearly impossible to affirm that the God of the covenant does act in history unless God's presence at Auschwitz can be recognized. Some scholars would suggest that following this line of development would mean favoring God's omnipotence at the expense of his divine love and mercy. Maybaum has hoped to defuse this conundrum by asserting that Auschwitz does not necessarily imply the absence of God's love and mercy toward the Jewish people, in light of the survival of the Jews as a people and the existence of the Republic of Israel as a political unit. Not surprisingly, Maybaum's position has been criticized. The Holocaust was horrific, but it did not annihilate the Jewish people, and this may be, according to some, a cause for rejoicing. The Third Reich was not an insignificant development, and the world as it exists today may not reflect God's "everlasting kindness." Maybaum has tried to find space for reflecting on the historical God of the covenant in a world that allows sanctioned murder. Some would make the point that the Final Solution is the disastrous consequence of the modernization of Europe's economy and society and so has implications for our whole culture as well as our relationship to God.[34] Maybaum has suggested that God may be signaling the importance of uniting all humanity to achieve a kind of tectonic shift in our culture, which would include expunging antisemitism.

Eliezer Berkovits

Eliezer Berkovits has responded to the Shoah by recalling the history of Christian antisemitism. After probing the classical antisemitic foundation of our culture, Berkovits explored selected biblical and rabbinic responses to suffering to test whether the Jewish tradition was strong enough to grapple with the problems posed in

Auschwitz. Through exploring martyrdom in the Jewish tradition, Berkovits has tried to uncover what can be offered to a contemporary reflection on the death camps. Martyrdom traditionally has signified the ultimate commitment of trust in God and has been faith's response to mystery. Berkovits seems to feel, however, that such acts may not afford unrefracted insights into the ultimate post-Holocaust issues. The question Berkovits asked went to the heart of the problem: If Nazi barbarism were to be equated with the absence of God, what could be said about the moral grandeur of the victims?[35] Can there be moral, even if not theological, statements without God?

Berkovits has maintained that there has to be a "faith after the Holocaust." An adequate Jewish understanding of the God-in-history has to be displayed so that our contemporary religious, social, and political environment can be morally evaluated. Only within a faith milieu can a dialogue about the theological relevance of the Holocaust be nourished. Jewish attempts to deal with Auschwitz, not nurtured by their historical faith-experience, Berkovits has argued, "suffer from one serious shortcoming: they deal with the Holocaust in isolation, as if there had been nothing else in Jewish history but this Holocaust."[36] Developing a nuanced sense of Jewish historical experiences, Berkovits has suggested that historically Auschwitz has been unique with its magnitude of destruction, but it has not posed any unusual theodicy issue for faith. He has intentionally dissociated himself from those who see the Holocaust as unique from the perspective of theodicy. If uniqueness were to be rejected, then the Jewish people would have to make responses based on tradition coupled with the current environment. If Auschwitz could be viewed as partially the repetition of an ancient pattern of bias and partially the result of religious antisemitism and modernization phenomena, then the theological reaction to Auschwitz could be "normalized" as the ongoing human reflection on evil. The event may be monstrous, but its religious ramifications would be in line with past disasters. The number of people murdered would no longer have an ontological significance, and God's moral role in human history would not need to be so rigorously examined.[37] Theologians could uncover the message in the event.

Along with many of the major thinkers, Berkovits has rejected any notion that the death camps are God's response to Jewish sins. For

Berkovits, the Holocaust is an injustice inflicted by Gentiles on Jews and merely accepted by God. Berkovits has tried to create a space in God's scheme for Auschwitz, although he has emphasized repeatedly that such carnage has to be unequivocably labeled a moral outrage. To accomplish this seemingly impossible goal, he has reintroduced the biblical concept of "the hiding face of God," in which God for mysterious reasons completely unrelated to human sin may turn from humanity. This "hiding face" perspective has the ability to retain God's presence and simultaneously to affirm God's hiddenness. In both conditions, God's redemptive role perdures as he interacts with humanity.[38] But there is a positive dimension in Berkovits' reflection.

Berkovits has argued that this nuanced perspective on God's hidden face is requisite for man's own moral development. God's concealment opens the way to ethical action because God's absence requires that human freedom, foundational for moral behavior, be fully actualized. For humans to develop a functional moral horizon, God has to accept human decisions as binding, which could mean that God may have to bracket his own power in order to legitimate human action. To have morality requires freedom, which is always open to abuse. "Free will" is necessary for morality, but, conversely, it may also result in barbaric acts. Consonant with this view, God may not necessarily punish wickedness and may indeed even appear deaf to the pleas of the victims. Paradoxically, the fact that humanity can shape a moral response may be because God does not continually exercise justice. His love for humanity may lie beyond strict justice because suffering and evil may have to impact on his creatures to develop their full potential. Berkovits has responded to the theodicy question in such a way that faith in both humanity and God can persist despite Auschwitz.[39]

At times, according to Berkovits, God may absent himself so that humankind can exist freely. Simultaneously, God may also communicate to and be with humanity to preclude the victory of meaninglessness. His presence in history, therefore, may at times be "hidden." His real power may become visible in history only through the self-limitation that forces us to act. The longest historical witness to God's control over humanity's action has been the Jewish people. Through the Jewish faith-experience can be discerned God's hidden, but still active, presence in and concern with the course of history. In joy and suffering Israel's persistent life has proven that God exists even at times of concealment. In the view of Berkovits, then, Jewish existence has opposed idolatry and promised God's redemption. It is a prophetic statement directed at expunging the moral corruption that has protruded throughout human history.[40]

By drawing the issue so starkly, Berkovits has made us reflect on whether the Holocaust signifies the "death of God" or is part of the story of his ongoing mercy toward sinners. By locating Auschwitz in the context of historical Jewish experience, he has encouraged us to make a more nuanced analysis. The crematoriums cannot be handled if the Shoah experience is seen as unique in the God-Israel relationship. Jews today may be confused and see in Auschwitz the absence of God, but they remain the descendants of the Sinai and the Red Sea people who once stood intimately in God's presence. Post-Auschwitz Jewish survival in Israel, a revelation event for Berkovits, also proclaims to all that evil has not triumphed. Although Berkovits' theology does not address the question of why Nazism was allowed, it does at least provide an environment out of which answers can be unveiled concerning humanity's own relation to God, freedom, and evil. In Auschwitz and in Israel, God is in fact speaking to humanity in history. This rebirth of a political Israel has to be appreciated both historically and eschatologically. "The return is the counterpart in history to the resolution in faith that this world is to be established as the Kingdom of God." Israel as a state has a destiny to help vindicate God's presence and his continuing concern with the human race.[41] Particularly interesting in the reflections offered by Berkovits is the stress on human freedom and its moral implications. God's absence and human suffering seem to make us truly human. The Holocaust was a unique and meaningful experience for Jews in their relationship to God and simultaneously has universal implications for all humanity.

Humanity and God as the Architects of Society

Focusing philosophically and theologically on the Holocaust does not seem to create a universally satisfying analysis that would have both meaning and integrity for everyone concerned. As in most analyses, the theological "facts" are selected by the questions asked and scholarly methodology used. Heterogeneous premises and asymmetrical queries have yielded an array of conclusions. Rubenstein has used psychoanalytical, anthropological, and then finally mystical foci that have yielded an ongoing reconfiguration of responses. He seems to conclude that except for a remnant of the Jewish people, the transcendental, although not anthropological and psychological, value of religion is no longer needed. Fackenheim begins with existentialist supernaturalism so that God is revealed even at Auschwitz. Maybaum exudes a confidence, rooted in post-Enlightenment liberalism, that humanity can progress. God acts in the whole course of history, including the barbarous Holocaust, to guide humanity toward moral goals. Berkovits has utilized traditional metaphysical tools to sculpt his data so that he can, even if only partially, justify God's acts. These above selected perspectives into the profound questions raised by the Shoah suggest that a conceptually "neat" solution to this complex issue probably will never emerge. Auschwitz has posed troubling phenomenological and existential issues for morality, theology, and political science, which have to be dissected even though the unsatisfying results never seem to lead to any kind of comfortable closure.[42]

Jewish Holocaust theology, however, has gone straight to the heart of faith and morality concerns. To say that the collective trauma that the Jewish people have lived has been *a*, or often *the*, formative event in a long Jewish history seems for most impossible. Caution, of course, must be taken in viewing the Shoah as unique. Holocaust theologians have, therefore, generally tried to locate the Shoah on a horizon along with other events in biblical Judaism as they ask whether God has overall been faithful to the covenant. Their theological referents have helped highlight an aspect of the sordid modernity characterized by mass dislocation and death. Most commentators insist that the event cannot be classified as unique, except perhaps from a technical standpoint, without opening to question the entire covenantal experience with its periods of death and destruction.[43]

In the midst of the lives and faiths shattered by the Shoah, Jewish theologians have reappropriated their own tradition to help reconfigure a future for the Jewish people that can be based on their history as a community. To survive Auschwitz and to continue in a covenantal relationship, they have restated what it means to be Jewish. Several have reappropriated older traditions to maintain continuity even in the face of this unprecedented horror so that a renewed Israel with a future could be reestablished. For them, the experiences and memories of the Holocaust have to be accepted in order to empower the struggle for the continuity of the Jewish people. Some commentators suggest that the Jewish people have been commanded by God and the victims to continue. These theologians have directly faced the modernity crisis that threatened to destroy the Jewish people. Responding to the cultural and religious issues, they have tried to construct a framework to connect with their tradition those persecuted in this purportedly progressive and liberal century.

Rubenstein has tried to explicate a theological basis that would make sense in this era. He initially, therefore, suggested a "death of God" in order to force humanity back to its original roots. With God's death we would be left to our own resources. In his more recent writings, he has favored a mystically rooted approach to determine an acceptable Jewish role in the post-1945 world. No matter where he directs his concerns, Rubenstein seems to return to the importance of human activity in shaping the world. Irving Greenberg also sees Judaism as a force for active redemption that is confronted by the existential world typified by a lack of social justice. As a sociopolitical phenomenon, modernity has tended to denigrate human dignity. In his opinion, the Exodus from Egypt could be seen as a paradigm of human liberation that has served to validate the promised perfection of the world. Greenberg has also maintained that in an age of power in Israel, Jews must act more responsibly as models that serve to show how society can be re-formed. The Holocaust has given them a special responsibility in this arena. The covenant supported by historical memory has to couple power with value and goals. For both Rubenstein and Greenberg, the supposedly impervious moral and political barrier against brutality erected in Western civilization after centuries of struggle was breached by the Nazis, who bureaucratically exterminated millions. Imitating the Nazis, other governments might now be more likely to try and resolve political issues through genocide. The Jewish victims, Greenberg has insisted, are compelled to cry out for a political system that can help avoid any future coalescence of inhumane values and political force that could lead to another Shoah. For these scholars, the horror is that past atrocities can still be replicated unless humans are ready to accept their moral responsibility to shape society.[44] This strong emphasis on humanity acting as cocreator with God has also resonated with the views of non-Jewish thinkers, who are seeking to prevent future genocides.

Jewish theologians have also nurtured an expansion beyond the Holocaust to the arena where religious meaning and political power meet. In the view of Marc Ellis, for example, Holocaust theology has failed in one important respect because it has not adequately analyzed the contemporary use of power, which is now in Jewish hands in Israel, and so has not properly reflected on the potential moral cost of empowerment. Although it could pose radical religious and ethical questions, Jewish theology has tended to organize a neoconservative set of principles. Frequently uncriticized by those on the left, who are fearful of having their nationalism challenged, Holocaust theologians seem to feel most comfortable at the conservative end of the political spectrum. Most Jewish thinkers, he has asserted, have not started out as politically motivated, but have ended, it should come as no surprise, in supporting Israel for religious and political reasons. Ellis has challenged the political sensibilities of Holocaust theology. He has sought the exploration of the ethical dimension that he feels has to emerge in a time of Jewish empowerment. The object is that Jews who have been persecuted in the past should now avoid becoming oppressors. He has acknowledged that new theological perspectives can be useful to the Jewish community and can be critical of contemporary political results. The current political and religious consensus may make problematic any hope of progress toward a more elevated level of reflection unless the issues posed by empowerment can be accepted as real. The historical feelings of abandonment and isolation, which have worried Jewish communities for centuries, may be the initially significant political variables in Israel. Understandably, Jews may now feel that only power can save them as a community. Renewed Jewish theologians and politicians who see the dynamics that led to the Holocaust should be sensitive to non-Jewish communities so that the potentially ugly results of Jewish empowerment can be controlled. Ellis has pointed out that the great paradox may be that in empowerment, Jewish leaders may require an in-depth understanding of the traditional persecutor, Christianity. In this line of thought, Jews may find that they can only avoid the repetition of the past mistakes of Christians by understanding where and how Christians made their own mistakes.[45] Ellis has focused on a very important point by suggesting that both Christians and Jews can learn from one another the dangers of power as a potentially destructive force behind moral behavior.

Building on the perspectives provided by Holocaust theologians and sensitive to the fact that the Jewish people now have political power, Ellis and others have now begun seeking legitimate ethical and prophetic values in the empowered Republic of Israel. Ellis has forcefully urged that Jewish theologians seek to uncover the dangerous tendencies within the empowerment phenomenon and articulate again those values that are rooted in the most profound experiences of the Jewish people in their covenant with God.[46] Do the paths of empowerment today help free humanity or do they merely duplicate those paths on which the Jewish victims were forced to march in the Third Reich? Can Jews make a better world, one that avoids Christian mistakes?

From another perspective, Amos Funkenstein has suggested that even the focus on the religious or theological meanings of the Holocaust may be essentially "wrong." What the Shoah teaches about God or ethical principles may be insignificant in light of what it teaches us about human brutality and compassion. As a human event, the Holocaust has demonstrated those possibilities that only humans and their society could devise.[47] From the experiences of the immediate past humans are being asked to create political systems that can prevent future genocides and can provide a milieu that will ennoble the species. Elie Wiesel[48] has shown that science and scholarship without an ethical foundation can become diabolical instruments of inhumanity. Rubenstein has stressed that we shape our natural world. Fackenheim has maintained that we cannot abdicate responsibility for sharing with God the condition of the world. Maybaum has promoted the idea that Israel should act in concert with other peoples to form a common destiny. Finally, Berkovits has shown that morality requires freedom so that both God and his creatures have responsibility.

Jewish theological reflections on humanity, the God-of-history, humans as cocreators, and the true meaning of freedom can resonate among Christians involved with similar concerns. Rather than discussing supersessionism and the meaning of antisemitism in the Christian Scriptures, which are certainly important, theologians might be more advised now to focus on such issues as human dignity in the community, freedom, empowerment, and the message that God through humanity is trying to communicate. Concerns with such issues might well open new areas of congruence and inspire a less defensive Jewish-Christian dialogue.

How can theology be rethought, restated, and rewritten to take into account the real relationship that can exist between Christians and Jews, who are both now concerned with politics, society, and moral values? Such an intellectual movement would necessitate a new self-understanding of what it means to be a Christian because the Jewish experience can no longer be marginalized. Increasingly, it has also become obvious that such theology would have ethical as well as political ramifications and can no longer be ahistorical because the "event" must now govern theology as well. This realization has stimulated the development of a political theology that, as we will see in the next chapter, also reflects some of the broader concerns of those working in the social sciences. A broad spectrum of current Christian theologians has been stimulated to use the Holocaust as a tool with which to probe the theological, political, and psychological dimensions of the human condition. The similarity of Christian insights to the reflections of Jewish thinkers suggests that a generation of intellectuals is in the process of redefining the critical values that, if institutionalized, could help ensure that political brutalization may be less frequent in the future. Naturally, there is a chasm that divides the creation of a normative framework and its institutionalization. But if antisemitism has been able to wreak such destruction, and genocide has become almost a normal part of twentieth-century politics, then an attempt to create a normative order would seem to be a necessary first step in avoiding future sanctioned murder. Jewish and Christian theologians have taken a step in this direction. Having the most baggage to shed, Catholic theologians have made particularly exciting advances.

Notes

1. Elie Wiesel, *One Generation After* (New York: Random House, 1970), 215.
2. Katz, *Post-Holocaust Dialogues*, 141-42. For a comprehensive analysis of the issue of theodicy from a Jewish perspective, see David Birnbaum, *God and Evil: A Unified Theodicy/Theology/Philosophy* (Hoboken, NJ: KTAV Pub. House, 1989). Katz offers probably the most nuanced study of post-Holocaust Jewish theology.
3. Katz, *Post-Holocaust Dialogues*, 142.
4. Ibid., 143-44.
5. Rubenstein, *After Auschwitz: Radical Theology*, 46-58, 223. See also Richard Rubenstein, *After Auschwitz: History, Theology, and Contemporary Judaism*, 2nd rev. ed. (Baltimore: Johns Hopkins University Press, 1992), in which there are nine new chapters. Unlike the original, which provoked such a debate, *After Auschwitz: History* takes into account the searching dialogue of the last twenty-five years and is not written in a spirit of opposition and revolt but of synthesis and reconciliation.
6. Katz, *Post-Holocaust Dialogues*, 146.
7. Martin Buber, *Eclipse of God: Studies in the Relation Between Religion and Philosophy* (New York: Harper, 1953).
8. Rubenstein, *After Auschwitz: Radical Theology*, 68, 119. To understand the original meaning of demythologizing, see Rudolf Bultmann, *Jesus and Mythology* (New York: Scribner, 1958); Rubenstein, *After Auschwitz: History*, xii, xiii.
9. Rubenstein, *After Auschwitz: Radical Theology*, 223ff.; Richard Rubenstein, *The Religious Imagination: A Study in Psychoanalysis and Jewish Theology* (Indianapolis: Bobbs-Merrill, 1968).
10. Rubenstein, *After Auschwitz: Radical Theology*, 93-111, 135ff., 240.
11. Ibid., 9.
12. Ibid., 73-74. See Rene Girard, "Is There Antisemitism in the Gospels?," a paper presented at Boston College, 15 March 1993.
13. Rubenstein, *After Auschwitz: Radical Theology*, 49.
14. Katz, *Post-Holocaust Dialogues*, 175-77.
15. To deal with the Holocaust requires familiarity with Jewish history in general, according to Eliezer Berkovits in his *Faith after the Holocaust*. For a socioreligious history of the Jews, see Baron, *A Social and Religious History*.
16. A. Roy Eckardt, "Is the Holocaust Unique?" *Worldview* (1974): 31-35; Rubenstein, *After Auschwitz: Radical Theology*, 21.

17. Rubenstein, *After Auschwitz: Radical Theology*, 131-42, 227-43.
18. Ibid., 153-54; Richard Rubenstein, "Naming the Unnameable; Thinking the Unthinkable: A Review Essay of Arthur Cohen's *The Tremendum*," *Journal of Reform Judaism* 31 (1984): 43-54; Richard Rubenstein and John Roth, *Approaches to Auschwitz: The Holocaust and its Legacy* (Atlanta: John Knox Press, 1987), 316.
19. Katz, *Post-Holocaust Dialogues*, 150. For Emil Fackenheim's scathing attack of Rubenstein, see Fackenheim, *God's Presence*, 72.
20. Katz, *Post-Holocaust Dialogues*, 151.
21. Fackenheim, *God's Presence*, 31.
22. Emil Fackenheim, "These Twenty Years," in Emil Fackenheim, ed., *Quest for Past and Future: Essays in Jewish Theology* (Bloomington: Indiana University Press, 1968), 3-26.
23. Emil Fackenheim, ed., *Quest for Past and Future: Essays in Jewish Theology* (Bloomington: Indiana University Press, 1968), 5, 10; Steven Katz, ed., *Jewish Philosophers* (New York: Bloch Pub. Co., 1975); Emil Fackenheim, "Buber's Doctrine of Revelation," in M. Friedman and P. Schilpp, eds., *The Philosophy of Martin Buber* (LaSalle, IL: Open Court, 1967).
24. Fackenheim, *God's Presence*, 8-11.
25. Ibid., 16ff., 20, 25-31.
26. Katz, *Post-Holocaust Dialogues*, 154.
27. Fackenheim, *God's Presence*, 84; Emil Fackenheim, "Jewish Faith and the Holocaust," *Commentary* 47 (1967).
28. Fackenheim, *God's Presence*, 82-92; Katz, *Post-Holocaust Dialogues*, 154-55.
29. M. Meyer, "Judaism after Auschwitz," *Commentary* 53 (1972); Seymour Cain, "The Questions and Answers after Auschwitz," *Judaism* 20 (1971).
30. Ignaz Maybaum, *The Face of God after Auschwitz* (Amsterdam: Polak & Van Gennep, 1965), 35, 135; Samuel R. Driver and Adolf Neubauer, *The Fifty-Third Chapter of Isaiah, According to the Jewish Interpreters* (New York: KTAV Pub. House, 1969).
31. Maybaum, *The Face of God*, 25ff.
32. Ibid., 32-67; Rubenstein, *After Auschwitz: Radical Theology*, 93-112.
33. Rubenstein and Roth, *Approaches to Auschwitz*, 307.
34. Ibid., 307-8. For a study of the Vatican's pre-1993-94 positions with respect to the Republic of Israel, in which Catholic dogma has little significance for this political issue, see Andrej Kreutz, *Vatican Policy on the Palestinian-Israeli Conflict: The Struggle for the Holy Land* (New York: Greenwood Press, 1990). For a brief commentary on this issue, see Eugene Fisher, "The Vatican and the State of Israel," *First Things* 1991:

11-12. For studies of modernity and the Holocaust, see Horowitz, *Taking Lives*; Bauman, *Modernity and the Holocaust*.

35. Menasheh Unger, *Seyfer Kdayshim: Rabeyim oyf Kidesh-Hashem* (New York: Schulzinger, 1967), 36; Katz, *Post-Holocaust Dialogues*, 164-65.
36. Berkovits, *Faith after the Holocaust*, 88.
37. Ibid., 90. For a contradictory view, see Katz, *Post-Holocaust Dialogues*, 287-318.
38. Berkovits, *Faith after the Holocaust*, 89, 94ff.; cf. Psalm 44.
39. Berkovits, *Faith after the Holocaust*, 106.
40. Ibid., 109ff.
41. Ibid., 134ff., 144-69.
42. Katz, *Post-Holocaust Dialogues*, 168; Steven Katz, "Critical Reflections on Holocaust Theology," paper presented at the Holocaust Symposium, Indiana University, 1980.
43. Marc Ellis, *Toward a Jewish Theology of Liberation* (Maryknoll, NY: Orbis Books, 1987), 7-24; Rubenstein, *After Auschwitz: Radical Theology*; Richard Rubenstein, *The Cunning of History: Mass Death and the American Future* (New York: Harper & Row, 1975).
44. For an exploration of survival as the commanding voice of Auschwitz, see Fackenheim, *God's Presence*. For a cogent expression of Jewish theology articulating a future for the Jewish people, see Irving Greenberg, "Cloud of Smoke, Pillar of Fire: Judaism, Christianity and Modernity after the Holocaust," in Fleischner, *Auschwitz: Beginning of a New Era?*, 7-55; Rubenstein, *The Cunning of History*, 28; Greenberg, "History, Holocaust and Covenant": 1-12.
45. Ellis, *Toward a Jewish Theology*, 25-37, 49-58; Nathan Perlmutter and Ruth Ann Perlmutter, *The Real Anti-Semitism in America* (New York: Arbor House, 1982); Gustavo Gutiérrez, *A Theology of Liberation: History, Politics and Salvation* (Maryknoll, NY: Orbis Books, 1973).
46. Marc Ellis, "Holocaust Theology and Latin American Liberation Theology: Suffering and Solidarity," paper presented at the "Remembering for the Future Conference," theme 1, Oxford, July 1988, pp. 584-97.
47. Amos Funkenstein, "Theological Interpretations of the Holocaust: A Balance," in Furet, *Unanswered Questions*, 302-3.
48. Elie Wiesel, "Die Massenvernichtung als literarische Inspiration," in Kogon, *Gott nach Auschwitz*, 45.

7

Political Theology and Foundational Values

Focusing on the historical nexus of faith and society, earlier Catholic moral theologians have tended to concentrate on individual guilt and responsibility, and so the church's traditional view of moral culpability has not, until recently, been prepared to deal with the issue of collective or social responsibility. In this historically conditioned moral theology, the basic presumption generally has been that for a specific evil act the total number of responsible participants has to be relatively small because theoretically any act could only be perpetrated by a person or by a limited number of persons. Thus, the total responsibility could only be assigned to a few individuals. This approach to "social justice" was rooted in the controlling influence of private confession, which was concerned primarily with individual guilt. Traditionalists have feared that those suggesting a different perspective would "exonerate" those perpetrating evil in society by introducing a social meaning to sin and by accepting the presumption that evil and guilt can exist as components of the institutions that are embedded in the social order as such. Moral theologians, however,

have increasingly been engaged in formulating an agenda that has
progressed beyond such individual moral issues as those concerned
with sexuality and have begun to address, for example, nuclear
warfare and world poverty on the national and international scales.
The earlier individualistic moral tradition has slowly been transformed
into a concern with macromoral challenges that can have implications
for the political issues of our time.[1]

In recent years Catholic thinkers have more aggressively insisted
that the ahistorical and staid concept of nature has led to theologically
defective sociopolitical conclusions because virtually no space for the
societal significance of God's plan had been cleared. The problems
with the traditional approach can be seen as the church has tried to
address the issues of the modern world using viable moral principles.
In *Humanae Vitae*, for example, Pope Paul VI made reference to the
problematic involved in the "principles of a moral teaching on
marriage which relies solely on natural law illuminated and enriched
by divine revelation."[2] Paul VI tried to suggest, although not too
successfully as the results indicate, that a "natural" law anthropology
as the foundation for moral reasoning could not respond to the
historical world in which "man is made a new creature who can
respond in love and genuine freedom to the plan of his creator and
Savior."[3] For contemporary scholars, the historical continuity of
God's providence seems to make obsolete the older conceptual
distinction that was philosophically developed to handle the
complementarity of nature and supernature. Many elements of this
encyclical have been vigorously disputed, although the stress on
personalism was greeted with applause and for a number of scholars
even helped undermine the controversial position on birth control.[4] On
the positive side, therefore, the encyclical focuses on the human
person who has developed within the community and who has been
initiated by God.

An evolving dissatisfaction with the traditional theological concept
of "nature" has helped serve to focus moral theory on the "human
person" or "human dignity" rather than simply on human nature. The
fathers at the Second Vatican Council, for example, fully realized that
traditional ethical principles have rested on the "law of nature," and
that there might be some problems with this. Post-Vatican II
theologians began dissolving the natural law paradigm by suggesting

that there could be devised objective moral standards on "the dignity of the human person," i.e., on the "nature of the person and his acts."[5] The council's "Decree on Religious Freedom" opened with the very crucial statement "A sense of the dignity of the human person has been impressing itself more and more deeply on the consciousness of man."[6] In revisiting the meaning of the human condition, they insisted that the right to religious freedom emanated from the very dignity of the individual person. Their discussions formalized the shift from nature to the person, wherein human dignity could now become the basis for moral reasoning. Significantly, in his encyclical *Redemptor Hominis*, Paul VI stated as well that divine revelation concerned the entire human person and did not merely reference the "supernatural" dimension. Humanity was to be viewed as holistic and as the object of God's love, design, and destiny. Such a perspective marks a significant sea shift in moral theology. Individuality was to distinguish each of us from one another, while personhood was to bind us to one another.[7]

This shift from individualistic atomism to an integrated communitarianism would now demand a perspective that could be capable of stressing the historical continuity of the multidimensioned pattern that represented the individual's moral history and life. In this holistic model, the person could become the central referent and the basis for generating objective moral criteria. In October 1980, for example, John Paul II urged that scientific research and experimentation be controlled by "respect for the person." He exhorted those in medicine, for example, to develop and then reinforce "a more unitary view of the patient." This personalistic stance has now become the controlling agenda that can be used to guide reflection on moral behavior and can be useful in analyzing situations that can incite a clash of values with their practical implications. Theologians have now begun delineating and refining their understanding of moral values by focusing on the interaction that occurs in life and experience. These men and women seem to be suggesting that the values that undergird society should emerge out of human interaction and should be continually reshaped through our consciousness of the historical event. Under the influence of Marxist thought and particularly the Frankfurt School, there has been an increasing realization that historical patterns have been embedded in sociopolitical structures that subsequently have had an impact on the social order. This altered perspective on the part of the magisterium and of many moral theologians has called for an increased identification with the poor and deprived, the so-called preferential option for the poor, and has been coupled with a rethinking of the so-called "sanctity" of private property, which many insist has even more social implications than Leo XIII originally suggested. In essence, structural oppression has been accepted as an existing evil. Out of this has come the moral need to imitate Christ and to identify with marginalized persons. Such paradigmatic speculations have also begun to suggest the need for values sustainable for societies as well as for individuals. Such a hierarchy of need had previously had its speculative foundation in the conceptual and ahistorical analysis of man's metaphysical nature, which resulted in the isolation of spiritual, physical, and property values that have now been categorized into a "hierarchy of urgencies."[8] The earlier perspective encouraged a very structured delineation along what seemed to be a restrictive continuum of values and was not fundamentally responsive to historical contingencies.

Since 1945, with the growing importance of "la nouvelle théologie," which has stressed existentialist and personalist thought along with reappropriation of a historical dimension in theology, an amazing number of theologians have viewed pluralism, change, and difference as positive contributions to human development. Referring to post-Vatican II moral theology, Joseph Fuchs, for example, has stressed that scholars should jettison that individualistic moral theology empowered by the Enlightenment and its philosophes who had insisted that Christ was merely a superior moral model and leader. In its own way, enlightened moral philosophy was as individualistic as traditional Catholic models because both used natural rights and law, even though differently conceived, as the basis for speculation. Fuchs has stressed that moral theology should now search into how, not why, mankind has been summoned personally to fulfill God's unfinished task. Moral theology, many feel, should now embody faith seeking expression in behavior and have as its concern the articulation of values that can be of service to society. Because humans are the image of God and, according to Christian theology, have one destiny, a shared moral program among persons gathered in communities presumably has to be devised and explicated as the primary creational task at every level of society.[9] To reach this understanding, such theologians as Metz have returned to the Christian message of compassion for the marginalized victims in society.

The Event and Authentic Theology

In light of the need for a coherent and meaningful theology that is responsive to political oppression, Johannes Metz has used Auschwitz as the reality that has epitomized brutalized oppression in this century. He has suggested that Auschwitz might seem initially unfathomable if we hypothesize that the executioners performed their evil deeds while God apparently remained silent. Even more disturbing than the outright murder, in Metz's opinion, was the compliance of subordinates and the silence of bystanders as the Jewish people were slaughtered. The Final Solution has compelled theologians to examine critically the moral values embedded in our tradition. Our historical acts can be condemned, but they should also help produce new standards for action. After Auschwitz, theologians cannot ignore the defects in Christianity that helped lead to oppression in the Third Reich. According to Metz, theologians now have to affirm that there is at least *one* authority (those who suffer) that can never again be rejected. The Holocaust, therefore, is not just another historical fact or arcane research specialty with no moral implications. The event itself helps create an authentic theology. With his sensitivity toward historical process, Metz sees the concrete world as the horizon for any consideration of God's creative activity. Incarnation, for example, is now seen to indicate that God acts in such a way in relation to the world that he accepts it irrevocably in his Son.[10]

In the context of Auschwitz, Christian theodicy, which may try to justify God or discourse on human meaning, would be blasphemous if the real victims were ignored. In essence, Auschwitz has created a breach in our Enlightenment understanding of theodicy and of history. We may be witnessing a change in the theological paradigm that has governed Catholic thought for centuries. Auschwitz has become the point of departure for the construction of any meaningful theological discourse that is sensitive to victimization. Auschwitz has demanded that meaningful theology be grounded on human experience, reveal evil, and conversely be the response of living faith. As the perpetrators of Auschwitz, Christians are now summoned to construct a *saving history* that will not continue supporting the triumphalistic metaphysic of a Christianity that purports to be the source of all salvation. The pre-Holocaust theological model tended to obviate catastrophes by transforming them into the fuel that was driving history, wherein disasters seemed to be rationally "good."[11] How can Christians penetrate into the deepest meaning of the Holocaust and not see it merely as one element in a Hegelian dialectic? To reach the most profound meaning, the event has to be allowed to speak through its victims. Christians may have been too aggressive in seeking dialogue, which may be a superficial means to cleanse their consciences. Christians have to reflect on the meaning of their own faith, and this may involve listening before speaking.

Victims are not offered a dialogue; they are the oppressed in the event. Responsible for the culture that made Auschwitz a reality, Christians should begin their reflection by listening to the Jewish victims and realizing that they do not have answers to every question. This process may lead Christians and Jews to analyze their past political as well as theological experiences and to reflect on the meaning of the Shoah for the future of humanity. In particular, Christians should avoid drawing religious, political, or social conclusions that are isolated from concrete memories and persons. Christians cannot appropriate Jewish experiences, which are unique, even though ultimately they may have universal ramifications as well. Dogmatic or theological treatises have certainly been more conciliatory than before 1945, but they can still misinform if Christians only speak and fail to listen closely. Much of the well-meaning literature, for example, exhibits a preference to speak about "Judaism," an abstraction, rather than the "Jews" as people, and to focus on dogma rather than persons. Some theologians seemed focused on how to save dogma, not people. Part of this can be seen as a cultural habit that will require constant monitoring.[12]

Alert to this theological pitfall, Metz has reminded us that Christians need to be cautious about which terminology they use and have to avoid sweeping comparisons, which may produce an intellectual assimilation of the Jewish faith. Christians have to focus on their own faith-experiences and the meaning derived from these encounters. After Auschwitz, which exhibited so much adaptation, how can Christianity consider itself a religion of the suffering without critically rethinking its own roots and traditions? Theological maxims by their nature may be abstract, but they should somehow be tied to people in their concrete environment if they hope to become existentially valid. In the post-Auschwitz universe, then, theological systems that do not address the concerns of living and dead people should be retired to libraries as inert relics from the past. Any systematic comparison of seemingly similar Jewish-Christian doctrines has to be conducted cautiously, even if well intentioned, and opened to virtually every nuance. Attempts to establish any "theological common ground" between Christians and Jews also should be viewed with suspicion. We have to recall that the "common ground" present at the inception of Christianity has not served to prevent disaster.[13] As he offers direction, Metz has laid out some caveats that have to guide theological speculation that is designed to protect both the Christian and Jewish faith-experiences.

Historically, Christians have posited their faith as a theological *Weltanschauung* that has provided universal answers. In hindsight, we can now see that it really avoided the agonizing questions that should have been posed as acts of cruelty were committed. Christians have historically viewed human suffering, for example, from the perspective of the cross, which allowed them to share discipleship with Christ as they approached the triumphal Second Coming. The unfortunate result of this attitude is that Christians have been insensitive and indifferent to the suffering of others because it somehow in their minds could be related to Christ's redemptive mission. Suffering had no atoning power unless it could somehow be connected to the cross, and then it was to be endured. The suffering that Christians inflicted on the Jewish people down through the ages was justified because church leaders saw it rooted in the Christian faith in the eschaton. For Metz, from a theological viewpoint, the relationship between the Christian faith and the world should be seen as a creative and militant eschatology that can induce reform. In fact, the gospel's message should have a polemical and liberating relation to a person's present and practical life in society.[14] Metz is asking that Christians now rethink the meaning of the human condition, freedom, faith, and suffering. Should Christians ever inflict suffering or assume the role of bystander? Is there a Christian tradition of opposition to oppression?

Christian history can present an exhibit of conflicts between the church and political powers, which could help refine our reflection on the history of the suffering and persecution of the Jews. Why did Christians not oppose the persecution of this people? As previous chapters have shown, the answer is all too clear. Unfortunately, in Nazi Germany, Christianity exhibited an alarming deficit of resistance to political oppression and accommodated itself to political evil.[15] Jesus foretold that his disciples would be tested. They were tested, have been found wanting, and have even inflicted suffering as they ignored the normative values in their own faith. Conscious of this betrayal of the meaning of Christianity, Metz and Dermot Lane have tried to construct a political theology that could help support a relentless opposition to any extreme interiorization of a religious salvific mission. Such a development has carried with it the danger of the uncritical and all-too-frequent reconciliation of Christianity with dominant political interests. The political theology that they propose has argued that it is nondialectic interiorizing of doctrine that historically has prompted Christianity to enter into uncritical alliances with morally hostile political regimes. In the past, Christianity has tended to focus solely on a spiritual faith, which encouraged it to ignore its sociopolitical environment as long as its "eternal values" were not impacted. Presumably, one lesson that can be derived from our experiences with Nazi Germany is that a Christianity true to its origins should never model the patterns of power constellations that have enjoyed historical triumph. This does not mean that Christianity should be strictly a spiritual phenomenon and ignore the concrete world. From the standpoint of praxis, Christianity has to operate in the world of power politics. But Christianity should simultaneously reflect on its spiritual essence so that it can take a critical stance. To achieve this, Christianity should probably assume a marginal position and never be part of the dominant power complex.[16]

In the past, Christianity has become obsessed with the correct statement of dogma. The Jewish faith, on the contrary, seems heavily oriented to activism in the real world and has eschewed an enforced doctrinal unity. This Jewish heritage could help balance the interiorizing model of Christianity. After it became institutionalized and separated from its Jewish roots, Christianity focused on the discussions and promulgations that aimed at defining doctrine. Such a historical development seems frequently to occur as a charismatic religious orientation becomes institutionalized. At its inception, however, Christianity was not just a doctrine that had to be preserved in an ossified and pure state but a praxis whose goal it was to transform persons as they experienced conversion to the message of Jesus. This praxis of love and suffering unfortunately failed to become the prominent controlling force behind the Christian faith in our culture. In fact, the original concept of praxis was submerged, and the authentic expression of this original faith living in the earliest Christian communities saw its place taken by dogmatic systems. A case could be made that the original Christian faith was to be enacted in the praxis of discipleship, but in reality this has not happened with any degree of frequency. As a cognitive faith, Christianity became a part of an institutional superstructure serving its own interests as well as those of specific groups. Christianity became an ideology and not a living discipleship. Karl Marx labeled this the opiate of the people. Not practicing compassion, it only preached compassion. This institutional spirituality led to a situation that found Christians believing and praying to God as they stood next to the walls of Auschwitz and ignored the Jewish victims. Bourgeois Christianity seemed to legitimate those who already possess, who already have abundant prospects, and who have a rich future. It failed to support those who have tried to confront victimization.[17] The implications for a faith that ignores praxis have become clear as the activities of the Third Reich are perused.

What Christian theologians can now *do* for the murdered Jews is to change the theology that has led to the barbarities perpetrated during the Second World War. Christians can avoid doing a theology that would seem unaffected by or neutral toward the barbarities of political oppression. If Christians and Jews hope to construct a relationship that originated in their root experiences, which can react to the horror of Auschwitz, they should avoid relying on a sense of reconciliation based solely on terminological and conceptual manipulation, or on a generalized friendliness that does not grapple with the significant issues that can serve to unite them on some levels as well as maintain their separate integrity on others. Both Jews and Christians have to recognize the reality that some issues will continue to separate. To avoid a superficial reform that verbally obfuscates major divisions, Christian theologians have begun to develop a concrete and foundational theology that can create a healing Christian consciousness. This theology would recognize that such legitimate separation may be an act of faith and may simultaneously provoke a realization that the Jewish faith-experience can still offer important dimensions for a Christian consciousness of God. Such a dialogical relationship would dictate an extension of pedagogy into everyday life, into Sunday homilies, and virtually into all grassroots institutions so that the sociopsychological mechanisms that confront bias can be built right into the religious structures. Theology has to become proactive. Auschwitz can then be remembered as an event that has had moral and theological repercussions and is not consigned to the history of humanity as just another tragedy.[18] As always, the question has to be posed: How can theology be made ethically normative? This stress on the dignity of the person in Catholic theology can help facilitate the entrance into this exciting theological dimension that requires dialogue with historians and social scientists. This interest in elucidating theology from the historical events in which we live has led to an intense focus on the theory-praxis polarity by such theologians as Lamb and Lane, who have found a conceptual opening through the work of Rahner, Lonergan, and Metz as the thinkers have tried to move theology into an attitude of compassion for victims.

Praxis and Theory

Inspired by the idea of a common human destiny, such Catholic theologians as Matthew Lamb and Dermot Lane have insisted that a self-conscious "solidarity with victims," to use Lamb's phrase, can lead to a moral theology responsive to a world sundered by violence and oppression. Following the very suggestive comments in John Paul II's encyclical *On Human Work*, such self-critical solidarity would demand reflection and action among the victims and those supporting reform "against the degradation of human beings." The oppressed should be enabled or empowered to become the appropriate agents for reform in their cultures. Such solidarity can be nurtured through dialogue and collaboration between the victims as well as the bystanders against the oppressors immutably pursuing their agenda., As research on the Holocaust suggests, a personal identification with the victims through some type of spiritual, empathetic process that touches both the individual bystander and the victim seems to be fundamental to altruistic behavior. Lamb and others would like to have this "private" conversion experience impact on the social order as well. This communitarian thrust is designed to oppose the modernistic emphasis of post-Enlightenment individualism that has featured an isolated ego involved in cognitive and moral speculation. This atomistic model culturally supported the traditional Christian stress on the private character of evil. [19]

Such an anthropocentric victimology has demanded that theologians reflect critically on the individual person living in the coils of the social order to expose the real meaning of evil. Political theology no longer need justify the status quo; it has now become foundational for reform because it is now being derived from criteria nourished by both faith and reason and concerned with the individual-societal nexus. This person-society dialectic can be designed to nurture faith as a form of knowledge. This faith has yet to be realized or actualized in historical society. The foundational criteria for the innovative theological speculation of today are derived from the need for a reappropriation of the Christian faith in the light of historical victimization. To accomplish this reappropriation, such theologians as David Tracy have favored a hermeneutics of recovery, which they feel can help establish the transcendent values that can only be birthed dialectically through sensitivity to historical human suffering. They have also found a hermeneutics of suspicion useful[20] in confronting the dehumanizing values embodied in the institutions that have powered human history.

Doing such political theology would, as we will see in the next chapter, involve actively collaborating with the sociologists and psychologists who are critically exploring the roots of racism and antisemitism. The brutality of Nazism, for example, has helped pose "the problem" by arrogantly proclaiming the superiority of some traits and the eugenic unhealthiness of others. Their efforts may well suggest that those prejudices are social pathologies. Political theologians have also been succored by those political scientists who have exposed the alienating politicization that has so typified this century, with its extended history of suffering. In light of all these insights, political theologians have begun focusing their work on transforming future human history by understanding the past and present. Their disciplined study is organized and nurtured by a felt need to create a subject-empowering life-giving environment that can counter the biases that have needlessly victimized millions. Comprehending such past social as well as religious sins as antisemitism, a component of our culture, and the Holocaust can sensitize us to our present environment and assist us in shaping the future. Understanding a past evil of this nature can serve as a lens to help us grapple with the present. Auschwitz has more and more been seen as the logical conclusion of the structural hubris that has helped control the sociopolitical identity that has been endemic to the Western socialization processes at the base of our culture.[21] How can we, however, move from theory to the real world?

From the perspective of political theology, the meaning of praxis, as a technical concept, has become substantially important as scholars have delved into the implications of such systemic evils as the Holocaust. Gustavo Gutiérrez, for example, has said that in a profound sense, praxis is dedicated to seeing the becoming of humanity as a process of emancipation through history. Humanity has a task to create a constantly improving society in which servitude can be eliminated. Humans are the artisans of the new humanity. A focus on praxis reminds us that theory and action exist in a symbiotic relationship. Theory at its best embodies the subject's orientation toward the object. Praxis represents human action with respect to what is currently done or could be done. In its fullest sense, praxis demands committed involvement because only morally oriented actions can make persons truly human. Praxis, then, encourages intersubjectivity because an individual's interactions will or will not produce authentic persons. Critical theory combined with liberating praxis can help create knowledge of the truth by in effect "doing the truth."[22] To be authentic, then, theory must be enacted. Given this principle, the dialectic relating theory and praxis goes to the very core of what it means to be human. Several theologians have probed the meaning of praxis, and a survey of their observations can help us probe the social and theological viability of this dialectic.

Committed to a cognitive theory that can be correlated with critical praxis, several prominent theologians have been acknowledging that the normative revelation contained in the Jewish and Christian traditions can transcend the results of pure reason. Pursuing this fruitful dimension, for example, Metz has maintained that the values contained in Judeo-Christian eschatological reflections reveal the cries of history's victims. Both Lonergan and Metz have insisted that the learned theological tomes, which call for explicating theology within the traditional ecclesial contexts, are too limiting. In fact, theory by itself has in the past wreaked evil on persons. After the degrading events of this century, theologians cannot advance their enterprise by merely including a reflection on the Holocaust as a supplement to an academic program and thus ignore the basic cognitive corpus that has been part of our culture. Only authentic religious, moral, and social praxis, in which theory responds to the concrete world, can provide an adequate foundation for doing theology and so help prevent future genocidal policies and sanctioned murder.[23]

Authentic praxis cannot be derived from theory alone. Lonergan, for example, has promoted a cognitive model that seeks to liberate persons by raising the individual's consciousness about his or her activities and whether they fit into a normative structure. Such an approach is designed to reappropriate from revelation the goals of legitimate human freedom. This reappropriation would ultimately demand that a realistic cognitive structure be devised to promote compassion. Political theology that has responded to the Holocaust and has focused on articulating a valid praxis seems to be both the goal and the foundation of critical theory. In general, today's political theologians have not emphasized that revelation can transcend human reason because they prefer to mediate faith dialectically through human activity. Faith seeks understanding, but at the same time it should have a transformative function with respect to human activity.[24] Historical events help shape faith and its concomitant theological understanding, which ideally should affect humans as they try to reconfigure their own world. By the fact of its massive intrusion into human history, the Holocaust may well have inspired a theology that is particularly sensitive to the degradation of the human person. Such theological sensitivization can be useful in the transformation of our culture. It is not surprising, then, that several theologians have pursued the goal of inserting praxis more aggressively into theology.

The theory-praxis polarity, of course, is not new, but its timely and emphatic reappropriation has been highlighted in the systems of

Rahner, Lonergan, and Metz. Rahner has viewed church doctrine as the expression of a praxis that is ideally rooted in and has grown from Christian activities in historical communities. While criticizing some aspects of Rahner's transcendental theology as metaphysically too conceptual, Metz has sought similar results by extending theological anthropocentrism into personal and social practice. In this context, Metz's own hermeneutics of suspicion can be seen as a necessary prerequisite for a hermeneutics of reform. He has insisted that theology should be grounded not merely on concepts and ideas but on dynamic interaction as real persons live out their conversion through moral, social, and religious imperatives.[25]

This transcendental focus in contemporary theological treatments discloses humans working out their salvation in God's presence, which virtually demands a transformative function for theology. Such an enterprise should support humans and help them become attentive, responsible, and loving subjects who as people of faith can respond to their historical and social experiences. Their presence and relation to God should summon these people of faith to be authentically responsible human subjects. Such social sins as racism as well as political and economic structural oppression cannot be confronted simply with pious ideals devoid of any driving force for their application. To counter social or systemic evils, therefore, would require conversion to a social and political praxis. By correlating the identity crisis that for almost two centuries has plagued a frequently irrelevant Christianity, with that of humanity after Auschwitz, the political theology of Metz and Lonergan can carry forward more concretely Rahner's insight into the meaning of the dying and risen Christ. The human condition thereby could achieve a God-centeredness. This anthropocentrism would be profoundly theocentric and would respond to the needs that the Holocaust seems to mandate.[26]

Metz's political theology has suggested a foundational theology that can help us reflect on those questions and challenges posed by the Marxist critical concern with our socioeconomic structure. Concrete historicity is the key to this new, more relevant political theology. According to Metz, because of his metaphysical overview, Rahner has somewhat discounted the problematic features of human experience in its social and historically dialectical dimensions. Rahner tended to surrender to the conceptual aspects of transcendental theology as he reflected on social issues. Rahner's overall accomplishments, therefore, may have to be complemented by the analytical and critical perspectives of the social sciences, which can help disclose the dynamics of the suffering that are tied to the struggles for liberation from systematic oppression. [27]

Lonergan has also suggested that people adhere to values even though they may not cognitively understand the nearly symbiotic connection between the person and the culture. Knowledge emanates from our loving or hating acts in society. Such knowledge is the result of human judgments rendered on real historical acts, whether these be compassionate or hateful. Seen from this perspective, in which knowledge and act are connected, persons respond to their surroundings in a transformative fashion that actually can change the way the empirical consciousness develops, which subsequently can affect the social and cultural forms of institutions. Since cognitive data is derived from what persons do with what they know, Lonergan's speculative method is intimately connected to praxis. He highlights the transformative sense of praxis when he suggests that decision and action precede as well as ground the knowledge of values. Such a decision and action nexus subsequently can lead to a hermeneutics of suspicion and recovery, which can then isolate the needed data that will shape consciousness. [28] His system is based on a dynamic interaction between act and theory.

Given the transformative role of praxis, Lonergan has offered a theory of orthopraxis, which theologically adds a new dimension to orthodoxy. From Lonergan's perspective, persons sincerely practicing their religion inculcate its meanings and values, which have enlivened their culture. The primary goal of valid orthopraxis would be to realize in concrete acts that an ongoing battle against sinful hate and indifference is foundational if a culture is to have prosocial values. A genuine praxis is seen as a dynamic force in a religious tradition because it is a combined product of God's grace and of the human response. Orthopraxis ideally should be foundational to the theological tradition. Sensitive to the meaning of orthopraxis, the religious person instrumentally would try to attach theology to the human consciousness that is continuously nourished in the real world. [29] Lonergan has written:

Religious communities are historical realities. Their authenticity is the resultant not only of the authenticity of their contemporary members but also of the heritage transmitted down through the centuries. Whatever the defects of such heritage, it comes to be accepted in good faith. Good faith is good, not evil. It needs to be purified, but the purification will be the slow product of historical research into the screening memories and defense mechanisms and legitimations that betray an original waywardness and a sinister turn.[30]

Faith is not just a cognitive act detached from the historical world but rather a response to God that has been refined through our interactions in our culture.

The Scriptures have revealed values that can serve a transformative function for our culture. The religious texts may have incorporated the cultural values of the specific historical societies in which they were birthed, but simultaneously they also have criticized their environments and so suggest a useful model. Acknowledging this, theologians today have been reflecting on the past dialectic between faith and its environment to open up ways of dealing with the future. Metz's social-critical dialectic, for example, has sought to move from the conservative, paternalistic ecclesial structure to a more liberating model that can critique culture. Lonergan has emphasized relating a historical or social science perspective with a dialectical, foundational, and critically practical method. Theological and sociological paths to knowledge are complementary and may provide as well a mutually corrective service. Lonergan's epistemology is designed to be sensitive to the transforming values explicit and implicit in the scriptural narratives and is to be coupled with the praxis that takes its theme from religious conversion. Faith could be depicted, therefore, as a leap into the value-oriented reason that can continue liberating Christians from biased, historically conditioned dehumanization and depersonalization. Instrumental reason as a critical tool revealing structural economic exploitation, racism, sexism, and militarism can be retrieved and provided with an appropriate theological dimension. Religious faith, hope, and love, even though not fully actualized, could be viewed as constitutive elements in a human society dedicated to empowering transformative value. Such a reliance uses the stresses and strains in a society to make theological reflection a natural act with very redeeming social values. The exploitative evils of class, race, and sex within Christian cultures stem from the failure to construct a legitimate orthopraxis tied to Christ's compassion for the marginalized victims of his day. Lonergan's multidimensional system therefore relies on dialectical methods to create a spiritually and historically powered orthopraxis. The goal is to reappropriate the values introduced at the very inception of Christianity, even if these have been at times sublimated or ignored.[31] Lonergan and Rahner laid the abstract epistemology for a systematic theology that can be useful in understanding how our Christian responsibilities can be discharged into our culture, but others have delved more deeply into the meaning and significance of praxis and critical theory.

Action as Concretized Knowledge

The behavioral sciences have provided evidence that a person belongs to a social network of human relationships that is composed of family, friends, country, and a religious tradition. From a religious tradition, for example, we can gain knowledge and "truth values" so that we may attempt to transform the world through implementing God's revelation. Knowledge and truth can be concretized through action and performance. The paradigm that is used to comprehend our secular society also appears in many of the foundational theologies that are now being formulated. Praxis by definition is concrete sociotheological activity. If social reality is perceived as static, for example, then theology would be formulated as a set of immutable principles. If, however, social reality were to be understood to be a dynamic and unfinished process, then theology would reflect an openness conducive to creativity.[32] From this vantage point theological principles are intimately connected to one's view of the social dynamic that organizes society.

Historical experience can serve as the concrete foundation for a theological understanding that can help create a praxis oriented theology. Relating theology to current experience, as was suggested formally at the Second Vatican Council, has ensured that praxis has now become central to those who "do" theology. The emerging emphasis on praxis has meant a decisive turn to the subject, which can allow the human condition to be comprehended inductively from the "inside out" rather than deductively. Human identity, dignity, and agency have become crucial in light of our concern with the person.[33]

Christianity's current historical crisis of identity is not so much related to the dicta of faith as it is to the practical meaning of imitating Christ. Particularly interesting is the work that has been done to relate praxis and the meaning of victim in the attempt to develop a transformative moral ethos. Metz, Lane, and Lamb have insisted that the dialectical tension between theory and praxis means that primacy should be given to reflective praxis, which would engage our reactions to the concrete events that connect humanity to God. The experience derived from such praxis subsequently would become the basis for human understanding of future actions. They have concluded that practical fundamental theology should be governed by the primacy of praxis. To base theology exclusively on abstract reflection is uncritical and can ultimately yield merely ossified academic constructs.[34] In this dialectical context, christological knowledge, informed by a praxis orientation, could effect change on living society. For these theologians, only when people imitate Christ through authentic praxis can they theologically comprehend their spiritual allegiance to Jesus because religion as such is not merely a cognitive act. From this standpoint, Metz has found flaws in most modern Christologies, because they do not further the praxis implications of Christology. With the exception of the spirit Christology, which connects God and the human person who is God's image, most of the modern Christologies utilize a nondialectical relationship that effectively severs theory from praxis. The Christian Scriptures, when relating to Jesus, demand the need for praxis. The narrative and the spiritual directive in the gospel accounts, he feels, should not be separated. The gospel narrative and the activity induced convey an understanding of Christ's message. Christ's idea (spiritual directive) and his concrete acts are both necessary for theological understanding.[35]

Metz and others have unveiled the meaning of Christian praxis and have drawn out some of its implications. Since the concern is for the person in society, Metz has insisted that valid praxis should always be ethically determined to ensure that an abstract or violent negation of the individual person's dignity cannot result. This normative requirement is vital in light of past political policies, which have frequently neglected the dignity of the individual person. Christian praxis as a social act has to use the gospel with its liberating memory of Jesus as its referent because a social praxis shaped solely by any prevailing political agenda could be lethal if it simply sustained the dominant viewpoint. Christian praxis, according to Metz, should institutionalize empathy so that it can oppose the contemporary apathy of society. To be legitimate, such praxis has to demand a solidarity with the past and present victims of suffering. Such solidarity as the normative principle that governs praxis would ensure that suffering cannot be rationalized as an acceptable component of the human condition. In light of this, Gregory Baum has insisted that praxis is a dialectic between action with its articulated response that is directed toward historical involvement and theory. Knowledge can be empowered to improve our total environment.[36] Contrary to past viewpoints, suffering can no longer be justified as good and necessary for human progress.

Historically, the Christian message, when proclaimed in the public forum, has been ineffective because of its stress on abstract dogma, which to many has seemed politically irrelevant. As the basis for political and liberation theology, concrete praxis can become the heralded corrective to the traditional almost exclusively speculative reflection that in the past has served as theologically foundational. This recent turn to praxis has signified the necessary involvement of theology with the event and has also suggested that Christianity can significantly contribute to the social and political process of reconstructing and renewing the social community. This more activist approach can undeniably affect how we live in society and experience social reality.[37] Being praxis-oriented demands that the Christian theologian use critical theory as a tool to analyze what sociopolitical groups do in order to direct society, science, and culture. The Holocaust has suggested that some dangerous fissures exist in our civilization; critical theory can be instrumental in dissecting our sociocultural environment. A praxis-oriented Christian consciousness has already begun shaping political, liberation, practical, and critical theology.[38] Theology fused to critical theory has offered men and women of faith a way to reveal systemic sin and a tool with which to engage in macrosocial correction.

Critical theory by its nature is directed toward the future because it is committed to the creation of those social, political, and economic conditions which can ensure that humanity "will for the first time be a conscious subject and actively determine its own way of life."[39] In correct praxis, "truth" is tied to changing historical conditions and should not simply be identified with historical success (the status quo) because this could have the effect of mutating a theologian into an apologist for the currently victorious sociopolitical process. Certainly this phenomenon has occurred in the past. In the sphere of critical theory, truth would be seen as political reality, a dynamic moment of the specific praxis that is working to transform the social conditions of reality. Basically, the theory — i.e., speculative theology — is actually validated due to its dialectical relationship with "true" praxis. In such a dialogical tension, theory directs the praxis that subsequently becomes the "truth" of theory. This dialectical tension holding together theory and praxis can generate a dynamically living truth, which philosophical speculation or mysticism cannot reveal. Theology is here only done in the context of the event. With his critical theory, Jürgen Habermas has been significant in guiding theologians along this theory-praxis path. [40]

Historical reality provides the critical tool to reveal the deficiencies of ahistorical hermeneutics. Habermas, for example, has critiqued any hermeneutics that interprets a text that is isolated from its historical environment and severed from the cultural issues that initially nurtured the text. Ignoring the generative historical experience would eliminate any real possibility of critically challenging the ideological agenda that birthed the text. The critique of the dominant ideology seems requisite for sociopolitical emancipation. [41]

For Habermas, theory is not something that can help justify current political action in a concrete situation, but it serves a critical function. Theoretical principles do not basically embody an absolute authority. A superficial understanding of history would destroy any legitimate dialectic between theory and praxis. To alert us to the meaning of this tension, Habermas has stated explicitly: "Decisions for the political struggle cannot at the outset be justified theoretically and then carried out organizationally; there can be no theory which at the outset can assure a world-historical mission in return for potential sacrifices." [42] Theory alone cannot change the world because this would reduce political activity to merely instrumental manipulation. In fact, as we can see in our own century, "scientific" theory has historically tended to become authoritarianism in practice. Theory needs the corrective of praxis. The history of the twentieth century has warned us about promoting any ideology as *the* system of principles that should be organizing society.[43] Habermas' discussion of political and social theory has informed Christian theologians as well.

Marx and Habermas have insisted that praxis can help reveal the radical elements that have informed social philosophy for both good and ill during the last century and a half. Among Christian theologians, Lamb has best explored the concrete possibilities offered by a theory-praxis relationship. From the perspective of Habermas among others, Lamb has maintained that theory helps orient the person toward an authentic subjectivity. Lamb has asserted that there exists for some a primacy of theory wherein normative human action finds its sustenance in theoretical knowledge. For others, the primacy of praxis finds its normative foundation in the concrete experiences of life. Fusion of these two mutually related perspectives would seem to be a valid goal. To achieve such a theological fusion, the primacy of the Christian faith-love principle can and should be rediscovered continually in Christ's paradoxical revelation. The norms that can guide action are revealed only through the mediative tension that binds Christian faith and life. Praxis is symbiotically connected to revelation and so becomes the goal and the foundation of theory, which simultaneously is articulated as the self-understanding of praxis. Although enlivened by theory, normative praxis also has the role to exercise a critical function to control theory so that the social order can experience an ongoing emancipation. Authentic self-transcendence can only result from the social, transformative, and liberating praxis that directs and then redirects theory. This relationship reveals the primacy of praxis and its radical possibilities within contemporary theology.[44]

Praxis as just the implementation of theory into concrete activity has generally been labeled technique. Praxis is not "putting faith into practice" or making Christianity relevant. Rather, praxis is delineated as reflective, dialectical, and intentionally transformative. Christ's own constructively conflictual responses to his culture help suggest that praxis at its best should critique the prevailing society and culture. Within its specific social context, liberating praxis has as its goal the commitment to and solidarity with other persons. Liberation and political theologies are today being asked to address the personal, social, and economic evils in the world while they stimulate a praxis of liberating transformation that can then address the restatement of an authentic theology. An authentic praxis incorporating religious self-transcendence, moral conversion, or intellectual growth can be assessed by evaluating the transformative effect it has in improving our social condition. Authentic praxis, therefore, should change both society and the person, because truth can be recovered in the very experience of furthering societal liberation. Such theologians as Metz and Lamb have argued for a social dynamism that has not previously characterized Christian theology.

Critical praxis makes it axiomatic that authentic theology find its referent in the historical, social, and cultural condition nurturing humanity. The Christian theology that supported antisemitism, for example, was rooted in specific models of Christology. To revisit the past and see Christianity as emanating from the Incarnation, however, could help critically correlate the gospel message with the human condition and so could help support a radically different cognitive development than that which supported marginalization. Human consciousness, which incorporates theology, is shaped within the social environment and cannot be immune to the ideologizing influences surrounding it. Ideological components fuel the social reality that nurtures institutionalized Christianity, and so Christians should question the ideologies emanating from earlier cultures that surround them to avoid infection by the ideologies underpinning past or present social reality. If praxis-theology is to sustain credibility, it should be engaged in constant questioning. To safeguard, protect, and maintain the present social reality as *the* normative condition could result in endorsing an oppressive social situation that could mean acquiescence, albeit unconsciously, to sin.[45] To achieve a correct theory-praxis model, critical theory demands an analysis of the reality that it (critical theory) has just affirmed. Authentic theology, which would be event driven, is directed to assist humans in developing their full potential as the image of God. What are some of the concrete ramifications that an authentic theory-praxis model can have?

Theory-Praxis and its Potential Impact

Scientific, social, ecological, nuclear, economic, political, and cultural crises have compelled us to rethink the historical developments that have challenged us in this century. Theology cannot be indifferent to the oppressions and tragedies that have marked our century because it is part of the crisis due to its role in creating some of the dominant social, political, and cultural agendas that have molded our tradition. In some ways, theology has persisted in supporting the institutions that have been instrumental in paving the way to some of this century's worst disasters. In 1971 Paul VI wrote:

> It is up to Christian communities to analyze with objectivity the situation that is proper to their own country, to shed on it the light of the gospel's unalterable words, to draw principles of reflection, norms of judgment and directives of action from the social teaching of the Church.[46]

But that social teaching has to be informed by a legitimate praxis theology.

Our civilization has been and still is characterized by such controlling values as individualism, alienation, and consumerism, which have been in part derived from the atomistic, substantialist, fragmented, and "objectivist" Enlightenment culture. What should have been a holistic reality has been segmented into discrete units for analysis. While such analytic methodologies are comprehensible, humans who are viewed as fragments can be exploited and manipulated without any ontological concern for their interconnectedness. This Enlightenment worldview has been characterized as an amalgam of such varied philosophical viewpoints as Aristotelian substantialism, objectivist ontologies, naive realism, Cartesian dualism, liberal individualism, and Newtonian mechanization. The resulting amalgam has resulted in a number of "alienating dualisms." Nature is divorced from humanity; matter is divided from spirit; persons are seen as objects. When viewed in this way, our entire civilization may well be comprehended as a stratified dualism that virtually has managed, at least until recently, to preclude the dialogical interaction that seems needed to resuscitate the whole.[47]

Discussions centering on authenticating existence have yielded an awareness that many of society's problems may be fundamentally structural and systemic. A universal vision of life, which would include a re-creation of a web of values, could help support the type of universal sense of obligation that such scholars as Helen Fein suggest could have prevented the Holocaust. The construction of an integral whole that holds its component human parts in a relational exchange, is a reaffirmation of community values and of human dignity.[48] This holistic construct would be the fruitful result of the theory-praxis dialectic.

In the healthiest dialectic, praxis has to be shaped by and directed toward the requirements of the community as well as toward the always pressing needs of the individual with an eye to balancing individual and societal agendas. No division between individual and social praxis or between the private domain and the public realm of transformative praxis can be maintained. This theory-praxis connection is the challenge to social praxis as a transformative act. Perceiving the world as an ongoing process has suggested to some theologians that social praxis has a place of prominence on the theological agenda of understanding God's revelation.[49]

Vatican II has urged that the signs of the times be scrutinized in light of the gospel. In formulating this challenge, the council has proposed a particular direction for doing theology in this fractured world. Theology is increasingly seen as receiving nourishment from its historical interactions in the world, which means that it is formulated within a particular context. Applying this perspective in the postconciliar period has enabled recent Catholic thinkers to construct praxis-oriented political and liberation theologies that take the event as the factor controlling the theological agenda.[50]

Listening to the revelatory message and in light of the Holocaust, many theologians seem to be suggesting that we are living in a situation where sin and injustice have impacted major institutions. Atomistic political theories, for example, have permeated the economic, social, and political institutions of society and have been labeled by some as "social sin." The concept of social or structural sin illuminates the fact that destructive and dehumanizing trends over the centuries have become organically a part of the very systems that control our social life. Such social sin may not be consciously planned and may emanate as a consequence of human blindness or personal greed, and it seems to contradict, at least in the opinions of many Jews and Christians, God's plan of creation and salvation. This plan, they suggest, is socially oriented and views the individual as an integral part of the whole. The Christian doctrine of creation seems to be mandating that the fruits of the earth are for the use of every human being and are not just for the exploitation by a powerful privileged few. Structural sin as a source of political, social, and gender oppression, if allowed to continue, would ultimately repudiate God's offer of salvation to all humanity. Viewed from this theory-praxis standpoint, the eschaton can be seen as the result of God's incarnational presence in the historical world. Reaction to this divine mission may be the engine that could power the collective authentication cause of men and women who seek to dwell in a community of love and justice.[51] More than almost any single event, the Holocaust has opened the eyes of Christian theologians to the fact that dogma and religious statements that ignore historical reality can lead to brutalization.

A notion of social sin can help sensitize those reflecting on sociopolitical issues so that they realize that the effects of cumulative individual sin have empowered the social systems and structures so typical of the twentieth century that have engaged in victimization. These sinful social structures have denied basic rights and inhibited freedom. The social mission of Christianity is to promote a praxis that affects theory and that is redemptively transformative.[52] To uncover the sinful social structures built by those who have historically institutionalized evil, the social sciences can offer perspectives and tools useful to theologians and others confronting the meaning of the Holocaust. In fact, it is provocative that so many individuals in such diverse fields as theology, psychology, and sociology have been reflecting on similar problems and reaching similar conclusions. Such a phenomenon would suggest that a new paradigm, or at least a new pattern of thought, may be indeed emerging. Marx continues, therefore, to remind us that understanding is not enough; the point is to change the world. This would seem to mean that ideas and concrete reality must engage in mutually corrective interaction.

Technology, bureaucracy, social mobility, and mass communication have made the public world seem alien and impersonal. Simultaneously, these very challenges heighten the impact that the structures of society actually have on the meaning of dignity in our lives. A narrow focus on private goods and individual interest can make the common good of social existence slip from the control of human freedom into the grip of powerful elites. Paradoxically, just as it has become increasingly difficult to sustain a vision of the common good, it is likewise more urgently important to succeed here if we hope to sustain democratic life. The basis of democracy is not rugged individualism. Democracy and freedom depend on the strength of the communal relationships that can give persons a measure of real power to shape their political environment.[53] To have the ability to shape our environment means that we have to understand the psychosocial dynamics that operate to explain behavior. Developing philosophical and theological values is useless unless they become part of the life of society.

Notes

1. Mahoney, *The Making of Moral Theology*, 33-35; James Brown Scott, *Francisco de Vitoria and His Law of Nations* (Oxford: Clarendon Press, 1934); Louis Monden, *Sin, Liberty and Law* (New York: Sheed & Ward, 1966), 45.
2. Pope Paul VI, *Humanae Vitae* in *Acta Apostolicae Sedis* 60 (1968): 483.
3. Ibid., 25: 498-99.
4. Ibid., 19: 495.
5. *Gaudium et Spes* in *Acta Apostolicae Sedis* 58 (1966): 1072.
6. *Declaration on Religious Freedom* in *Acta Apostolicae Sedis* 58 (1966): 929.
7. *Redemptor Hominis* in *Acta Apostolicae Sedis* 71 (1979): 277, n. 12, 280, n. 13, 283; John Mahoney, SJ, "The Challenge of Moral Distinctions," *Theological Studies* 53 (1992): 678.
8. John Paul II in *Acta Apostolicae Sedis* 72 (1980): 1126-29; J.-M. Aubert, "Hierarchie de valeurs et histoire," *Revue des Sciences Religieuses* 44 (1970): 5-22.
9. Karl Rahner, "Pluralism in Theology and the Unity of the Creed," in *Theological Investigations* 1966: 3-23; Josef Fuchs, "Moral Theology according to Vatican II," in Josef Fuchs, *Human Values and Christian Morality* (Dublin: Gill and Macmillan, 1970), 8; Mahoney, *The Making of Moral Theology*, 340-46. For the most recent analysis of "the new theology," see Joseph A. Komonchak, "Theology and Culture at Mid-Century: The Example of Henri de Lubac," *Theological Studies* 1990: 579-602.
10. Metz, *The Emergent Church*, 18. A great deal of revisionist historical literature can be found in *The Journal of Historical Review*. For an analytical survey of some revisionist issues, see Deborah Lipstadt, "Deniers, Relativists, and Pseudo-Scholarship," *Dimensions* 6 (1991): 4-

9; Johannes Metz, *Theology of the World* (London: Burns & Oates, 1969), 21-22, 128-29.

11. Metz, *The Emergent Church*, 19-20; Ammicht-Quinn, *Von Lissabon bis Auschwitz*.

12. Metz, *The Emergent Church*, 21; Johannes Metz, *Jenseits bürgerlicher Religion: Reden über die Zukunft des Christentums* (München: Kaiser, 1980), 37-39.

13. Metz, *The Emergent Church*, 22.

14. Ibid., 23-24; Johannes Metz, *Theology of the World* (London: Burns & Oates, 1969), 91, 95.

15. For analyses of the sociopolitical accommodation policies of the Christian churches during the Third Reich, see the books of Dietrich, Conway, Lewy, and Zahn. For a recent study of the relationship of knowledge and power, see Marc Lalonde, "Power/Knowledge and Liberation: Foucault as a Parabolic Thinker," *Journal of the American Academy of Religion* 61 (1993): 81-100.

16. Metz, *The Emergent Church*, 27; Charles Davis, *Theology and Political Society* (Cambridge: Cambridge University Press, 1980); Dermot Lane, *Foundations for a Social Theology: Praxis, Process and Salvation* (New York: Paulist Press, 1984).

17. Johannes Metz, "Political Theology of the Subject as a Theological Criticism of Middle Class Religion," in Johannes Metz, ed., *Faith in History and Society: Toward a Practical Fundamental Theology* (New York: Seabury Press, 1980), 32-48; Johannes Metz, ed., *Christianity and the Bourgeoisie* (New York: Seabury Press, 1979).

18. Metz, *The Emergent Church*, 28, 30, 32; Max Horkheimer and Theodor Adorno, "Elements of Anti-Semitism: Limits of the Enlightenment," *Continuum* 1975: 168-208.

19. Lamb, *Solidarity with Victims*, ix, 2-3; Lane, *Foundations;* Georges Gusdorf, *De l'histoire des sciences à l'histoire de la pensée* (Paris: Payot, 1966), 93-126; Georges Gusdorf, *La révolution galiléenne* (Paris: Payot, 1969), 17-122; Samuel Oliner, *Restless Memories: Recollections of the Holocaust Years*, 2nd ed. (Berkeley: Judah L. Magnes Museum, 1986).

20. Lynn White, *Medieval Religion and Technology: Collected Essays* (Berkeley: University of California Press, 1978), 329-38; Hasting Rashdall, *The Universities of Europe in the Middle Ages*, 2nd ed., ed. by F.M. Powicke and A.B. Emden (Oxford: Clarendon Press, 1936), vol. 1; J. Leclercq, *The Love of Learning and the Desire for God* (London: SPCK, 1970). For a brief as well as explicative analysis of the "hermeneutics of suspicion," see Elisabeth Schüssler Fiorenza and David

Tracy, "The Holocaust as Interruption and the Christian Return to History," in Fiorenza and Tracy, *The Holocaust as Interruption*, 83-86.

21. Metz, *The Emergent Church*, 52; Ernest Becker, *The Denial of Death* (New York: Free Press, 1973); Ernest Becker, *Beyond Alienation: A Philosophy of Education for the Crisis of Democracy* (New York: G. Braziller, 1969), 165-225. For an analysis of elites engaged in political manipulation, see Jürgen Habermas, *Legitimation Crisis* (Boston: Beacon Press, 1975), 1-32, 95-143; Thomas McCarthy, *The Critical Theory of Jürgen Habermas* (Cambridge: MIT Press, 1978), 1-39, 358-86; Theodor Adorno, *Negative Dialectics* (New York: Continuum, 1973), 362; M. Horkheimer, *Critique of Instrumental Reason* (New York: Seabury Press, 1974); Richard Lerner, *Final Solutions: Biology, Prejudice, and Genocide* (University Park, PA: Pennsylvania State University Press, 1992). Lerner's work offers the thesis that to destroy a group we must first dehumanize it. While referring to it as a disease, we can justify its eradication.

22. Gustavo Gutiérrez, *A Theology of Liberation: History, Politics and Salvation* (Maryknoll, NY: Orbis Books, 1973), 88; Jürgen Habermas, *Theory and Practice* (Boston: Beacon Press, 1973), 253-82; Jürgen Habermas, *Knowledge and Human Interests* (Boston: Beacon Press, 1971), 301-17; Lonergan, *Method in Theology*, 265-92.

23. Lonergan, *Method in Theology*, 24, 125-45, 332, 355-68; Johannes Metz, and Trutz Rendtorff, eds., *Die Theologie in der Interdisziplinären Forschung* (Düsseldorf: Bertelsmann Universitäts—Verlag, 1971); Bernard Lonergan, "The Ongoing Genesis of Methods," *Studies in Religion* 6/4 (1977): 341, 351; Lamb, *Solidarity with Victims*, 84.

24. Matthew Lamb, *History, Method and Theology: A Dialectical Comparison of Wilhelm Dilthey's Critique of Historical Reason and Bernard Lonergan's Meta-Methodology* (Missoula, MT: Scholars Press for the American Academy of Religion, 1978), 2-210, 479-536; Lonergan, *Method in Theology*, 20-25; Jürgen Habermas, *Theory and Practice* (Boston: Beacon Press, 1973), 253-82; Lamb, *Solidarity with Victims*, esp. chap. 5.

25. Johannes Metz, ed., *Faith in History and Society: Toward a Practical Fundamental Theology* (New York: Seabury Press, 1980), 60-73, 161-63, 219-28; Lonergan, *Method in Theology*, 140. For Derrida's deconstructionist interpretation of the hermeneutics of suspicion, which is analyzed as an incompleteness of the interpretive act, the thought that behind every mask there is another mask, see Kevin Hart, *The Trespass of the Sign: Deconstruction and Philosophy* (New York: Cambridge University Press, 1989), 48.

26. Lamb, *Solidarity with Victims*, 120-21. For a study of compassion, see Karl Morrison, *"I Am You": The Hermeneutics of Empathy in Western Literature, Theology, and Art* (Princeton: Princeton University Press, 1988).

27. Volker Spülbeck, *Neomarxismus und Theologie: Gesellschaftskritik in Kritischer Theorie und Politischer Theologie* (Freiburg: Herder, 1977); Roger Johns, *Man in the World: The Political Theology of Johannes B. Metz* (Missoula, MT: Scholars Press for the American Academy of Religion, 1976), 132-49; Marcel Xhaufflaire, ed., *La pratique de la théologie politique: analyse critique des conditions practiques de l'instauration d'un discours chrétien libérateur* (Tournai: Casterman, 1974); Johannes Metz, ed., *Faith in History and Society: Toward a Practical Fundamental Theology* (New York: Seabury Press, 1980), 154-68; Johannes Metz, "An Identity Crisis in Christianity? Transcendental and Political Responses," in William J. Kelly, ed., *Theology and Discovery: Essays in Honor of Karl Rahner, S.J.* (Milwaukee: Marquette University Press, 1980), 121-41 (see the responses of Tracy and Lamb on pp. 142-51; Lamb, *History, Method and Theology*, 1-54.

28. Bernard Lonergan, "The Ongoing Genesis of Methods," *Studies in Religion* 6/4 (1977): 348-52; R. Doran, *Subject and Psyche: Ricoeur, Jung, and the Search for Foundations* (Washington, DC: University Press of America, 1977), 253-309; Lamb, *History, Method and Theology*, 422-53.

29. Bernard Lonergan, "Theology and Praxis," *Catholic Theological Society of America Proceedings* 32 (1977): 1-16; Lonergan, *Method in Theology*, 85-99, 105-7, 237-44, 267-71; Bernard Lonergan, "Mission and Spirit," in Peter Huizing and William Bassett, eds., *Experience and the Spirit, Concilium* (New York: Seabury, 1976), 699-778; Bernard Lonergan, "Healing and Creating in History," in *Bernard Lonergan: Three Lectures* (Montreal: Thomas More Institute for Adult Education, 1975), 55-68.

30. Bernard Lonergan, "The Ongoing Genesis of Methods," *Studies in Religion* 6/4 (1977): 353.

31. Rosemary Haughton, *The Catholic Thing* (Springfield: Templegate, 1979), 17; Edward K. Braxton, *The Wisdom Community* (New York: Paulist Press, 1980), viii; Q. Quesnell, "Beliefs and Authenticity," in Matthew Lamb, ed., *Creativity and Method: Essays in Honor of Bernard Lonergan* (Milwaukee: Marquette University Press, 1981), 173-83; Allen W. Wood, *Kant's Moral Religion* (Ithaca: Cornell University Press, 1970); David Mueller, *An Introduction to the Theology of Albrecht Ritschel* (Philadelphia: Westminster Press, 1969); N. Gottwald, *The Tribes of Yahweh: A Sociology of the Religion of Liberated Israel, 1250-*

1050 B.C. (Maryknoll, NY: Orbis Books, 1979); Gerd Thiessen, *Urchristliche Wundergeschichten* (Philadelphia: Fortress Press, 1983); Richard J. Cassidy, *Jesus, Politics and Society: A Study of Luke's Gospel* (Maryknoll, NY: Orbis Books, 1978); Hans Küng and Johannes Metz, "Perspektiven für eine Kirche der Zukunft," *Publik-Forum* 9/13 (June 1980): 15-21; R. Siebert, "The Church from Below: Küng and Metz," *Cross Currents* 31 (1981): 62-84; Alfred Schindler, ed., *Monotheismus als politisches Problem? Erik Peterson und die Kritik der politischen Theologie* (Gütersloh: Gütersloher Verlagshaus Mohn, 1978); Schubert Miles Ogden, *Faith and Freedom: Toward a Theology of Liberation* (Nashville: Abingdon, 1979), 33-37, 44-65, 115-24. For works that would challenge Ogden's thesis, see Karl Rahner, ed., *Befreiende Theologie: der Beitrag Lateinamerikas zur Theologie der Gegenwart* (Stuttgart: W. Kohlhammer, 1977); D. Keefe, "The Ordination of Women," *New Oxford Review* 47 (1980): 12-14. Although inadequate, several authors have analyzed the sociocritical reconstruction of historical criticism. See, for example, H. Baumgartner, *Kontinuität und Geschichte zur Kritik und Metakritik der historischen Vernunft* (Frankfurt: Suhrkamp, 1972); K.-O. Apel, *Towards a Transformation of Philosophy* (Boston: Routledge and Kegan Paul, 1980), 136-79, 225-300; Lamb, *Solidarity with Victims*, 139-42.

32. Lane, *Foundations*, 1, 3; Paul Sigmund, *Liberation Theology at the Crossroads: Democracy or Revolution?* (New York: Oxford University Press, 1990).

33. Henri de Lubac, *Surnaturel: Études Historiques* (Paris: Aubier, 1946); Henri de Lubac, *Catholicism: A Study of Dogma in Relation to the Corporate Destiny of Mankind* (New York: Sheed & Ward, 1958); Dermot Lane, *The Experience of God: An Invitation to Do Theology* (New York: Paulist Press, 1981), chap. 1; Bernard Lonergan, "The Subject," in William F.J. Ryan and Bernard J. Tyrell, eds., *A Second Collection: Papers by Bernard Lonergan* (London: Darton, Longman, and Todd, 1974), 69-85; Karl Rahner, *Foundations of Christian Faith: An Introduction to the Idea of Christianity* (New York: Seabury Press, 1978), 26-31; Johannes Metz, ed., *Faith in History and Society: Toward a Practical Fundamental Theology* (New York: Seabury Press, 1980), 60-70.

34. Johannes Metz, ed., *Faith in History and Society: Toward a Practical Fundamental Theology* (New York: Seabury Press, 1980), 50-51, 165, 167.

35. Ibid., 79; Johannes Metz, *Followers of Christ: The Religious Life and the Church* (New York: Paulist Press, 1978), chap. 2.

36. Metz, *Faith in History and Society*, 56-58; Gregory Baum, *Theology and Society* (New York: Paulist Press, 1987), 123.

37. Metz, *Faith in History and Society*, 212.

38. On critical theory and theology, see Schillebeeckx, *The Understanding of Faith*, chap. 7; Edward Schillebeeckx, "Critical Theories and Christian Political Commitment," in Alois Muller, ed., *Political Commitment and Christian Community* (New York: Herder and Herder, 1973); Francis Fiorenza, "Critical Social Theory and Christology," *C.T.S.A. Proceedings* 30 (1975): 63-110.

39. Max Horkheimer, *Critical Theory: Selected Essays* (New York: Herder and Herder, 1972), 233.

40. H. Horkheimer, "Zum Problem der Wahrheit," *Zeitschrift für Sozialforschung, IV* 3 (1935): 345; Theodor Adorno, *Kierkegaard: Konstruktion des Aesthetischen* (Frankfurt: Suhrkamp, 1966), 111.

41. D. Misgeld, "Critical Theory and Hermeneutics: The Debate between Habermas and Gadamer," in John O'Neill, ed., *On Critical Theory* (New York: Seabury Press, 1976).

42. Jürgen Habermas, *Theory and Practice* (Boston: Beacon Press, 1973), 33.

43. Richard J. Bernstein, *The Restructuring of Social and Political Theory* (New York: Harcourt Brace Jovanovich, 1976), 217; J. Hellesness, "Education and the Concept of Critique," *Continuum* 1970: 40.

44. Matthew Lamb, "The Theory-Praxis Relationship in Contemporary Christian Theologies," *C.T.S.A. Proceedings* 31 (1976): 149-78; William Shea, "Seminar on Theology and Philosophy: Matthew Lamb's Five Models of Theory-Praxis and the Interpretation of John Dewey's Pragmatism," *C.T.S.A. Proceedings* 32 (1977): 140; Lamb, *Solidarity with Victims*, 103; Dermot Lane, *The Experience of God: An Invitation to Do Theology* (New York: Paulist Press, 1981), 63-65; Charles Davis, "Lonergan's Appropriation of the Concept of Praxis," *New Blackfriars* (1981): 114-26.

45. P. Berger and T. Luchmann, *The Social Construction of Reality: A Treatise on the Sociology of Knowledge* (New York: Doubleday, 1967), 9; Dermot Lane, *The Experience of God: An Invitation to Do Theology* (New York: Paulist Press, 1981), 77-78.

46. Pope Paul VI, *Octogesima Adveniens*, a.4.

47. Lane, *Foundations*, 44-45.

48. Ibid., 94-95; Hans Küng and David Tracy, eds., *Paradigm Change in Theology: A Symposium for the Future* (New York: Crossroad, 1989); Fein, *Accounting for Genocide*.

49. Alfred North Whitehead, *Modes of Thought* (New York: Free Press, 1968), 60.

50. *Gaudium et Spes* in *Acta Apostolicae Sedis* 58 (1966), a. 4.

51. Lane, *Foundations*, 111, 123.

52. P. Henriot, "Social Sin and Conversion: A Theology of the Church's Social Involvement," *Chicago Studies* 11 (1972): 3-18; *Gaudium et Spes* in *Acta Apostolicae Sedis* 58 (1966), a. 25; U.S. Catholic Conference, "The Church in the Present-Day Transformation of Latin America in the Light of the Council," conference paper, Washington, DC, 1970, pp. 28-40; Canadian Catholic Bishops, "Sharing National Income," *Catholic Mind* (October 1972): 59. For a warning against inflating the church's social mission, see Langdon Gilkey, *Reaping the Whirlwind: A Christian Interpretation of History* (New York: Seabury Press, 1978), 236.

53. Samuel Huntington, *The Third Wave: Democratization in the Late Twentieth Century* (Norman, OK: University of Oklahoma Press, 1991); John A. Coleman, "Religious Liberty in America and Mediating Structures," in John Coleman, *An American Strategic Theology* (New York: Paulist Press, 1982), 226.

8

The Holocaust and Modernity

After World War II, most scholars still felt comfortable in asserting that modern, liberal democratic society was basically sane and healthy. The Nazi era, most felt, was an interruption in the otherwise normal progress of history, a cancerous growth that had been excised, or a momentary divergence from sanity. This equanimity resulted in part from a conviction that the Shoah was a specifically Jewish tragedy that could not be the natural result of the historical development launched during the Enlightenment. The values undergirding modern society would ensure, presumably, that the Holocaust could not be replicated. Some scholars and commentators also consigned the Shoah to the Jewish people to avoid trivialization as well as to justify the Republic of Israel. The cumulative result was that for several years universalization of the Holocaust was avoided, and the tragedy was merely included in the list of unfortunate twentieth-century horrors. Such a tendency served initially to ban the Holocaust from having a significant impact on those who were reflecting on the human condition.[1] The focus of research, however, began shifting as a variety of scholars suggested that the Shoah could only have been implemented because of serious fissures or faults in our cultural, social, economic, and political infrastructure. Modernity, they suggested, had perhaps cleared a path for political destruction on a monumental scale.

While virtually everyone today agrees that the Holocaust was a Jewish tragedy, most now feel as well that it was not simply an event in Jewish history but that it has profound implications for our entire culture. The Holocaust was nurtured in and implemented by modern, "rational" society, and so the social, cultural, and political nexus that led to barbarism may well be endemic to our civilization. The sociological, psychological, political, and theological infrastructure that supported sanctioned massacre created the institutions that performed the act. The Holocaust, therefore, cannot be perceived merely as the culmination of European-Christian antisemitism and thereby simply the result of a warped intellectual development. Such a cultural simplification may be attractive, because it could answer the challenge to our civilization's broader values, but it would not be accurate. Certainly antisemitism provided concrete content to the ideological intensity that became supranational Nazism and helped mobilize local and cultural grievances. The Holocaust, however, was more than the outgrowth of the religious antisemitism that helped prepare the groundwork for this disaster. To suggest that the Holocaust was a historically unique phenomenon or was caused only by antisemitism would not forward our understanding of *normal* modern society. To catalogue and analyze the centuries of theological contempt, legal discrimination, ghettoization, pogroms, and persecutions would only show ethnocentric and religious hatred as endemic to our culture. Such a perspective could actually defuse the challenge to modernity and suggest that no major reforms of our society are needed, given that a solution to antisemitic hatred that could be offered might just focus on reeducating people to stop hating Jews. Preventing a genocide is more complicated than simply taming rogue, intellectual prejudice. [2] Clearly, the volumes of research after 1945 suggest that scholars have seen the Shoah as more than just a historical aberration and more than just the result of religious antisemitism.

The Holocaust and Nazi Germany

Increasingly the Holocaust has been analyzed as a product of modernity and not simply as a historical disaster resulting from specific group hatreds. Bureaucratic procedures and such cultural values as rationalism seem to be interconnected. A brief summary of these interconnections can be useful before we explore more thoroughly the psychosocial dynamics that support genocidal policies, because to prevent future genocides, the values of the culture have to be shaped to control murderous political behavior. Fortunately, such phenomena as the Holocaust have been rare. But the Holocaust does offer us a closed case that can allow us to examine the structural value system underpinning modern society and the sanctioned murders that have been all too frequent. Genocide as public policy has helped undermine our faith in rationalized procedure and has provided some shattering insights into the "twisted road to Auschwitz," the product of a political policy in a civilized state. To a considerable extent, the choice of physical extermination was the result of routine bureaucratic procedures galvanized and incited by the orders of Hitler and his radical minions, who since 1933 had been seeking some type of "final solution to the Jewish problem." But even such an observation is too limited to explain this tragedy. How were ordinary Germans and other Europeans transformed into murderers? Some psychological research suggests that moral inhibitions that can prevent atrocities can be eroded after three conditions have been met:

1. Violent acts have to be *authorized* by official and legal orders.
2. The legal acts have to be *routinized* and assigned to the proper officials.
3. The victims have to be culturally *dehumanized* so that the population can be indoctrinated.[3]

All of these modes of operation seem necessary, but first a specific group has to be identified. The Jewish people had historically been preselected.

Our standard image is that the civilizing process is an ongoing historical suppression of irrational antisocial drives coupled with a rational and methodical elimination of violence from social life. The goal of this process is safe stability. Historically, this goal has been achieved through the concentration of power in the state, whose mission has been defense of the nation's borders and legitimation of the historically composed sociopolitical order. At least theoretically, power and order have been based on our presumption that civilized society is a moral force. Traditionally, we have viewed society as a system of interactive institutions that were to cooperate and complement one another as part of the process of establishing a normative order and the rule of law. This bureaucratic order was designed to establish conditions supporting social peace and individual security. As part of the dominant stream of political theories in European culture, this image of the state as political and social arbiter has unfortunately diverted attention from the destructive potential of this very same modernity process. Since the eighteenth century, our obsession with "progress" has frequently silenced and marginalized critics who could see the possibilities for evil in the sociopsychological interaction that presumably was preserving our civilization. The Holocaust has forced us to question this modernization process. Legal violence has been justified by moral values, and bureaucratic rationalization has left behind the guidance of ethical norms and moral inhibitions. Phrases like "sanctity of human life" or "moral duty" have now become as problematic in a university seminar as in faceless bureaucracies.[4] Within the parameters of this now-suspect civilizing process, what role did religious/cultural antisemitism play in propelling Europeans into politically sanctioned murder? For authorized routinization to have an effect, the victims had to be dehumanized. Previously, we have seen how Christian theological contempt had become part of the social, political, and cultural structure of Christian Europe. To understand how Hitler's hatred could fall on such fertile ground, we have to study, albeit briefly, the parameters of modern antisemitism that became part of the culture of post-Enlightenment Europe.

Initially, few causal links stand out more clearly than those that exist between the Holocaust and antisemitism. Extensive research, however, has undermined such a reductionistic conclusion.[5] Evidence can also be marshaled[6] that indicates that before the Nazi "revolution," and long even after the consolidation of Hitler's rule, popular antisemitism in Germany ran a poor second to fear of bolshevism and support for nationalism.[7] Rarely, in the Third Reich during this grisly process did popular antisemitism, in contrast to the racial antisemitism of the ruling elite, play an instrumentally determinative role. Although we may understand how virulently antisemitic leaders could shape a policy, our problem comes down to why or how so many went along. Popular and theological antisemitism may have contributed obliquely to the active perpetration of mass murder by reinforcing the already existing apathy toward the victims among the bystanders who daily witnessed the spiraling destruction. For centuries the Jewish people had been considered outsiders.

Historically, European culture had created the religious notion that the Jews were different and, therefore, dangerous. Such a stereotype, when combined with the threatening sociopolitical factors present in Weimar Germany, served to dehumanize the Jews into a group that could be politically marginalized. In effect, the bystanders had been inoculated by their own culture against protesting antisemitism. Some bystanders also presumably felt that the legalization of antisemitism and subsequently the implementation of the "resettlement" policies presented career and economic benefits. Such scholars as Walter Laqueur have explained such passive cooperation by suggesting that the bystanders and even the activists may not have had any articulated convictions about the anthropological nature of the Jewish people. They all probably had cultural biases that could inoculate them against helpfulness. Very few people seemed to have an activist interest in the fate of the Jews, who had gradually been removed from their midst anyway. It is difficult to have compassion for those with whom we have no contact. Antisemitism proved to be an unpleasant topic of conversation for those who tried to avoid political entanglements. Any public discussion of the fate of the Jews by the very nature of the system had to remain muted and relatively nonexistent.[8] Religious/cultural antisemitism helped in the process of the depersonalization and marginalization of this so-called hostile group.

To explain the Holocaust just by appealing to religious or racial antisemitism alone, however, would be problematic. In its various forms, antisemitism – religious or racial, cultural or economic, virulent or mild – has existed for nearly two thousand years as a component of European civilization, but no assault matching that of the Holocaust occurred even in the Middle Ages, when the church, which fostered antisemitism, was dominant. Apparently, government policy and specific officials, who have a personal interest vested in the bias, are the crucial variables necessary for sponsored mass murder.[9] A scholarly consensus has been emerging that the Holocaust cannot be seen as solely the culmination of anti-Jewish sentiments or as a virulent eruption of popular resentment against the Jews, but the bias did serve to isolate a group that could be oppressed and finally murdered for reasons of state more closely associated with social engineering techniques.

Post-Enlightenment modernity inherited a religious image of "the Jew" and gradually developed a secularized stereotype that bore little resemblance to the real Jewish men and women who inhabited the towns and villages of Europe. The stereotype had historically proven its worth as a mode of response to threatening conditions. The prejudice was valuable as a tool to channel anger and to relieve social anxiety. Useful in the contrapuntal role of alter ego to the church in Christian society, the stereotype could be used from the Enlightenment onward to help support the secular agencies working for social integration. At least theoretically, the modernistic goals urged the sublimation of differences through the assimilation of peoples. For varied sociopsychological reasons, however, many still tried to retain selected societal and cultural distinctions to support their own personal and group identities even in the face of the awesome eroding power of social and legal equality. Egalitarianism and antisemitism, therefore, managed to live side by side. Ultimately, uniformity was sought through totalitarian methods by those who could no longer handle the cultural dissonance.

In our modern era, the religious roots of the boundary between Christians and Jews could not legitimately support ethnic or racial distinctions because conversion to Christianity could only resolve the religious issue, which would be irrelevant to those imbued with the secularistic spirit. Thus, the modern rationale behind the distinctiveness of the Jews had to be established on a new foundation that ultimately would prove more potent than such variables as culture and religious self-determination. Judaism had to be replaced with Jewishness: "Jews had been able to escape from Judaism into conversion; from Jewishness there was no escape."[10] Science could support this metamorphosis and seemingly eliminate the relativism of culture. Eugenic racism became a tool of social engineering, which was to help design a secular society that might be seen as a worthy successor of the desired homogeneous religious society. Biological policies for purifying society, which were supported by the educated elite, were institutionalized prior to the Final Solution and softened the consciences of many. Long before gas chambers were physically constructed, the Nazis had also inaugurated extermination of the mentally ill and bodily impaired German citizens through "mercy killing," i.e., euthanasia. Equally as subversive, such policies as *Lebensborn* were to encourage the breeding of a superior race through the organized fertilization of superior Aryan women by racially certified men. From 1933 on, negative eugenic policies were used to sterilize "inferior" persons. All of these policies can be seen as incremental landmarks on the slippery slope to Auschwitz. The murder of the Jews could then be seen as another rationalization tool to manage society toward political ends.[11] Bureaucracy, science, and state power served to establish the Final Solution as policy; antisemitism culturally isolated the group.

Christian theologians, of course, had never developed an extermination program, but they could support the exclusion and ghettoization policies that for centuries had served to remind Christians of their salvation. In its "scientific" form, the traditional segregation of the Jews was expanded and racially defined into an exercise in sanitation. Modern Jew-hatred saw in this socioreligious group a biologically ineradicable flaw. Committing spiritual wrongs, sinners could repent, and the Jewish people could convert. In a biologically racial context, those with unacceptable blood would have to be expunged from the body politic.[12]

Such racial extermination was facilitated by using ethnocentric and racial imagery from premodern and modern historical experiences so that new policies seemed to be based on older values. The Holocaust as a policy suggests that an entrenched conceptualization of the use of medicine and surgery accompanied by a model of health and normality provided at least one premise for a strategy of separation, which could build on the centuries-old policy of isolating Jews from the Christian communities. This supplied a consistency that could be cognitively appealing. The Holocaust as a policy resembles the engineering and biological models of society that the educated elite felt could legitimate the prescribed social order. Crucial as well in the process was the modern ethos of institutional expertise that had grown out of the scientific management of social interaction. This nexus of impulses produced the policy. The Shoah can be viewed as a thoroughly modern phenomenon rooted in the modernization process, but nurtured and modeled already in the premodern environment.[13]

From hindsight, the Holocaust seems to be the monstrous result of a comprehensible process. The bureaucratic and scientific ethos, which was instrumental in actualizing the Holocaust, has not disappeared, as other genocidal disasters can prove. What nonantisemitic factors can also be cited? As distinct from sporadic pogroms, systematic murder apparently can be implemented only by a powerful government that can orchestrate the social forces and tensions so typical of modern society. The stresses and anxieties growing out of a lost war or emerging from traditional political tensions seem to be necessary to implement policies of ethnic cleansing. Procedurally organized exclusion and murder also seem to require the cooperation of the military and the bureaucracy.

Several factors led to the Holocaust, which served to integrate religious and racial antisemitism into the practical policy-making apparatus of a centralized state. The "state of emergency" growing out of the war allowed the Nazis to commit the legalized murder that presumably would have been opposed in times of peace, even though this biopolitical policy was very logical in a culture that supported eugenic racism. The Nazi state and the accompanying total war are not necessarily intrinsic to modern state development, but certainly such likenesses have been made more easily possible in the twentieth century. The sociopolitical, psychological, economic, and cultural factors potentially leading to genocide seem present in virtually every modern social organization endemic to our civilization.[14] Religious antisemitism or anti-Judaism, therefore, created the vocabulary, popular imagery, and theological theses that served to reinforce the secular agendas leading to the Shoah. The culture was supportive of the exclusionary and murderous policies that social scientists have profitably been analyzing.

The Holocaust and the
Psychosocial Dynamics of a Normal Society

What are the controlling social and political forces as well as psychosocial dynamics in modern society that social scientists studying mass murder have isolated? As an unprecedented event, the Holocaust demands political, social, moral and religious analyses that intersect and illuminate the human predicament in modern society.

The nation-state, which in our century has instrumentally promoted genocide, compels our questioning its historical evolution since the French Revolution. As scholars have faced the horrors of this century, they have tried to define "genocide" and "Holocaust." Genocide as a somewhat limited ethnocentric policy has offered an unfortunate plethora of examples in this century, whereas the Holocaust was unique because the Nazis hoped to murder an entire people wherever they lived in the world. Helen Fein has suggested a definition that may be of service in helping us understand both.

> Genocide is sustained purposeful action by a perpetrator to physically destroy a collectivity directly or indirectly, through interdiction of the biological and social reproduction of group members, sustained regardless of the surrender or lack of threat offered by the victim.[15]

Formulating definitions can be bizarre and may seem insignificant. Distinguishing between genocide and the Holocaust seems to involve differentiating between delineating people as subhuman for use as economic slaves or to be executed, and designating them as nonhuman, which was the case with the Holocaust. It is probably a sign of our rationalist/scientific era that some scholars have tried to distinguish between genocide as a regularly exercised option of state power and the Holocaust as a specific implementation of the Nazi worldview. The Holocaust can be seen as genocide with an added twisted dimension rooted in an all-encompassing ideology.

Nazi Germany can help illustrate the effects of a culturally transmitted bias that can aid in understanding why racial antisemitism was effective as we remember that the biological mooring was central and superseded the older religious stereotype. The Nazi state was interested in some kind of Final Solution and was able to build a broad range of societal support for itself because the prejudice against the Jewish people runs deeply in our society. Penetration by Nazis into the social structure gradually occurred as they promoted along with antisemitism such ideas as cleanliness or hard work, which traditionally had been held to be respectable and virtuous by members of the middle class. Even though powered by hatred, therefore, the Nazi political program appeared respectable. The Nazis supported a broad range of social virtues, and many Germans could support

Nazism despite the rabid antisemitism of some of its leaders. Basically, the Nazi goal was to weave antisemitism into the web of civic virtue. Mass extermination was the fruit of the bureaucratically engineered dehumanization that aimed at converting citizens into aliens by impugning their lack of civic and racial virtue, which in fact were considered identical. A potent tendency in Nazi Germany was to create juridical-legal divisions between citizens and aliens, or "dominant and backward races," which they hoped could scientifically be shown as rooted in moral and/or anthropological soil. Such "scientifically proven distinctions" could help condition the population, they felt, to accept the legalization of genocide as public policy.[16] Creating public policy and a political ethos can have consequences.

In the genocidal environments that we have witnessed, the substantive issues seem to revolve around how individuals concerned with rights to self-definition can live in communities with other groups. This is a particularly timely issue because states have the power, presumed legal and moral, to destroy enemies that threaten their existence. Why people are executed becomes a measure of what societies value. Studying genocide can help sensitize us to the potential dangers of state power. Generally, more state authority would signal a reduction in individual survival possibilities. Put another way, a greater capacity to develop personal potential would seem to suggest a more circumscribed state authority. Embedding the principle of personal dignity at the center of moral and political values can help serve as a counterbalance to the awesome sociopolitical power at the heart of totalitarian societies. Such powers can also be engaged in democratic societies in the name of state efficiency. What is debated in medical literature under the rubric of societal health, for example, ended up being transformed into support for euthanasia even during the Weimar Republic. Similarly, the antisemitism that theologically had been embedded in Christian European culture could and did suggest to some that religious distinctions had been sanctioned by God and so could be extended politically.[17]

Is there an essential and growing contradiction between the growing bureaucratization rooted in societal hierarchy and the principle of participatory equality, which was theoretically at the basis of the liberal democratic order? Bureaucracy historically has consigned people to slots, which reflects the institutionalization of domination hierarchies. Participatory modes of government suggest a grass-roots source of power. As nineteenth- and twentieth-century governing institutions have gained in size and dynamism, however, they have frequently curtailed political participation because they could no longer support the traditional liberating values in a complex social order that seemed to cry for organization. The major emerging principle forging modern and postindustrial societies has worked toward having decisions removed from the political arena into bureaucracies that can be controlled by ideologically driven elite groups. Technology has frequently driven this decision-making process.[18] The Holocaust, then, seems to suggest that even a democratic culture must be sensitized to new patterns of administration that can remove political authority from a responsible group into a faceless bureaucracy controlled by an individual who controls the power of the state.

The Holocaust has reemphasized the need to highlight the person as *the* central factor in the social order to counterbalance state power. Social scientists have focused on the nature of the social system with respect to its murderous potential. Sensitive to the horrors wreaked in the twentieth century, they have suggested that systems should take as given a person's right to live. Such a basic principle would ensure that death did not become the result of an efficiently running state. Several political principles would follow if the *person* as an embodiment of dignity were at the center of the system. Obligations to the state would be ontologically related to the right to live and would not be connected to the reasons for living. In this context, the managed society would command obedience only when it became necessary for communal survival and was not just being imposed for technocratic efficiency. Proclaiming the rights of the individual person and how that person should live is not the primary concern of the state. Too much normative theorizing on *the* social good that is not counterbalanced by an awareness of the sanctity of the person could end in a Hobbesian doctrine of obligations. Political theory in the nineteenth and twentieth centuries has been muddied by a juridical assertion of atomistic individual rights and obligations that serve the state but do not counterbalance the right to life as *the* basic right within a state. Any stress on the atomistic individual or on the organic community as the primary arbiter of rights misses the point of the sanctity of human dignity, which flows into the construction of person-centered communal relations. Darrell Fasching even goes so far as to suggest that a theological-ethical maxim that requires that we welcome the stranger and audaciously protect this person's rights and well-being may be basic for a social order that can protect us all.[19] Perhaps that welcoming attitude is the key to evaluating a societal system.

Cognizance of the widespread practice of genocide as a political program may help lead us to conclude that extreme caution should be exercised when supporting the nation-state. Brutal fanaticism and rampant chauvinism have been generated by mindless adherence to national goals. Political elites have instrumentalized genocide as a tool that has proven useful with unfortunate frequency in the pursuit of national and social policy. Genocide as a technique for achieving national solidarity has historically been implemented in a variety of forms across the political spectrum.[20] Even understanding the political and bureaucratic instruments behind the policy still leaves a gap in our understanding of sanctioned murder. What are the psychosocial dynamics driving ordinary people into committing crimes? Why do normal people perform extraordinarily evil acts? Ervin Staub and Herbert Kelman have pursued this issue, which gets to the root of how genocide can be part of "normal" political life.

Genocide does not simply begin in isolation as a stated policy without any historical precedents and preparation. Rather, it seems to be the end of a progression of actions. Staub and others have suggested psychological principles that can help track the trajectory that seems to lead to brutal political murder. Involved specifically in the Holocaust was a long-term historical devaluation of the Jewish people. This historical scapegoating is a particularly important dimension because blaming others diminishes the responsibility that might accrue to the perpetrators. Scapegoating can also help the perpetrators gain a sense of community. On a personal level, devaluation of a subgroup can psychologically help enhance one's own low self-esteem and thereby serve a socially integrating function. Joined with the adoption of a popular ideology, displacing hatred and anxiety can help shape a new world and possibly a utopian vision that can help the individual deal with a dismal or oppressive world. Joining with others in a group can serve to help erase a depressing self-image while assuming a constructive communal identity. In times of stress, groups that hope to attract members generally support an ideological blueprint for the future. As part of the process of shaping group identity, an enemy is usually identified, persecuted, and perhaps even annihilated to realize an ideology that promises a better world that can replace a social order that is disappointing. A potent nationalism frequently blossoms and is nourished by the experiences of shared trauma, suffering, and humiliation, which had initially caused debilitating self-doubt. This nationalism can then stimulate hope for a "paradise regained."[21] Given the stress and the hope for positive change, normal inhibitions seem to recede into the background as ethical sensitivities weaken.

Moral constraints seem to exert less powerful controls for groups than for individuals, who find that in serving the interests of the group as a whole, a sense of personal moral obligation tends to recede. Frequently, a diffusion of responsibility will reduce ethical inhibitions. In the group political process, members generally relinquish authority to the group and its leader. They become less compassionate and can find it easy to abandon their decision-making responsibilities to the group or its leader. With their moral sensitivities deadened, they may even sacrifice their lives.[22] This altruistic self-sacrifice for group identity seems to be a factor in reinforcing opposition to that segment of the population that seems to threaten the community. The group's power to repress dissent can now take a quantum leap forward in the potential for evil. The rise and brutal success of Nazism have provided the historical data that can be used to root popular psychological theories in the historical milieu.

In the last two decades, historians have devised increasingly complex analyses of the economic and political forces that preceded the Holocaust. The role of elites, the relationship between big business and Hitler, the nature and impact of mass politics, the factors that led to the collapse of the Weimar Republic, the unification of Germany under Bismarck within a highly authoritarian political framework, and rapid industrialization have all been examined to discern their roles in the rise of Hitler and implementation of the Final Solution. The basic nutrients of the Holocaust, however, appear to be an antisemitic cultural environment that respected authority and was stimulated by the stressful life conditions that demanded change to achieve political, economic, and social stability. Hitler had the ability to manipulate the population and to articulate the nationalist political purpose that, at least on the surface, seemed able to respond to these needs. His own political agenda was embraced by most Germans even though they may not have been enthusiastically antisemitic. In fact, during the final electoral battles in the Weimar Republic, the Nazis were supported *despite* and not because of their antisemitism, which concealed Hitler's own activist racial agenda. Channeling frustration, uncovering scapegoats, and formulating respectable political ideologies fused Germans in support of one leader who promised a return to an idealized past. Thus, psychological hungers and carefully crafted political purpose coincided disastrously in Germany. This resonance between the motives of the members of the group and their leader proved satisfying and able to drive the state.[23] This symbiosis between Hitler and the German people generated an almost unstoppable political power, which demanded a culture that was conducive to this resonance and formed the bedrock for the disastrous policies of World War II.

In twentieth-century states, the citizens' response to sociopolitical hardship is mediated through their culture and institutions. Culture conditions what ideals emerge and whether fulfillment can be achieved through opposition toward internal subgroups and external enemies. Culture can also inform citizens why their society is in a stressful state and how the situation might be improved. Traditional values can be mediated through the historically conditioned symbolic environment that shapes the ideals for such institutions as the military, schools, and the family with its child-rearing practices. As a web of processes, culture socializes the individual personality. The clarity of earlier dominant values has receded in modern complex societies because of the attempt to bind together groups with differing agendas.[24] A specific society's goals, for example, epitomize treasured values as well as shape the existing culture and institutions that socialize the children who will maintain the future society. Historical differences among subgroups within a society can affect values, goals, and ways of life, which may lead to conflict until one set of goals becomes normative. Within the pluralistic culture, individuals try to refine an ethical grid in order to make social decisions.

Moral configurations seem to emerge through social interaction within the parameters of specific cultures. Individuals and cultures, for example, differ in their concern for others' welfare. Typically, European civil societies have stressed rule-centered moral orientations that focus on norms, conventions, and the maintenance of society. Community survival takes priority over the personal welfare of the individual. A person-centered orientation, however, is directed toward the well-being of persons within the group. Ideally, of course, the interests of the person and the community should be balanced. Guided by respect for the person, moral rules could be devised to serve individual survival. When the group has become the focus of concern, however, historically the individual has tended to be denigrated. As a result, in European societies specific individuals or such subgroups as the Jewish people have frequently been excluded by the dominant group from the universe of moral concern or obligation. Given the normative belief in a just world,[25] victims have usually been viewed as deserving their fate.

The grid of moral values, which is used by individuals to make their personal decisions, is given its controlling force through the standards and rules that embody the will of the dominant group. Deviation from these moral obligations is felt to have serious social consequences. Conscious burdens may also be lightened, however, because we obey laws that have been almost unconsciously inculcated through socialization processes. Still, morality supported by the group can take a lethal direction that previously did not originally seem likely or even potential. Religious antisemitism, for example, never proposed physical extermination, yet the connection now seems clear. In general, we try to adjust our personal values to meet variations in our psychosocial environment. Subgroups that do not seem to conform to the dominant definition of the "good society" may be excised from "humanity" as the Final Solution prescribed.[26] The dynamics of group interaction, which take place in the ethical grid that governs society, can help us understand how sanctioned massacres can occur.

Human beings seem to have almost a psychological need to divide their social world into "us" and "them." Crucial for supporting this ethnocentrism, for example, is the nearly axiomatic need we have to categorize by highlighting trivial distinctions to create ingroups and outgroups. Reinforcing the ingroup-outgroup discrimination are the fear and anxiety, which seem to be our response when we confront the different and equate the familiar with the good. Essential to the psychological dimension is the fact that familiar sociocultural configurations seem to offer the indispensable foundation for a normal social existence. A child's parents, community, and nation, as well as religion, race, and social tradition, are the primary agents involved in the socialization process. On a day-to-day level we would be swamped by uncertainty and anxiety if we had to react socially with no guidance from the past. Categorization derived from socialization seems to be the basis for stereotypes, i.e., exaggerated beliefs about groups, which generally are negative. Merely defining people as "them" can cause immediate devaluation. Such distinguishing characteristics as race, religion, status, wealth, power, and political views help reinforce the primary ingroup-outgroup differentiation. [27]

How a culture reinforces its members' evaluation, categorization, and labeling is significant because devaluation makes mistreatment likely. In the context of the Holocaust, for example, guilt-free massacre was built on the ability to deny the victim's humanity. As the history of the Jews in Europe has shown, negative stereotypes can result in discriminatory social institutions. Helen Fein, for example, has indicated that the Nazis exterminated more Jews in those states where discriminatory antisemitism was already a powerful force and was supported by local institutions rooted in the culture. [28]

Once a specific group has been victimized, albeit only slightly, the resultant psychological state that occurs nearly always ensures greater harmdoing. One psychological result of social aggression, for example, seems to be a felt need to further devalue the victim. Embedded in this just-world theory is the axiom that the victims deserve their suffering by their actions or character. [29] Faith in this just-world theory can easily result in derogating impoverished persons, underprivileged groups, or minorities. The importance of legalistic convention as distinct from empathy and concern with human welfare arises as just-world theory and dehumanization processes intersect in the day-to-day activities of persons in society.

Genocide or mass murder cannot be directly correlated only with stressful conditions, with their psychologically depressing effects. Necessary to the genocidal act, according to Staub, is an incremental progression along a "continuum of destruction." People both learn and change by *doing*, when they frame discriminatory laws or mold a biased culture. Casual, everyday activities can serve to bind a person into a destructive system. Initiatory acts may inflict only limited harm, but they may ultimately introduce psychological changes that can virtually eliminate inhibition, which can reinforce the devaluation of the outgroup and make possible even more serious victimology. Finding support for their actions, the perpetrators may end up even more oppressive toward their victims.[30] Supporting discriminatory stereotypes seems to reduce socially developed commitments to the welfare of others. The inhibitions prohibiting killing gradually dissolve. Such inhibitions, moreover, can be further reduced when the political leaders accept responsibility for the murderous acts. Accountability can be reduced by shifting responsibility to others so that the compartmentalization of acts allows the perpetrators to deny their conscious participation in murderous policies. Such a dynamic reinforces the need to follow orders.

Such a devaluation of individuals with distinguishing differences generally occurs only within a delineated framework. Such devaluation develops gradually over decades or even centuries and can permeate the whole culture prior to the perpetration of genocide. Cultural devaluation of a designated group, therefore, historically has "preselected" the victimized group for persecution. In a society under stress, leaders may argue the need to protect the individual and group self-concept by harming others. Devaluation of specific subgroups can be seen as a necessary cultural tool for facilitating harmdoing as well as a criterion for organizing the framework for selecting victims.[31]

The Shoah was the end-product of a continuum of hate, fear, and discrimination. A historical continuum in "steps" of antisemitism originated, even if such was not the original intent of the authors, in the scriptural passages that were composed in response to specific historical contexts and subsequently were filtered through the traditions of Christian communities and the works of Christian authors down through the ages. Some of these formulations were removed from the specific historical context and universalized, especially after the destruction of the temple in 70 C.E. These initial formulae justified and were embedded into a history of persecution, pogroms, and such cultural manifestations as Passion Plays and thereby normalized the prejudicial process that culminated in Nazi Germany with boycotts, legal exclusion from the professions, sterilization, euthanasia, and, finally, Auschwitz.[32]

Sanctioned massacres cannot be sufficiently explained simply by referring to psychological forces that shape behavior. The institutional components that perpetrate legalized violence are also at fault and go a long way toward explaining the behavior of those who do not hate but are only "doing their job." These institutions have historically been designed to rationalize the policies for the efficient governing of society. The unintended result, however, has been to concentrate power in the hands of technocrats who have no political responsibility to the citizenry. Why were so many people willing to devise, condone, and perpetrate policies that demanded the mass killing of seemingly defenseless victims? According to Herbert Kelman, the personal motives for violence should certainly be examined, but only within the context of the situational environment that seems able to mute the traditional moral inhibitions against violence. As mentioned above, three social processes that support implementation of genocidal policy have been isolated: authorization, routinization, and dehumanization.[33] Authorization absolves the individual from moral responsibility for harmdoing. Routinization breaks the action into component parts so that no opportunity for even asking moral questions can emerge. Dehumanization historically shapes cultural attitudes toward the target so that it becomes neither necessary nor likely that the perpetrators would review the action in moral terms.

Sanctioned massacres are generally launched by an overwhelming authority, which helps legitimize the abrogation of personal moral principles in favor of societal viewpoints. When violence has been officially ordered, subtly urged, tacitly condoned, or just allowed by the proper authorities, individuals who have been culturally conditioned, apparently have no problem with acting brutally. Authorization obviates the need to form judgments because the so-called normal moral principles seem to be set adrift as a new ethical grid is devised. When the actions are explicitly ordered, a perverse morality now seems to stress that the person should obey superior orders rather than protect human life.[34]

In the presence of a dominant legal authority, individuals tend to capitulate to superior orders, even if such demands contradict what has been considered normative. For responsible citizens, no choice really has to be made as long as, at least superficially, the legitimacy of the authorities and their orders are centered in the sociopolitical environment. It is difficult to predict under what conditions individuals will challenge a "legitimate" order and at what level that response will be. It is difficult for most persons to argue that an order is illegal, or that the authorities have superseded their bounds, or that official policy can violate, except accidentally, basic human rights and fundamental societal values. To sustain legitimate authority requires that citizens respond with obedience, even if their personal preferences may have to be altered. Our social bias seems to favor authority rather than personal preference. Only by successfully challenging the governing authority as legitimate can citizens disobey. Historically we have found it fairly easy to obey unquestioningly, even though our behavior may well entail extreme personal sacrifice or even bodily harm to others.[35]

Structurally crucial to the authority issue is the fact that psychologically individuals prefer to bracket themselves in order to escape personal responsibility even for killing others. If they can perceive themselves as constrained, then they seem not to feel personally responsible for what others usually consider crimes. The perpetrators do not see themselves as evil but rather as merely extensions of legal authority. Since responsibility is not carefully delineated, guilt-free massacres can occur. Antisocial behavior ranging from boycotts to extermination, and that may be formally illegal, can be legitimated by the legal authorities.[36] Legal orders can create an environment that eases people into violent actions while ignoring their moral implications by encouraging automatic behavioral responses. Taking the initial step can create a psychological and social habit that can reinforce continuation. Forces that might normally have preserved moral integrity now appear to dissolve as individuals make a commitment to obey under the aegis of the state.[37] Authorization complements the routinization of assigning responsibilities.

Although there seem to be some explanations for guilt-free harmdoing, the nature of such a horror as Auschwitz is so overwhelming that we might anticipate that our deep-seated moral scruples would intervene. Unfortunately, the possibility of moral resistance becomes greatly reduced when ordered actions are compartmentalized into routine, mechanical, standardized operations. Routinization obviates the need to make independent decisions and deadens our ability even to have moral quandaries. Standardized mechanization also shelters the perpetrator from the implications of a job because the details of the task become the obsession, and moral ramifications can be ignored. If the implementation of the policy can be divided into a series of discrete steps, which can be taken virtually automatically, it can be easy to forget the nature of the act.[38] Such a diffusion of responsibility serves to limit the scope of necessary decision making. Each participant's actions are part of the legitimate process. Such routines as stamping and filing papers, exchanging memos, implementing orders serve to reinforce the individuals who are part of the process. The reinforced conception that state officials and civil servants have legal authority can help others in the bureaucracy to focus totally on such mundane issues as the efficiency of their offices and the productivity process.[39]

Normalizing atrocities would be next to impossible if there were constant reminders that legal murder has moral connotations. Bureaucrats, therefore, characteristically invent language that can assist in camouflaging ethical nuances. The SS, for example, established *Sprachregelungen*, or "language rules," which gave them the ability to discuss the extermination program through verbal euphemisms. The term "language rule" was a code name that meant to lie. Such code words or euphemisms for killing and liquidation as "final solution," "resettlement," and "special treatment" helped those administrators involved adhere to their own ethical grids.[40]

Even utilizing authorization and routinization techniques, the inhibitions against murder are so powerful that the victims have to be dehumanized to make systematic killing "normal."[41] Sanctioned massacres become legitimized when victims can be deprived of their humanity. An identity as a distinctive person possessing intrinsic value seems crucial to preserving the individual. Equally important is the role of the community wherein the individual finds his or her identity. For optimal results, this community should be an interconnected network of caring individuals who can provide respect and support.[42] When a group of people has historically been categorized as subhuman and so can be excluded from the dominant community, the moral restraints against killing virtually seem to dissolve.

In war, dehumanization of the enemy seems fairly common. As part of a normal political process, sanctioned massacres seem to require dedicated dehumanization, which means the declaration of an "internal war." To promote genocide, the conflict usually redefines the very category of membership in a group. The battlefield then involves the struggle of an elite group to destroy the "enemy" that purportedly is undermining the society. In such a society, systematic destruction becomes a desirable political end. Homicidal dehumanization seems to emerge as a policy when the target group can easily be labeled because it has been historically stigmatized in the dominant culture. The stigmatized group is seen as the sinister enemy undermining social intercourse. Labels have historically served to deprive victims of an identity within the dominant community. The above can describe the history of antisemitism.[43] But this historical isolation process, which preselects, is only the beginning.

The massacre process demands further dehumanization of the victims if the perpetrator's activities are to be justified. The bureaucracy in Nazi Germany, for example, increasingly designated the victims as statistical entries for reports and the end results of productivity quotas. The perpetrators can also find reinforcement for their dehumanization tactics by observing the victimization phenomenon. The "just-world theory" helps "prove" to them that the victims are subhuman and deserve to be extirpated. Dehumanization is a process that seems to need continuous reinforcement.[44] In essence, why would a group be assaulted unless it deserved persecution?

Kelman and Hamilton have stated that obedience to authority needs social reinforcement as well.[45] In virtually all the social psychological research,[46] the individual is portrayed as an autonomous, inner-directed person as well as someone subject to external forces. The potency of social influence would seem to suggest that societal and cultural influences support a person's committing heinous acts. Most recent work cautions focusing exclusively on the role of dispositional factors. Situational environments seem crucial.[47] Human actors make moral decisions to assist survival within their environments. Even a powerful commitment to so-called objective ethical principles within the individual may not be sufficiently potent in a threatening situational context. The ethical values that we seemingly have cherished proved very fragile, for example, in Nazi Germany.

Particularly provocative in the context of Staub's "continuum of destruction" model are some of the strategies that have been devised to mitigate the contextually ingrained habits of obedience and destruction. At the societal level, Staub has maintained that the established norms that help amplify a universe of obligation have to be developed and then strengthened to guard against any routine acceptance of dehumanizing cruelty. Failure to challenge murderous policies, for example, can only contribute to their normalization and legitimization. In a context of continuing obedience, people can habitually and routinely obey diabolical orders as legitimate. Research on aggression also suggests that seeing sanctioned violence can desensitize participants.[48] Can something be done to mitigate "everyday" discrimination, as well as violence supported by political groups? Corrective efforts could include obsessively enforcing laws against discrimination and educating citizens so that violations of human rights cannot become normalized. Such counterforces, instrumentalized through watchdog organizations as well as legal structures and embedded in educational systems, can help mold social norms and moral sensitivities. In turn, these norms and sensitivities could activate and reinforce prosocial responses to crimes of obedience.

Dehumanization in combination with the messianic conviction of transcendent political missions can be particularly lethal. Highlighting the salience of victims as victims with an intrinsic value as human beings may be useful in opposing sanctioned brutality. Individuals have to be systematically placed in the forefront of communal obligation to ensure that their basic dignity is recognized. Political elites have to reflect on the consequences of the law, so that focusing on some transcendent goal can be obviated if it impacts negatively on any specific group. Faceless victims can be provided a political salience by using the law or publicity. When the potential victims have the ability to assert their own agenda values, they can help focus the decision makers' attention and avoid vulnerable situations.[49] In some circumstances, of course, such aggressive public behavior may elicit negative responses from the ruling elite. In a liberal democratic society, however, passive resistance or legal prosecution of violators has traditionally helped lead to new laws and social awareness and so to the improvement of the environment supporting victims rather than victimizers.

In those societies where a specific group has already been dehumanized, research directed to understanding the dynamics of prejudice, stereotyping, and ethnocentrism could also support strategies that emphasize that both the potential perpetrators and victims are human. If the "perpetrator" and the potential victim can engage in peaceful and noncompetitive contact as equals, it seems to be more difficult to dehumanize individuals. In ameliorating relationships between groups, leaders have to nourish an understanding sensitive to the needs and anxieties present in both groups along with a clear perspective of the ideology that is shaping society. The goal should be to nurture a realistic empathy that can integrate all of those in the state into the community.[50] Such a mutual defusing of cognitive categorization does not seem to develop naturally.

In society, political structures, educational programs, media initiatives, and advocacy groups sensitive to humanizing values have to be supported. Ethnocentric categorizations have to be countered because almost inevitably they lead directly to victimization. Targeting a group as the embodiment of social vice creates potential victims. Individualization techniques work against victimization because it seems easier to persecute a stereotype than an individual. Policies or actions that remove anyone from the human community should be opposed, especially if the legal authorities attempt to legitimize the pariah status of a group.[51] Virulent ideologies that aim at creating the "new man" in our century have been particularly prone to justifying crimes of obedience or to engaging in ethnic cleansing.

A poignant example of how dehumanization policies can be confronted was provided by the French Protestant villagers of Le Chambon who extended refuge for persecuted Jews from 1940 to 1944. Their Huguenot tradition in Catholic France and the character of their pastor, André Trocme, help explain their courageous behavior. Their resistance seems to have been a communally shared and traditional concern for individuals who were facing persecution. Villagers cared for and responded to the needs of the Jewish refugees from Nazi persecution. Informed by an official that the Nazis wanted to deport the Jews, for example, Trocme countered: "We do not know what a Jew is. We know only men."[52] The diverse accounts of altruistic behavior all seem to verify that some kind of consciousness of human dignity motivated those who rescued those Jews who were fleeing Nazi persecution.

Focusing on past historical experiences seems to suggest that nurturing prosocial values can help lay the foundations for long-term humanization policies. The right of the individual to say "no" should probably be legally supported to counter bureaucratic decisions and organized administrative environments. Such a response would necessitate ongoing reexamination of our institutionalized structures, which could provoke a sense of personal responsibility, a realization that ideas have consequences, and a compassion toward our fellow citizens. Such a critical response demands the everyday control of authority to mitigate excessive awe and the technique to avoid entrapment in its mystique.[53] Political participation at local and national levels can be supportive in this enterprise.

The Development of Prosocial Values

What has historically developed through cultural, social, and political interaction can presumably be dismantled by reinforcing prosocial values. The relationship between Jews and Christians, for example, must be reconsidered to reorient Christian theology around the concept that God's revelation is not group specific. Several strategies have been suggested. Starting with individualizing those we meet, an advance to political actions that constructively relate the person and community along with an intellectual restructuring and rethinking of Christian theology can all help articulate concern and a consciousness of our political universe of obligation. To counter the possibility of genocide and war, prosocial values ultimately have to be inclusive and treat all persons as having intrinsic value. As citizens experience the satisfactions inherent in prosocial acts, they may begin to see themselves as more caring. The social goal is to reinforce continuously even more altruism. Prosocial behavior should be sought as the moral premise that can humanize political life.[54]

Only in political action can social change be institutionally affected and a prosocial community structured. To promote equality, government practices have to be motivated to avoid the us-them dichotomy. Since laws can support a status quo or can facilitate social change, historically we have tended to rely on legal measures to advance our welfare. Converting a social agenda into law conforms with our historical dispositions and may help provide enduring reforms to mitigate civil strife.[55] If the law forbids discrimination, for example, then normal citizens seem to find it easier to follow moral norms that are supported by political and presumably social reinforcement mechanisms.

Laws, of course, need enforcement because inequitable practices usually find support in entrenched majority groups. When legal prohibitions merely oppose popular attitudes and activities, such laws may well be disobeyed, circumvented, or poorly administered. Simply having a law does not necessarily mean that an abuse can be countered. A fairly massive legal assault on discrimination may be needed to actualize existing statutes designed to further social reform. Laws enforced on a day-to-day basis can eventually shift cultural attitudes. Legal mechanisms that reinforce social change can help sustain a society's capacity for reform by legally protecting the opponents of discriminatory behavior from unauthorized coercion.[56] Laws seem to be able to change a social order that relies on discrimination, however, only if a socially critical mass can be methodically constructed.

Complex issues generally do not yield to a single solution for reducing the level of destructiveness. Both individual corrective initiatives and group action seem useful in changing the practices of established social systems. Since murderous aggression is not rooted in our nature but seems to be a product of aggression-promoting conditions, presumably we can counter potential destructive behavior by reinforcing prosocial behavior. Some historical experiences and social science research have suggested that an ameliorative social order can be constructed. Social experiences have to be directed toward personal dignity and then programmed so that a prosocial orientation and a sense of security can become institutionalized. Such a prosocial orientation certainly seems to rest on rejoicing in persons as persons.[57] A vision of the future with ideals that are rooted in the welfare of the person, who has a unique dignity, rather than in either religious or secular visions for improving "humanity," seems basic. Intermediate and achievable goals in the process and the courage to express reform ideas seem essential if we hope to develop an agenda characterized by nonaggression, cooperation, caring, and human connection. Social scientists as well as theologians can be part of creating this new paradigm, which can project the dignity, sanctity, and integrity of the person as central to the social order and the protection of as well as support for each person in the sociopolitical community as vital to nonaggressive human progress in relating the individual to the community.

Notes

1. Bauman, *Modernity and the Holocaust*, vii, 7; John K. Roth, "Holocaust Business," *Annals of the AAPSS* 450 (July 1980): 70.
2. Bauman, *Modernity and the Holocaust*, x, 1-2; Israel Charny, *How Can We Commit the Unthinkable?* (Boulder: Westview Press, 1982); Stellar Flory, "The Psychology of Antisemitism," in Michael Curtis, ed., *Antisemitism in the Contemporary World* (Boulder: Westview Press, 1986); George M. Kren and Leon Rappoport, *The Holocaust and the Crisis of Human Behavior* (New York: Holmes and Meier, 1980), 2.
3. For the well-balanced work that synthesizes the contributions stemming from the intentionalist/functionalist debate, see Richard Breitman, *The Architect of Genocide: Himmler and the Final Solution* (New York: Knopf, 1991). Breitman leans toward intentionalism but recognizes the need for the functionalist stress on a bureaucracy seeking the means to overcome obstacles. Herbert Kelman, "Violence Without Moral Restraint," *Journal of Social Issues* 29 (1973): 29-61; Rubenstein, *The Cunning of History*, 91, 195; Christopher Browning, "The German Bureaucracy and the Holocaust," in Alex Grobman and Daniel Landes, *Genocide: Critical Issues of the Holocaust* (Los Angeles: Simon Wiesenthal Center, 1983), 148; Leo Kuper, *Genocide: Its Political Use in the Twentieth Century* (New Haven: Yale University Press, 1981), 161.
4. Hilberg, *The Destruction*; John Lachs, *Responsibility of the Individual in Modern Society* (Brighton: Harvester Press, 1981), 12-13, 58; Colin Gray, *The Soviet-American Arms Race* (Farnborough: Saxon House, 1976), 39-40.
5. Katz, *From Prejudice to Destruction*; Friedrich Heer, *God's First Love: Christians and Jews Over Two Thousand Years* (New York: Weybright and Talley, 1970); Michael Kater, "Everyday Antisemitism in Prewar Nazi Germany: The Popular Bases," *Yad Vashem Studies* 16 (1984): 129-59. For a recent study using a traditional intellectual history approach, see Shmuel Almog, "'Judaism as Illness': Antisemitic Stereotype and Self-Image," *History of European Ideas* 13 (1991): 793-804.
6. Sarah Gordon, *Hitler, Germans, and the "Jewish Question"* (Princeton: Princeton University Press, 1984); Karl Schleunes, *The Twisted Road to*

Auschwitz: Nazi Policy Toward the German Jews: 1933-1939 (Urbana: University of Illinois Press, 1970).

7. Fein, *Accounting for Genocide*; Harry Feingold, *Menorah*, Judaic Studies Programme of Virginia Commonwealth University 4 (Summer 1985): 2.

8. Cohn, *Warrant for Genocide*, 267-68; Harry Feingold, *Menorah*, Judaic Studies Programme of Virginia Commonwealth University 4 (Summer 1985), 5; Laqueur, *The Terrible Secret*; Robert Gellately, *The Gestapo and German Society: Enforcing Racial Policy, 1933-1945* (Oxford: Clarendon Press, 1990).

9. Cohn, *Warrant for Genocide*, 266-67.

10. Bauman, *Modernity and the Holocaust*, 39, 58; Cohn, *Warrant for Genocide*, 252.

11. For conversion as a religious issue, see Tal, *Christians and Jews in Germany*; Hannah Arendt, *The Origins of Totalitarianism* (New York: Harcourt Brace Jovanovich, 1973), 87. For doctors and eugenics, see Robert Jay Lifton, *The Nazi Doctors: Medical Killing and the Psychology of Genocide* (New York: Basic Books, 1986); Proctor, *Racial Hygiene*; Paul Weindling, *Health, Race, and German Politics between National Unification and Nazism, 1870-1945* (Cambridge: Cambridge University Press, 1989). For sexism related to racism, see Gisela Bok, "Racism and Sexism in Nazi Germany: Motherhood, Compulsory Sterilization and the State," *Signs* 8 (1983): 400-21. For eugenics as rational political management, see Weiss, *Race Hygiene*.

12. Mosse, *Toward the Final Solution*, 134; Hannah Arendt, *The Origins of Totalitarianism* (New York: Harcourt Brace Jovanovich, 1973), 87. For Nazi terminology associating "Jew" with such terms as cancer and vermin, see Richard Koenigsberg, *Hitler's Ideology: A Study in Psychoanalytic Sociology* (New York: Library of Social Science, 1975); Merkl, *Political Violence under the Swastika*.

13. Proctor, *Racial Hygiene*, 1-47; Weindling, *Health, Race, and German Politics*.

14. Gordon, *Hitler, Germans*, 48-49; Bauman, *Modernity and the Holocaust*, 84-95.

15. For a sociological analysis of genocide, see Horowitz, *Taking Lives*, 16; Yehuda Bauer, "Against Mystification," in Yehuda Bauer, *The Holocaust in Historical Perspective* (Seattle: University of Washington Press, 1978), 30-49; Helen Fein, "Genocide: A Sociological Perspective," *Current Sociology* 1 (1990); 24. See also Fein, *Genocide Watch*, 3.

16. Mosse, *Toward the Final Solution*, 232-35; Horowitz, *Taking Lives*, 27,

57. For a multicausal analysis of the emergence of the Holocaust as policy, see Dietrich, "Holocaust as Public Policy": 445-62.

17. Henry Steele Commager, *The American Mind: An Interpretation of American Thought and Character Since the 1880's* (New Haven: Yale University Press, 1950), 176-77; Peter Glock, "Individualism, Society, and Social Work," *Social Casework* 58 (1977): 579-84; Michael Foucault, *Discipline and Punish: The Birth of the Prison* (New York: Pantheon Books, 1977), 3-5; Hannah Arendt, *Eichmann in Jerusalem: A Report on the Banality of Evil* (New York: Viking Press, 1963), 232; Horowitz, *Taking Lives*, 83, 86.

18. Daniel Bell, *The Coming of Post-Industrial Society: A Venture in Social Forecasting* (New York: Basic Books, 1973); Daniel Bell, *The Cultural Contradictions of Capitalism* (New York: Basic Books, 1976); Irving Louis Horowitz, "A Funeral Pyre for America," *Worldview* 19 (1976); Aaron Wildavsky, *Budgeting: A Comparative Theory of Budgetary Processes* (Boston: Little, Brown, 1975), 155-57; Joseph LaPalombara, ed., *Bureaucracy and Political Development* (Princeton: Princeton University Press, 1963), 48-55.

19. Horowitz, *Taking Lives*, 177, 184; Michael Walzer, *Obligations: Essays on Disobedience, War and Citizenship* (Cambridge: Harvard University Press, 1970), 98; Fasching, *Narrative Theology*, 2.

20. Ralf Dahrendorf, *Society and Democracy in Germany* (Garden City, NJ: Doubleday, 1967), 205-9; Michael Walzer, *Obligations: Essays on Disobedience, War and Citizenship* (Cambridge: Harvard University Press, 1970), 98; Horowitz, *Taking Lives*, 190-91. For an analytical survey of genocidal incidents, see Frank Chalk and Kurt Jonassohn, *The History and Sociology of Genocide: Analyses and Case Studies* (New Haven: Yale University Press, 1990).

21. Staub, *The Roots of Evil*, 17, 19; Herbert Kelman and V. Lee Hamilton, *Crimes of Obedience: Toward a Social Psychology of Authority and Responsibility* (New Haven: Yale University Press, 1989); J. Mack, "Nationalism and the Self," *Psychohistory Review* 2 (1983): 47-69.

22. Wallach, "Group Influences": 75-86; Latane and Darley, *The Unresponsive Bystander*; C. Mynatt and S.J. Sherman, "Responsibility Attribution in Groups and Individuals: A Direct Test of the Diffusion of Responsibility Hypothesis," *Journal of Personality and Social Psychology* 32 (1975): 1111-18.

23. Karl Dietrich Bracher, *The German Dictatorship: The Origins, Structure, and Effects of National Socialism* (New York: Praeger Publishers, 1970); Abraham, *The Collapse*; Weinstein, *The Dynamics of Nazism*; Golo Mann, *The History of Germany Since 1789* (London: Chatto & Windus,

1968); Marrus, *The Holocaust*; Dietrich, "National Renewal": 385-411; Hamilton, *Who Voted for Hitler?*

24. Stanley Milgram, "Nationality and Conformity," *Scientific American* 205 (1961): 45-51; S. Perrin and C. Spencer, "Independence and Conformity in the Asch Experiments as a Reflection of Cultural and Situational Factors," *British Journal of Psychology* 20 (1981): 205-9.

25. For a sociological analysis of society as a universe of moral concern, see Fein, *Accounting for Genocide*; Carol Gilligan, *In a Different Voice: Psychological Theory and Women's Development* (Cambridge: Harvard University Press, 1982); M.L. Hoffman, "Conscience, Personality, and Socialization Technique," *Human Development* 13 (1970): 90-126. For the "just world" theory, see Melvin Lerner, *The Belief in a Just World: A Fundamental Delusion* (New York: Plenum Press, 1980), esp. chap. 6.

26. Staub, *The Roots of Evil*, 58.

27. H.A. Hornstein, "Out of the Wilderness," *Contemporary Psychology* 29 (1984): 11-12; H. Tajfel et al., "Social Categorization and Intergroup Behavior," *European Journal of Social Psychology* 1 (1971): 149-77; Tajfel, *Social Identity*; R.B. Zajonc, "Attitudinal Effects of More Exposure," *Journal of Personality and Social Psychology, Monograph Supplement 1*, 9 (1968); Gordon Allport, *The Nature of Prejudice* (Cambridge, MA: Addison-Wesley Pub. Co., 1954), 28.

28. T. Duster, "Conditions for Guilt-Free Massacre," in C. Comstock and Nevitt Sanford, *Sanctions for Evil: Sources of Social Destructiveness* (San Francisco: Jossey-Bass, 1971), 27; Fein, *Accounting for Genocide*.

29. Melvin J. Lerner and C.H. Simmons, "Observer's Reaction to the 'Innocent Victim': Compassion or Rejection?" *Journal of Personality and Social Psychology* 4 (1966): 203-10; L.A. Peplau and Z. Rubin, "Belief in a Just World and Reactions to Another's Lot: A Study of Participants in the National Draft Lottery," *Journal of Social Issues* 29 (1973): 73-93; L.A. Peplau and Z. Rubin, "Who Believes in a Just World," *Journal of Social Issues* 29 (1975): 65-89.

30. Staub, *The Roots of Evil*, 17-18.

31. Tajfel, "Social Categorization": 149-77; M.B. Brewer, "Ingroup Bias on the Minimal Intergroup Situation: A Cognitive-Motivation Analysis," *Psychological Bulletin* 86 (1978): 307-24. For an analysis of Weimar Germany, see Karl Dietrich Bracher, *Die Auflösung der Weimarer Republik. Eine Studie zum Problem des Machtverfalls in der Demokratie*, 3rd ed. (Villingen/Schwarzwald: Ring-Verlag, 1960); Hamilton, *Who Voted for Hitler?*

32. Ervin Staub, "Individual and Societal (Group) Values in a Motivational

Perspective and Their Role in Benevolence and Harmdoing," in Ervin Staub et al., eds., *Social and Moral Values: Individual and Societal Perspectives* (Hillsdale: L. Erlbaum Associates, 1989), 55. For studies of antisemitism in the history of European civilization, see Gager, *The Origins of Anti-Semitism*; Neusner, *Judaism and Christianity in the Age of Constantine*; Obermann, *The Roots of Anti-Semitism*; Katz, *From Prejudice to Destruction*; Bruce Richard Bramlett, "Images of the Passion in Post-Shoah Theological Reflection? Dilemmas of Language, Remembrance and History in the Age After Auschwitz," Ph.D dissertation, Graduate Theological Union, 1992.

33. Kelman and Hamilton, *Crimes of Obedience*, 15-16; Albert Bandura, "Social Learning Theory of Aggression," in J.F. Knutson, ed., *Control of Aggression: Implications from Basic Research* (Chicago: Aldine Pub. Co., 1973); Robert Jay Lifton, *Home from the War—Vietnam Veterans: Neither Victims nor Executioners* (New York: Simon and Schuster, 1973).

34. Kelman and Hamilton, *Crimes of Obedience*, 16.

35. Stanley Milgram, "Behavioral Study of Obedience," *Journal of Abnormal and Social Psychology* 67 (1963): 371-78; Stanley Milgram, "Group Pressure and Action Against a Person," *Journal of Abnormal and Social Psychology* 69 (1964): 137-43.

36. Kelman and Hamilton, *Crimes of Obedience*, 17.

37. Kurt Lewin, "Group Decision and Social Change," in E.L. Hartley and T.M. Newcomb, eds., *Readings in Social Psychology* (New York: H. Holt, 1947).

38. Kelman and Hamilton, *Crimes of Obedience*, 18.

39. For the classic study of "groupthink," see Irving L. Janis, *Victims of Groupthink: A Psychological Study of Foreign-Policy Decisions and Fiascoes* (Boston: Houghton, Mifflin, 1972).

40. Arendt, *Eichmann in Jerusalem*, 85.

41. Kelman and Hamilton, *Crimes of Obedience*, 18-19.

42. Kelman, "Violence Without Moral Restraint": 25-61; D. Bakan, *The Duality of Human Existence: An Essay on Psychology and Religion* (Chicago: Rand McNally, 1966).

43. Kelman and Hamilton, *Crimes of Obedience*, 19.

44. Robert Jay Lifton, "Existential Evil," in Comstock and Sanford, *Sanctions for Evil*.

45. Arthur Miller, "Book Review: A Perspective on Kelman and Hamilton's *Crimes of Obedience*," *Political Psychology* 11 (1990): 189-201.

46. S.E. Asch, "Studies of Independence and Conformity: A Minority of One Against a Unanimous Majority," *Psychological Monographs* 70 (1956); P.G. Zimbardo, "The Human Choice: Individuation, Reason, and Order

versus Deindividuation, Impulse, and Chaos," in W.J. Arnold and D. Levine, eds., *Nebraska Symposium on Motivation* (Lincoln: University of Nebraska Press, 1969): 237-307.

47. Arendt, *Eichmann in Jerusalem*, 6; Stanley Milgram, *Obedience to Authority: An Experimental View* (New York: Harper & Row, 1974).

48. Kelman and Hamilton, *Crimes of Obedience*, 335-36; Albert Bandura, "Social Learning Theory of Aggression," in Knutson, *Control of Aggression*.

49. C.D. Stone, *Where the Law Ends: The Social Control of Corporate Behavior* (New York: Harper & Row, 1975).

50. Allport, *The Nature of Prejudice*; Tajfel, *Social Identity*; R.K. White, *Fearful Warriors: A Psychological Profile of U.S.–Soviet Relations* (New York: Free Press, 1984); Herbert Kelman, "The Political Psychology of the Israeli-Palestinian Conflict: How Can We Overcome the Barriers to a Negotiated Solution?" *Political Psychology* 8 (1987): 347-63.

51. Kelman, "Violence Without Moral Restraint": 54.

52. P.P. Hallie, *Lest Innocent Blood Be Shed: The Story of the Village of Le Chambon, and How Goodness Happened There* (New York: Harper & Row, 1979), 103. For analyses of Christian altruism toward the Jews during the Second World War, see Nechama Tec, *When Light Pierced the Darkness: Christian Rescue of Jews in Nazi-Occupied Poland* (New York: Oxford University Press, 1986); Samuel P. Oliner and Pearl Oliner, *The Altruistic Personality: Rescuers of Jews in Nazi Europe* (New York: Free Press, 1988). According to the Oliners, rescuers were conditioned to care.

53. Kelman and Hamilton, *Crimes of Obedience*, 21-22, 338.

54. Staub, *The Roots of Evil*, 276-77; Albert Bandura, *Aggression: A Social Learning Analysis* (Englewood Cliffs, NJ: Prentice-Hall, 1973), 320.

55. Bandura, *Aggression*, 322; G. Hawkins and F. Zimring, "The Legal Threat as an Instrument of Social Change," *Journal of Social Issues* 27 (1971): 33-48.

56. L.M. Friedman, "Legal Rules and the Process of Social Change," *Stanford Law Review* 19 (1967): 786-840.

57. Bandura, *Aggression*, 323; Staub, *The Roots of Evil*, 282.

9

Conclusion

Scholars have been trying to deal rationally with such political traumas of our century as the Holocaust, which was rooted in a nationalistic and bureaucratic environment. The Shoah as an event has alerted us to the fissures in our civilization. In feminist, political, and liberation theology, Christian theologians have worked to develop a hermeneutics where the subject matter — the event — can once again be allowed to rule. As an event, the Holocaust has compelled intellectuals in diverse disciplines to reflect on the values at the base of our culture. It has not been easy to deal with the Holocaust because this brutality has called into question a traditional view of both human and divine behavior.[1] Some Jewish scholars have responded to this shattering challenge by reaffirming God's continuing presence in history. Others have preferred to rely more on the freedom of men and women as they confront the human predicament. Christian theologians have reexamined early Christian antisemitism to find the context wherein it emerged and have sought to make speculative systems responsible to the concrete world of political power.[2] To meditate fully on the "human condition" in this post-Holocaust era seems to require that the Shoah be diagnosed by scholars who are sensitive to

Christian antisemitism, to the theological possibilities present in Jewish and Christian thought, and to social science research. Scholars in these areas have discerned that the values embedded in our theological and secular culture have to be questioned and transformed so that we may establish a defense against the possibility of future sanctioned massacres.

In this final decade of the twentieth century, after countless Holocaust studies, a critical nexus for future reflection on the issue of sanctioned murder can be discerned. The theological, historical, cultural, and sociopolitical environment that formed the necessary soil for the Holocaust, as well as the murderous actors operating individually or through institutions, have been studied in depth.[3] Scholars have now been working to face the challenge of understanding the divine and human meaning of the event with its implications for moral values and theological statements. Their theological, philosophical, and sociopsychological reflections seem to be creating a critical mass that may tell us how to reshape the structural values at the very foundation of our culture and civilization. Understanding the weaknesses of our culture is not enough, however, when human life is at stake. Philosophical and theological speculation will have to engage politics to avoid future tragedy.

Probing beneath the everyday surface of our civilization has become imperative because Auschwitz has insisted that we question the basic value assumptions at the very core of our culture — the nature of progress, the effect of science and technology on culture, the significance of the nation-state, the role of religion in our civilization, and certainly the concept of individualistic morality, which for too long has absolved corrupt institutions. Along with uncovering historical facticity and reflecting on the conceptual moral structures that have undergirded civilization, understanding the sociopsychological principles that seemingly support the behavior of those perpetrating murderous deeds can guide us as we begin reshaping our moral and cultural universe so that a future Auschwitz can be avoided. The actual transformation of values, of attitudes, and of our bureaucratic institutions is a task substantially more complex and demanding than merely identifying how we have erred in the past.[4] We have to rethink the individual and social meaning of morality in light of the God-humanity relationship and the psychological perspectives that have been suggested in earlier chapters. The analysis of our culture from the perspective of the Holocaust has offered several explanatory directions that can continue to be explored.

Since antisemitism is deeply rooted in our history, it is important to see that the early Christian search for an identity that was *not* Jewish inadvertently sponsored a potent bias against Jews in the two-thousand-year history of our culture.[5] This religious antisemitism was reinforced down through the centuries by the social, political, and economic interactions that contributed to the formation of our European civilization. Equally pernicious, at least in hindsight, has been the concept that moral questions are specific to individuals but not to cultures or institutions. In light of the Shoah, gender oppression, and marginalization tactics, it has become increasingly more compelling to look toward the uncovering of systemic and institutional evils that have been woven into our culture and society. Such a suggestion seems to mandate a reexamination of our moral culture. Among Catholic moral theologians who are responding to our overall culture, for example, there is currently emerging a dissatisfaction with the individualistic and traditional view of "nature" as the conceptual abstraction defining moral parameters. Such a traditional approach stressed the ahistorical world at the expense of the real world. The current disenchantment with abstract nature has helped move the moral focus from "human nature" to the "human person or human dignity." The participants at Vatican II, for example, were familiar with the whole Catholic moral tradition centered on the law of nature, when they suggested that moral standards should now be more responsive to the "dignity" of the human person, which could then be the basis for a more incisive sociopolitical critique. In *Pacem in Terris*, John XXIII also expressed this viewpoint well: "At the basis of any human coexistence that should be well ordered and fruitful must lie the principle that every human being is in essence a person." Stress on the person as a developing entity has become the crucial criterion used to judge the morally right or wrong act. The result is that human activity more and more can be judged insofar as it resonates with the human person as an integral entity. We seem increasingly, therefore, committed to an inductive method in deliberating about the rightness or wrongness of those acts in which our historical experience plays an indispensable role. Sin can be viewed as not simply an isolated deed of an individual but also as an act having institutional and structural dimensions. The "sins" of one generation can really become the restrictive conditions in our culture and its institutions.[6] Even the meaning of freedom and responsibility has to be examined. The charge of moral relativism can potentially be levied here unless the relationship between theory and praxis is carefully understood. Theory or the foundational principles of theology are uncovered or revealed more fully when we expand the meaning of revelation through the "reality test" of concrete activity. In this sense, then, praxis becomes the ensemble of theory and action.

One primary ethical issue challenging us after the Shoah has been how we are to respond to the concept of human liberation and the capability of structuring our sociopolitical environment. The notion of human liberation was inherent in the Nazi worldview and is at the basis of current democratic societies. Human liberation has led to brutal massacres when its proponents have asserted that they can make the "new man." Freedom has been lethal when combined with the instruments of control, which have been prevalent in this century. Paradoxically, the more liberated we have become, the more hazardous we have been toward our own species, because we feel free to direct our development. Such a notion was at the root of Nazi biopolitics. Until recently, our moral tradition has not dealt well with the concept of collective responsibility for significant sociopolitical issues. This micromoral orientation produced a social justice in the Catholic Church, for example, in which confession led to a myopic obsession with individuals, coupled with a reluctance to recognize the more socially or historically developed meaning of sin. As we now more and more realize, an element of sinfulness can exist in specific institutions or even in the social and cultural underpinnings of society. As Christian theologians have faced the post-Holocaust world of environmental degradation, political brutalization, and social oppression, to list only the most obvious abuses, a concept of evil embedded in an individual's relation to God does not seem sufficient because it cannot explain macroevil. Although uneven in quality, liberation theology, which concentrates on the sociopolitical implications of scripture, does suggest some directions for future speculation. Theologians and ethicists are now being asked to get involved in the overall political and cultural process of shaping society.[7]

This recent holistic, relational analysis of the individual person in society is critical of considering moral values in remote abstraction from the totality of lived experiences. The salubrious result has been that the hierarchy of values — which in the past emanated from a conceptual reflection on our metaphysical nature as it was actualized in its religious, social, and cultural manifestations — has now placed in the forefront a hierarchy of urgencies that takes into account our sociopolitical environment.[8] The human condition and its foundational values are intimately connected to the control fostered by the institutional environment. Social psychologists are equally convinced that we can create values that govern our cultural and moral universe and, conversely, that there are sociopsychological principles that can help illuminate the process of moral development as well as of diabolical behavior. These principles have reaffirmed that persons cannot be compartmentalized from their society.

From a social psychological perspective, the evidence seems to indicate that there is a critical interaction between the person and society that needs to be understood before the development and formulation of a moral grid can be accomplished. The behavior of whole societies reflects the collective nature of the goals and values of the persons involved. The more important a positive or negative value is for societal integration, and the stronger the power activating it, the more likely it may be realized. Such negative values as antisemitism, for example, have historically been powerful motivational determinants because they can respond to an array of threatening conditions. This bias historically has seemed relevant to the interactions of men and women in society. From the standpoint of social psychology, opposing values can coexist, but then the social spheres that respond to "good" and "bad" values have to be delineated. Christianity, which purportedly has been a religion embodying love and compassion, has misdeveloped by supporting antisemitism. Such values as those supportive of human dignity and compassion need not be universal even if such were desirable. They can be selectively viewed as inapplicable to a wide range of people, events, or environmental conditions. Members of outgroups, for example, have typically been classified as beyond the range of even basic human compassion. Their exclusion from the moral realm allows ideological formulations to justify physical abuse.[9] The goal would seem to be to extend that moral realm.

Psychologists as well as theologians have been confronting the moral challenges posed by the Holocaust as they have responded to current sociopolitical issues. Socialization research suggests that people can manifest one or both of the two primary moral orientations. One orientation focuses on the welfare of persons, the other on moral principles and rules. The two are not mutually exclusive, but one may dominate. A focus on moral principles follows from our concern with human welfare. As this personalistic response has historically been formalized into principles and rules, the intensive focus on the person's welfare has frequently lost its incisive edge because principles can become distanced from their original purpose. Therein lies the danger. Laws can end up camouflaging the original concrete reasons for the rule because universals obscure the nuances of real life. Equally as significant, reflection on moral issues in our culture has historically focused on the individual as a member of society, and to the individual has ascribed guilt. Ideally, of course, moral concerns should focus on both individuals and the group to which they belong. Obsession with the individual historically has established a focus that is legalistic and not sensitive to social evil. But should the group replace the individual as a focal point of concern? The danger of such group-centered morality as that prescribed in Nazi Germany is that concern about the member parts may vanish. Individuals may be sacrificed to group welfare or in the name of group goals; in this century this has led to unprecedented barbarity. The horrors of the past and present would seem to suggest that a positive evaluation of each human person's dignity in society is vital. Unfortunately, as we have seen, those who may positively evaluate human beings in general have frequently proceeded to destroy marginalized members of society if group-centered morality prevails. Resistance to barbarism, according to Metz and Bonhoeffer, can only emerge from the praxis of active and "costly discipleship." This theology of emancipation can focus on both individual humans and their institutions.[10] Psychological dynamics can help explain the marginalization process as well as how a conscience can be deadened; it then becomes incumbent on us to reconstruct our society and theology.

Psychologically, the us-them differentiation is a central source of devaluation. As part of the identity process, apparently there evolve stereotypical conceptions of other groups, which are frequently devaluative in nature. These stereotypes, which project negative images, are then usually taught to children as part of the socialization process through such media as literature and the arts. What seems to happen is that the cultural devaluation of a specific group historically "preselects" this very group for subsequent mistreatment. When conditions of life in a society are stressful, for example, the need to protect the individual and the dominant group self-concept may nearly demand that others be harmed as part of the process. Devaluation of subgroups makes doing harm to the selected victims more likely.[11] Unfortunately, the suffering of other people tends to reinforce their devaluation. "Just world" thinking can induce the perpetrators and bystanders to explain that the victims' sufferings are due to their character or actions. Empathy rarely arises for devalued victims. Real life and experimental evidence indicate that devaluation facilitates harming behavior. Theological and historical antisemitism created a culture that was structurally poisoned, that preselected a target group, and that theologically as well as morally eased the consciences of those actors in the drama of the Third Reich by historically supporting the virtues of ethnic and cultural citizenship.[12] What can now be done to re-create a new culture that can offer resistance to sanctioned massacre? No easy answers can be given, but there are indicators that can guide this enterprise.

To increase caring, connection, and compassion, and to diminish the number of times that members of a group mistreat "outsiders," research from the social sciences suggests that cultural and socialization practices have to be shaped to support the essential humanity of each person. Every person has needs and hopes. In particular, the research cautions us about the incremental development of values, attitudes, and behavior that depersonalize. Governments do not just promote a policy of genocide without antecedents that have prepared the way. Genocide and mass killings appear at the end of what Staub has labeled a "continuum of destruction." Theological and historical antisemitism softened the consciences of Europeans and enabled them to mistreat Jews for centuries. In Nazi Germany, then, boycotts and the exclusion of Jews from career opportunities did not seem unusual behavior. Ultimately this legal discrimination led to physical isolation and then to destruction. The cultural content nourished the sociopolitical continuum. Each step, successfully accomplished, facilitated the totalistic process. Undergirding this political behavior was the historical continuum of antisemitism rooted in scriptural passages and patristic reflections, which was funneled through medieval culture into the present so that the modern biological or racist stereotype was given a religious and cultural underpinning.[13] What has historically developed through interaction and cultural construction can presumably be dissolved and replaced by prosocial values, which means that the relationship between Jews and Christians as members of religious groups would have to be reconsidered with an eye to reducing the in-out group phenomenon by treating people as persons with an inherent dignity and by seeing both Judaism and Christianity as two paths for God's revelation, each with its own integrity. Sensitive to this transformative need, theologians and ethicists have been methodically reformulating the traditional configurations that guided Christian and Jewish life for centuries. This has meant reexamining the human condition and the meaning of God for humankind. Even though the Holocaust was a Christian deed, Jewish thinkers have also been quick to respond to the issues at hand. Lessons learned from the improvement of Jewish-Christian relations should be transferable to other antagonistic situations, especially those that may involve xenophobia.

Within a religious context, to discuss morality is to reflect on God and humanity. As we have seen, some Jewish scholars of the Holocaust have accused God of severing the covenant, and some have seen humanity in Auschwitz as a suffering servant. But this has proven unsatisfying in light of their tradition because we usually insist on seeing men and women as free agents of their destiny. Thus, in recent years the focus has methodically shifted to each person's free relationship to God, as well as the ability and responsibilities of humans to structure their political society through group interaction. Such a perspective would seem to demand that we must strive to keep the future history free of Nazi-like evil. But how? In exercising free responsibility, humanity has been viewed by some Jewish and Christian scholars as having a positive role in restoring the divine image, which would mean that we have a distinct role in the process of salvation. The Holocaust has stressed that the survival of humanity may well be preeminently a human duty. Through reflecting on the Holocaust, theologians of both faiths have suggested that we can experience God as a healing and affirming person as well as one who shares the responsibility for creation. God along with the Shoah as the event have helped expose the destructive power of hatred when combined with instrumentalized rationalism. In a very real sense, then, this God has displayed a vulnerability as well as a faith in humanity both on the cross and in Auschwitz.[14] While freedom is to be cherished, history has shown that it can be dangerous when not rooted in legitimate human values.

When the Nazis exalted the "new man" as a creature exercising total freedom, they in fact rejected God and perverted the meaning of true freedom. Sensitivity to this perversion, then, has supported a new consciousness of humanity's relationship to God. The Jewish people's experience has illustrated the demonic possibility of radical, unfettered human freedom when it is severed from transcendent authority. Such freedom, which in Nazi Germany stressed eugenic control, became a manipulative and dehumanizing force that could not be challenged by ahistorical theological abstractions that had failed to counter centuries of prejudice. A new meaning of and role for humanity has been taking form. In essence, those who have been reflecting on this issue have consciously begun to elevate a sense of human dignity that realizes its limitations. An adequate ethic requires a new appreciation of the profound link between history and human consciousness as it has meditated on the co-creational activity of God and humankind. In assuming power and recognizing responsibility for the species, we need to create a better mechanics of self-criticism, correction, and repentance as well as, to use Tracy's phrase, a "hermeneutics of suspicion."

The dialogue on Holocaust-related moral issues has been expanding yearly and seems to be shaping at least a tentative perspective that we must bear a major responsibility for our own activities, including sanctioned massacre. Searching for a theodicy that struggles to explain God's role in the Holocaust has directed us to move aggressively into political, social, and spiritual enterprises to prevent destruction. Those theologians engaged in Holocaust studies have found an attentive audience in those exploring personalistic ethical systems as well as liberation and political theologies. Since the presumption is that we all bear a primary responsibility for a society that is safe and nurturant, it has become incumbent on us to understand the sociocultural dynamics that have historically shaped modern political communities so that we may more effectively move into a safer future.

Moral theologians and social scientists can now profitably join issue in analyzing the Holocaust and proposing a moral grid that can serve to help prevent sanctioned murder.[15] Such an ethical grid, according to Haas, would be a system of values and convictions within which actions can be classified as good or evil. In the context of genocide, political power, individualism, collectivism, bureaucracy, and terrorism, sociopolitical phenomena that we have experienced have been related to oppressive and controlling national states. The role and power of the nation-state in the twentieth century, therefore, has to be questioned. The state that can foster murder is at least potentially evil, and virtually every political institution in the modern state has that possibility in specific circumstances. Although there are different foundational traditions behind the theological and sociopolitical principles that have helped produce genocide, scholars in varied disciplines have been working to develop a normative framework that is designed to protect the individual person's life, not just to produce social stability. Helen Fein, for example, has maintained that genocide as a political policy in the Third Reich has thrived in those communities that have systematically tried to exclude a portion of the population from what she labels "the universal sense of obligation" that persons feel for their fellow citizens.[16] In other words, there is a process of dehumanization and marginalization at work in genocidally prone societies. Such crimes as the Holocaust are not just spontaneous events. Theologians as well as social scientists, then, seem to have recognized this and to be working toward inculcating into our social order moral values that can prevent another brutal disaster. The key seems to be our understanding of what it means to be human, and, for those religiously inclined, what it means to be a creature of God.

This God-human relationship and the freedom to shape the destiny of our social order have emerged to the forefront of this post-Holocaust dialogue that is being sponsored by ethicists, theologians, and social scientists. For centuries, theologians have interpreted the significance of human creation in the image of God and have advanced the ramifications of that divine spark. For the most part, humankind's powers of reason and free choice, which differentiate our species from the rest of creation, have been stressed. Along these lines, personalist moral theory has urged that what is unique to humans is the capacity for personal relationships, which axiomatically also lies at the very heart of the Trinity as well. God and human beings are interpersonal realities. Such a privilege places before humans not only a common destiny but also the shared moral program of a fellowship of persons in society as a creational force.[17] In Jewish thought, the creation story has suggested an interesting interpretation which bears on this issue. It revolves around the frequently quoted but curious statement in Gen. 1: 26: "Let us make man." Whom is God addressing? Some Jewish sages have thought that God was talking to the potential Adam, whom God's plan envisages, but who can only be fully actualized if God and his creation cooperate. This initial covenant made the free person a partner with God to fulfill creation's destiny or to destroy it.[18]

Following the Holocaust as well as the other incidents of sanctioned massacre that we have seen, theological reflections have demanded a rethinking of the God-humanity relationship as it impacts on morality and politics. In moral theology, there has been a growing rejection of micromorality with its myopic categorist thinking and with its anthropology not anchored in values that accentuate the personal dignity of the individual or in the sanctity of human interrelationships. A religious anthropology that posits humanity as coresponsible with God for the survival of the species would perceive that religious institutions with their memberships have a moral duty to apply power in shaping the values within our societal environment. Feminist, Afro-Americans, and liberation theologies as well as our engagement in dialogue on the meaning of the Holocaust have forced Christians to examine their own complicity in sociopolitical evil and have inspired us to suggest remedies. This "ideology critique" has proven fundamental as Christians explore the meaning of God's revelation at the end of the twentieth century. Encountering the Holocaust and its sociopolitical implications has challenged theologians to clarify and explore the Christian message so that it may prove as meaningful today as it did for the first Christian communities.[19]

This "return to history and the world" has been supported by political and liberation theology, which has become accustomed to directing a hermeneutics of suspicion toward established societies and any version of Christian salvation that purports to mold political systems. The Holocaust can help shatter any artificial ecclesiologies that might prescribe churches as institutions existing apart from human history. This return to history can help mobilize speculation on an ethics grounded in solidarity with those persons marginalized by oppressive political forces. Neither religious nor political societies can rely merely on the exercise of brute control or on stability as sources for their normative values. [20]

Just as destructive systems seem to mature incrementally, remedies to institutionalize compassion have to advance by methodical steps. We cannot unlearn stereotypes and prejudices overnight. Any societal metamorphosis would seem to require both individual corrective effort and group action to change the practices of dominant social systems. Aggression is not an inevitable component of the human condition. Such brutal behavior as that shown in the Holocaust seems to be a product of aggression-promoting conditions combined with the skewed theological and moral vision that supported modern political principles. Reflecting on the above theological and social science discourse, a moral obligation to exercise power in order to reduce the level of violence in the political environment and ultimately to try to reduce potential aggression may well be a sine qua non for our survival. Along with other challenges, the Holocaust has effected the theologians' encounter with the world of marching soldiers.[21] In this process, Christians, who first formed an identity in the Jewish milieu wherein they developed an antisemitic bias, have now found that they have to re-form their identity in light of the pain and death inflicted on the Jewish people in a nominally Christian civilization. The specific horrors of the Holocaust have been leading us to rethink our traditional cultural/religious values and to attempt to reconfigure the moral ethos of our civilization in light of the Shoah. A growing intellectual consensus has posed the thesis that political power, coupled with a redirected theology, can reveal values useful to individuals in society and can help stop political, economic, social, and ecological tragedies from robbing humanity of its birthright — survival. To the amazement of all, this hope has become a controlling theme as the third millennium approaches. Certainly the collapse of fascism, Nazism, and communism and the apparent triumph of liberal democracy can be used to reinforce this theme of the sanctity of the human person.

Auschwitz was and remains an assault on our Christian and Jewish religious heritage. Christianity was grafted onto Judaism, and our mutual history has dissolved unfortunately into a tragedy that has compelled us to reexamine our consciousness of the essence of humanity. We have been groping for a new understanding of God and of the intrinsic relationship of creation to its creator. As Christians reappropriate their past, they need to examine the possibilities it once seemed to contain and to explore how they might construct in a healing way their Christianity that unfortunately helped support the barbaric treatment of the Jewish people during World War II. "Love of neighbor" suggests that the *need* of others should help define a universe of obligation. In differing contexts, both Jews concerned with the fate of Israel and their covenant and Christians concerned with the political role of their churches and their covenant have to find a reaffirming faith that can intersect with public policy. The social sciences have uncovered some of the dynamics operating among values, attitudes, and behavior. Perhaps that search will provide the future foundation for an enduring and fruitful Jewish-Christian symbiosis as well as for a more optimistic future for humanity "as God's image," which in the Jewish and Christian texts helps shape the individual and social dimensions of life. Vatican II and other ecclesial meetings have raised these dimensions to a new and now more elevated level of importance. *Gaudium et Spes*, issued by Vatican II, for example, challenges an ethics restricted to individual rights when it states that "one of the salient features of the modern world is the growing interdependence of human persons one on the other, a development very largely promoted by modern technical advances." The social nature of human beings makes it evident that the sanctity of the human person is hinged to the advance of society. The goal of all social institutions is the development of human person, which by its very nature needs a social life.[22] Human rights need to be concerned with a community dimension and cannot merely focus on the individual. Essentially, individuality distinguishes us from one another; personhood is what binds us to each other.

Human rights have been labeled the minimum conditions for life in community and entail a relational meaning from the very start. Among others, the American bishops spelled it out very carefully when they said that basic justice demands that minimum participatory levels in the life of the human community for all persons be established. Injustice is for a person or a group to be treated actively or abandoned passively, as if they were nonmembers of the human race.[23] Any persecution that attacks acts of social participation, which are crucial to a just society, can be designated immoral. Such normative statements give a new impetus to historians and social scientists, who have been working to understand how marginalization occurs and what it can mean. Changing the way we think is generally the necessary prelude to changing the way we act. If Christian antisemitism led to contempt, then it is important to revise theology and the values that it sustains. Such a process can instruct us how to deal with other incidents of xenophobia and ethnocentrism. In light of the potential for brutalization, such a journey is mandated because religious symbols and doctrines can and do inform political and ethical discussion. Knowing what values are crucial to sustain the human person, and understanding how such values can be destroyed, ought to give us clues to institutionalizing the normative moral values that can form the foundation for a society that allows men and women to develop their full potential. That is our challenge in giving the Holocaust a universal meaning.

Notes

1. Elisabeth Schüssler Fiorenza and David Tracy, "The Holocaust as Interruption and the Christian Return into History," in Fiorenza and Tracy, *The Holocaust as Interruption*, 84-85. For the most recent work on the historical intertwining of Jewish-Christian relations, see Eugene Fischer, ed., *Interwoven Destinies: Jews and Christians through the Ages* (New York: Paulist Press, 1993).
2. Fackenheim, *The Jewish Return*, 279; Fackenheim, *God's Presence*, 84-92; Amos Funkenstein, "Theological Interpretations of the Holocaust: A Balance," in Furet, *Unanswered Questions*, 302.
3. Marrus, *The Holocaust*; Bauer, *Remembering for the Future*.
4. Kren and Rappoport, *The Holocaust and the Crisis*, 125-43; Alan Rosenberg and Paul Marcus, "The Holocaust as a Test of Philosophy," in Alan Rosenberg and Gerald Myers, eds., *Echoes from the Holocaust:*

Philosophical Reflections on a Dark Time (Philadelphia: Temple University Press, 1988); Roy Bhaskar, "Emergence, Explanation and Emancipation," in P. F. Secord, ed., *Explaining Human Behavior: Consciousness, Human Action and Social Structure* (Beverly Hills: Sage Publications, 1982), 275-310.

5. R.S. MacLennan, *Early Christian Texts on Jews and Judaism* (Atlanta: Scholars Press, 1990).

6. *Gaudium et Spes* in *Acta Apostolicae Sedis* 58 (1966): 1072; John XXIII, *Pacem in Terris* (Boston: Daughters of St. Paul, 1963), 8-9; Richard McCormick, "Moral Theology, 1940-1989: An Overview," *Theological Studies* 50 (1989): 16, 19; Vatican Council II, *Dignitatis Humanae* (Declaration on Human Freedom), in Abbott, *The Documents of Vatican II*; R. M. Hare, *Moral Thinking: Its Levels, Method and Point* (Oxford: Clarendon Press, 1981); Basil Mitchell, *Morality; Religious and Secular: The Dilemma of the Traditional Conscience* (Oxford: Clarendon Press, 1980); Charles Elliott Vernoff, "After the Holocaust: History and Being as Sources of Method within the Emerging Interreligious Hermeneutic," *Journal of Ecumenical Studies* 21 (1984): 639-63; van Buren, *Discerning the Way*, 181; Hans Georg Gadamer, *Truth and Method*, trans. by Garrett Borden and John Cumming (New York: Seabury Press, 1975).

7. Mahoney, *The Making of Moral Theology*, 32-35, 333-34; John J. Noonan, "Development in Moral Doctrine," *Theological Studies* 54 (1993): 662-77.

8. Aubert, "Hierarchie de valeurs et histoire": 5-22; John Harris, *The Value of Life* (London: Routledge and Kegan Paul, 1985).

9. Ervin Staub, "Individual and Societal (Group) Values in a Motivational Perspective and Their Role in Benevolence and Harmdoing," in Staub, *Social and Moral Values*, 47-48.

10. Ervin Staub, "Individual and Societal (Group) Values in a Motivational Perspective and Their Role in Benevolence and Harmdoing," in Staub, *Social and Moral Values*, 49-51; Staub, *The Roots of Evil*; L. Berkowitz and K.G. Luttermann, "The Traditional Socially Responsible Personality," *Public Opinion Quarterly* 32 (1968): 169-85. For examples of the early church fathers and antisemitism, see Bratton, *The Crime of Christendom*; Blumenkranz, *Die Judenpredigt Augustins*, 99-100; Johannes Metz, *Zeit der Orden: Zur Mystik und Politik der Nachfolge* (Freiburg: Herder, 1977), 39; Dietrich Bonhoeffer, *Nachfolge*, 13th ed. (München: Kaiser, 1981), 22.

11. Brewer, "Ingroup Bias": 307-24; H. Tajfel et al., "Societal Categorization and Intergroup Behavior," *European Journal for Social Psychology* 1 (1971): 149-77.

12. Lerner, *The Belief in a Just World*; D. Regan and J. Totten, "Empathy and Attribution: Turning Observers into Actors," *Journal of Personality and Social Psychology* 32 (1975): 850-56; A. Bandura et al., "Disinhibition of Aggression through Diffusion of Responsibility and Dehumanization of Victims," *Journal of Research in Personality* 9 (1975): 253-69; T. Duster, "Conditions for Guilt-Free Massacre," in Comstock and Sanford, *Sanctions for Evil*. To see how Christians adapted to National Socialism, see Conway, *The Nazi Persecution*; Dietrich, *Catholic Citizens*.
13. Ervin Staub, "Individual and Societal (Group) Values in a Motivational Perspective and Their Role in Benevolence and Harmdoing," in Staub, *Social and Moral Values*, p. 55; Schleunes, *The Twisted Road*; Katz, *From Prejudice to Destruction*. For a study of non-German antisemitism, see Tony Kushner, *The Persistence of Prejudice: Antisemitism in British Society During the Second World War* (Manchester: Manchester University Press, 1989).
14. Maybaum, *The Face of God*; Rubenstein, *After Auschwitz: Radical Theology*; Fackenheim, *The Jewish Return*, 251; Arthur Cohen, *The Tremendum: A Theological Interpretation of the Holocaust* (New York: Crossroad, 1981), 97; Pawlikowski, "Christian Ethics": 662.
15. John Pawlikowski, "The Shoah: Its Challenges for Religious and Secular Ethics," *Holocaust and Genocide Studies* 3 (1988): 443-55; Leo Kuper, *The Prevention of Genocide* (New Haven: Yale University Press, 1985); Charny, *How Can We Commit the Unthinkable?*; Franklin H. Littell, "Essay: Early Warning," *Holocaust and Genocide Studies* 3 (1988): 483-90. For historical treatments that support the theses of Littell and Horowitz, see Werner Mosse, ed., *Entscheidungsjahre 1932. Zur Judenfrage in der Endphase der Weimarerrepublik* (Tübingen: Mohr Siebeck, 1966); Dietrich, *Catholic Citizens*, especially chaps. 2 and 3.
16. Horowitz, *Taking Lives*, 209; George Z.F. Bereday, "The Right to Live and the Right to Die: Some Considerations of Law and Society in America," *Man and Medicine* 4 (1979): 233-56; Fein, *Accounting for Genocide*; Haas, *Morality after Auschwitz*, 3.
17. Mahoney, *The Making of Moral Theology*, 345-46.
18. André Neher, "The Silence of Auschwitz," in Berenbaum and Roth, *Holocaust*, 12-13.
19. Gregory Baum, "The Holocaust and Political Theology," in Fiorenza and Tracy, *The Holocaust as Interruption*, 36; Francis Fiorenza *Foundational Theology: Jesus and the Church* (New York: Crossroad, 1984); Lamb, *Solidarity with Victims*.
20. Pawlikowski, "The Shoah": 453-55.

21. Bandura, *Aggression*, 322-324; Mussner, *Tractate*; Johannes Baptist Metz, "Facing the Jews. Christian Theology after Auschwitz," in Fiorenza and Tracy, *The Holocaust as Interruption*, 27.

22. Vatican Council II, *Gaudium et Spes* in *Acta Apostolicae Sedis* 58 (1966), nos. 23, 25.

23. National Conference of Catholic Bishops, *Economic Justice for All: Pastoral Letter on Catholic Social Teaching and the U.S. Economy* (Washington, DC: Office of Publishing and Promotion Services, United States Catholic Conference, 1986), nos. 77, 79; Peter Hayes, ed., *Lessons and Legacies: The Meaning of the Holocaust in a Changing World* (Evanston: Northwestern University Press, 1991).

Bibliography

Books

Abbott, Walter, ed. *The Documents of Vatican II*. New York: Herder and Herder, 1966.

Abraham, David. *The Collapse of the Weimar Republic*. New York: Holmes and Meier, 1986.

Adler, Hermann. *Vater ... vergib! Gedichte aus dem Ghetto*. Berlin: Im Christian-Verlag, 1950.

Adorno, Theodor. *Kierkegaard: Konstruktion des Aesthetischen*. Frankfurt: Suhrkamp, 1966.

———. *Negative Dialects*. New York: Continuum, 1973.

Agus, Jacob Bernard. *Dialogue and Tradition: The Challenge of Contemporary Judaeo-Christian Thought*. London: Abelard-Schuman, 1971.

Allport, Gordon. *The Nature of Prejudice*. Cambridge, MA: Addison-Wesley Pub. Co., 1954.

Almog, Schmuel, ed. *Antisemitism through the Ages*. Oxford: Pergamon Press, 1988.

Amir, Yehoshua. *Deraschot: Jüdische Predigten*. Berlin: Institut Kirche und Judentum, 1983.

Ammicht-Quinn, Regina. *Von Lissabon bis Auschwitz: Zum Paradigmawechsel an der Theodizeefrage*. Freiburg: Herder, 1992.

Anderson, Gerald H. and Stransky, Thomas, eds. *Christ's Lordship and Religious Pluralism*. Maryknoll, NY: Orbis Books, 1981.

Apel, K.-O. *Towards a Transformation of Philosophy*. Boston: Routledge and Kegan Paul, 1980.

Arendt, Hannah. *Eichmann in Jerusalem: A Report on the Banality of Evil*. New York: Viking Press, 1963.

————. *Elemente und Ursprünge totaler Herrschaft*. Frankfurt: Europäische Verlagsanstalt, 1955.

————. *The Origins of Totalitarianism*. New York: Harcourt Brace Jovanovich, 1973.

Arnold, William J. and Levine, David, eds. *Nebraska Symposium on Motivation*. Lincoln: University of Nebraska Press, 1969.

Auerbach, Leopold. *Das Judentum und seine Bekenner in Preussen und in anderen deutschen Bundesstaaten*. Berlin: S. Mehring, 1890.

Bakan, D. *The Duality of Human Existence; An Essay on Psychology and Religion*. Chicago: Rand McNally, 1966.

Bandura, Albert. *Aggression: A Social Learning Analysis*. Englewood Cliffs, NJ: Prentice-Hall, 1973.

Baron, Salo. *A Social and Religious History of the Jews*. New York: Columbia University Press, 1952.

Barth, Markus. *Israel and the Church; Contribution to a Dialogue Vital for Peace*. Richmond: John Knox Press, 1969.

———— et al. *Paulus – Apostat oder Apostle? Jüdische und christliche Antworten*. Regensburg: Pustet, 1977.

Bartoszewski, Wladyslaw. *The Convent at Auschwitz*. New York: G. Braziller, 1991.

Baudis, Andreas et al., eds. *Richte unsere Füsse auf den Weg des Friedens: Gollwitzer zum 70. Geburtstag*. München: Kaiser, 1979.

Bauer, Walter. *Orthodoxy and Heresy in Earliest Christianity*. Philadelphia: Fortress Press, 1971.

Bauer, Yehuda. *A History of the Holocaust*. New York: F. Watts, 1982.

————. *The Holocaust in Historical Perspective.* Seattle: University of Washington Press, 1978.

———— et al., eds. *Remembering for the Future: The Impact of the Holocaust and Genocide on Jews and Christians.* Oxford: Pergamon Press, 1989.

Baum, Gregory. *Is the New Testament Anti-Semitic? A Re-examination of the New Testament.* Glen Rock, NJ: Paulist Press, 1965.

————. *Theology and Society.* New York: Paulist Press, 1987.

Bauman, Zygmunt. *Modernity and the Holocaust.* Ithaca, NY: Cornell University Press, 1989.

Baumgartner, H. *Kontinuität und Geschichte. Zur Kritik und Metakritik der historischen Vernunft.* Frankfurt: Suhrkamp, 1972.

Bea, Augustin. *The Church and the Jewish People.* New York: Harper & Row, 1966.

Becker, Ernest. *Beyond Alienation; A Philosophy of Education for the Crisis of Democracy.* New York: G. Braziller, 1967.

————. *The Denial of Death.* New York: Free Press, 1973.

Beker, Johan Christian. *Paul the Apostle: The Triumph of God in Life and Thought.* Philadelphia: Fortress Press, 1980.

Bell, Daniel. *The Coming of Post-Industrial Society: A Venture in Social Forecasting.* New York: Basic Books, 1973.

————. *The Cultural Contradictions of Capitalism.* New York: Basic Books, 1976.

Berdyaev, Nicholas. *Christianity and Anti-Semitsm.* Kent, England: Hand and Flower Press, 1952.

Berenbaum, Michael and Roth, John K. *Holocaust: Religious and Philosophical Implications.* New York: Paragon House, 1989.

Berger, P. and Luchmann, T. *The Social Construction of Reality: A Treatise on the Sociology of Knowledge.* New York: Doubleday, 1967.

Berkovits, Eliezer. *Faith after the Holocaust.* New York: KTAV Pub. House, 1973.

————. *Major Themes in Modern Philosophies of Judaism.* New York: KTAV Pub. House, 1974.

Bernstein, Richard J. *The Restructuring of Social and Political Theory.* New York: Harcourt Brace Jovanovich, 1976.

Bethge, Eberhard. *Am Gegebenen Ort*. München: Kaiser, 1979.

Bienert, Walther. *Martin Luther und die Juden*. Frankfurt: Evangelisches Verlagswerk, 1982.

Birnbaum, David. *God and Evil: A Unified Theodicy/Theology/Philosophy*. Hoboken, NJ: KTAV Pub. Housc, 1989.

Bishop, Claire Huchet. *How Catholics Look at Jews: Inquiries into Italian, Spanish, and French Teaching Materials*. New York: Paulist Press, 1974.

Blumenkranz, Bernhard. *Die Judenpredigt Augustins: Ein Beitrag zur Geschichte der Jüdisch-Christlichen Beziehungen in den ersten Jahrhunderten*. Paris: Études Augustiniennes, 1973.

Boadt, Lawrence et al., eds. *Biblical Studies: Meeting Ground of Jews and Christians*. New York: Paulist Press, 1980.

Bockmuehl, Markus and Burkhardt, Helmut. *Gott Lieber und Seine Gebote Halten*. Giessen: Brunner Verlag, 1991.

Bonhoeffer, Dietrich. *Nachfolge*, 13th ed. München: Kaiser, 1981.

Bowker, John. *Jesus and the Pharisees*. Cambridge: The University Press, 1973.

Bracher, Karl Dietrich. *Die Auflösung der Weimarer Republik; Eine Studie zum Problem des Machtverfalls in der Demokratie*, 3rd ed. Villingen: Ring-Verlag, 1960.

————. *The German Dictatorship: The Origins, Structure, and Effects of National Socialism*. New York: Praeger Publishers, 1970.

Braham, Randolph, ed. *The Origins of the Holocaust: Christian Anti-Semitism*. New York: Columbia University Press, 1986.

Bratton, Fred. *The Crime of Christendom; the Theological Sources of Christian Anti-Semitism*. Boston: Beacon Press, 1969.

Braxton, Edward K. *The Wisdom Community*. New York: Paulist Press, 1980.

Breitman, Richard. *The Architect of Genocide: Himmler and the Final Solution*. New York: Knopf, 1991.

Brocke, Michael and Jochum, Herbert. *Wolkensäule und Feuerschein: Jüdische Theologie des Holocaust*. München: Kaiser, 1982.

Brown, Peter. *The World of Late Antiquity, AD 150-750*. New York: Harcourt Brace Jovanovich, 1971.

Brown, Raymond. *The Community of the Beloved Disciple*. New York: Paulist Press, 1979.

————. *The Death of the Messiah*. 2 vols. New York: Doubleday, 1994.

————, ed. *The New Jerome Biblical Commentary*. Englewood Cliffs, NJ: Prentice-Hall, 1990.

———— et al., eds. *Mary and the New Testament*. Philadelphia: Fortress Press, 1978.

———— et al., eds. *Peter in the New Testament*. New York: Paulist Press, 1973.

Buber, Martin. *Eclipse of God; Studies in the Relation Between Religion and Philosophy*. New York: Harper, 1953.

Buber, Martin. *Two Types of Faith*. London: Routledge and Kegan Paul, 1951.

Buchberger, Michael, ed. *Lexikon Für Theologie und Kirche*, 2nd ed. Freiburg: Herder, 1930.

Bultmann, Rudolf. *Jesus Christ and Mythology*. New York: Scribner, 1958.

Camps, Arnulf, *Partners in Dialogue: Christianity and other World Religions*. Maryknoll, NY: Orbis Books, 1983.

Cargas, Harry James. *A Christian Response to the Holocaust*. Denver: Stonehenge Books, 1982.

————. *Reflections of a Post-Holocaust Christian*. Detroit: Wayne State University, 1989.

————. *Shadows of Auschwitz: A Christian Response to the Holocaust*. New York: Crossroads, 1990.

————, ed. *When God and Man Failed: Non-Jewish Views of the Holocaust*. New York: Macmillan, 1981.

Cassidy, Richard J. *Jesus, Politics, and Society: A Study of Luke's Gospel*. Maryknoll, NY: Orbis Books, 1978.

Chalk, Frank and Jonassohn, Kurt. *The History and Sociology of Genocide: Analyses and Case Studies*. New Haven: Yale University Press, 1990.

Charlesworth, James H. *Jesus within Judaism. New Light from Exciting Archaeological Discoveries*. New York: Doubleday, 1988.

————, ed. *Jesus' Jewishness: Exploring the Place of Jesus within Early Judaism*. Philadelphia: American Interfaith Institute, 1991.

————, ed. *Jews and Christians: Exploring the Past, Present, and Future*. New York: Crossroad, 1990.

Charny, Israel. *How Can We Commit the Unthinkable?* Boulder: Westview Press, 1982.

Chazan, Robert. *Barcelona and Beyond: The Disputation of 1263 and Its Aftermath.* Berkeley: University of California Press, 1992.

————. *Daggers of Faith: Thirteenth-Century Missionizing and Jewish Response.* Berkeley: University of California Press, 1988.

Cobb, John B. *Christ in a Pluralistic Age.* Philadelphia: Westminster Press, 1975.

Cohen, Arthur. *The Tremendum: A Theological Interpretation of the Holocaust.* New York: Crossroad, 1981.

———— and Mendes-Flohr, Paul, eds. *Contemporary Jewish Religious Thought: Original Essays on Critical Concepts, Movements, and Beliefs.* New York: Scribner, 1987.

Cohen, Jeremy. *The Friars and the Jew: The Evolution of Medieval Anti-Semitism.* Ithaca: Cornell University Press, 1982.

Cohen, Martin A. and Croner, Helga, eds. *Christian Mission — Jewish Mission.* New York: Paulist Press, 1982.

Cohn, Norman. *Warrant for Genocide: The Myth of the Jewish World-Conspiracy and the Protocols of the Elders of Zion.* New York: Harper & Row, 1967.

Coleman, John. *An American Strategic Theology.* New York: Paulist Press, 1982.

Commager, Henry Steele. *The American Mind: An Interpretation of American Thought and Character Since the 1880s.* New Haven: Yale University Press, 1950.

Comstock, Craig and Sanford, Nevitt. *Sanctions for Evil: Sources of Social Destructiveness.* San Francisco: Jossey-Bass, 1971.

Conway, John. *The Nazi Persecution of the Churches, 1933-1945.* New York: Basic Books, 1968.

Croner, Helga. *Stepping Stones to Further Christian-Jewish Relations.* London: Stimulus Books, 1977.

————, ed. *More Stepping Stones to Jewish-Christian Relations: An Unabridged Collection of Christian Documents, 1975-1983.* New York: Paulist Press, 1985.

Curtis, Michael, ed. *Antisemitism in the Contemporary World.* Boulder: Westview Press, 1986.

Dahrendorf, Ralf. *Society and Democracy in Germany.* Garden City, NJ: Doubleday, 1967.

Danielou, Jean. *The Dead Sea Scrolls and Primitive Christianity*. Baltimore: Helicon Press, 1958.

———. *Dialogue with Israel*. Baltimore: Helicon Press, 1968.

———. *The Theology of Jewish Christianity*. London: Darton, Longman, and Todd, 1964.

——— and Chouraqui, André. *The Jews: Views and Counterviews — A Dialogue*. Westminster, MD: Newman Press, 1967.

Davies, Alan. *Anti-Semitism and the Christian Mind: The Crisis of Conscience after Auschwitz*. New York: Herder and Herder, 1969.

———, ed. *Antisemitism and the Foundations of Christianity*. New York: Paulist Press, 1979.

Davies, William David. *Jewish and Pauline Studies*. Philadelphia: Fortress Press, 1984.

Davis, Charles. *Theology and Political Society*. Cambridge: Cambridge University Press, 1980.

Davidowicz, Lucy. *The War Against the Jews, 1933-1945*. New York: Holt, Rinehart, and Winston, 1975.

D'Costa, Gavin. *Theology and Religious Pluralism: The Challenge of Other Religions*. Oxford: Blackwell, 1986.

de Corneille, Roland. *Christians and Jews: The Tragic Past and the Hopeful Future*. Toronto: Longmans Canada, 1966.

de Lubac, Henri. *Catholicism: A Study of Dogma in Relation to the Corporate Destiny of Mankind*. New York: Sheed & Ward, 1958.

———. *Surnaturel: Études Historiques*. Paris: Aubier, 1946.

Deschner, John et al., eds. *Our Common History as Christians: Essays in Honor of Albert C. Outler*. New York: Oxford University Press, 1975.

Dietrich, Donald J. *Catholic Citizens in the Third Reich: Psycho-Social Principles and Moral Reasoning*. New Brunswick: Transaction Books, 1988.

———. *The Goethezeit and the Metamorphosis of Catholic Theology in the Age of Idealism*. Berne: Lang, 1979.

Doering, Bernard. *Jacques Maritain and the French Catholic Intellectuals*. Notre Dame: University of Notre Dame Press, 1983.

Donaldson, James and Roberts, Alexander. *Ante-Nicene Christian Library: Translations of the Writings of the Fathers Down to A.D. 325*. Edinburgh: T. and T. Clark, 1882.

Doran, R. *Subject and Psyche: Ricoeur, Jung, and the Search for Foundations*. Washington, DC: University Press of America, 1979.

Driver, Samuel R. and Neubauer, Adolf. *The Fifty-Third Chapter of Isaiah, According to the Jewish Interpreters*. New York: KTAV Pub. House, 1969.

Dupuy, Bernard and Hoch, Marie-Therese, eds. *Les Églises devant le Judaisme*. Paris: Éditions du Cerf, 1980.

Dupuy, Bernard and Halperin, Jean, eds. *Juifs et Chrétiens "pour une entente nouvelle."* Paris: Éditions du Cerf, 1986.

Eckardt, Arthur Roy. *Elder and Younger Brothers: The Encounter of Jews and Christians*. New York: Schocken Books, 1973.

————. *Jews and Christians, the Contemporary Meeting*. Bloomington: Indiana University Press, 1986.

————. *Reclaiming the Jesus of History: Christology Today*. Minneapolis: Fortress Press, 1992.

————. *Your People, My People: The Meeting of Jews and Christians*. New York: Quadrangle, 1974.

Eckert, Willehad Paul and Henrix, Hans Hermann, eds. *Jesus Jude — Sein als Zugang zum Judentum: Eine Handreichung für Religionsunterricht und Erwachsenenbildung*. Aachen: Einhard-Verlag, 1976.

Edwards, John. *The Jews in Christian Europe, 1400-1700*. London: Routledge, 1988.

Effroymson, David et al., eds. *Within Context: Essays on Jews and Judaism in the New Testament*. Collegeville, MN: Liturgical Press, 1993.

Ellis, Marc. *Toward a Jewish Theology of Liberation*. Maryknoll, NY: Orbis Books, 1987.

Evans, Craig A. and Hager, Donald A., eds. *Anti-semitism and Early Christianity: Issues of Polemic and Faith*. Minneapolis: Fortress Press, 1993.

Fackenheim, Emil. *God's Presence in History. Jewish Affirmation and Philosophical Reflections*. New York: New York University Press, 1970.

————. *The Jewish Return Into History: Reflection in the Age of Auschwitz and a New Jerusalem*. New York: Schocken Books, 1978.

————, ed. *Quest for Past and Future: Essays in Jewish Theology*. Bloomington: Indiana University Press, 1968.

Falaturi, Aboldjavad, et al., eds. *Three Ways to One God: The Faith Experience in Judaism, Christianity, and Islam*. New York: Crossroad, 1987.

Fasching, Darrell J. *Narrative Theology After Auschwitz: From Alienation to Ethics*. Minneapolis: Fortress Press, 1992.

Fein, Helen. *Accounting for Genocide: National Responses and Jewish Victimization During the Holocaust*. New York: Free Press, 1979.

————, ed. *Genocide Watch*. New Haven: Yale University Press, 1992.

————, ed. *The Persisting Question: Sociological Perspectives and Social Contexts of Modern Anti-Semitism*. New York: DeGruyter, 1987.

Feldman, Louis. *Jew and Gentile in the Ancient World: Attitudes and Interactions from Alexander to Justinian*. Princeton, NJ: Princeton University Press, 1993.

Festinger, Leon. *A Theory of Cognitive Dissonance*. Stanford, CA: Stanford University Press, 1957.

Fiedler, Peter. *Das Judentum im Katholischen Religionsunterricht*. Düsseldorf:: Patmos-Verlag, 1980.

Field, Geoffrey. *Evangelist of Race: The Germanic Vision of Houston Stewart Chamberlain*. New York: Columbia University Press, 1981.

Filthaut, Theodor. *Israel in der christlichen Unterweisung*. München· Kösel-Verlag, 1963.

Finkel, Asher. *The Pharisees and the Teacher of Nazareth: A Study of Their Background, Their Halachic and Midrashic Teachings, the Similarities and Differences*. Leiden: E.J. Brill, 1964.

Fiorenza, Elisabeth Schüssler and Tracy, David. *The Holocaust as Interruption*. Edinburgh: T and T Clark, 1984.

Fiorenza, Francis. *Foundational Theology: Jesus and the Church*. New York: Crossroad, 1984.

Fisher, Eugene. *Faith Without Prejudice: Rebuilding Christian Attitudes Toward Judaism*. New York: Crossroad, 1977.

————. *Seminary Education and Christian-Jewish Relations: A Curriculum and Resource Handbook*. Washington, DC: National Catholic Educational Association, 1983.

————, ed. *Interwoven Destinies: Jews and Christians through the Ages*. New York: Paulist Press, 1993.

————, et al., eds. *Twenty Years of Jewish-Christian Relations*. New York: Paulist Press, 1986.

Fitzmyer, Joseph. *Paul and His Theology: A Brief Sketch*. 2nd ed. Englewood Cliffs, NJ: Prentice Hall, 1989.

Flannery, Edward H. *The Anguish of the Jews: Twenty-Three Centuries of Anti-Semitism*. New York: Macmillan, 1965; New York: Paulist Press, 1985.

Fleischner, Eva. *Judaism in German Christian Theology Since 1945: Christianity and Israel Considered in Terms of Mission*. Metuchen, NJ: Scarecrow Press, 1975.

————, ed. *Auschwitz: Beginning of a New Era?* New York: KTAV Pub. House., 1977.

Foucault, Michael. *Discipline and Punish: The Birth of the Prison*. New York: Pantheon Books, 1977.

Freyne, Sean. *The World of the New Testament*. Wilmington, DE: Michael Glazier, 1980.

Friedländer, Saul. *Pius XII and the Third Reich*. New York: Knopf, 1966.

Friedman, Maurice and Schilpp, Paul A., eds. *The Philosophy of Martin Buber*. LaSalle, IL: Open Court, 1967.

Fuchs, Josef. *Human Values and Christian Morality*. Dublin: Gill and Macmillan, 1970.

Furet, Francois, ed. *Unanswered Questions: Nazi Germany and the Genocide of the Jews*. New York: Schocken Books, 1989.

Gadamer, Hans Georg. *Truth and Method*. New York: Seabury Press, 1975.

Gager, John. *The Origins of Anti-Semitism. Attitudes Toward Judaism in Pagan and Christian Antiquity*. New York: Oxford University Press, 1983.

Gaston, Lloyd. *Paul and the Torah*. Vancouver: University of British Columbia Press, 1987.

Gellately, Robert. *The Gestapo and German Society: Enforcing Racial Policy, 1933-1945*. Oxford: Clarendon Press, 1990.

Gilbert, Arthur. *The Vatican Council and the Jews*. Cleveland: World Pub. Co., 1968.

Gilkey, Langdon. *Reaping the Whirlwind: A Christian Interpretation of History*. New York: Seabury Press, 1976.

Gilligan, Carol. *In a Different Voice: Psychological Theory and Women's Development*. Cambridge: Harvard University Press, 1982.

Ginzel, Günther B., ed. *Auschwitz als Herausforderung für Juden und Christen*. Heidelberg: L. Schneider, 1980.

Glatzer, Nahum. *Franz Rosenzweig: His Life and Thought*. New York: Farrar, Strauss, and Young, 1953.

Gordon, Sarah. *Hitler, Germans, and the "Jewish Question."* Princeton, NJ: Princeton University Press, 1984.

Gottlieb, Roger, ed. *Thinking the Unthinkable: Meanings of the Holocaust*. New York: Paulist Press, 1990.

Gottwald, N. *The Tribes of Yahweh: A Sociology of the Religion of Liberated Israel, 1250-1050 B.C.* Maryknoll, NY: Orbis Books, 1979.

Gray, Colin. *The Soviet-American Arms Race*. Farnborough: Saxon House, 1976.

Grayzel, Solomon. *The Church and the Jews in the XIIIth Century, vol. 2, 1254-1314*. Detroit: Wayne State University Press, 1989.

Gritsch, Eric W. *Luther and the Jews: Toward a Judgment of History*. New York: Lutheran Council in the USA, 1983.

———. *Martin – God's Court Jester: Luther in Retrospect*. Philadelphia: Fortress Press, 1983.

Grobman, Alex and Landes, Daniel. *Genocide: Critical Issues of the Holocaust*. Los Angeles: Simon Wiesenthal Center, 1983.

Gudorf, Christine. *Victimization: Examining Christian Complicity*. Philadelphia: Trinity Press International, 1992.

Gusdorf, Georges. *De l'histoire des sciences à l'histoire de la pensée*. Paris: Payot, 1966.

———. *La révolution galiléenne*. Paris: Payot, 1969.

Gutiérrez, Gustavo. *A Theology of Liberation: History, Politics, and Salvation*. Maryknoll, NY: Orbis Books, 1973.

Haas, Peter. *Morality after Auschwitz: The Radical Challenge of the Nazi Ethic*. Philadelphia: Fortress Press, 1988.

Habermas, Jürgen. *Knowledge and Human Interests*. Boston: Beacon Press, 1971.

————. *Legitimation Crisis*. Boston: Beacon Press, 1975.

————. *Theory and Practice*. Boston: Beacon Press, 1973.

Hall, Sidney. *Christian Antisemitism and Paul's Theology*. Minneapolis: Fortress Press, 1993.

Hallie, Philip Paul. *Lest Innocent Blood be Shed: The Story of the Village of Le Chambon, and How Goodness Happened There*. New York: Harper & Row, 1979.

Halpérin, Jean and Sovik, Arne, eds. *Luther, Lutheranism, and the Jews*. Geneva: Dept. of Studies, Lutheran World Federation, 1984.

Hamilton, Richard. *Who Voted for Hitler?* Princeton, NJ: Princeton University Press, 1982.

Harder, Günther, ed. *Kirche und Israel: Arbeiten zum Christlich-jüdischen Verhältnis*. Berlin: Selbstverlag Institut Kirche und Judentum, 1986.

Hare, Douglas. *The Theme of Jewish Persecution of Christians in the Gospel According to St. Matthew*. Cambridge: Cambridge University Press, 1967.

Hare, Richard M. *Moral Thinking: Its Levels, Method, and Point*. Oxford: Clarendon Press, 1981.

Harrington, Daniel. *God's People in Christ: New Testament Perspectives on the Church and Judaism*. Philadelphia: Fortress Press, 1980.

Harris, John. *The Value of Life*. London: Routledge and Kegan Paul, 1985.

Hart, Kevin. *The Trespass of the Sign: Deconstruction and Philosophy*. New York: Cambridge University Press, 1989.

Hartley, Eugene L. and Newcomb, Theodore M., eds. *Readings in Social Psychology*. New York: H. Holt, 1947.

Haughton, Rosemary. *The Catholic Thing*. Springfield, IL: Templegate, 1979.

Hayes, Peter, ed. *Lessons and Legacies: The Meaning of the Holocaust in a Changing World*. Evanston, IL: Northwestern University Press, 1991.

Haynes, Stephen. *Prospects for Post-Holocaust Theology: "Israel" in the Theologies of Karl Barth, Jürgen Moltmann, and Paul van Buren*. Atlanta: Scholars Press, 1991.

Heer, Friedrich. *God's First Love: Christians and Jews Over Two Thousand Years*. New York: Weybright and Talley, 1970.

———. *Offener Humanismus*. Bern: Scherz, 1962.

Heinemann, Isaak. *Antisemitismus*. Stuttgart: J.B. Metzler, 1929.

Heinz, Friedrich Wilhelm. *Die Nation greift an: Geschichte und Kritik des Soldatischen Nationalismus*. Berlin: Verlag Das Reich, 1933.

Hertzberg, Arthur. *The French Enlightenment and the Jews*. New York: Columbia University Press, 1968.

Herzl, Theodor. *Complete Diaries*. ed. Raphael Patai. New York: Herzl Press, 1960.

Heschel, Abraham Joshua. *God in Search of Man: A Philosophy of Judaism*. New York: Farrar, Strauss, and Cudahy, 1955.

———. *The Prophets*. New York: Harper & Row, 1962.

Heyer, Robert, ed. *Jewish/Christian Relations*. New York: Paulist Press, 1974.

Hilberg, Raul. *The Destruction of the European Jews*. New York: Holmes and Meier, 1985.

Horkheimer, Max. *Critical Theory: Selected Essays*. New York: Herder and Herder, 1972.

———. *Critique of Instrumental Reason: Lectures and Essays since the End of World War II*. New York: Seabury Press, 1974.

Horowitz, Irving Louis. *Taking Lives: Genocide and State Power*, 3rd ed. New Brunswick, NJ: Transaction Books, 1982.

Hovannisian, Richard G., ed. *The Armenian Genocide in Perspective*. New Brunswick, NJ: Transaction Books, 1986.

Howard, George. *Paul: Crisis in Galatia. A Study in Early Christian Theology*, 2nd ed. New York: Cambridge University Press, 1989.

Hruby, Kurt. *Juden und Judentum bei der Kirchenvätern*. Zurich: Theologischer Verlag, 1971.

Hsia, R. Po-chia. *The Myth of Ritual Murder: Jews and Magic in Reformation Germany*. New Haven: Yale University Press, 1988.

Hubner, Hans. *Das Gesetz bei Paulus*. Göttingen: Vandenhoeck und Ruprecht, 1978.

Huizing, Peter and Bassett, William, eds. *Experience and the Spirit, Concilium*. New York: Seabury, 1976.

Huntington, Samuel. *The Third Wave: Democratization in the Late Twentieth Century*. Norman: University of Oklahoma Press, 1991.

Huss, Hermann and Schroeder, Andreas, eds. *Antisemitismus: Zur Pathologie der Bürgerlichen Gesellschaft*. Frankfurt: Europäische Verlagsanstalt, 1965.
Isaac, Jules. *Genèse de l'anti-sémitisme; Essai historique*. Paris: Calmann-Lévy, 1956.
———. *Jesus and Israel*. New York: Holt, Rinehart, and Winston, 1971.
———. *The Teaching of Contempt*. New York: Holt, Rinehart, and Winston, 1964.
Jacob, Walter. *Christianity Through Jewish Eyes: The Quest for Common Ground*. New York: Hebrew Union College Press, 1974.
Janis, Irving L. *Victims of Groupthink: A Psychological Study of Foreign-Policy Decisions and Fiascoes*. Boston: Houghton-Mifflin, 1972.
Jochum, Herbert and Kremers, Heinz, eds. *Juden, Judentum und Staat Israel im christlichen Religionsunterricht in der Bundesrepublik Deutschland*. Paderborn: Schöningh, 1980.
Jocz, Jakob. *Christians and Jews: Encounter and Mission*. London: SPCK, 1966.
———. *The Jewish People and Jesus Christ: A Study in the Controversy Between Church and Synagogue*. London: SPCK, 1962.
Johns, Roger. *Man in the World: The Political Theology of Johannes B. Metz*. Missoula, MT: Scholars Press for the American Academy of Religion, 1976.
Journet, Charles. *Destinée d'Israël, A Propos du salut par les Juifs*. Paris: Egloff, 1945.
Käsemann, Ernst. *Commentary on Romans*. Grand Rapids, MI: Eerdmans, 1980.
———. *Perspectives on Paul*. Philadelphia: Fortress Press, 1971.
Kasper, Walter and Küng, Hans, eds. *Christians and Jews*. New York: Seabury Press, 1974.
Katz, Jacob. *From Prejudice to Destruction: Anti-Semitism, 1700-1933*. Cambridge: Harvard University Press, 1980.
———. *Out of the Ghetto: The Social Background of Jewish Emancipation: 1770-1870*. Cambridge: Harvard University Press, 1973.

Katz, Steven. *Post-Holocaust Dialogues: Critical Studies in Modern Jewish Thought*. New York: New York University Press, 1983.
————, ed. *Jewish Philosophers*. New York: Block Pub. Co., 1975.
Kelly, William J., ed. *Theology and Discovery: Essays in Honor of Karl Rahner, S.J.* Milwaukee: Marquette University Press, 1980.
Kelman, Herbert and Hamilton, V. Lee. *Crimes of Obedience: Toward a Social Psychology of Authority and Responsibility*. New Haven: Yale University Press, 1989.
Klein, Charlotte. *Anti-Judaism in Christian Theology*. Philadelphia: Fortress Press, 1978.
————. *Theologie und Anti-Judaismus: Eine Studie zur deutschen theologischen Literatur der Gegenwart*. München: Kaiser, 1975.
Knight, George A.F., ed. *Jews and Christians: Preparation for Dialogue*. Philadelphia: Westminster Press, 1965.
Knitter, Paul. *No Other Name? A Critical Survey of Christian Attitudes toward the World Religions*. Maryknoll, NY: Orbis Books, 1985.
Knutson, J.F., ed. *Control of Aggression: Implications from Basic Research*. Chicago: Aldine Pub. Co., 1973.
Koenig, John. *Jews and Christians in Dialogue: New Testament Foundations*. Philadelphia: Westminster Press, 1979.
Koenigsberg, Richard. *Hitler's Ideology: A Study of Psychoanalytic Sociology*. New York: Library of Social Science, 1975.
Kogon, Eugen, et al., eds. *Gott nach Auschwitz: Dimensionen des Massenmords am jüdischen Volk*. Freiburg: Herder, 1979.
Kohn, Johanne. *Haschoah: Christlich-jüdische Verständigung nach Auschwitz*. München: Kaiser, 1986.
Kraus, Hans Joachim. *Reich Gottes, Reich der Freiheit: Grundriss Systematischer Theologie*. Neukirchen: Neukirchener Verlag, 1975.
Kremers, Heinz. *Die Juden und Martin Luther — Martin Luther und die Juden*. Neukirchen: Neukirchener Verlag, 1985.
Kren, George M. and Rappoport, Leon. *The Holocaust and the Crisis of Human Behavior*. New York: Holmes and Meier, 1980.
Kreutz, Andrej. *Vatican Policy on the Palestinian-Israeli Conflict: The Struggle for the Holy Land*. New York: Greenwood Press, 1990.
Kulka, Otto and Mendes-Flohr, Paul R. *Judaism and Christianity under the Impact of National Socialism*. Jerusalem: Historical

Society of Israel and Zalman Shazar Center for Jewish History, 1987.

Küng, Hans. *The Church.* New York: Sheed & Ward, 1967.

———. *Judaism between Yesterday and Tomorrow.* New York: Crossroad, 1992.

——— and Tracy, David, eds. *Paradigm Change in Theology: A Symposium for the Future.* New York: Crossroad, 1989.

Kuper, Leo. *Genocide: Its Political Use in the Twentieth Century.* New Haven: Yale University Press, 1981.

———. *The Prevention of Genocide.* New Haven: Yale University Press, 1985.

Kushner, Tony. *The Persistence of Prejudice: Antisemitism in British Society During the Second World War.* Manchester: Manchester University Press, 1989.

Lachs, John. *Responsibility and the Individual in Modern Society.* Brighton: Harvester Press, 1981.

Lamb, Matthew. *History, Method, and Theology: A Dialectical Comparison of Wilhelm Dilthey's Critique of Historical Reason and Bernard Lonergan's Meta-Methodology.* Missoula, MT: Scholars Press for the American Academy of Religion, 1978.

———. *Solidarity with Victims: Toward a Theology of Social Transformation.* New York: Crossroad, 1982.

———, ed. *Creativity and Method: Essays in Honor of Bernard Lonergan, S.J.* Milwaukee: Marquette University Press, 1981.

Lane, Dermot. *The Experience of God: An Invitation to Do Theology.* New York: Paulist Press, 1981.

———. *Foundations for a Social Theology: Praxis, Process, and Salvation.* New York: Paulist Press, 1984.

Langmuir, Gavin. *History, Religion, and Antisemitism.* Berkeley: University of California Press, 1990.

———. *Toward a Definition of Antisemitism.* Berkeley: University of California Press, 1990.

LaPalombara, Joseph, ed. *Bureaucracy and Political Development.* Princeton, NJ: Princeton University Press, 1963.

Lapide, Pinchas. *The Resurrection of Jesus: A Jewish Perspective.* Minneapolis: Augsburg Pub. House, 1983.

——— and Luz, Ulrich. *Jesus in Two Perspectives: A Jewish-Christian Dialogue.* Minneapolis: Augsburg Pub. House, 1985.

Lapomarda, Vincent. *The Jesuits and the Third Reich*. Lewiston: E. Mellen Press, 1989.

Laqueur, Walter. *The Terrible Secret: An Investigation into the Suppression of Information about Hitler's "Final Solution."* London: Weidenfeld and Nicolson, 1980.

Latane, Bibb and Darley, John M. *The Unresponsive Bystander: Why Doesn't He Help?* New York: Appleton-Century Crofts, 1970.

Latourelle, Rene, ed. *Vatican II: Assessment and Perspectives. Twenty-Five Years After (1962-1987)*. New York: Paulist Press, 1988.

Leclercq, Jean. *The Love of Learning and the Desire for God*. London, SPCK, 1978.

Lenhardt, Pierre. *Auftrag und Unmöglichkeit eines Legitimen christlichen Zeugnisses gegenlüber den Juden: Eine Untersuchung zum theologischen Stand des Verhältnisses von Kirche und jüdischen Volk*. Berlin: Selbstverlag Institut Kirche und Judentum, 1980.

Lerner, Melvin J. *The Belief in a Just World: A Fundamental Delusion*. New York: Plenum Press, 1980.

Lerner, Richard. *Final Solutions: Biology, Prejudice, and Genocide*. University Park: Pennsylvania State University Press, 1992.

Levy, Samson, H. *The Messiah: An Aramaic Interpretation: The Messianic Exegesis of the Targum*. Cincinnati: Hebrew Union College, 1974.

Lewy, Guenter. *The Catholic Church and Nazi Germany*. New York: McGraw-Hill, 1964.

Liebeschütz, Hans. *Das Judentum im Deutschen Geschichtsbild von Hegel bis Max Weber*. Tübingen: Mohr, 1967.

Lifton, Robert Jay. *Home From the War — Vietnam Veterans: Neither Victims nor Executioners*. New York: Simon and Schuster, 1973.

———. *The Nazi Doctors: Medical Killing and the Psychology of Genocide*. New York: Basic Books, 1986.

Lindemann, Andreas. *Paulus im ältesten Christentum*. Tübingen: Mohr, 1979.

Lindström, Theodor. *Paul de Lagarde. Deutschsozialer Reform, Antisemitisches Jahrbuch*. Berlin: Humboldt, 1898.

Littell, Franklin. *The Crucifixion of the Jews*. New York: Harper & Row, 1975.

——— et al., eds. *In Answer — The Holocaust: Is the Story True? Why did the World Community Not Respond? What Are the Lessons?* West Chester, PA: Sylvan, 1988.

Loewe, Raphael, ed. *Studies in Rationalism, Judaism, and Universalism; In Memory of Leon Roth.* London: Routledge and Kegan Paul, 1966.

Lonergan, Bernard. *Bernard Lonergan: Three Lectures.* Montreal: Thomas More Institute for Adult Education, 1975.

———. *Doctrinal Pluralism.* Milwaukee: Marquette University Press, 1971.

———. *Method in Theology.* New York: Herder and Herder, 1972.

Long, Bruce, ed. *Judaism and the Christian Seminary Curriculum.* Chicago: Loyola University Press, 1966.

Lovsky, Fadiey. *Antisémitisme et mystère d'Israël.* Paris: A. Michel, 1955.

Maccoby, Hyam. *The Mythmaker: Paul and the Invention of Christianity.* New York: Harper & Row, 1986.

MacLennan, Robert S. *Early Christian Texts on Jews and Judaism.* Atlanta: Scholars Press, 1990.

Mahoney, John. *The Making of Moral Theology: A Study of the Roman Catholic Tradition.* Oxford: Clarendon Press, 1987.

Maguire, Daniel. *The Moral Core of Judaism and Christianity: Reclaiming the Revolution.* Minneapolis: Fortress Press, 1993.

Malamud, Bernard. *The Fixer.* New York: Farrar, Strauss, and Giroux, 1966.

Mann, Golo. *The History of Germany Since 1789.* London: Chatto and Windus, 1968.

Manuel, Frank. *The Broken Staff: Judaism through Christian Eyes.* Cambridge: Harvard University Press, 1992.

Marcus, Jacob R., ed. *The Jew in the Medieval World: A Source Book, 315-1791.* Cincinnati: The Sinai Press, 1938.

Markus, Marcel, et al., eds. *Israel und Kirche Heute: Beiträge zum Christlich-jüdischen Dialog.* Freiburg: Herder, 1991.

Marquardt, Friedrich Wilhelm. *Das christliche Bekenntnis zu Jesus, dem Juden: eine Christologie.* München: Kaiser, 1990.

———. *Die Wiederentdeckung des Judentums für die christliche Theologie. Israel im Denken Karl Barths.* München: Kaiser, 1967.

————. *Verwegenheiten: Theologische Stücke aus Berlin*. München: Kaiser, 1981.

————. *Von Elend und Heimsuchung der Theologie-Prologemena zur Dogmatik*. München: Kaiser, 1988.

Marrus, Michael. *The Holocaust in History*. Hanover, NH: University Press of New England, 1987.

Martyr, Justin. *The Dialogue with Trypho*. New York: Macmillan, 1930.

Maybaum, Ignaz. *The Face of God after Auschwitz*. Amsterdam: Polak and van Gennep, 1965.

McCarthy, Thomas. *The Critical Theory of Jürgen Habermas*. Cambridge: MIT Press, 1978.

McGarry, Michael B. *Christology after Auschwitz*. New York: Paulist Press, 1977.

McKenzie, John. *A Theology of the Old Testament*. Garden City, NJ: Doubleday, 1974.

McNamara, Martin. *Targum and Testament; Aramaic Paraphrases of the Hebrew Bible: A Light on the New Testament*. Shannon: Irish University Press, 1972.

Meeks, Wayne A. *The First Urban Christians: The Social World of the Apostle Paul*. New Haven: Yale University Press, 1983.

———— and Wilken, Robert. *Jews and Christians in Antioch in the First Four Centuries of the Common Era*. Missoula, MT: Scholars Press, 1978.

Melito, Saint of Sardis. *Sermon "On the Passover."* Trans. by Richard White. Lexington, MA: Lexington Theological Seminary Library, 1976.

Merkl, Peter. *Political Violence under the Swastika: 581 Early Nazis*. Princeton, NJ: Princeton University Press, 1975.

Metz, Johannes. *The Emergent Church: The Future of Christianity in a Post-Bourgeois World*. New York: Crossroad, 1981.

————. *Followers of Christ: The Religious Life and the Church*. New York: Paulist Press, 1978.

————. *Jenseits bürgerlichen Religion: Reden über die Zukunft des Christentums*. München: Kaiser, 1980.

————. *Theology of the World*. London: Burns and Oates, 1969.

————. *Zeit der Orden: Zur Mystik und Politik der Nachfolge*. Freiburg: Herder, 1977.

————, ed. *Christianity and the Bourgeoisie*. New York: Seabury Press, 1979.

————, ed. *Faith in History and Society: Toward a Practical Fundamental Theology*. New York: Seabury Press, 1980.

———— and Rendtorff, Trutz, eds. *Die Theologie in der Interdisziplinären Forschung*. Düsseldorf: Universitätsverlag, 1971.

Milgram, Stanley. *Obedience to Authority: An Experimental View*. New York: Harper & Row, 1974.

Miller, Ronald. *Dialogue and Disagreement: Franz Rosenzweig's Relevance to Contemporary Jewish-Christian Understanding*. Lanham, MO: University Press of America, 1989.

Miskotte, Kornelis Heiko. *When the Gods Are Silent*. London: Collins, 1967.

Mitchell, Basil. *Morality, Religious and Secular: The Dilemma of the Traditional Conscience*. Oxford: Clarendon Press, 1980.

Moltmann, Jürgen. *The Crucified God; The Cross of Christ as the Foundation and Criticism of Christian Theology*. New York: Harper & Row, 1974.

Monden, Louis. *Sin, Liberty, and Law*. New York: Sheed & Ward, 1965.

Moore, James. *Theology after the Shoah: A Reinterpretation of the Passion Narratives*. Lanham, MO: University Press of America, 1993.

Morley, John. *Vatican Diplomacy and the Jews during the Holocaust, 1939-1943*. New York: KTAV Pub. House, 1980.

Morrison, Karl. *"I am You": The Hermeneutics of Empathy in Western Literature, Theology, and Art*. Princeton, NJ: Princeton University Press, 1988.

Mosis, Rudolf, ed. *Exil, Diaspora, Rückkehr: zum theologischen Gespräch zwischen Juden und Christen*. Düsseldorf: Patmos-Verlag, 1978.

Mosse, George. *The Crisis of German Ideology: Intellectual Origins of the Third Reich*. New York: Schocken Books, 1981.

————. *Germans and Jews: The Right, the Left, and the Search for a "Third Force" in Pre-Nazi Germany*. New York: H. Fertig, 1970.

————. *Toward the Final Solution: A History of European Racism*. New York: H. Fertig, 1978.

Mosse, Werner, ed. *Entscheidungsjahre 1932. Zur Judenfrage in der Endphase der Weimarerrepublik*. Tübingen: Mohr Siebeck, 1966.

Mueller, David. *An Introduction to the Theology of Albrecht Ritschel*. Philadelphia: Westminster Press, 1969.

Muller, Alois, ed. *Political Commitment and Christian Community*. New York: Herder and Herder, 1973.

Müller, Ingo. *Hitler's Justice: The Courts of the Third Reich*. London: Tauris and Co., 1991.

Mussner, Franz. *Tractate on the Jews: The Significance of Judaism for Christian Faith*. Philadelphia: Fortress Press, 1984.

National Conference of Catholic Bishops. *Economic Justice for All: Pastoral Letter on Catholic Social Teaching and the U.S. Economy*. Washington, DC: Office of Publishing and Promotion Services, United States Catholic Conference, 1986

Neusner, Jacob. *Jews and Christians: The Myth of a Common Tradition*. Philadelphia: Trinity Press International, 1991.

———. *Judaism and Christianity in the Age of Constantine: History, Messiah, Israel, and the Initial Confrontation*. Chicago: University of Chicago Press, 1987.

———. *The Rabbinic Tradition About the Pharisees before 70*. Leiden: E.J. Brill, 1971.

——— et al., eds. *Judaisms and Their Messiahs at the Turn of the Christian Era*. Cambridge: Cambridge University Press, 1987.

——— et al., eds. *The Social world of Formative Christianity and Judaism. Essays in Tribute to Howard Clark Kee*. Philadelphia: Fortress Press, 1988.

Nietzsche, Friedrich. *Aufzeichnungen über Geschichte und historische Wissenschaften*. München: Musarion Gesamtausgabe, 1922.

Noth, Martin. *The History of Israel*. New York: Harper, 1958.

Obermann, Heiko. *The Roots of Anti-Semitism in the Age of the Renaissance and Reformation*. Philadelphia: Fortress Press, 1984.

Oesterreicher, John, ed. *Brothers in Hope*. New York: Herder and Herder, 1970.

Ogden, Schubert Miles. *Faith and Freedom: Toward a Theology of Liberation*. Nashville: Abingdon, 1979.

Oliner, Pearl and Oliner, Samuel P. *The Altruistic Personality: Rescuers of Jews in Nazi Europe*. New York: Free Press, 1988.

Oliner, Samuel. *Restless Memories: Recollections of the Holocaust Years*, 2nd ed. Berkeley: Judah L. Magnes Museum, 1986.

Olson, Bernhard. *Faith and Prejudice: Intergroup Problems in Protestant Curricula*. New Haven: Yale University Press, 1963.

O'Neill, John, ed. *On Critical Theory*. New York: Seabury Press, 1976.

Opsahl, Paul and Tannenbaum, Marc. *Speaking of God Today: Jews and Christians in Conversation*. Philadelphia: Fortress Press, 1974.

Oyer, John S. *Lutheran Reformers against Anabaptists: Luther, Melanchton, and Menius, and the Anabaptists of Central Germany*. The Hague: M. Nijhoff, 1964.

Parkes, James William. *The Conflict of the Church and the Synagogue: A Study in the Origins of Antisemitism*. London: The Soncino Press, 1934.

———. *The Foundations of Judaism and Christianity*. Chicago: Quadrangle Books, 1960.

———. *Judaism and Christianity*. London: Victor Gollancz, 1948.

———. *Prelude to Dialogue: Jewish-Christian Relationships*. New York: Schocken Books, 1969.

Pawlikowski, John. *The Challenge of the Holocaust for Christian Theology*. New York: Center for Studies on the Holocaust, 1978.

———. *Christ in the Light of the Christian-Jewish Dialogue*. New York: Paulist Press, 1982.

———. *Jesus and the Theology of Israel*. Wilmington, DE: Michael Glazier, 1989.

———. *What Are They Saying about Christian-Jewish Relations*. New York: Paulist Press, 1980.

Peck, Abraham, ed. *Jews and Christians after the Holocaust*. Philadelphia: Fortress Press, 1982.

Pelikan, Jaroslav. *The Emergence of the Christian Tradition (100-600)*. Chicago: University of Chicago Press, 1971.

Perlmutter, Nathan and Perlmutter, Ruth Ann. *The Real Anti-Semitism in America*. New York: Arbor House, 1982.

Perrin, Norman. *New Testament: An Introduction; Proclamation and Parnesis, Myth and History*. New York: Harcourt Brace Jovanovich, 1974.

Poliakov, Leon. *Harvest of Hate: The Nazi Program for the Destruction of the Jews of Europe*. Syracuse, NY: Syracuse University Press, 1954.

————. *The History of Anti-Semitism*. New York: Schocken Books, 1974.

Pope John XXIII. *Pacem in Terris*. Boston: Daughters of St. Paul, 1963.

Pope Paul VI. *Octogesima Adveniens*. Boston: Saint Paul Editions, 1971.

Presbyterian Church 1987 General Assembly (USA). *A Theological Understanding of the Relationship between Christians and Jews*. New York: Office of the General Assembly, 1987.

Proctor, Robert. *Racial Hygiene: Medicine under the Nazis*. Cambridge: Harvard University Press, 1988.

Pross, Harry. *Die Zerstörung der Deutschen Politik, Dokumente 1871-1933*. Frankfurt: Fischer Bücherei, 1959.

Pulzer, Peter G.J. *The Rise of Political Anti-Semitism in Germany and Austria*. New York: Wiley, 1964.

Rahner, Karl. *Foundations of Christian Faith: An Introduction to the Idea of Christianity*. New York: Seabury Press, 1978.

————. *Theological Investigations*. New York: Seabury, 1976; Baltimore: Helicon Press, 1961, 1969.

————. *Theological Investigations*, vol. 1, *Christ, Mary, and Grace*. London: DLT, 1969.

————. *Theological Investigations*, vol. 4, *More Recent Writings*. London: DLT, 1966.

————. *Theological Investigations*, vol. 5, *Later Writings*. Baltimore: Helicon Press, 1966.

————, ed. *Befreiende Theologie: Der Beitrag Lateinamerikas zur Theologie der Gegenwart*. Stuttgart: W. Kohlhammer, 1977.

Rashdall, Hastings. *The Universities of Europe in the Middle Ages*, 2nd ed., edited by Emden, A.B. and Powicke, F.M. Oxford: Clarendon Press, 1936.

Rendtorff, Rolf and Stegemann, Ekkehard, eds. *Auschwitz — Krise der christlichen Theologie: eine Vortragsreihe*. München: Kaiser, 1980.

Rengstorf, Karl H. and von Kortzfleisch, Siegfried, eds. *Kirche und Synagogue. Handbuch zur Geschichte von Christen und Juden. Darstellung mit Quellen*. Stuttgart: Klett, 1968.

Richards, E. Randolph. *The Secretary in the Letters of Paul.* Tübingen: J.C.B. Mohr, 1991.

Richardson, Peter, ed. *Anti-Judaism in Early Christianity.* Waterloo, Ontario: Wilfrid Laurier University Press, 1986.

Rivkin, Ellis. *A Hidden Revolution.* Nashville: Abingdon, 1978.

Rose, Paul. *Revolutionary Antisemitism from Kant to Wagner.* Princeton, NJ: Princeton University Press, 1990.

Rosenberg, Alan and Myers, Gerald, eds. *Echoes from the Holocaust: Philosophical Reflections on a Dark Time.* Philadelphia: Temple University Press, 1988.

Rosenberg, Stuart. *The Christian Problem: A Jewish View.* Montreal: Deneau, 1986.

Rosenstock-Huessy, Eugen. *Judaism Despite Christianity: The Letters on Christianity and Judaism Between Eugen Rosenstock-Huessy and Franz Rosenzweig.* University, AL: University of Alabama Press, 1969.

Rosenzweig, Franz. *The Star of Redemption.* New York: Holt, Rinehart, and Winston, 1971.

Roth, John. A *Consuming Fire: Encounters with Elie Wiesel and the Holocaust.* Atlanta, GA: John Knox Press, 1979.

———. *Ethics: An Annotated Bibliography.* Pasadena, CA: Salem Press, 1991.

——— and Sontag, Frederick, eds. *The Defense of God.* New York: Paragon House, 1985.

Rothschild, Fritz, ed. *Between God and Man: An Interpretation of Judaism from the Writings of Abraham J. Heschel.* New York: Free Press, 1959.

Rousseau, Richard, ed. *Christianity and Judaism: The Deepening Dialogue.* Montrose, PA: Ridge Row Press, 1983.

Rubenstein, Richard. *After Auschwitz: History, Theology, and Contemporary Judaism,* 2nd rev. ed. Baltimore: Johns Hopkins University Press, 1992.

———. *After Auschwitz: Radical Theology and Contemporary Judaism.* Indianapolis: Bobbs-Merrill, 1966.

———. *The Age of Triage: Fear and Hope in an Overcrowded World.* Boston: Beacon Press, 1983.

———. *The Cunning of History: Mass Death and the American Future.* New York: Harper & Row, 1975.

————. *The Religious Imagination; A Study in Psychoanalysis and Jewish Theology.* Indianapolis: Bobbs-Merrill, 1968.

Rubenstein, Richard and Roth, John. *Approaches to Auschwitz: The Holocaust and Its Legacy.* Atlanta: John Knox Press, 1987.

Ruether, Herman and Ruether, Rosemary. *The Wrath of Jonah: The Crisis of Religious Nationalism in the Israeli-Palestinian Conflict.* San Francisco: Harper & Row, 1989.

Ruether, Rosemary. *Faith and Fratricide: The Theological Roots of Anti-Semitism.* New York: Seabury Press, 1974.

Rürup, Reinhard. *Emanzipation und Antisemitismus.* Göttingen: Vandenhoeck und Ruprecht, 1975.

Ryan, William F.J. and Tyrell, Bernard J. eds. *A Second Collection: Papers by Bernard Lonergan.* London: Darton, Longman, and Todd, 1974.

Saldarini, Anthony. *Pharisees, Scribes and Sadducees in Palestinian Society: A Sociological Approach.* Wilmington, Delaware: M. Glazier, 1988.

Sanders, E.P. *Paul and Palestinian Judaism: A Comparison of Patterns of Religion.* Philadelphia: Fortress Press, 1977.

————. *Paul, the Law, and the Jewish People.* Philadelphia: Fortress Press, 1983.

Sandmel, Samuel. *Anti-Semitism in the New Testament?* Philadelphia: Fortress Press, 1978.

————. *The First Christian Century in Judaism and Christianity: Certainties and Uncertainties.* New York: Oxford University Press, 1969.

————. *Two Living Traditions: Essays on Religion and the Bible.* Detroit: Wayne State University Press, 1972.

Sandnes, Karl Olav. *Paul — One of the Prophets? A Contribution to the Apostle's Self-Understanding.* Tübingen: J.C.B. Mohr, 1991.

Schillebeeckx, Edward. *Christ: The Experience of Jesus as Lord.* New York: Crossroad, 1981.

————. *The Church with a Human Face: A New and Expanded Theology of Ministry.* New York: Crossroad, 1985.

————. *Jesus: An Experiment in Christology.* New York: Seabury Press, 1979.

————. *The Understanding of Faith: Interpretation and Criticism*. New York: Seabury Press, 1974.

Schindler, Alfred, ed. *Monotheismus als politisches Problem? Erik Peterson und die Kritik der politischen Theologie*. Gütersloh: Gütersloher Verlagshaus Mohn, 1978.

Schlcunes, Karl. *The Twisted Road to Auschwitz: Nazi Policy Toward German Jews: 1933-1939*. Urbana: University of Illinois Press, 1970.

Schmidt, Karl Ludwig. *Die Judenfrage im Lichte der Kapital 9-11 Römerbriefes*. Zürich: Evangelischer Verlag, 1943.

Schoenbaum, David. *Hitler's Social Revolution: Class and Status in Nazi Germany, 1933-1939*. Garden City, NJ: Doubleday, 1966.

Scholem, Gershom Gerhard. *The Messianic Idea in Judaism and Other Essays on Jewish Spirituality*. New York: Schocken Books, 1971.

Schweitzer, Frederick. *A History of the Jews since the First Century A.D.* New York: Macmillan, 1971.

Scott, James Brown. *Francisco de Vitoria and His Law of Nation*. Oxford: Clarendon Press, 1934.

Secord, P.F., ed. *Explaining Human Behavior: Consciousness, Human Action and Social Structure*. Beverly Hills: Sage Publications, 1982.

Segal, Alan. *Paul the Convert: The Apostolate and Apostasy of Saul the Pharisee*. New Haven: Yale University Press, 1990.

————. *Rebecca's Children: Judaism and Christianity in the Roman World*. Cambridge: Harvard University Press, 1986.

Seltzer, Sanford and Stackhouse, Max, eds. *The Death of Dialogue and Beyond*. New York: Friendship Press, 1969.

Sigmund, Paul. *Liberation Theology at the Crossroads: Democracy or Revolution?* New York: Oxford University Press, 1990.

Simon, Marcel. *Verus Israel: A Study of the Relations between Christians and Jews in the Roman Empire*. New York: Oxford University Press, 1986.

The Sixteen Documents of Vatican II. Boston: Daughters of St. Paul, 1966.

Sloyan, Gerard Stephen. *Jesus on Trial: The Development of the Passion Narratives and Their Historical and Ecumenical Implications*. Philadelphia: Fortress Press, 1973.

Snyder, Mary Hebrow. *The Christology of Rosemary Radford Ruether: A Critical Introduction*. Mystic, CT: Twenty-Third Publications, 1988.

Spülbeck, Volker. *Neomarxismus und Theologie: Gesellschaftskritik in Kritischer Theorie und Politischer Theologie*. Freiburg: Herder, 1977.

Starck, Helmut and von Klappert, Bertold, eds. *Umkehr und Erneuerung: Erläuterungen zum Synodalbeschluss der Rheinischen Landessynode 1980 "zur Erneuerung des Verhältnisses von Christen und Juden."* Neukirchen: Neukirchen Verlag, 1980.

Staub, Ervin. *Positive Social Behavior and Morality*. Vol. 1, *Social and Personal Influences*. Vol. 2, *Socialization and Development*. New York: Academic Press, 1978.

———. *The Roots of Evil: The Origins of Genocide and Other Group Violence*. Cambridge: Cambridge University Press, 1989.

——— et al., eds. *Social and Moral Values: Individual and Societal Perspectives*. Hillsdale, NJ: L. Erlbaum Associates, 1989.

Stendahl, Krister. *Paul among the Jews and Gentiles, and Other Essays*. Philadelphia: Fortress Press, 1976.

Stern, Fritz. *The Politics of Cultural Despair; A Study on the Rise of the Germanic Ideology*. Berkeley: University of California Press, 1961.

Stone, Christopher D. *Where the Law Ends: The Social Control of Corporate Behavior*. New York: Harper & Row, 1975.

Strauss, Herbert A., et al., eds. *Der Antisemitismus der Gegenwart*. Frankfurt: Campus Verlag, 1990.

Sullivan, Francis A., SJ. *Salvation Outside the Church? Tracing the History of the Catholic Response*. New York: Paulist Press, 1992.

Swidler, Leonard, et al. *Death or Dialogue? From the Age of Monologue to the Age of Dialogue*. Philadelphia: Trinity Press International, 1990.

Synan, Edward. *The Popes and the Jews in the Middle Ages*. New York: Macmillan, 1965.

Tajfel, Henri, ed. *Social Identity and Intergroup Relations*. Cambridge: Cambridge University Press, 1982.

Tal, Uriel. *Christians and Jews in Germany: Religion, Politics, and Ideology in the Second Reich, 1870-1914*. Ithaca: Cornell University Press, 1975.

Talmage, Frank E. *Disputation and Dialogue: Readings on the Jewish-Christian Encounter*. New York: KTAV Pub. House, 1975.

Tec, Nechama. *When Light Pierced the Darkness: Christian Rescue of Jews in Nazi-Occupied Poland*. New York: Oxford University Press, 1986.

Thackeray, H., trans. *Josephus*. Cambridge: Harvard University Press, 1926.

Thieme, Karl, ed. *Judenfeindschaft: Darstellung und Analysen*. Frankfurt: Fischer Bücherei, 1963.

Thiessen, Gerd. *Urchristliche Wundergeschichten*. Philadelphia: Fortress Press, 1983.

Thoma, Clemens. *A Christian Theology of Judaism*. New York: Paulist Press, 1980.

———. *Christliche Theologie des Judentums*. Aschaffenburg: P. Pattloch Verlag, 1978.

Townsend, John T. *The Study of Judaism: Bibliographical Essays*, vol. 2. New York: Anti-defamation League of B'nai B'rith, 1976.

Trachtenberg, Joshua. *The Devil and the Jews: The Medieval Conception of the Jew and its Relation to Modern Antisemitism*. New Haven: Yale University Press, 1943.

Tracy, David. *Blessed Rage for Order: The New Pluralism in Theology*. New York: Seabury Press, 1975.

Unger, Menasheh. *Seyfer Kdayshim: Rabeyim oyf Kidesh-Hashem*. New York: Schulzinger, 1967.

van Buren, Paul. *The Burden of Freedom: Americans and the God of Israel*. New York: Seabury Press, 1976.

———. *A Christian Theology of the People of Israel*. New York: Seabury Press, 1983.

———. *Christ in Context*. New York: Harper & Row, 1988.

———. *Discerning the Way: A Theology of the Jewish Christian Reality*. New York: Seabury Press, 1980.

———. *A Theology of the Jewish Christian Reality*. San Francisco: Harper & Row, 1987.

von Balthasar, Hans Urs. *Church and World*. New York: Herder and Herder, 1967.

von der Osten-Sacken, Peter. *Christian-Jewish Dialogue: Theological Foundation*. Philadelphia: Fortress Press, 1986.

———. *Grundzüge Einer Theologie im Christlich-Jüdischen Gesprach*. München: Kaiser, 1982.

Waite, Robert. *Vanguard of Nazism: The Free Corps Movement in Postwar Germany, 1918-1923*. Cambridge: Harvard University Press, 1952.

Walzer, Michael. *Obligations: Essays on Disobedience, War, and Citizenship*. Cambridge: Harvard University Press, 1970.

Weindling, Paul. *Health, Race, and German Politics Between National Unification and Nazism, 1870-1945*. Cambridge: Cambridge University Press, 1989.

Weinstein, Fred. *The Dynamics of Nazism: Leadership, Ideology, and the Holocaust*. New York: Academic Press, 1980.

Weinstein, Fred I. and Polsby, Nelson, eds. *Macropolitical Theory*, Vol. 3, *Handbook of Political Science*. Reading, MA: Addison-Wesley Pub. Co., 1975.

Weiss, Sheila. *Race Hygiene and National Efficiency: The Eugenics of Wilhelm Schallmayer*. Berkeley: University of California Press, 1987.

Welch, David. *Propaganda and the German Cinema, 1933-1945*. Oxford: Clarendon Press, 1983.

Wellhausen, Julius. *Prolegomena to the History of Ancient Israel*. New York: Meridian Books, 1957.

White, Lynn Townsend. *Medieval Religion and Technology: Collected Essays*. Berkeley: University of California Press, 1978.

White, Ralph K. *Fearful Warriors: A Psychological Profile of U.S. — Soviet Relations*. New York: Free Press, 1984.

Whitehead, Alfred North. *Modes of Thought*. New York: Free Press, 1968.

Whitney, Barry. *Theodicy: An Annotated Bibliography of the Problem of Evil, 1960-1990*. Hamden, CT: Garland Publishing, 1993.

Wiesel, Elie. *A Jew Today*. New York: Random House, 1978.

———. *One Generation After*. New York: Random House, 1970.

Wigoder, Geoffrey. *Jewish-Christian Relations Since the Second World War*. Manchester, UK: Manchester University Press, 1988.

Wildavsky, Aaron. *Budgeting: A Comparative Theory of Budgetary Processes*. Boston: Little, Brown, 1975.

Wiles, Maurice. *Christian Theology and Interreligious Dialogue*. Philadelphia: Trinity Press International, 1992.

Wilken, Robert. *John Chrysostom and the Jews: Rhetoric and Reality in the Late Fourth Century*. Berkeley: University of California Press, 1983.

Willebrands, Johannes Cardinal. *Church and the Jewish People: New Considerations*. New York: Paulist Press, 1992.

Williams, A. Lukyn. *Adversus Judaeos: A Bird's-Eye View of Christian Apologiae Until the Renaissance*. London: Cambridge University Press, 1935.

Williamson, Clark. *Has God Rejected His People? Anti-Judaism in the Christian Church*. Nashville: Abingdon, 1982.

Wood, Allen W. *Kant's Moral Religion*. Ithaca: Cornell University Press, 1970.

Xhaufflaire, Marcel, ed. *La pratique de la théologie politique: analyse critique des conditions pratiques de l'instauration d'un discours chrétien libérateur*. Tournai: Casterman, 1974.

Zimmermann, Moshe. *Wilhelm Marr: The Patriarch of Anti-Semitism*. New York: Oxford University Press, 1986.

Articles

Aagard, Johannes. "The Church and the Jews in Eschatology." *Lutheran World* 11 (1964): 270-78.

"Address to Rome's Chief Synagogue." *Origins* 15 (1986): 279, 731-33.

Agus, Jacob. "The Covenant Concept – Particularistic, Pluralistic, or Futuristic." *Journal of Ecumenical Studies* 18 (1981): 217-30.

———. "Revelation as Quest." *Journal of Ecumenical Studies* 9 (1972): 521-43.

Almog, Schmuel. "Judaism as Illness: Antisemitic Stereotype and Self-Image." *History of European Ideas* 13 (1991): 793-804.

Asch, S.E. "Studies of Independence and Conformity: A Minority of One Against a Unanimous Majority." *Psychological Monographs* 70 (1956).

Aubert, J.M. "Hierarchie de valeurs et histoire." *Revue des Sciences Religieuses* 44 (1970): 5-22.

Bandura, A. et al. "Disinhibition of Aggression through Diffusion of Responsibility and Dehumanization of Victims." *Journal of Research in Personality* 9 (1975): 253-69.

Baum, Gregory. "The Doctrinal Basis for Jewish-Christian Dialogue." *The Month* 224 (1967): 232-45.

————. "The Jews, Faith, and Ideology." *The Ecumenist* 10 (1971/72): 71-76.

Bea, Augustin. "Antisemitismus, Rassentheorie, und Altes Testament." *Stimmen der Zeit* 100 (1920): 171-83.

Bereday, George Z.F. "The Right to Live and the Right to Die: Some Considerations of Law and Society in America." *Man and Medicine* 4 (1979): 233-56.

Berkhof, H. "Israel as a Theological Problem in the Christian Church." *Journal of Ecumenical Studies* 6 (1969): 329-47.

Berkovits, Eliezer. "Facing the Truth." *Judaism* 27 (1978): 324-26.

Berkowitz, L. and Luttermann, K.G. "The Traditional Socially Responsible Personality." *Public Opinion Quarterly* 32 (1968): 169-85.

Bernardin, Joseph. "Emerging Catholic Attitudes toward Judaism." *Journal of Ecumenical Studies* 26 (1989): 445-46.

Bok, Gisela. "Racism and Sexism in Nazi Germany: Motherhood, Compulsory Sterilization and the State." *Signs* 8 (1983): 400-471

Bowleen, Maurice. "Rosenzweig on Judaism and Christianity – the Two Covenant Theory." *Judaism* 22 (1963): 475-81.

Boys, Mary et al. "Symposium: Why Do the Ruethers so Furiously Rage? Christian Critiques." *Continuum* 1 (1990): 116-27.

Brener, Pynchas et al. "*Nostra Aetate* Twenty Years On: A Symposium." *Christian-Jewish Relations* 18 (1985): 5-46.

Brewer, M.B. "Ingroup Bias on the Minimal Intergroup Situation: A Cognitive-Motivation Analysis." *Psychological Bulletin* 86 (1978): 307-24.

Bronfman, Edgar et al. "Catholic-Jewish Relations – Tension and Intention." *Christian-Jewish Relations* 20 (1987): 33.

Brown, Raymond. "Does the New Testament Call Jesus God?" *Theological Studies* 26 (1965): 538-51.

Cain, Seymour. "The Questions and Answers after Auschwitz." *Judaism* 20 (1971): 263-78.

Campbell, N.S. "Christianity and Judaism: Continuity and Discontinuity." *Christian-Jewish Relations* 18 (1985): 3-14.

Canadian Catholic Bishops. "Sharing National Income." *Catholic Mind* (October 1972): 59.

Chirico, Peter. "Christian and Jew Today from a Theological Perspective." *Journal of Ecumenical Studies* 7 (1970): 37-51.

Cook, Michael. "Jesus and the Pharisees: The Problem as it Stands Today." *Journal of Ecumenical Studies* 15 (1978): 441-60.

Culpepper, R.A. "The Gospel of John and the Jews." *Review and Expositor* 84 (1987): 273-88.

Davies, Alan T. "The Jews in an Ecumenical Context." *Journal of Ecumenical Studies* 5 (1968): 488-506.

Davis, C. "Lonergan's Appropriation of the Concept of Praxis." *New Blackfriars* (1981): 114-26.

D'Costa, Gavin. "Elephants, Popes, and a Christian Theology of Religions." *Theology* 68 (1985): 259-68.

Dietrich, Donald J. "Holocaust as Public Policy: The Third Reich." *Human Relations* 34 (1981): 445-62.

———. "National Renewal, Anti-Semitism, and Political Continuity: A Psychological Assessment." *Political Psychology* 9 (1988): 385-411.

Eckardt, A. Roy. "Christians and Jews: Along a Theological Frontier." *Encounter* 40 (1979): 89-127.

———. "End to the Christian-Jewish Dialogue." *Christian Century* 83 (1966): 393-95.

———. "Is the Holocaust Unique?" *Worldview* (1974): 31-35.

———. "Is There a Way Out of the Christian Crime? The Philosophic Question of the Holocaust." *Holocaust and Genocide Studies* 1 (1986): 121-26.

———. "Recent Literature on Christian-Jewish Relations." *Journal of the American Academy of Religion* 49 (1981): 99-111.

———. "Toward an Authentic Jewish-Christian Relationship." *Journal of Church and State* 13 (1971): 271-82.

Eckardt, Alice. "Post-Holocaust Theology: A Journey Out of the Kingdom of Night." *Holocaust and Genocide Studies* 1 (1986): 229-40.

Eckardt, Alice and Eckardt, A. Roy. "The Holocaust and the Enigma of Uniqueness: A Philosophical Effort at Practical Clarification." *Annals of the American Academy of Political and Social Science* 450 (1980): 165-78.

Epp, E.J. "Anti-Semitism and the Popularity of the Fourth Gospel in Christianity." *Journal of the Central Conference of American Rabbis* 22 (1975): 35.

Estes, Joseph. "Jewish-Christian Dialogue as Mission." *Review and Expositor* 68 (1971): 5-16.

"The Evanston Report (1954)." *Lutheran World* 11 (1964): 358.

Fein, Helen. "Genocide: A Sociological Perspective." *Current Sociology* 1 (1990): 1-126.

Feingold, Harry. "Menorah." *Judaic Studies Programme of Virginia Commonwealth University* 4 (Summer 1985): 2.

Finkel, Asher. "Yavneh's Liturgy and Early Christianity." *Journal of Ecumenical Studies* 18 (Spring 1981): 231-50.

Fiorenza, Francis. "Critical Social Theory and Christology." C.T.S.A. Proceedings 30 (1975): 63-110.

Fisher, Eugene. "Ani Ma'amin: Theological Responses to the Holocaust." *Interface* (December 1980): 1-8.

———. "Continuity and Discontinuity in the Scripture Readings." *Liturgy* (May 1978): 30-37.

———. "The Evolution of a Tradition: From *Nostra Aetate* to the 'Notes'." *Christian-Jewish Relations* 18 (1985): 32-47.

———, "The Holy See and the State of Israel: The Evolution of Attitudes and Policies." *Journal of Ecumenical Studies* 24 (1987): 191-211.

———. "A New Maturity in Christian-Jewish Dialogue: A Bibliographical Essay." *Face to Face* 11 (Spring 1984): 29-43.

———. "A New Maturity in Christian-Jewish Dialogue: An Annotated Bibliography, 1975-1978." *Shofar* 3 (1985): 1: 5-43.

———. "The Vatican and the State of Israel." *First Things* (1991): 11-12.

Fitzmyer, Joseph. "Antisemitism and the Cry of all the People (Matt. 27: 25)." *Theological Studies* 26 (1965): 667-71.

———. "Jesus the Lord." *Chicago Studies* 17 (1978): 87-90.

Friedman, F.G. and Rahner, Karl. "Unbefangenheit und Auspruch." *Stimmen der Zeit* 173 (1966): 81-97.

Friedman, L.M. "Legal Rules and the Process of Social Change." *Stanford Law Review* 19 (1967): 786-840.

Fuchs-Kreimer, Nancy. "Christian Old Testament Theology: A Time for New Beginnings." *Journal of Ecumenical Studies* 18 (1981): 90-92.

Gappelt, Leonard. "Israel and the Church in Today's Discussion and in Paul." *Lutheran World* 10 (1963): 364.

Glock, Peter. "Individualism, Society, and Social Work." *Social Casework* 58 (1977): 579-84.

Goldmann, Felix. "Das Irrationale Im Antisemitismus." *Der Morgan* (August 1927): 314.

Greenberg, Irving. "History, Holocaust, and Covenant." *Holocaust and Genocide Studies* 1 (1990): 1-12.

Haight, Roger, SJ. "The Case for Spirit Christology." *Theological Studies* 53 (1992): 257-87.

Hartman, David. "Jews and Christians in the World Tomorrow." *Immanuel* 6 (1976): 79.

Hawkins, Gordon and Zimring, Franklin. "The Legal Threat as an Instrument of Social Change." *Journal of Social Issues* 27 (1971): 33-48.

Hellwig, Monika. "Christian Theology and the Covenant of Israel." *Journal of Ecumenical Studies* 7 (1970): 39, 44-51.

Henriot, P. "Social Sin and Conversion: A Theology of the Church's Social Involvement." *Chicago Studies* 11 (1972): 3-18.

Hoffman, M.L. "Conscience, Personality, and Socialization Technique." *Human Development* 13 (1970): 90-126.

Horkheimer, H. "Zum Problem der Wahrheit." *Zeitschrift für Sozialforschung IV* 3 (1935): 345.

Hornstein, H.A. "Out of the Wilderness." *Contemporary Psychology* 29 (1984): 11-12.

Horowitz, Irving Louis. "A Funeral Pyre for America." *Worldview* 19 (1976).

Hruby, Kurt. "Jesus, Disciple of Moses: The True Relationship of Christianity and Judaism." *Encounter Today* 8 (1972): 6-12.

———. "Peoplehood in Judaism and Christianity." *Theology Digest* 22 (1974): 11.

Hvalvik, Reidar. "A 'Sonderweg' for Israel: A Critical Examination of a Current Interpretation of Romans 11: 25-27." *Journal for the Study of the New Testament* 38 (1990): 87-107.

"Important Declarations of John Paul II." *SIDIC* 15 (1982): 27.

John Paul II. "The 20th Anniversary of *Nostra Aetate.*" *Origins* (5 December 1985): 409-11.

Kater, Michael. "Everyday Antisemitism in Prewar Nazi Germany: The Popular Bases." *Yad Vashem Studies* 16 (1984): 129-59.

Katz, Steven. "Issues in the Separation of Judaism and Christianity." *Journal of Biblical Literature* 103 (1984): 43-76.

Keefe, D. "The Ordination of Women." *New Oxford Review* 47 (1980): 12-14.

Kelman, Herbert. "The Political Psychology of the Israeli-Palestinian Conflict: How Can We Overcome the Barriers to a Negotiated Solution?" *Political Psychology* 8 (1987): 347-63.

————. "Violence Without Moral Restraint." *Journal of Social Issues* 29 (1973): 29-61.

Kershaw, Ian. "The Persecution of the Jews and German Popular Opinion in the Third Reich." *Leo Baeck Yearbook* 26 (1981): 261-89.

Komonchak, Joseph A. "Theology and Culture at Mid-Century: The Example of Henri de Lubac." *Theological Studies* (1990): 579-602.

Küng, Hans and Metz, Johannes. "Perspektiven für eine Kirche der Zukunft." *Publik-Forum* (June 1980): 15-21.

Kuschel, Karl-Josef. "Ecumenical Consensus on Judaism in Germany? A Theological Analysis of Recent Catholic and Protestant Statements on the Jewish Question." *Christian-Jewish Relations* 17 (1984): 3-20.

Lalonde, Marc. "Power/Knowledge and Liberation: Foucault as a Parabolic Thinker." *Journal of the American Academy of Religion* 61 (1993): 81-100.

Lamb, Matthew. "The Theory-Praxis Relationship in Contemporary Christian Theologies." *C.T.S.A. Proceedings* 31 (1976): 149-78.

Leibig, Janis. "John and 'the Jews': Theological Antisemitism in the Fourth Gospel." *Journal of Ecumenical Studies* 20 (1983): 226-27.

Lerner, M.J. and Simmons, C.H. "Observer's Reaction to the 'Innocent Victim': Compassion or Rejection?" *Journal of Personality and Social Psychology* 4 (1966): 203-10.

Levin, Nora. "A Jewish View of the Dialogue." *Christian-Jewish Relations* 17 (1984): 35-42.

Lindscy, R.L. "Salvation and the Jews." *International Review of Missions* 61 (1972): 20-37.

Lipstadt, Deborah. "Deniers, Relativists, and Pseudo-Scholarship." *Dimensions* 6 (1991): 4-9.

Littell, Franklin H. "Essay: Early Warning." *Holocaust and Genocide Studies* 3 (1988): 483-90.

———. "A Milestone in Post-Holocaust Church Thinking: Reflection on the Declaration by the Protestant Church of the Rhineland Regarding Christian-Jewish Relations." *Christian News From Israel* 27 (1980): 113-16.

Lonergan, Bernard. "The Ongoing Genesis of Methods." *Studies in Religion* 6/4 (1977): 341-351.

———. "Theology and Praxis." *Catholic Theological Society of America Proceedings* 32 (1977): 1-16.

Lowry, Richard. "The Rejected Suitor Syndrome: Human Sources of the New Testament's Antisemitism." *Journal of Ecumenical Studies* 14 (1977): 219-32.

Mack, J. "Nationalism and the Self." *Psychohistory Review* 2 (1983): 47-69.

Mahoney, John, SJ. "The Challenge of Moral Distinctions." *Theological Studies* 53 (1992): 663-82.

Martin, B. "Paul Tillich and Judaism." *Judaism* 15 (1966): 180-88.

McCormick, Richard. "Moral Theology, 1940-1989: An Overview." *Theological Studies* 50 (1989): 3-24.

Milgram, Stanley. "Behavioral Study of Obedience." *Journal of Abnormal and Social Psychology* 67 (1963): 371-78.

———. "Group Pressure and Action Against a Person." *Journal of Abnormal and Social Psychology* 69 (1964): 137-43.

———. "Nationality and Conformity." *Scientific American* 205 (1961): 45-51.

Miller, Arthur. "Book Review: A Perspective on Kelman and Hamilton's *Crimes of Obedience*." *Political Psychology* 11 (1990): 189-201.

Mynatt, C. and Sherman, S.J. "Responsibility Attribution in Groups and Individuals: A Direct Test of the Diffusion of Responsibility Hypothesis." *Journal of Personality and Social Psychology* 32 (1975): 111-18.

Noonan, John. "Development in Moral Doctrine." *Theological Studies* 54 (1993): 662-77.

"Orientierungspunkte zum Themen 'Christen und Juden'." *Berliner Theologische Zeitschrift* 1 (1984): 370-72.

Osborn, Robert. "The Christian Blasphemy." *Journal of the American Academy of Religion* 53 (1985): 339-63.

Papademetriou, George. "Jewish Rite in the Christian Church: Ecumenical Possibility." *Scottish Journal of Theology* 26 (1973): 466-87.

Pawlikowski, John. "Christian Ethics and the Holocaust: A Dialogue with Post-Auschwitz Judaism." *Theological Studies* 49 (1988): 649-70.

———. "Christian-Jewish Relations and Catholic Teaching Materials." *Catholic Library World* 45 (1973): 227-32.

———. "The Church and Judaism: The Thought of James Parkes." *Journal of Ecumenical Studies* 6 (1969): 573-97.

———. "The Shoah: Its Challenges for Religious and Secular Ethics." *Holocaust and Genocide Studies* 3 (1988): 443-55.

———. "Toward a Theology for Religious Diversity: Perspectives from the Christian-Jewish Dialogue." *Journal of Ecumenical Studies* 26 (1989): 138-53.

Peplau, L.A. and Rubin, Z. "Belief in a Just World and Reactions to Another's Lot: A Study of Participants in the National Draft Lottery." *Journal of Social Issues* 29 (1973): 73-93.

———. "Who Believes in a Just World." *Journal of Social Issues* 29 ((1975): 65-89.

Perrin, S. and Spencer, C. "Independence and Conformity in the Asch Experiments as a Reflection of Cultural and Situational Factors." *British Journal of Psychology* 20 (1981): 205-9.

Pope John Paul II, Giacomo Saban and Chief Rabbi Elia Toaff. "Documentation: Pope John Paul II's Visit to the Synagogue in Rome." *Christian-Jewish Relations* 19 (1986): 46-56.

Pope Paul VI. *Humanae Vitae*. *Acta Apostolicae Sedis* 60 (1968): 483.

Regan, D. and Totten, J. "Empathy and Attribution: Turning Observers into Actors." *Journal of Personality and Social Psychology* 32 (1975): 850-56.

Rengstorf, K.H. "The Place of the Jew in the Theology of the Christian Mission." *Lutheran World* 11 (1964): 194-200.

Rijk, Cornelius. "The Holy Year and the Reconciliation between Christians and Jews." *SIDIC* 7 (1974): 21-23.

———. "Some Observations on a Christian Theology of Judaism." *SIDIC* 5 (1972): 3-17.

Roth, John K. "Holocaust Business." *Annals of the AAPSS* 450 (July 1980): 70.

———. "The Ruethers Wrath of Jonah: An Essay Review." *Continuum* 1 (1990): 105-15.

Roth, Norman. "Bishops and Jews in the Middle Ages." *The Catholic Historical Review* 80 (1994): 1-17.

Rubenstein, Richard. "Naming the Unnameable; Thinking the Unthinkable: A Review Essay of Arthur Cohen's *The Tremendum*." *Journal of Reform Judaism* 31 (1984): 43-54.

Ruether, Rosemary. "An Invitation to Jewish-Christian Dialogue: In What Sense Can We Say that Jesus was 'The Christ'?" *The Ecumenist* 10 (1972): 17-24.

———. "Theological Anti-Semitism in the New Testament." *The Christian Century* 85 (1968): 191-96.

Rylaarsdam, J. Coert. "Common Ground and Difference." *Journal of Religion* 43 (1963): 264.

———. "Jewish-Christian Relationship: The Two Covenants and the Dilemmas of Christology." *Journal of Ecumenical Studies* 9 (1972): 249-70.

Saldarini, Anthony. "Delegitimation of Leaders in Matthew 23." *Catholic Biblical Quarterly* 54 (1992): 659-80.

———. "Jews and Christians in the First Two Centuries: The Changing Paradigm." *Shofar* 10 (1992): 16ff.

Sanders, James A. "An Apostle to the Gentiles." *Conservative Judaism* 25 (1973): 61-63.

Shea, William. "Seminar on Theology and Philosophy: Matthew Lamb's Five Models of Theory-Praxis and the Interpretation of John Dewey's Pragmatism." *C.T.S.A. Proceedings* 32 (1977): 140.

Siebert, R. "The Church From Below: Küng and Metz." *Cross Currents* 31 (1981): 62-84.

Siegel, S. "Election and the People of God: A Jewish Perspective." *Lutheran Quarterly* 21 (1969): 437-50.

Stegemann, E. "Alt und Neu bei Paulus und in den Deutero-Pauliner (Kol/Eph)." *Evangelische Theologie* 37 (1977): 508-36.

Stroh, H. "Gibt es eine Verständigung zwischen Juden und Christen?" *Zeitschrift für Theologie und Kirche* 71 (1974): 227-38.

Swidler, Leonard. "The Pharisees in Recent Catholic Writing." *Horizons* 10 (1983): 267-87.

Tajfel, H. et al. "Social Categorization and Intergroup Behavior." *European Journal of Social Psychology* 1 (1971): 149-77.

Tal, Uriel. "On the Study of the Holocaust and Genocide." *Yad Vashem Studies* 13 (1979): 7-52.

van Buren, Paul. "The Context of Jesus Christ: Israel." *Religion and Intellectual Life* 3 (1986): 31-50.

Vawter, Bruce. "Are the Gospels Anti-Semitic?" *Journal of Ecumenical Studies* 5 (1968): 473-87.

Vernoff, Charles Elliott. "After the Holocaust: History and Being as Sources of Method within the Emerging Interreligious Hermeneutic." *Journal of Ecumenical Studies* 21 (1984): 639-63.

Vogel, Manfred. "The Problem of Dialogue Between Judaism and Christianity." *Journal of Ecumenical Studies* 4 (1967): 684-99.

von der Osten-Sacken, Peter. "Die paulinische Theologia Crucis als Form apokalyptischer Theologie." *Evangelische Theologie* 39 (1979): 477-96.

Wallach, M.A. et al. "Group Influences on Individual Risk Taking." *Journal of Abnormal and Social Psychology* 65 (1962): 75-86.

Weber, Eugen. "Jews, Antisemitism, and the Origins of the Holocaust." *Historical Reflections* 5 (1978): 1-17.

Weyman, Ernst. "Die deutsche Sendung als Leitgedanke im Geschichtsunterricht in der höheren Schulen." *Tribüne* 5 (1966): 1820ff.

Willebrands, Johannes Cardinal. "Is Christianity Antisemitic?" *Christian-Jewish Relations* 18 (1985): 8-20.

———. "Vatican II and the Jews: Twenty Years Later." *Christian-Jewish Relations* 18 (1985): 16-30.

Williamson, Clark. "The *Adversus Judaeos* Tradition in Christian Theology." *Encounter* 39 (1978): 273-96.

Zahn, Gordon. "The Unpublished Encyclical – An Opportunity Missed." *National Catholic Reporter* 8 (15 December 1972): 9.

Zajonc, R.B. "Attitudinal Effects of More Exposure." *Journal of Personality and Social Psychology, Monograph Supplement 19* (1968).

Public Documents

Document produced through the Commission on Faith and Order of the National Council of Churches and the Secretariat for Catholic-Jewish Relations of the National Conference for Catholic Bishops, issued 19 June 1973.

Parkes, James. "Judaism and the Jewish People in Their World Setting at the End of 1973." Pamphlet distributed by the Canadian Council of Christians and Jews, Toronto, 1974.

World Council of Churches. Documents published by the World Council of Churches, Programme Unit in Faith and Witness, March 1974.

———. Report on Consultation on the Church and the Jewish People, 10-14 February 1986.

Unpublished Material

Bramlett, Bruce Richard. "Images of the Passion in Post-Shoah Theological Reflection? Dilemmas of Language, Remembrance, and History in the Age after Auschwitz." Ph.D dissertation, Graduate Theological Union, 1992.

Cunningham, Philip. "A Content Analysis of the Presentation of Jews and Judaism in Current Roman Catholic Religion Textbooks." Ph.D dissertation, Boston College, 1991.

"Christen und Juden: Eine Schwerpunkt-Tagung der Landessynode der Evangelischen Landeskirche in Baden, 10-11 November 1980." *In Bad Herrenalb: Referate, Diskussionen, Bekenntnisse, Konsequenzen,* 1981, Karlsruhe.

"The Church in the Present Day Transformation of Latin America in the Light of the Council." Conference paper, U.S. Catholic Conference, 1970, Washington, DC

D'Costa, Gavin. "Jews and Christians: Reflections on 'Covenant' and 'Fulfillment' Towards a Theology of Christian-Jewish Relations." Paper presented October 1989, Harvard University.

Deutscher Koordinierungsrat der Gesellschaften für christlich-jüdische Zusammenarbeit e.v. ed. *Im Blick auf Morgan: Juden und Christen in der Verantwortung*, 1985, Frankfurt.

Eckardt, A. Roy. "The Resurrection and the Holocaust." Paper presented at the Israel Study Group, 4 March 1978, New York.

Ellis, Marc. "Holocaust Theology and Latin American Liberation Theology: Suffering and Solidarity." Paper presented at "Remembering for the Future Conference," Theme I, July 1988, Oxford.

"Erwangungen zur kirchlichen Handsreichung zur Erneuerung des Verhältnisses von Christen und Juden." Evangelisch-Theologisches Seminar der Rheinischen Friedrich Wilhelm Universität, May 1980, Bonn.

Girard, Rene. "Is There Antisemitism in the Gospels?" Paper presented at the McCarthy Lecture Series, 15 March 1993, Boston College.

Hellwig, Monika. "Proposal Towards a Theology of Israel as a Religious Community Contemporary with the Christian." Ph.D dissertation, Catholic University of America, 1968.

John Paul II. Address to the American Jewish Committee Representatives, 15 February 1985.

———. Address to Representatives of Catholic Bishop's Conference and Other Christian Churches, 6 March 1982, National Catholic News Service, trans. 17 March 1982.

Pope Paul VI. *Octogesima Adveniens*, a. 4.

Katz, Steven. "Critical Reflections on Holocaust Theology." Paper presented at the Holocaust Symposium, November 1980, Indiana University.

Michnik, Adam. "Poland and the Jews." Address given at Central Synagogue, April 1991, New York.

Pawlikowski, John. "Christ and the Jewish-Christian Dialogue: An Evaluation of Contemporary Perspectives." Paper presented at the American Academy of Religion, 26 October 1974, Washington, DC

———. "Ethical Issues in the Israeli-Palestinian Conflict: One Christian Viewpoint." Unpublished paper, 1988.

Rossano, Pietro, rector of the Pontifical Lateran University, Rome. Address in Jerusalem, 1987: 67.

Ruether, Rosemary. *Messiah of Israel and the Cosmic Christ: A Study of the Development of Christology in Judaism and Early Christianity*. Unpublished manuscript, 1972.

van Buren, Paul. "The Church and Israel: Romans 9-11." Opening address at the Third Frederick Neumann Symposium, 13-16 October 1989, Princeton Theological Seminary.

Index

Antisemitism and the Final Solution are the integrating themes of this book. To include in the index each page where these themes appear would mean including virtually every page in one or both categories. Thus, the index has been designed to include authors and concepts that can be related to the interaction between antisemitism and the Final Solution.